WOMEN AGAINST THE VOTE

Women Against the Vote

Female Anti-Suffragism in Britain

JULIA BUSH

OXFORD
UNIVERSITY PRESS

OXFORD

UNIVERSITY PRESS

Great Clarendon Street, Oxford OX2 6DP

Oxford University Press is a department of the University of Oxford.
It furthers the University's objective of excellence in research, scholarship,
and education by publishing worldwide in

Oxford New York

Auckland Cape Town Dar es Salaam Hong Kong Karachi
Kuala Lumpur Madrid Melbourne Mexico City Nairobi
New Delhi Shanghai Taipei Toronto

With offices in

Argentina Austria Brazil Chile Czech Republic France Greece
Guatemala Hungary Italy Japan Poland Portugal Singapore
South Korea Switzerland Thailand Turkey Ukraine Vietnam

Oxford is a registered trade mark of Oxford University Press
in the UK and in certain other countries

Published in the United States
by Oxford University Press Inc., New York

British Library Cataloguing in Publication Data

Data available

Library of Congress Cataloging in Publication Data

Data available

Typeset by Laserwords Private Limited, Chennai, India
Printed in Great Britain
on acid-free paper by
Biddles Ltd, King's Lynn, Norfolk

ISBN 978-0-19-924877-3

3 5 7 9 10 8 6 4 2

for Raymonde Hainton and Joanna Bazley

Acknowledgements

Thanks are due to a number of historians who have advised and encouraged me, with the usual proviso that academic responsibility for the book rests with me alone. I am grateful to Brian Harrison for the inspiration which his classic book on the anti-suffrage movement has always afforded me, and for his supportive advice when my book was on the drawing board, as well as to Janet Howarth, Myriam Boussahba-Bravard, and Lucy Delap for their constructive comments on draft chapters and articles. Members of the Women's History Network offered further useful advice at successive annual conferences. Sheila Fletcher's books have continued to help me after her death in 2001, and I remain grateful for her scholarly friendship. I am also grateful to fellow historians at the University of Northampton for their support, especially Sally Sokoloff, Elizabeth Tingle, and Peter King, and to the University for two periods of research leave. Other friends and family have completed my circle of support. Thanks to Harriet Webzel and to my daughter Ruth Bush for reading chapters and (in Ruth's case) providing much-needed technical advice. My son Tom Bush and my friends Sylvia Collicott and Joy Howkins have been a continuous source of encouragement over the years. My mother Raymonde Hainton and my sister Joanna Bazley have been a mainstay in good times and bad, and this book is jointly dedicated to them.

I owe a considerable debt to the professional assistance of many librarians and archivists. I would like to thank the staff of the Women's Library, the Bodleian Library, Pusey House Library, Lady Margaret Hall Library, the British Library, the British Library of Polical and Economic Science, London Metropolitan Archives, the National Archives, University College London Archives, Lambeth Palace Library, the University of Birmingham Archives, the University of Newcastle Archives, the University of Northampton Library, the Girls' Friendly Society, the Mothers' Union, and the Victoria League. Thanks are also due to Ruth Parr, Anne Gelling, Timothy Saunders, and Rupert Cousens at Oxford University Press for their guidance and support.

Finally, I wish to acknowledge the kind permission of copyright holders to quote from documents within their care: the Earl of Cromer (Cromer papers), Mrs Halcyon Palmer (Markham papers), Ms Rebekah Ingall and Mr Robert Ingall, on behalf of the late Mrs Gillian Ingall (Bryce papers), Lady Margaret Hall (Wordsworth papers), Pusey House (Mary Ward papers), University College London (Dorothy Ward papers), the London School of Economics (Harrison papers), the British Library Board (Curzon papers), London Metropolitan Archives (Jersey papers), Lambeth Palace (Creighton papers), the Special Collections Librarian, Robinson Library Special Collections, University of Newcastle (Gertrude Bell papers), the Head of Special Collections, Main Library, University of Birmingham (Chamberlain papers).

Julia Bush

November 2006

Contents

Abbreviations

ORGANIZATIONS

GFS	Girls' Friendly Society
JAC	Joint (Parliamentary) Advisory Committee
LCC	London County Council
LGAC	Local Government Advancement Committee
NCW	National Council of Women
NLOWS	National League for Opposing Woman Suffrage
NUSEC	National Union of Societies for Equal Citizenship
NUWSS	National Union of Women's Suffrage Societies
NUWW	National Union of Women Workers
WI	Women's Institute
WLGS	Women's Local Government Society
WNASL	Women's National Anti-Suffrage League
WSPU	Women's Social and Political Union

ARCHIVES

BL	British Library
BLPES	British Library of Political and Economical Science
Bodl.	Bodleian Library, Oxford
LMA	London Metropolitan Archives
LMH	Lady Margaret Hall, Oxford
LSE	London School of Economics
UCL	University College London

1

An Introduction to Women's Anti-Suffragism

British women who opposed their own enfranchisement were ridiculed by the supporters of votes for women and have since been neglected by historians. These two dimensions of their negative reputation are closely linked. Campaigners for the vote were early and prolific historians of their own movement. During the campaign, and especially in the aftermath of the 1918 Representation of the People Act, they made extensive efforts to memorialize the path to victory through published life histories and tales of suffrage adventure,[1] providing later researchers with influential retrospective accounts to set alongside the lively sketches and parodies of anti-suffragism which had multiplied in suffrage publications during the heat of the battle. The suffragist leader Mrs Fawcett wrote in 1912 of the 'inherent absurdity of the whole position of anti-suffrage women', claiming their 1889 manifesto 'had the effect which similar protests have ever since had of adding to the numbers and activity of the suffragists'.[2] In her adulatory 1928 account of *The Cause,* Ray Strachey claimed that the anti-suffrage Leagues formed in 1908 and 1910 'soon began to afford great delight and comfort to their opponents by the ineptitude and futility of their ways'.[3] The image of women's anti-suffragism emerging from early suffrage histories was one of bizarre, narrow-minded irrelevance. It suited suffragists to portray an opposition

---

[1] See e.g. M. Fawcett, *What I Remember* (London: T. Fisher Unwin,1925); A. Kenney, *Memories of a Militant* (London: Edward Arnold, 1924); C. Hamilton, *Life Errant* (London: Dent, 1935); C. Lytton, *Prisons and Prisoners* (London: William Heinemann, 1914); D. Montefiore, *From a Victorian to a Modern* (London: Edward Archer, 1927); M. W. Nevinson, *Life's Fitful Fever* (London: A. and C. Black, 1926); C. Pankhurst, *Unshackled: The Story of How We Won the Vote* (London: Hutchinson, 1959); E. Pankhurst, *My Own Story* (London: Eveleigh Nash, 1914); E. S. Pankhurst, *The Suffragette Movement* (London: Longman, 1931); ead., *Life of Emmeline Pankhurst* (London: Longman, 1934); E. Pethwick Lawrence, *My Part in a Changing World* (London: Victor Gollancz, 1938); M. Richardson, *Laugh a Defiance* (London: Weidenfeld and Nicolson, 1953); E. Sharp, *Unfinished Adventure* (London: John Lane, 1933); R. Strachey, *The Cause: A Short History of the Women's Movement in Great Britain* (London: G. Bell and Sons, 1928); H. Swanwick, *I Have been Young* (London: Victor Gollancz, 1935).

[2] M. Fawcett, *Women's Suffrage: A Short History of a Great Movement* (London: T. C. and E. C. Jack, 1912), 45. She went on to predict, correctly, that 'future generations will probably mete out no very kindly judgment to the women who petitioned against women'. Ibid. 46.

[3] R. Strachey, *The Cause: A Short History of the Women's Movement in Great Britain* (1928; London: Virago Press, 1978), 319.

dominated by stubborn male politicians and brutal male law-enforcers, rather than by fellow women. Basic assumptions about the counterproductive nature of organized anti-suffragism, and the anomalous stance of its women leaders, have certainly strongly influenced later accounts. Modern histories of suffragism all too often ignore its committed female critics, and fail to evaluate the widespread support for their views. Thus the women anti-suffragists have become eclipsed within an opposition which was itself marginalized by historical failure.

Though not hard to explain, the limited and unflattering reputation of women anti-suffragists is in other respects rather surprising. Women's roles in the British anti-suffrage movement were important, and in some ways distinctive. Women provided a good deal of the initiative and most of the hard work behind the organized opposition, as well as the majority of its declared supporters. In 1913 more than two-thirds of the direct subscribers to the anti-suffragists' central office were women; at branch level the proportion of women subscribers rose to more than five out of every six.[4] Their ideas and activism were often overshadowed by a self-consciously masculine leadership in the years before the First World War, but did not go unrecorded. Women oppositionists also wrote life histories.[5] Some provided rueful, self-explanatory reflections on the lost cause. All offered indirect evidence of the social and political milieu which encouraged substantial numbers of intelligent, energetic women to commit themselves to anti-suffragism. A minority of leading women antis contributed powerfully to contemporary theoretical debates over the nature of womanhood and women's potential contribution to national life, producing books and articles which deserve the same careful reading as those of suffragist authors.[6] Larger numbers participated in the public debate on the Woman Question through contributions to newspapers and periodicals, including the daily press, the many monthly journals aimed at both male and female middle-class readerships, and the *Anti-Suffrage Review*, published from 1908 to 1918. Some women expressed their hostility to the vote by collective resistance through the 1889 Appeal Against Women's Suffrage,[7] and later through the Women's National Anti-Suffrage League (1908–10) and the National League for Opposing Woman

---

[4] Edward Mitchell-Innes, in an unnamed newspaper dated 29 Apr. 1913, replying to an article by the suffragist Lady Chance which criticized the NLOWS for being 'financed and controlled by a few rich men'; 1,005 men and 2,375 women subscribed to the central office, while 145 NLOWS branches (of 270 in total) listed men and women separately, totalling 2,830 men and 16,148 women. Bodl., NLOWS Scrapbook 24, 2474d70.

[5] See e.g. L. Creighton, *Memoir of a Victorian Woman*, ed. J. T. Covert (Bloomington: Indiana University Press, 1994); V. Markham, *Return Passage* (London: Oxford University Press, 1953); M. Ward, *A Writer's Recollections* (London: W. Collins and Sons, 1918); B. Webb, *My Apprenticeship* (London: Pelican Books, 1938).

[6] See esp. the writings of Ethel Colquhoun, Louise Creighton, Ethel Harrison, Violet Markham, Gladys Pott, and Mary Ward.

[7] 'An Appeal Against Female Suffrage', *Nineteenth Century*, 25 (June 1889), 781–8.

Suffrage (1910–18). Women provided (and collected) nearly half a million anti-suffrage petition signatures before the war, and formed the vast majority of the 42,000 enrolled membership of the Women's League and the mixed-sex National League, which joined forces in 1910.[8]

These numbers compare not unfavourably with the signed-up membership of the main suffrage societies in the same period. The Women's Social and Political Union had around 5,000 members and the National Union of Women's Suffrage Societies around 50,000 members in 1914.[9] However, there was a sharp contrast between suffragists and their opponents in terms of political visibility, whether in the form of publications and speech-making, or including the more spectacular exploits of legal and illegal militancy. Anti-suffrage women were usually reluctant to court publicity for their political beliefs. Organized campaigning for the anti-suffrage cause was continuously handicapped by the refusal of its female supporters to mount platforms, attend meetings, pen leaflets, or sometimes even sign petitions. This was partly a logical extension of their reluctance to take to the stage of parliamentary politics. It was also a reflection of their positive commitment to a paradigm of womanhood characterized by altruistic femininity, devotion to family duties, and inconspicuous public service in the extended domestic setting of local communities.

From the 1870s up to the moment of enfranchisement, both male and female anti-suffragists claimed emphatically that the majority of British women did not want the parliamentary vote. This claim has considerable plausibility, despite the suffragists' best efforts to disprove it and the relative political passivity of many anti-suffragists. A history of women's opposition to the vote must attempt to test the movement's unflagging confidence in its mass female support. Large numbers of women were publicly silent on the subject of the vote, but demonstrated their loyalty to 'true' rather than 'new' womanhood through alternative channels. This study will extend beyond the organized anti-suffrage movement into other socially conservative women's organizations, including religious, philanthropic, and imperialist associations and the National Union of Women Workers, the main 'umbrella' organization for female social service. It would obviously be unjustifiable to appropriate all these organized women retrospectively to the anti-suffrage cause. Each of the non-political women's organizations also contained many suffragist members. By 1913 the suffragists had even succeeded in provoking a public schism by asserting their superior strength at leadership level within the National Union of Women Workers. Many other women's organizations had ruled suffrage debate out of order, in

---

[8] Membership figures and numbers of signatories were given sporadically in the *Anti-Suffrage Review*, e.g. in the report on the Annual Council Meeting of the NLOWS in July 1914, when Lady Tullibardine claimed 42,367 subscribing members and 15,810 non-subscribing 'adherents' for the League. These figures included the Scottish membership. *Anti-Suffrage Review*, 69 (July 1914), 110.

[9] Membership figures for these organizations are discussed in M. Pugh, *The March of the Women* (Oxford: Oxford University Press, 2000), 210–11 and 254–5.

recognition of divided opinions and in order to avoid diverting their members' attention from constructive work for other causes. These organizations provide evidence of widely shared women's interests, activities, and gender beliefs which together afforded a favourable setting for anti-suffrage propaganda, or at the very least for indifference to suffragism.

The non-political women's movement gives insight into the shared views of suffragist and anti-suffragist women on issues other than the vote, enabling us to revisit the franchise debate from a less confrontational perspective. From the socially conventional viewpoint of the main middle- and upper-class women's organizations, anti-suffrage arguments seemed far from absurd. Instead, they can be reinterpreted as part of mainstream female opinion on desirable gender roles and on women's positive role in national life. In 1914 the largest non-political women's organizations were the Anglican Mothers' Union (1875), the Girls' Friendly Society (1876), and the National Union of Women Workers (1895); after 1918 they shared their place with the non-denominational Women's Institutes (1915) and Townswomen's Guilds (1928). Though the leadership of all these organizations was mainly middle class, members included large numbers of working-class women influenced by similar gender ideals. Womanly responsibilities for home and family took very different forms for poorer women but were often a considerable source of pride and self-respect, and a bulwark of unarticulated gender conservatism.

Suffrage as well as anti-suffrage discourse acknowledged the power of women's domestic devotion. But the evidence of social historians and contemporary social commentators, as well as of mass-membership women's organizations, seems to show that suffragism remained a minority preoccupation across all social classes. Women's reluctance or inability to become involved in national politics was a source of great encouragement for the opponents of votes for women. Beyond the more conservative women's organizations lay a still broader hinterland of wholly unorganized female support, or prospective support, for anti-suffragism. Most 'ordinary women' have left very limited direct evidence of their political and social outlook. Our understanding of their views rests mainly upon indirect evidence, and upon the interpretative skills of modern historians working from diverse sources to restore their lives to the historical record. This book will relate its conclusions to research now available on the apolitical stance of many poorer women,[10] as well as drawing upon research into middle-class and working-class women's organizations. It will also relate anti-suffrage ideals to the fictional worlds enjoyed by many middle-class women, now widely acknowledged to have defined as well as expressed important aspects of their social outlook and

---

[10] e.g. E. Roberts, *A Woman's Place: An Oral History of Working Class Women 1890–1940* (Oxford: Basil Blackwell, 1984), introd. She acknowledges the diversity of the working class, whilst drawing important general conclusions upon gender outlook which many other historians working in different regions of Britain have tended to substantiate.

self-image.[11] It is suggestive that some of the most widely read Victorian novelists, and some of those whose reputations have declined most steeply since the turn of the century, were committed anti-suffragists.[12] These women writers reasssured a generation of socially conventional women readers by providing a view of womanhood which they enjoyed and with which they could empathize: only to be cast out into the wilderness as later generations found new heroines and new inspirations.

To some extent, the opinions of the silent majority will always remain a mystery. How far were the anti-suffragists justified in counting upon uncommitted, non-suffragist women (as opposed to declared suffragists or anti-suffragists) as rank-and-file opponents of votes for women? The confidence of organized anti-suffragism in its passive supporters is demonstrated by the anti-suffrage Leagues' enthusiasm for a referendum on the franchise issue. By this means, passive women would be prodded into voicing their views. The referendum issue emerged in a variety of forms during the suffrage debate, without ever securing parliamentary support.[13] Meanwhile female anti-suffragists attempted to fill the evidence gap by organizing their own tests of public opinion. Polling of women municipal voters on the franchise issue produced remarkably consistent results around the country in the pre-war years. When unofficial ballots were conducted by anti-suffrage women canvassers, or sometimes by pre-paid postcards, opposition voters generally outnumbered supporters of women's franchise by two to one.[14] This outcome was only slightly marred by the suffragists' success in producing smaller-scale results equally favourable to their own cause, sometimes in the same districts.[15] Despite their strenuous attempts to invalidate anti-suffragist tests of public opinion, suffragists were usually to be found arguing that the vote would

[11] Literary sources have been used by many historians researching middle-class attitudes, e.g. J. A. Hammerton, ' "The Perils of Mrs Pooter": Satire, Modernity and Motherhood in the Lower Middle Classes in England, 1870–1920', *Women's History Review*, 8/2 (1999), 261–76. Again, the diversity of the middle classes demands acknowledgement, as does the evidence of nuanced changes of domestic outlook over the decades. M. J. Peterson, *Family, Love and Work in the Lives of Victorian Gentlewomen* (Bloomington: Indiana University Press, 1989) investigates the opposite end of the middle-class spectrum. K. Flint, *The Woman Reader 1837–1914* (Oxford: Clarendon Press, 1993) provides an interesting discussion of the (far from straightforward) relationship between middle-class women's reading and their evolving opinions.

[12] e.g. Charlotte Yonge, Eliza Lynn Linton, Mary Ward, and Marie Corelli.

[13] There was some support for a referendum from members of Asquith's cabinet in 1911–12, and also from sections of the national press. The anti-suffragists moved from canvassing for petition signatures to advocating a referendum, but there were uncertainties over who should vote in it. The referendum idea resurfaced for a final time in 1917, when the NLOWS argued that major constitutional reform should not be introduced without a direct mandate. It seems likely that, in the pre-war period at least, the antis were influenced by the encouraging outcomes of suffrage referenda in the United States, rather than simply by despair over their lack of parliamentary support as Martin Pugh suggests in *March of the Women*, 165.

[14] Results were published in the *Anti-Suffrage Review* as they were received, and summarized in *The Anti-Suffrage Handbook* (London: National Press Agency, 1912).

[15] See Fawcett, *Women's Suffrage*, 52. The suffragists also did their best to discredit the antis' results by collecting evidence of malpractice. See K. Courtney's circular letter to NUWSS members

benefit all women in practice, rather than that all women actively wished to have the vote. The demand for an official referendum of women found little favour in suffrage ranks, suggesting that they were far less confident than the antis in the breadth of their female support.

This book will focus more extensively upon the lives and opinions of the anti-suffrage movement's women leaders, though some attempt must be made to reassess general support for the anti-suffrage cause. Leadership is defined here to include distinguished writers and opinion-formers, as well as collective, organized activism by influential women within the anti-suffrage campaign itself. The emphasis upon a prominent minority rests partly upon the availability of evidence, but is also justified in other ways. Women leaders were important because they helped to shape and articulate the convictions of their women followers. Their reasons for opposing the vote, and for eventually founding an organization specifically devoted to its defeat, require more thorough analysis than they have so far received either from contemporary critics or from many later historians. Far from being the pawns of male antis, the leading ladies of anti-suffragism drew their enthusiasm from deeply rooted convictions about womanhood, nation, and empire. Their views developed over many years, and did not remain static. Importantly, their views on the suffrage issue were meshed into beliefs, attitudes, and activities in many other areas of their lives.

In order to understand their political thinking and its influence, it is necessary to follow the trajectory of their activities beyond public affairs and into family life. Historical controversy continues over the significance of 'separate spheres' ideology during the Victorian age and after. This study contributes to the debate by showing how, for many socially conservative and anti-suffragist women, public work and family duties were overlapping and mutually reinforcing, rather than in tension with each other. For other anti-suffrage women, the political platform of the opposition may have helped to provide an escape from the dilemmas involved in a pursuit of less 'womanly' paths in their personal lives. As adult women, anti-suffrage leaders were usually participants in multiple causes and extensive social networks, so that the influence of family life and personal experience became part of a web of wider encounters with ideas, organizations, and individuals. Some also participated, both as readers and writers, in the transnational literary networks which played an influential part in shaping contemporary views on the Woman Question.[16] No single woman personified the essence of anti-suffragism, but analysis of the shared ideas and affiliations of the leading women shows common threads, as well as underlining the need

---

on 10 Mar. 1911, and responses, in London Society for Women's Suffrage papers, Women's Library, 2/LSW, 298/3.

[16] These networks provide the focus for Lucy Delap's forthcoming book, *The Feminist Avant-Garde: Transatlantic Encounters, 1900s to the 1920s* (Cambridge: Cambridge University Press, 2007). I am grateful for her generosity in permitting me to read this important book before publication.

to acknowledge diversity of individual outlook. Retrospectively, it is possible to reconstruct broad groupings of individuals, motivations, and ideas within a many-sided discussion of womanhood which extended far beyond the narrow issue of the parliamentary vote.

The choice of anti-suffrage commitment was not always a lasting one. Women who changed their minds on the vote feature prominently in the history of anti-suffragism.[17] Most conversions swelled the suffragist ranks, especially in the later stages of the campaign, though a few women are to be found moving in the opposite direction. For the purposes of this book, women have been included within the scope of anti-suffragism if they expressed open opposition to votes for women at any stage in their lives. A small number of influential women have also been included whose opposition to women's suffrage was muted or indirect, but adequately evidenced and of contemporary significance to the anti-suffrage cause.[18] Of course it is necessary to clarify the extent or the limitations of anti-suffrage commitment with reference to each of the individuals concerned, so far as available evidence permits. Reasons for changing sides also require careful consideration, for they reflect the impact of changing times upon the anti-suffrage movement as a whole as well as upon individuals. Often the move from opposition to support for the vote involved a much less dramatic shift of opinion than might be expected. Levels of commitment were also very variable, and sometimes hard to measure. The suffrage controversy was not usually the main priority even for the leading anti-suffrage women activists. Other women who had little or no enthusiasm for female suffrage deliberately abstained from any form of activism on this issue. Their work and interests lay elsewhere, and in some cases they were reluctant to enter into divisive political debate as a matter of principle.[19] Women who took opposing views on the female franchise usually respected and even admired each other's wider public work. At the height of divisive suffragette militancy, anti-suffrage and suffrage women worked amiably together for a wide range of social and political causes, and maintained personal friendships which were underpinned by shared values.[20]

Diversity was an important characteristic of the anti-suffrage movement and is well illustrated by a study of its leadership. Both male and female leaders took up their roles for a variety of reasons, and attempted to imprint the movement with their own ideas. Internal debate was inevitable, though unwelcome within the campaigning Leagues as they attempted to present a united front to their suffragist opponents. Especially unfortunate for Edwardian anti-suffragism was

---

[17] e.g. Louise Creighton, Beatrice Webb, and eventually Violet Markham.
[18] e.g. Elizabeth Wordsworth and Florence Bell.
[19] Evidence of political abstention is difficult to locate, but exists in the correspondence among women attempting to gather signatures for the 1889 Appeal. See Ch. 6, below.
[20] Close friendships across the suffrage divide included those between Louise Creighton and Kathleen Lyttelton (before 1906), Mary Ward and Louise Creighton (after the latter's conversion to suffragism in 1906), Florence Bell and Elizabeth Robins, Violet Markham and May Tennant.

the emergence of internal debate along gendered lines. The organized anti-suffrage movement became a site for difficult negotiations between men and women leaders between 1910 and 1914, despite the public deference of the female antis to masculine wisdom. The existing historiography of the anti-suffrage movement remains overwhelmingly dominated by Brian Harrison's classic study, published in 1978, which presents an unrivalled analysis of the male leadership and of the parliamentary context of the suffrage campaign.[21] This book introduces fresh perspectives on the movement as a whole by restoring female leaders and women supporters to their due prominence. Harrison presciently observed in his concluding Bibliographical Note that many important areas of women's history remained under-researched, including the history of 'the unorganised woman, in home and workplace' and 'the social and political role of the upper class woman'.[22] Elsewhere in his book, and with particular reference to disagreements between men and women in the National League, he referred to the gender imbalance of his own primary sources.[23] The current book has the advantage of being informed by nearly three decades of subsequent women's history research. This has provided the essential context for a study which focuses on women's ideas and activism, and draws largely upon female sources, despite their relative paucity alongside the parliamentary record and the extensive publications and archived correspondence of the male anti-suffragists.

Debates between male and female anti-suffragists throw a particularly dramatic light upon the diversity of their cause. However, the diversity among anti-suffrage women themselves is another important aspect of the present analysis, and has received even less historical attention. Anti-suffrage women prided themselves on the unity of their movement, in contrast to the proliferating, squabbling suffrage societies, but their unity was far from complete. Divisions of outlook, policy, and tactics within the suffrage movement have been carefully researched in recent years. The 1990s were a particularly productive decade in suffrage history as historians redefined the chronology, location, ideas, and activities of the movement.[24] The present book shares the academic directions of this work, in that it aims to discover what drew individuals and groups of women

---

[21] B. Harrison, *Separate Spheres: The Opposition to Women's Suffrage in Britain* (London: Croom Helm, 1978). More recent work includes Pugh, *March of the Women*, ch. 7; M. Faraut, 'Women Resisting the Vote: A Case of Anti-Feminism?', *Women's History Review*, 12/4 (2003), 605–21; M. Joannou, 'Mary Augusta Ward (Mrs Humphry) and the Opposition to Women's Suffrage', *Women's History Review*, 14/3&4 (2005), 561–80.

[22] B. Harrison, *Separate Spheres*, 258 and 259.   [23] Ibid. 136.

[24] See e.g. C. Bolt, *The Women's Movements in the United States and Britain from the 1790s to the 1920s* (Hemel Hempstead: Harvester Wheatsheaf, 1993); C. Daly and M. Nolan (eds.), *Suffrage and Beyond: International Feminist Perspectives* (Auckland: Auckland University Press, 1994); C. Hall, K. McClelland, and J. Rendall, *Defining the Victorian Nation: Class, Race, Gender and the Reform Act of 1867* (Cambridge: Cambridge University Press, 2000); S. Holton, *Suffrage Days: Stories from the Women's Suffrage Movement* (London: Routledge, 1996); M. Joannou, and J. Purvis (eds.), *The Women's Suffrage Movement: New Feminist Perspectives* (Manchester: Manchester University Press, 1998); A. John and C. Eustance (eds.), *The Men's Share? Masculinities, Male Support and Women's*

towards a gendered political viewpoint, what issues divided them, what caused some to become active in support of their views, and what shaped the nature and outcomes of their activism. Suffrage history has been greatly enriched by the growth of a more complex understanding of women's political motivation and methods, and can be further enhanced by a more complex analysis of its opponents. Suffragism and anti-suffragism developed within the same historical context and in close reciprocal relationship to each other. It is certainly necessary to explore the mutually defining nature of these opposing movements. However, it is still more important to understand their connectedness within a single spectrum of debate which was highly variegated rather than dichotomized into contrasting opposites.[25] Suffrage historians have led the way in exploring the diversity of ideas and self-expression amongst those who supported votes for women. Anti-suffrage women now deserve equally respectful analysis, based upon their life histories, their writings, and the full range of their public work.

Many of the new approaches which have shaped revisionist histories of suffragism are of equal relevance to the history of its female opponents. To begin with, the development of both suffrage and anti-suffrage ideology evidently needs to be more fully contextualized within the intellectual, political, and social history of its period. Debates over religious faith, imperialism, social evolutionism, social science, and the nature and consequences of democracy are as important to the histories of suffragism and anti-suffragism as controversy over gender itself. The campaign methods of each movement need to be understood as the product of a modernizing society, in which a growing range of media catered for the demands of an increasingly educated, urban public, as well as challenging the two movements' creativity and will to innovate. The social class dimensions of both suffragism and anti-suffragism have much to teach us about their supporters and their politics. Whilst suffrage history has reclaimed its working-class heroines and its connections to the labour movement, anti-suffragism consolidated behind an upper middle-class leadership with strong links to the political aristocracy, but only a token interest in enrolling working-class women to fight their own fight against enforced democracy. Women anti-suffrage leaders sought to emphasize the social mission underlying their anti-suffragism, but rarely doubted their duty to speak on behalf of poorer women, rather than alongside them. Local contexts are revealing in the study of anti-suffragism, as well as suffragism. Both movements were led from London, the seat of the political establishment which would decide the issue of votes for women. Both also set out to foster regional and local organization, with contrasting degrees of success. The anti-suffrage Leagues never fully succeeded in establishing a national network of branches with

---

Suffrage in Britain, 1890–1920 (London: Routledge, 1997); J. Purvis and S. Holton (eds.), *Votes for Women* (London: Routledge, 2000); Pugh, *March of the Women*.

[25] This point is strongly argued in L. Delap, 'Feminist and Anti-Feminist Encounters in Edwardian Britain', *Historical Research*, 78/201 (2005), 377–99.

a vibrant political life of their own: but they made a serious attempt, and evidence survives to suggest that at least some of the stronger branches took on a distinct identity and proved capable of standing up to the anti-suffrage headquarters as well as to suffragism. Scottish, Welsh, and Irish anti-suffragism will eventually require histories of their own, furthering this book's attempt to follow suffrage historians' example in redressing the metropolitan imbalance.[26]

Both suffragists and anti-suffragists recognized the potential value of support and inspiration drawn from overseas. As recent suffrage histories remind us, the enfranchisement of women was (and is) a worldwide cause, and its historians would do well to abandon a 'standard model' centred upon developments in Britain and America.[27] There was no attempt by women anti-suffragists to parallel the International Women's Suffrage Association (1897). On the whole male and female antis were proud to claim an imperialist model of British exceptionalism, but this did not mean that they turned their backs on like-minded women elsewhere. In February 1910 the Women's National Anti-Suffrage League announced the appointment of Miss Seeley as 'Honorary International Secretary of our League, to keep us informed of the progress which the Anti-Suffrage movement is making in foreign countries'.[28] The *Anti-Suffrage Review* also invited transatlantic sympathizers to 'seek hospitality in our columns'.[29] The American anti-suffrage societies were heavily dominated by women and provided an important inspiration for the British League. These much larger organizations have inspired several interesting recent studies, none of which does full justice to the connections between Britain and America (a subject which, like many others, has been covered much more thoroughly from the perspective of suffrage organizations).[30] The Australasian governments' decisions to grant the vote to women at an early date provided ammunition

---

[26] Apart from various regional and local studies, suffrage historians have provided full-scale accounts of the campaigns in Wales, Scotland, and Ireland. See A. John (ed.), *Our Mothers' Land: Chapters in Welsh Women's History 1830–1939* (Cardiff: University of Wales Press, 1991); L. Leneman, *A Guid Cause: The Women's Suffrage Movement in Scotland* (Aberdeen: Aberdeen University Press, 1991); C. Murphy, *The Women's Suffrage Movement and Irish Society* (Hemel Hempstead: Harvester Wheatsheaf, 1989).

[27] See Daly and Nolan (eds.), *Suffrage and Beyond*, ch. 1. Also J. Hannam, M. Auchterlonie, and K. Holden, *International Encyclopedia of Women's Suffrage* (Santa Barbara: ABC-CLIO, 2000), introd.

[28] *Anti-Suffrage Review*, 15 (Feb. 1910), 4. Despite her connection to the leading academic exponent of British imperialism, Miss Seeley did not persist in her new responsibilities. Internationalism was almost entirely transatlantic, and was mainly Mary Ward's enthusiasm.

[29] Ibid. American anti-suffragists took up this invitation over the following years. There was considerable anti-suffragist news-sharing, with news travelling in both directions across the Atlantic.

[30] On American anti-suffragism, see J. Camhi, *Women Against Women: American Anti-Suffragism 1880–1920* (New York: Carlson, 1994); T. Jablonsky, *The Home, Heaven and Mother Party: Female Anti-Suffragists in the United States 1868–1920* (New York: Carlson, 1994); S. Marshall, *Splintered Sisterhood: Gender and Class in the Campaign Against Woman Suffrage* (Wisconsin: University of Wisconsin Press, 1997). On links between British and American Suffragism, see P. Harrison, *Connecting Links: The British and American Women's Suffrage Movements 1900–1914* (Westport: Greenwood Press, 2000) as well as C. Bolt, *The Women's Movements*.

for both suffragists and anti-suffragists. Enfranchised women from New Zealand and Australia appeared frequently on suffrage platforms, and added a colourful imperial flair to demonstrations (along with their unenfranchized Indian 'sisters'). Meanwhile information on Australasian social progress and policy-making on 'women's issues' was carefully combed over by leading British women, and quoted in support of both sides in the suffrage debate. Indian women also had their uses for both sides. Recent research has shown how deeply many suffragists were imbued with their own maternal, philanthropic vision of British imperialism, especially in the aftermath of the South African War and in relation to the future of India.[31] The imperialism of the women anti-suffragists now needs to be restored to the equation, and reconsidered as a factor in relationships with the male leadership of the National League, as well as a cherished aspect of these women's own ideals. Anti-suffrage women had their own positive vision of feminine, nurturing imperialism. But it was accompanied by general acceptance of the view that Britain's empire depended ultimately upon masculine 'physical force', and therefore upon male parliamentary government.[32]

Suffrage history has been revised in the context of a wider rediscovery and reinterpretation of Victorian and Edwardian women's history. The suffrage campaign is now generally understood as a manifestation of extended social and political change, and as a facet of accompanying ideological debate over the nature and roles of women. Detailed studies of Victorian campaigns to improve women's status in marriage, education, and employment, and to address the consequences of double standards of sexual morality, have provided a wealth of evidence revealing how intensely female gender roles were debated during the second half of the nineteenth century.[33] By the end of the century, the perplexing controversies at the heart of this widespread discussion were often collectively

---

[31] See, e.g. A. Burton, *Burdens of History* (Chapel Hill: University of North Carolina Press, 1994); J. Bush, *Edwardian Ladies and Imperial Power* (London: Leicester University Press, 2000); N. Chaudhuri and M. Strobel (eds.), *Western Women and Imperialism: Complicity and Resistance* (Bloomington: Indiana University Press, 1992); I. Grewal, *Home and Harem: Nation, Gender, Empire, and the Cultures of Travel* (London: Leicester University Press, 1996); C. Midgely (ed.), *Gender and Imperialism* (Manchester: Manchester University Press, 1998); K. Pickles, *Female Imperialism and National Identity: Imperial Order Daughters of the Empire* (Manchester: Manchester University Press, 2002).

[32] The expression 'physical force' was used extensively by anti-suffragists to refer not only to the power of Britain's armed forces and other law enforcement agencies, but also to the superior physical strength of most individual men over most individual women.

[33] See e.g. P. Bartley, *Prostitution: Prevention and Reform in England, 1860–1914* (London: Routledge, 2000); L. Bland, *Banishing the Beast: English Feminism and Sexual Morality 1885–1914* (London: Penguin Books, 1995); B. Caine, *Victorian Feminists* (Oxford: Oxford University Press, 1992); ead., *English Feminism 1780–1980* (Oxford: Oxford University Press, 1998); C. Dyhouse, *Feminism and the Family in England 1880–1939* (Oxford: Basil Blackwell, 1989); ead., *No Distinction of Sex? Women in British Universities 1870–1939* (London: UCL Press, 1995); S. Kingsley Kent, *Sex and Suffrage in Britain 1860–1914* (Princeton: Princeton University Press, 1987); P. Levine, *Feminist Lives in Victorian England: Private Roles and Public Commitment* (Oxford: Basil Blackwell, 1990).

referred to as the Woman Question. Women themselves were major contributors, but were also attentive to male discourse in the same arena. A study of female anti-suffragism provides important reminders of the dangers of separating out women's history and of interpreting it mainly in terms of the successful advance of feminism. Nevertheless, the ideas of the women antis clearly formed part of the extended debate on the Woman Question to which the history of feminism belongs.

The history of feminism has become an important subject in its own right. It has been greatly enriched by the late twentieth-century renaissance of suffrage history, characterized as this is by an analysis of diverse suffragist theory in relation both to women's lives and to their political practice. But the boundaries of feminist history are severely stretched by the inclusion of more conservative women thinkers, some of whom were beginning, at the turn of the century, to identify themselves as 'anti-feminists'.[34] Women's history now needs to encompass more fully the 'border regions' identified by Barbara Caine[35] and other historians who have begun to venture into the problematic territory of socially conservative women's public activism. This book owes a considerable debt to the work of Jane Lewis, Barbara Caine, and Carol Dyhouse on some of the more conservative Victorian women thinkers and their relationship to both feminism and suffragism.[36] However, the history of women's anti-suffragism provides a pressing invitation to move away from interpretation of women's ideas primarily in relation to feminism.[37] The present book will make very limited and cautious use of this term. Respect for contemporary usage precludes commentary upon the 'feminism' of the more progressive female anti-suffragists, despite the fact that they shared common views with suffragists on many social issues.[38] On the other hand, some antis' openly expressed hostility towards their opponents' 'feminism' demands

---

[34] See e.g. Ethel Colquhoun's recommendation of her book to Lord Cromer as 'the first Anti-Feminist Book by a woman', on 30 Oct. 1913 (National Archives Cromer papers, FO 633/22/165). Her book was *The Vocation of Woman* (London: Macmillan, 1913). Other women anti-suffragists explicitly attacked feminism in journal articles, e.g. E. Harrison, 'Abdication', *The Nineteenth Century and After*, 74 (1913), 1328–35; H. Hamilton, 'Suffragette Factories', *National Review*, 60 (1912–13), 591–8; Author of *An Englishwoman's Home*, 'Feminine versus Feminist', *National Review*, 58 (1911–12), 938–45.

[35] Caine, *English Feminism*, 4.

[36] See J. Lewis, *Women and Social Action in Victorian and Edwardian England* (Stanford: Stanford University Press, 1991); Caine, *Victorian Feminists*; C. Dyhouse, *Girls Growing Up in Late Victorian and Edwardian England* (London: Routledge and Kegan Paul, 1981).

[37] Delap, 'Feminist and Anti-Feminist Encounters', highlights the ambiguity of 'feminism'/'anti-feminism' in the early 20th cent., and warns against anachronistic and overgeneralized usage. At the same time she concludes that 'it seems sensible to continue to use these terms, but with greater awareness of their lack of conceptual distinctness, more attention to the specific content of arguments, and greater sensitivity to the historical context in which they were deployed' (p. 399).

[38] Martin Pugh describes the more progressive female antis as 'feminists' in *March of the Women*, pp. 4 and 145–67.

careful attention. For these women, feminism was the social evil lurking behind the more superficial political errors of the female suffrage cause. Such fears seem rarely to have prevented anti-suffrage women from welcoming both suffragist and anti-suffragist women's inclusion within a broad-based women's movement. The dual concepts of a socially important Woman Question, and of an inclusive women's movement, were familiar to all leading women anti-suffragists, and will therefore be further explored and developed throughout this book.

Victorian discussion of the Woman Question developed in relation to a number of key issues which together defined the thinking of women at all points across the extended spectrum of the suffrage debate. The shared middle ground between pro-suffrage and anti-suffrage views on womanhood deserves at least as much attention as the opposed extremes of opinion which existed at each end of the spectrum. The most fundamental issue was the extent to which women differed from men in mind and body, and the related question of whether this difference was biologically determined or socially constructed. There was no simple correlation between women's views on the suffrage and on these questions, though the antis tended almost universally to assume that major differences between the sexes were natural, God-given, and therefore worthy of deep respect.[39] Suffragists and anti-suffragists often converged in the belief that the differences between men and women were socially beneficial, though some suffragists instead chose to emphasize the shared qualities of a common humanity.[40] Differentiated gender roles were believed to be particularly necessary within a highly civilized society which had judiciously removed many social and legal impediments to the full expression of women's distinctive strengths, as well as improving their educational opportunities. Social evolution was a major preoccupation of the late Victorian and Edwardian intelligentsia, and became another important influence on women's self-positioning within the suffrage spectrum. Supporters and opponents of votes for women often shared a belief that the advance of human societies (and especially British society) was accompanied by the evolution of a more influential role for women, both as biological bearers of racial strength and as guardians of moral values.[41] Yet this benign view of social evolution was counterbalanced, for most anti-suffragists, by vague fears of the consequences of failing the evolutionary test, whether for the British Empire, for British society, or for women as a sex. Diversion of women's social role away from the natural functions of motherhood, for

---

[39] This view is explained in A. Lovat, 'Women and the Suffrage', *The Nineteenth Century and After*, 62 (1907), 64–73 and in C. Stephen, 'Women and Politics', *The Nineteenth Century and After*, 61 (1910), 227–36.

[40] A contrasting emphasis upon shared humanity is to be found in J. Harrison, *"Homo Sum": Being a Letter to an Anti-Suffragist from an Anthropologist* (London: NUWSS, n.d., [*c*.1910]).

[41] See, e.g. anti-suffragist E. Colquhoun, 'Woman and Morality', *The Nineteenth Century and After*, 75 (1914), 128–140, and suffragists H. and M. Bernard, *Woman and Evolution* (London: Frank Palmer, 1909).

example through their future absorption into the male world of parliamentary government, could have catastrophic results both for individuals and for the progress of British civilization.[42]

The theme of motherhood was central to suffragism and to its opposition, serving both to unite and to divide. Whether or not women were to be direct participants in parliamentary government, their interests as mothers needed promotion and protection. Arguments circled around the best way to achieve this outcome, based upon a broad consensus over the importance of sound, healthy maternity for social cohesion and national efficiency. No issue was more vital to the later stages of the suffrage debate. The warnings of eugenicists, and of all those who regarded social evolution primarily in biological terms, were strongly accentuated by the setbacks of the South African War, then the demographic toll of the First World War. However, the most prominent women anti-suffragists shared the faith of many suffrage leaders in motherhood as a morally uplifting, civilizing force rather than simply a matter of healthy reproduction. There was unlimited scope for collaborative work among women to spread the force of intelligent, nurturing maternity beyond individual family homes out into the wider communities of nation and empire.[43]

Maternity was at the core of women's social action from the 1880s onwards, whether this took the form of individual charity, collective philanthropy, or involvement in the expanding work of local government. Social action by women and on behalf of mothers extended to include a wide range of related areas, including the emotive subjects of sexual conduct and social purity. Womanly social work was understood as drawing upon women's innate maternal qualities, whether or not they had children themselves. It was also very evidently a means of asserting the superiority of some mothers over others. The shared social class background of many suffrage and anti-suffrage women leaders served to consolidate their joint social action, both in theory and in practice. Middle-class womanly solidarity was powerfully symbolized at the annual gatherings of the National Union of Women Workers, which brought together women from all over the country to discuss practicalities and ideas concerning voluntary 'women's work'. No wonder the more determined and radical suffragists set out to capture the National Union for their cause; and no wonder they encountered stiff resistance, not only from anti-suffrage women, but also from many within the suffrage movement itself who were reluctant to break the ranks of true womanhood for the sake of a transient political cause.

Social action by genteel, motherly women was sometimes applauded from the sidelines by male anti-suffrage leaders. But it is apparent that they failed to grasp

---

[42] See e.g. E. Colquhoun, *Vocation of Woman*, ch. 11; A. Kenealy, 'Woman as Athlete', *The Nineteenth Century*, 45 (1899), 636–45, and 'Woman as Athlete: A Rejoinder', ibid. 915–29.

[43] This was advocated not merely by individual suffragists and anti-suffragists, but also by female imperialist societies including the Victoria League, the British Women's Emigration Association, the GFS, and the Mothers' Union.

the full significance of this defining aspect of womanhood for many of their female colleagues. They were on firmer shared ground when it came to resisting the threatening advance of democracy. Leading anti-suffrage women linked their views on women's social role to a positive concept of feminine gentility, and also to a profoundly negative fear of the ignorant masses.[44] The suffrage issue had always been inherently linked to the expansion of democratic government in Britain, and to debates over its social causes and consequences. The choice between various forms of limited female enfranchisement, and between a limited male and female franchise and full adult suffrage, was a difficult one for many suffragists. Organized anti-suffragism often chose to cast itself in the role of last remaining bulwark of civilization and rational government, holding back democratic forces which endangered far more than merely the efficiency of parliament: the abandonment of restraints upon democracy would be rapidly followed by subversion of the gender order and of society itself.

By definition, both male and female anti-suffragists were also anti-democrats, and many of them made no secret of their equally deep hostility to the labour movement and to socialism.[45] The heightened temperature of public debates over the Woman Question in the 1890s reflected these underlying concerns, as well as the potential threats to marriage and motherhood posed by the 'New Woman'.[46] Her incipient sexual revolt, whether in fact or fiction, was nearly as unwelcome to the more conservative suffragists as to the anti-suffrage women. For anti-suffragists of both sexes, it provided a confirmation of their worst fears about the corrupting influences of an increasingly democratic society. Women's lives were being perverted from their naturally beneficial social function by the twin evils of socialism and feminism, and women's suffrage would compound the danger to national life. Many suffragists and anti-suffragists were in broad agreement on the dangers of ill-considered, large-scale constitutional reform, given internal threats of class conflict and the extent of Britain's imperial responsibilities. The pre-war alliance between the National Union of Women's Suffrage Societies and the Labour party gave the women antis a golden opportunity to condemn conservative, anti-democratic suffragists for their inconsistency. Meanwhile the imperial duties of British womanhood provided common ground in some directions and weapons for attack in others, as suffragists and antis continued to rival each other's claims to the moral and political high ground in national life.

One aspect of democratic reform which united most suffrage and anti-suffrage women was their general welcome for women's expanding role in

---

[44] See e.g. the NLOWS provision to its speakers of alarming (and heavily emboldened) statistics on the numbers of prospective women voters in *The Anti-Suffrage Handbook*, 10–11.

[45] For examples of hostility to socialism, see Lord Cromer, 'Feminism in France', *National Review*, 62 (1913–14), 403–8; and C. Dawbon, 'Feminisme in France', *The Nineteenth Century and After*, 61 (1906), 816–22.

[46] For the 1890s New Woman debate, see A. Richardson, and C. Willis (eds.), *The New Woman in Fiction and in Fact: Fin-de-Siecle Feminisms* (Houndmills: Palgrave, 2001).

local government. The antis were sometimes accused of hypocrisy by suffragist contemporaries, but their enthusiasm for local government was entirely consistent with their general views on social action.[47] During the late nineteenth century it was by no means obvious that local government would become more and more yoked to parliamentary decision-making, and less and less dependent upon the voluntary social service provided by middle-class and upper-class women. The early twentieth century proved a turning point in this respect, as the Liberal government's social reform programme was followed by an onslaught of centralizing wartime bureaucracy. But the anti-suffrage proponents of 'womanly' local government lacked the benefit of historical hindsight as they tried to remain true to their long-established faith in women's gendered citizenship. The Women's National Anti-Suffrage League stoutly defended its 'second objective' of promoting women's contribution to local government within the merged League of 1910–18, despite the hostility of male leaders who dismissed this issue as an unwelcome diversion.[48]

The problematic merger of the male and female anti-suffrage Leagues in 1910 provides further evidence of the women anti-suffragists' views on both gender and citizenship. Despite their confidence in womanly strength, and in women's distinctive contribution towards a successful society, female anti-suffragists were deeply committed to working alongside men. Women's qualities could only flower within such a collaborative relationship. The idea of a 'sex war' (allegedly promoted by the 'feminists' and their suffragist allies) was anathema to those who sought a complementary gender role for women within an organic, stable society.[49] Many moderate suffragists were also trying hard to avoid fostering hostility between the sexes. There was further genuinely shared ground on this fundamental issue, though anti-suffrage polemicists sometimes tried to prove otherwise. Meanwhile the anti-suffrage women themselves were open to criticism for inconsistency as they discussed the most appropriate organizational means of combining their belief in gender collaboration with their belief in gender differentiation. Most felt strongly that the complementarity of male and female qualities should be expressed through joint organization for some social and political purposes, but that there were other spheres of public work which belonged either to men or to women alone. The imperial work of the British Houses of Parliament belonged to the male sphere. This claim was central to both male and female anti-suffragism. Despite the overlaps of work and beliefs

---

[47] The local government argument was first expressed in the 1889 Appeal, then reiterated in many later women's anti-suffragist speeches and articles. Local government was 'the domestic work of the nation' and called for the qualities of 'a good housewife', according to the *Anti-Suffrage Review* (Mar. 1909), 2.

[48] See Ch. 9, below, and J. Bush, 'British Women's Anti-Suffragism and the Forward Policy, 1908–1914', *Women's History Review*, 11/3 (2002), 431–54.

[49] See e.g. E. Colquhoun, 'Modern Feminism and Sex Antagonism', *Quarterly Review*, 219 (1913), 143–66.

between the more conservative suffragists and the more progressive, socially concerned women antis, a clear division emerged between those women who wanted to vote in parliamentary elections and thus share directly in national government, and those dedicated to the defence of gender separation within the most powerful arena of public life.

The extended debate over woman's nature, capabilities, and social functions during the suffrage campaign helped to determine its conduct and outcomes. Whilst the suffrage campaign contributed to the argument in various ways, it was as much a product of the Woman Question as a cause. New thinking about the qualities and duties of womanhood took place at many levels of society, though its most coherent expression remained dominated by educated leaders and opinion-formers. Inevitably, a multifaceted public discussion resulted in a huge range of different, conflicting viewpoints. In simplified forms, these percolated through the press, the pulpit, the schoolroom, and many other means of communication to virtually every home in Britain. The Woman Question was lived out by Victorian and Edwardian women, whether or not they chose to become active, organized participants within either its suffragist or anti-suffragist dimensions. Even small-scale domestic decisions were often unconsciously influenced by the large-scale gender debate raging elsewhere. Most women remained unorganized, and from their perspective it seems particularly apparent that the suffrage issue was not necessarily the most important aspect of the Woman Question. Though media attention ensured that the demand for votes for women was universally discussed during the years before the First World War, both suffrage and anti-suffrage organizations failed to mobilize more than a small minority of women as active adherents. The Girls' Friendly Society, the Mothers' Union, and the many other non-political societies affiliated to the National Union of Women Workers were conspicuously more successful in this respect.[50] They tapped into existing social structures and belief systems which made few challenging demands upon women's understanding of their prescribed role in life, and provided valued companionship and support. Rather than polarizing opinion around a single issue (such as the vote), they deliberately set out to cultivate the common ground among women which in many respects had been reinforced by an extended public debate over the nature of true womanhood.

Would votes for women fundamentally alter anything? Both suffragists and anti-suffragists faced an uphill struggle in convincing British women that this was the case. Whilst debating the Woman Question within their own organizations and with each other, they needed also to demonstrate its relevance to ordinary women's lives. At their most successful, women activists on both sides of the suffrage divide linked the franchise question to broader concerns over education,

---

[50] By 1914 the GFS claimed nearly 200,000 members, and the Mothers' Union over 400,000. See Ch. 3, below, for more information on the development of these organizations in relation to anti-suffragism.

employment, marriage, sexual behaviour, the hardships of working-class families, and the prospects of Britain as a world power. These subjects were recurrent within the pre-war history of women's anti-suffragism and remained prominent during the war years, when party politics and the suffrage question itself were in temporary abeyance. By the end of the war, the anti-suffrage cause was lost. But the broader social issues to which the suffrage debate had always been linked had never been more pressing. Women antis took comfort in the continuing relevance of their commitment to gendered social action, to maternity, and to the development of influential womanly citizenship. Though citizenship was to take the unwelcome form of the female parliamentary franchise, women voters might yet be persuaded to prioritize those aspects of womanhood which were their most precious contribution to society. During and after the war, suffrage supporters and their opponents found new opportunities to work together towards common ends. The rapid and largely successful mending of fences after 1918 serves to underline once again the extent to which the divisive pre-war campaign had mobilized women who shared many common ideals, despite having campaigned against each other over the vote.

The structure of this book aims to provide adequate space both for individual women anti-suffragists and for their organizations, in order to evaluate their place within the broad spectrum of the suffrage campaign and their role in wider women's history. The next four chapters introduce some of the leading protagonists. Women who became active in the cause of anti-suffragism generally made this commitment in relation to other aspects of their lives. They can be broadly categorized through their wider activities, which often resulted in anti-suffrage female friendship networks paralleling those of the better-known suffragist women. Anti-suffragism was rarely, if ever, a single-issue campaign for women. It was also fundamentally a social rather than merely a political cause. Even those whose commitment to anti-suffragism was temporary, or of less personal significance than other activities, can be related to the three loose groupings identified here: the maternal reformers, the women writers, and the imperialist ladies. In a few exceptional cases women worked within all these areas simultaneously, but usually their primary interests and activities lay within one or another.

The retrospective grouping-together of women leaders has been adopted as a device for exploring the intersection of individuals' lives as well as of their ideas. It rests upon the assumption that attitudes towards votes for women were conditioned by personal experience, as well as by the powerful currents of opinion which swirled around the Woman Question. The leading anti-suffrage women were participants in contemporary intellectual debates over the position of women and the role of gender in society. However, their decision to make a stand on the specific issue of the parliamentary franchise was often the outcome of circumstance as well as of ideological conviction. Personal life histories contribute towards an understanding of how and why some women came to believe that female enfranchisement was a serious threat to British women and to British society. At the same time many women's gendered collective work, pursued alongside the campaign against the vote, reveals much about their sense of priorities as well as the contexts which shaped both suffragism and anti-suffragism. Consideration of these women's lives, both as individuals and as members of associative networks, helps us to explore the ways in which anti-suffrage motivation and opportunities for activism related to personal choices as well as to social and intellectual milieu. The leading women decided to oppose suffragism for their own reasons. Many of them held decided views on the Woman Question which did not simply mirror those of male anti-suffragists. They applied their beliefs about women's gender role to a range of current social concerns, and drew strength and commitment to anti-suffragism from their parallel involvement in womanly work for nation and empire. At the same time, male antis often encouraged the women in their lives to take an interest in the movement. A shadowy fourth category emerges of women in lesser leadership roles whose main reason for activism was indeed a strong desire to identify closely with male anti-suffragism.

The organizational history of women's opposition to the vote is then analysed in the five chapters which follow. The ideas and motives of anti-suffrage women provide an underlying thread of discussion throughout the book, but detailed consideration of women's activism within the organized extra-parliamentary campaign is also essential to a study which seeks to redress the balance of earlier work centred mainly upon its masculine, parliamentary dimensions. By gender definition, the campaign within the male imperial Parliament is beyond the direct remit of the present work. However, the intersection between male and female activities beyond Parliament is a central concern of this book, and of course indirectly related to events and debates in Parliament itself. In the wake of the current study of female anti-suffragism, a revisionist study is needed of the movement as a whole, fully integrating parliamentary and extra-parliamentary dimensions. A more detailed analysis of women's contribution to organized anti-suffragism, both as leaders and supporters, provides new dimensions to our understanding of the movement's ideology and methods and reveals some of the ways in which anti-suffrage campaigning related to wider debates over the Woman Question. Organizational history and the history of ideas are closely connected, but their interconnections require detailed exploration and cannot simply be taken for granted. Relationships between men and women, and between leaders and followers, are particularly fruitful areas for discussion. Chapters 6, 7, and 8 focus upon defining moments in the history of organized anti-suffragism, including evaluation of their longer-term outcomes. In chronological order, attention is given to the earliest stages of organized female opposition in the 1880s, to the origins and achievements of the Women's National Anti-Suffrage League which existed from 1908 to 1910, to the merger decision of 1910 and its consequences, and to the strengths and deficiencies of the mixed-sex

National League for Opposing Woman Suffrage from 1910 to 1918. Chapter 9 reverts to a broader consideration of ideas within the anti-suffrage movement. Underlying the organizational successes and failures of pre-war anti-suffragism were interesting debates over female citizenship, related to underlying views on sexual politics and on constitutional reform, as well as to the immediate strategy and tactics of the anti-suffrage campaign. In Chapter 10 the leading women's wartime experience provides a further opportunity to relate anti-suffrage attitudes to social activism, and to investigate the continuing work of organized anti-suffragism within an increasingly difficult context. Last-gasp efforts by male and female diehards to prevent enfranchisement in 1917–18 were made in the face of defections from the cause by both men and women. Personal pride was at stake, but the remaining women antis also had firm grounds for believing that the war had not been entirely unfavourable to the ongoing cause of conservative womanhood. The broader social aims of female anti-suffragism still seemed worth defending.

The final chapter assesses the continuing relevance of female anti-suffragists' ideas in post-war Britain, rather than merely cataloguing their failures. Those who persisted in public life after the war soon found new outlets for what had previously been anti-suffrage views, whether within the women's movement or within the mainstream of British politics and government. This tends to reinforce the central conclusions of the present study. Women opposed their own enfranchisement for constructive as well as negative reasons, and they did so in very large numbers. Women against the vote deserve more attention within histories of anti-suffragism and of suffragism alike, for the relationship between these opposing movements was more than merely reciprocal. Suffragists and anti-suffragists defined each other's ideas and activities through collaboration as well as through conflict. A study of the manifold connections between women who supported and women who opposed the vote helps to set the suffrage debate in perspective as an aspect of the multi-dimensional late Victorian and Edwardian women's movement, rather than necessarily the keystone of the arch. The importance of women within the anti-suffrage movement, together with the many interesting connections they made between anti-suffragism, gender conservatism, and the wider women's movement, indicates that this much-maligned body of female opinion should now be restored to the mainstream of British women's history.

PART I

THE LEADING WOMEN
ANTI-SUFFRAGISTS

2

Maternal Reformers and Education

ANTI-SUFFRAGISM AND THE MATERNAL IDEAL

The maternal reformers were the most important leadership group among the women anti-suffragists. Their views on the centrality of motherhood to anti-suffragism, and on maternity's relationship to educational and social reform, helped to provide female opposition to the vote with a voice of its own. Not all maternal reformers were anti-suffragists, of course. The discourse of social maternalism suffused a wide variety of late Victorian and Edwardian reform campaigns, including the campaign for female enfranchisement itself. Yet leading women who opposed the vote drew insistently upon maternal ideals to support the case for alternative, more appropriate forms of womanly civic duty. Arguing from similar premises to many suffragists, anti-suffrage women reached different conclusions on the most appropriate means of extending beneficial maternal influence through society. They also distanced themselves from male anti-suffrage colleagues by their emphasis upon the inseparable ties between anti-suffragism and active support for women's participation in philanthropy, education, and local government. Maternal reformism underpinned what became known, after 1908, as the forward policy: a version of anti-suffragism shaped and supported by women who were determined to construct a positive opposition to the vote which would harness women's talents and enhance their future citizenship in a manner fully consonant with respect for gender difference. The forward policy was no mere tactical ploy. It symbolized the self-confidence and self-respect of anti-suffrage women, and their connectedness to the wider women's movement. For supporters of the forward policy, anti-suffragism was a logical extension of an existing commitment to motherly social action. This commitment, in turn, helped to position anti-suffragism at the heart of current social concerns. Women's opposition to the vote was intertwined with their strong views on the condition of British society, as well as the condition of British womanhood. The fact that anti-suffragism rested upon many ill-founded assumptions should not be allowed to conceal the depth and breadth of its support among women active in educational and social reform.

Before turning to individual life histories to illustrate the emergence of the maternal reformers' anti-suffrage beliefs, the particular importance attached to motherhood during this period requires brief introduction. The origins of public reverence for the maternal role, and of its claims to special social and national status, can be traced as far back as the late eighteenth century. Linda Colley has highlighted Rousseau's contribution towards a more polarized understanding of separate gender roles, linked in turn to the well-being of the state.[1] Women's involvement in early nineteenth-century reform movements was widely (though not exclusively) construed in terms of gender difference, and the responsibilities of virtuous wives and mothers.[2] Leonore Davidoff and Catherine Hall concluded from their study of early nineteenth-century family life that 'the language of class formation was gendered', and that many middle-class women gradually found themselves more rigidly contained within their prescribed marital sphere.[3] This provided a context for mid-Victorian criticisms of patriarchy, whilst also establishing a case for women's vital civic importance in the fulfilment of their family duties. Mothers were at the heart of the Victorian home, as educators, moral guardians, and care-givers, and over the decades which followed, the domestic roles of women were increasingly defined in relation to a spiritual mission of wifehood and maternity. Ruskin's *Sesame and Lilies*, published in 1865, became the most popular of his books, with its much-quoted definitions of women's 'true queenly power', exercised 'not in their households merely, but over all within their sphere'.[4]

The message that strongly differentiated gender roles were beneficial to civic society, as well as a source of satisfaction and empowerment for women themselves, was taken up in the late nineteenth century by suffragists and women anti-suffragists alike. The dignity of womanhood provided the central didactic message for innumerable sermons, books, papers, and speeches, and percolated as an ideal through all social classes. Towards the end of the century the maternal role became valued above all other womanly roles by leading opinion-formers in Britain. The reasons for this have been analysed by a number of historians.[5] They include the fact that motherhood's moral and educative functions were believed indispensable to the task of civilizing an urbanizing, modernizing Britain and

[1] L. Colley, *Britons: Forging the Nation 1717–1837* (New Haven: Yale University Press, 1992), 273–4.

[2] See e.g. K. Gleadle and S. Richardson (eds.), *Women in British Politics, 1760–1869: The Power of the Petticoat* (Basingstoke: Macmillan, 2000); C. Midgley, *Women Against Slavery: The British Campaigns 1780–1870* (London: Routledge, 1992).

[3] L. Davidoff, and C. Hall, *Family Fortunes: Men and Women of the English Middle Class 1780–1850* (London: Hutchinson, 1987), 450–2.

[4] J. Ruskin, *Sesame and Lilies*, ed. J. Bryson (London: J. M. Dent and Sons, 1970), 49.

[5] See e.g. A. Davin, 'Imperialism and Motherhood', *History Workshop Journal*, 5 (1978), 9–65; J. Harris, *Private Lives, Public Spirit: Britain 1870–1914* (London: Penguin Books, 1994); S. Koven and S. Michel, *Mothers of a New World: Maternalism, Politics and the Origins of Welfare States* (London: Routledge, 1993). Suffragist and feminist links with social maternalism have been researched much more extensively than non-suffragist or anti-suffragist equivalents: e.g. G. Bock and P. Thane, *Maternity and Gender Policies: Women and the Rise of the European Welfare States 1880s–1950s* (London: Routledge, 1991).

its expanding empire; at the same time its reproductive, physically caring side was equally essential to future national efficiency and imperial strength. The home as the centre of domestic life, and the mother as the domestic ruler of that home, were powerfully symbolized by Queen Victoria's chosen public image, and reinforced at the opposite end of the social scale by male workers' collective demands for a 'family wage' to secure the respectability of well-cared-for families as well as the economic status of male breadwinners. Meanwhile middle-class and upper-class women became increasingly self-conscious experts in maternity. The literature on social and scientific aspects of motherhood expanded, alongside growing opportunities for leisured, educated women to apply their maternal wisdom beyond their own homes.

The late nineteenth century witnessed a huge expansion of women's philanthropic activity, inspired by maternalist ideals as well as by social investigation and evangelical religious duty. Louisa Hubbard, editor of *The Englishwoman's Yearbook*, estimated that by 1893 half a million women were working 'continuously and semi-professionally' in philanthropy, in addition to 20,000 paid officials of charities, 20,000 nurses, and several hundred thousand women donating their social effort through the Mothers' Union and other Christian societies.[6] Frank Prochaska has demonstrated both the myriad forms of organized female philanthropy and the importance of its small-scale local dimensions, which connected closely to private charity and domestic life.[7] Further impetus to women's philanthropy was given by the gradual extension of state intervention into social welfare. Voluntary social action was undoubtedly encouraged, rather than threatened, by Victorian developments in Poor Law administration and elementary education, and the advent of elected local councils with welfare roles in town and country.[8] Women found themselves with an extended choice of philanthropic and educational work, assisted by a wider range of funding, and potentially leading on to positions of greater public responsibility. By the end of the century, the scope for maternal reform included membership of School Boards and Boards of Guardians, and of innumerable local and national voluntary societies devoted to care of the poor, social purity, educational and religious improvement, and health reform, alongside the more traditional Church work and family duties. The enhancement of female education in the second half of the nineteenth century can be read as part of the same wave of social action, led by women and directed towards the improvement of women's lives. Though there were other reasons for educating women, including their urge towards

---

[6] A. Burdett-Coutts (ed.), *Woman's Mission* (London: Samson, Low, Marston and Co., 1893), 361.

[7] F. Prochaska, *Women and Philanthropy in Nineteenth Century England* (Oxford: Clarendon Press, 1980).

[8] See G. Finlayson, *Citizen, State and Social Welfare in Britain 1830–1990* (Oxford: Oxford University Press, 1994), 166–75; F. Prochaska, *The Voluntary Impulse and Philanthropy in Modern Britain* (London: Faber and Faber, 1988).

self-fulfilment and (in some cases) aspirations towards professional opportunity, the publicly stated rationale for female education was often linked to wider social improvement and to educated women's ability to contribute towards this end. The process of opening up girls' schools and university education for women was a complex one resting upon many different sources of male as well as female support. Amongst other sources, it drew upon the philanthropic impulse and upon women's desire to influence social progress through the exercise of feminine civic virtue.

Experiences of organized philanthropy and of collective action in the cause of female education led some women towards the female suffrage campaign. Millicent Fawcett stated plainly in *Home and Politics* (1894): 'I advocate the extension of the franchise to women because I wish to see the womanly and domestic side of things weigh more and count for more in all public concerns'.[9] However, other women shared the contrasting conclusions drawn by anti-suffragist maternal reformers. Women were primarily responsible for home and family, so their vocation for spiritual and practical mothering could find its most fruitful fulfilment in their own families. Local communities and wider civic society stood to benefit from the special qualities of maternal social care only if certain boundaries were respected. The parliamentary vote was therefore a dangerous diversion from more suitable work close at hand. At the turn of the century the maternal excellence judged vital to the physical and moral welfare of the British imperial race was believed to rest heavily upon women's own domestic efforts. In a 1905 article titled 'The True Foundations of Empire', leading anti-suffragist Violet Markham claimed that 'the greatness of any nation is proportionate to the strength of its family life'.[10] When Mary Ward launched the Woman's National Anti-Suffrage League three years later, she stated: 'Women's true sphere is already secured to her, both in the home and the State, and what she has to do now is to fill and possess it'.[11] The Quaker anti-suffragist Caroline Stephen claimed to write on behalf of a 'great though silent multitude of women' as she expressed her belief that women's time and energies should be devoted first and foremost to 'discharging those duties which she alone is capable of undertaking . . . who can underestimate the importance to the whole nation of the right and unhindered performance of those duties?'[12] Other opponents of women's suffrage shared her faith in 'the purest and noblest type of womanhood . . . largely developed by the experiences and habits of motherhood'. There was a pressing need for 'feminine and motherly influences on public affairs', but this could only be met by those who 'before all things remain feminine and motherly', extending their sway

[9] M. Fawcett, *Home and Politics* (London: Women's Printing Society, 1894), 8.
[10] V. Markham, 'The True Foundations of Empire: the Home and the Workshop', *Nineteenth Century and After*, 59 (1905), 575.
[11] M. Ward, 'The Women's Anti-Suffrage Movement', *Nineteenth Century and After*, 64 (1908), 352.
[12] C. Stephen, 'Women and Politics', *Nineteenth Century and After*, 61 (1907), 227, 229.

through family nurture and inconspicuous social service rather than through the misguided experiment of sharing masculine parliamentary politics.[13]

Maternal values were energetically contested between suffragists and their opponents, in a period when public veneration of motherhood was accompanied by growing concern over the 'racial' consequences of women's failure to live up to the maternal ideal. Who were the women who yoked social maternalism to the anti-suffrage cause? To a greater or lesser extent, they included most of the leading women anti-suffragists. The trope of ideal motherhood was almost always present when the case against the vote was argued by women; it was also (though less frequently) pressed into service by anti-suffrage men. Opposition to the vote was invariably multifaceted, in the case of each woman supporter as well as in the collective experience of a lengthy, diverse campaign. It was also the outcome of multiple causes, including the powerful contexts of personal and family life, as well as the influences of direct argument and of broader ideological conviction. Unidimensional and monocausal explanations of individuals' anti-suffragism must be carefully avoided. However, against a background of widespread anti-suffrage enthusiasm for maternal reform, a number of leading women can be identified whose outlook was particularly framed by their views on motherhood and gendered social responsibility. They included the five women whose upbringing, family life, and public work is considered in the present chapter and the one which follows: Mary Ward, Louise Creighton, Ethel Harrison, Elizabeth Wordsworth, and Lucy Soulsby. These five maternal reformers have been grouped together because they shared some fundamental ideas in common. Their lives also intersected, both through their educational work in late Victorian Oxford and through their work for a variety of other social causes. It can be concluded that shared enthusiasm for educational and social reform, linked to a shared faith in maternalism, contributed towards their dislike of female suffrage, though in other respects these women led contrasting rather than similar lives.[14]

The most obvious contrasts among the women include their different levels of engagement with organized anti-suffragism. Mary Ward, Louise Creighton, and Ethel Harrison were the main authors and organizers of the 1889 Appeal Against Women's Suffrage. By 1908, when the Women's League again took up cudgels on behalf of female anti-suffragism, Louise Creighton had publicly recanted her opposition to votes for women, without, however, departing from her faith in maternal reformism, and her desire to build bridges between women on both sides of the suffrage divide. Mary Ward and Ethel Harrison, on the other hand, both became members of the Women's National Anti-Suffrage

---

[13] Ibid. 233, 234.

[14] See J. Bush, ' "Special strengths for their own special duties": Women, Higher Education and Gender Conservatism in Late Victorian Britain', *History of Education*, 34:4 (July 2005), 387–405, for a more detailed discussion of conservative women's contribution towards women's higher education in Oxford.

League executive committee. Mary Ward remained the main inspiration behind organized women's anti-suffragism until the final defeat of 1918. Elizabeth Wordsworth stands apart from the other four women as a non-suffragist, or an undeclared anti-suffragist, during most of her long life. As the distinguished Principal of Lady Margaret Hall, Oxford, she took no part in organized anti-suffragism, despite her friendships with many leading male and female antis. Her anti-suffrage sympathies were occasionally indicated in her private correspondence, while her broadly conservative gender outlook was influentially expressed through her educational work at Oxford and through her writings and speeches. Lucy Soulsby was another devoutly Anglican educator, and one of Elizabeth Wordsworth's friends. She was a resolute and lifelong anti-suffragist; a signatory of the 1889 Appeal; and a maternalist bridge-builder alongside Louise Creighton, in the National Union of Women Workers, as well as a committed member of the Edwardian anti-suffrage Leagues. The unmarried status of Elizabeth Worsdworth and Lucy Soulsby was no impediment to their advocacy of maternal educational and social reform; on the other hand Mary Ward, Louise Creighton, and Ethel Harrison made a conscious attempt to develop and exemplify their views on maternalism through their own lives as wives and mothers. Turning from contrasts to commonalities, these women all believed that the socially valuable aspects of innate maternal instinct needed appropriate enhancement through education. All were active in promoting educational causes, including the secondary education of girls and the higher education of women. All believed that maternal duty extended beyond the home, and that it played a central role in defining women's potentially influential and respected status as unenfranchised citizens. All helped to promote female philanthropic work, and welcomed women's growing involvement in local government as an extension of their voluntary social action.

The analysis which follows focuses upon the shared ideas and joint activity of these women, whilst also revealing their diversity. In the current chapter an outline is presented of each woman's formative years, suggesting the varying influences of family life and early education upon social and political outlook. The women's experiences of Oxford University, and of the advent of women's higher education, provide an opportunity to explore some further dimensions of maternal reformism in a setting which more famously inspired strong male anti-suffragism. In Chapter 3 the same group of maternal reformers are followed out into the wider world of social action, through their involvement in a range of organizations which extended into the heartlands of the British women's movement. Their ideas and activism connect with the histories of the largest British women's organizations, demonstrating the compatibility of anti-suffrage views with the maternalist ethos of these organizations as well as illustrating the varied ways in which the non-political British women's movement responded to the suffrage campaign. Together, the lives of these women help us to understand the influences which shaped anti-suffrage maternal reformism as a convincing, and far more attractive, alternative to suffragism for many intelligent, socially aware late-Victorian ladies.

GIRLS GROWING UP

Autobiographies are prone to dwell upon the formative years of childhood and those of the anti-suffrage women leaders are no exception. Both Mary Ward and Louise Creighton left memoirs which provide direct and indirect evidence of their experiences of being 'mothered'.[15] Certainly the young Mary Ward did not experience the kind of ideal mothering which anti-suffragists so strongly commended to others. Born in Tasmania in 1851, she was the daughter of a troubled marriage. Her father, Thomas Arnold, was a son of the illustrious mid-Victorian headmaster of Rugby School, but his religious travails as a twice-converted Catholic resulted in career blight as well as domestic strife. Her mother struggled with financial insecurity coupled with incessant pregnancies, separated from her husband in middle age, and was only too relieved to offload her responsibilities for a volatile eldest daughter onto several inadequate English boarding schools.[16] Mary Ward vividly depicted her own schooldays in her novel *Marcella*, whose heroine was 'the plain naughty child, whom nobody cared about, whose mother never wrote to her, who in contrast to every other girl in the school had not a single "party frock", despite having a distinguished uncle who had been Speaker of the House of Commons'. As a young adult, Marcella's short stay in London produced 'the chief excitement and motive-power of her new life . . . in the birth of social and philanthropic ardour, the sense of a hitherto unsuspected social power'.[17]

Mary Ward's own social conscience was certainly closely connected to her experience of family life both as a daughter and a mother herself. Somewhat starved of affection, she developed a strong need for the approval of others, an equally strong sense of family duty, and a commitment to the welfare of neglected children. After suffering a schooling which was 'practically wasted',[18] Mary's career as a reformer began with the expansion of educational opportunities for young women at Oxford, herself included. For anti-suffrage educators,

[15] M. Ward, *A Writer's Recollections* (London: W. Collins and Sons, 1918); L. Creighton, *Memoir of a Victorian Woman*, ed. J. T. Covert (Blomington: Indiana University Press, 1994). See also biographers of Mary Ward: J. Trevelyan, *The Life of Mrs Humphry Ward* (London: Constable, 1923); E. Huws Jones, *Mrs Humphry Ward* (London: Heinemann, 1973); J. Sutherland, *Mrs Humphry Ward: Eminent Victorian, Pre-Eminent Edwardian* (Oxford: Oxford University Press, 1991); and of Louise Creighton: J. Covert, *A Victorian Marriage: Mandell and Louise Creighton* (London: Hambledon and London, 2000).

[16] John Sutherland's biography places particular emphasis on the parental deprivation suffered by Mary Ward, concluding that in later life she sought out strong father figures. *Mrs Humphry Ward*, 26.

[17] M. Ward, *Marcella* (London: Virago Press, 1984 edn.), 7, 15.   [18] Ward, *Recollections*, 96.

training for womanhood and motherhood naturally involved more than mere book-learning. Somehow the feeding of minds must be accompanied by the maternal cultivation of girls' femininity. It is interesting to note that Mary's autobiographical account of her childhood, while dutifully silent on her mother's maternal deficiencies, includes an idealized portrait of her paternal grandmother, 'wife of Dr Arnold of Rugby'. During a thirty-year widowhood, this lady brought up her nine children so successfully that 'she possessed their passionate reverence and affection, and . . . each and all of them would have acknowledged her as among the dearest and noblest influences in their lives'.[19] Here was the mother Mary Ward had never had, and was never herself to become despite her best efforts to live up to the maternal ideal. In adulthood, an uneasy coexistence developed between the strong, successful woman novelist and social reformer, and the nostalgically remembered 'complete' mother she commended through her anti-suffrage campaign.[20]

Louise Creighton may have stronger claims than most to the mantle of ideal maternity. Yet her autobiography is remarkably unsentimental about the motherhood which so dominated her life and ideas. Instead, it offers fascinating insights into some of the tensions between her family life and work, even within one of the most apparently successful of Victorian companionate marriages. She, too, was born into a slightly unconventional upper middle-class family. Her moderately wealthy father was a Baltic trader, of German origins but naturalized and settled in London, where he married the only daughter of a Scottish businessman. Her mother produced a family of thirteen children. Despite being 'worn out with her large family', she superintended Louise's home education, encouraged her to read, and ensured that she became fluent in French and German as well as a proficient artist. Eight older brothers and sisters helped to fill the gaps, carrying Louise off to classes at the nearby Crystal Palace and enlivening the house with their friends and acquaintances. But it was her mother's reliable presence which counted for most in her childhood: 'The strongest feeling about her that I had was, I think, that it was upon her whom every thing depended and that I was absolutely sure of her.' Reflecting back as a successful maternal reformer, Louise judged that her mother had possessed a 'finer intelligence' than her father, though 'the strain of her large family must have made it impossible for her to maintain any definite habits of reading and study'. Her father's ideas 'ruled the home; but it was her character that made those ideas effective'.[21]

With the encouragement of a family friend, Louise joined the Self-Help Essay Society, a useful precursor of university extension classes and higher education for women. In 1869 she established her own small essay society devoted to art

[19] Ward, *Recollections*, 25–6.
[20] Mary Ward wrote, 'nothing could have been more "complete", more rounded, than my grandmother's character and life'. Ibid. 25.
[21] Creighton, *Memoir*, 3, 17.

history, and when London University's first Higher Examination for Women was fortuitously advertised in the same year, 'I immediately decided to go in for it'. In old age the pleasure of a pass 'with honours' had not yet worn off; neither had her gratitude towards a mother who 'encouraged my studies and never tried to get me to spend much time over sewing'.[22] As a young married woman, Louise Creighton was to continue her education alongside Mary Ward at Oxford, and to promote the education of other women. She gradually moved into a wider range of social reform activities, but never lost her belief in the importance of reconciling womanly and motherly roles with women's own intellectual development. Possession of the parliamentary vote seemed a remote issue to both these close friends, alongside the immediate practicalities of maternal education and social welfare. But it is significant that Louise Creighton's daughters eventually received a university education, while Mary Ward's did not.

Ethel Harrison left no autobiography and relatively few letters. Her husband, the Positivist philosopher Frederic Harrison, composed a short memoir after her death in 1916, and her son's account of his father's life and ideas adds limited further information.[23] Ethel's anti-suffrage views are more fully explained in her journalism and her 1908 book, *The Freedom of Women*, which was adopted as one of the favourite texts of the women's anti-suffrage movement.[24] As an adult, she became a convinced Positivist as well as an anti-suffragist. This encouraged her to represent herself as a retiring wife and mother, whose spiritual influence was exerted primarily through the men in her life. However, it remains to be considered how she reached this position, and whether her anti-suffragism was purely the outcome of her husband's overwhelming influence. Born in 1851, she passed a sheltered childhood in the comfortable home of a wealthy West Indies merchant. Her parents shared literary and musical interests, and Ethel was entirely home-educated by governesses and her extended family. Though detailed information is unavailable on her childhood, it appears to have been a happy and studious one. Her first cousin was Frederic Harrison, a brilliant scholar who initially devoted his Oxford education and his legal training largely to the welfare of the working classes. A full twenty years older than Ethel, he was part of her life from childhood onwards, and an increasingly powerful influence upon her as she reached the teenage years. They read together, developed the 'tender relations'[25] which so frequently arose between highly educated Victorian men and very much younger women, and by the age of 17 Ethel had both converted to Positivism and engaged herself to marry.

---

[22] Ibid. 28.

[23] F. Harrison, *Memoir and Essays of Ethelbertha Harrison* (Bath: Sir Isaac Pitman and Sons, 1917); A. Harrison, *Frederic Harrison: Thoughts and Memories* (London: William Heinemann, 1926).

[24] E. Harrison, *The Freedom of Women* (London: Watts and Co., 1908).

[25] This expression was used by Louise Creighton to describe historian J. R. Green's fondness for young protégées, including herself.

It is difficult to avoid the conclusion that this intelligent young woman had willingly agreed to subordinate her life and ideas to those of her husband. Harrison himself joined the Positivist 'religion of Mankind' in 1866, and was in the first flush of enthusiasm for this rationalist, socially improving creed at the time of his courtship. The only hint that Ethel may have exercised some reciprocal influence, even at this early stage of her life, appears in her husband's posthumous memoir. In a somewhat backhanded tribute, he insisted that Ethel's literary and social work had been 'all entirely her own in design as well as in execution', adding that he had 'needed to learn from her how women of high intelligence and noble nature felt and thought about the voting of women. Even before our marriage, as a girl of seventeen, in this question she rather held me back, when I was much under the influence of Mr John Stuart Mill'.[26] It is interesting to find that the youthful Ethel had already formed definite opinions on one of the key issues of the day, and that these views were apparently discussed at an intellectual rather than purely religious or emotional level between the engaged couple. In later life her anti-suffragism was to form her most forthright intervention into the public affairs of the nation.

Elizabeth Wordsworth's biographer describes her as 'one of the great figures of the women's movement, a cause in which she took not the faintest interest'.[27] This neatly summarizes her lack of enthusiasm for suffragism, allied to an important role in the educational advancement of women, but understates her involvement in wider debates over the Woman Question. As a leading university woman, she shared other maternal anti-suffragists' belief in the supreme importance of safeguarding femininity whilst at the same time fostering women's intellectual development. Her surviving correspondence is in the archive of Lady Margaret Hall: a reminder not only of her status within the university, but also of the way in which the College became her extended family, as she had always intended that it should. Elizabeth Wordsworth was the great-niece of the poet and daughter of Christopher Wordsworth, Headmaster of Harrow School, Canon of Westminster, and Bishop of Lincoln. Her grandfather had been Master of Trinity College Cambridge, and her theologian brother became Bishop of Salisbury.[28] Elizabeth's upbringing was strongly influenced by the Tractarian debates over the doctrines and practices of the Anglican Church, and its relationship to the Church of Rome. In contrast to conventional Victorian views on parental roles, her mother apparently left her education mainly in her husband's hands, once the governesses had completed their work. She spent a single year at boarding school, but was eager to return to the far more intellectually stimulating

[26] F. Harrison, *Memoir*, 21.

[27] G. Battiscombe, *Reluctant Pioneer: A Life of Elizabeth Wordsworth* (London: Constable, 1978), 11.

[28] John Worsdworth, Elizabeth's brother, was initially opposed to the foundation of women's colleges. Mary Ward wrote a polemical attack against his theological position in a series of Oxford lectures in 1881, and was never subsequently friendly with Elizabeth.

environment of her family home. According to her biographer, her mother was 'a soft cushion' who 'deprecated any show of interest in scholarship as something highly unbecoming in a woman'.[29]

This role model was less appealing to Elizabeth Wordsworth than the prospect of becoming her father's chief assistant as he wrote his theological commentary upon the entire Bible. The Wordsworths were wealthy: there seems to have been little pressure upon her to marry and no expectation at all that she should develop a means of earning her own living. Unlike Mary Ward, Louise Creighton, and Ethel Harrison, Elizabeth Wordsworth enjoyed an extended period as the unmarried daughter-at-home, developing social graces and domestic management skills alongside her academic training. She began to write poems, tracts, and stories from a young age, and published some through Charlotte Yonge's magazine for young women, *The Monthly Packet*. It was not until the age of 30 that she made friends with this most successful of Victorian women writers. Their friendship was to be an important influence on her life, steering her firmly towards a conservative view of woman's duty.[30]

Lucy Soulsby was another admirer of Charlotte Yonge, and in due course came to know and admire Elizabeth Wordsworth too. Like both these women, she held views on womanhood which were closely bound up with her Anglican Christianity. However, her childhood was a much less privileged one, and her religious faith more ecumenical. Born in 1856, she experienced 'years of privation and hardship' when her parents emigrated to New Zealand in search of better economic opportunities.[31] Her father was the impoverished younger son of Northumberland gentry, scraping a living as a land agent in England and no more fortunate on the other side of the world, where supplementary income from his wife's private teaching was needed to sustain the family. Two sons died in infancy, and in 1867 illness carried off Lucy's father as well. The two surviving children were brought back to England by their mother, a resilient, resourceful woman who brought them up alone and extended her maternal dominance over the whole of her daughter's adult life. An unusually full and intimate picture survives of this particular mother–daughter relationship, in the form of a privately published volume of letters between them and a second volume of collected reminiscences, both produced as a posthumous tribute by pupils of the select girls' school which Lucy Soulsby headed in later life.[32]

---

[29] Battiscombe, *Reluctant Pioneer*, 21.

[30] See letters from Charlotte Yonge to Elizabeth Worsdworth dated 14 May 1872, 30 Oct. and 26 Nov. 1874, 17 Nov. 1877. LMH archives, E. Wordsworth papers, box 1, 50, 62, 63, 74. Charlotte Yonge's book on womanly duty, *Womankind* (London: Mozley and Smith, 1876), is discussed in Ch. 4, below.

[31] E.A. and B.H.S. (eds.), *Impressions of L.H.M.S.* (Brondesbury: Manor House School, 1927), p. viii.

[32] E.A., B.H.S., and P.H. (eds.), *The Letters of S.S.S. and L.H.M.S. (Mrs and Miss Soulsby)* (Brondesbury: Manor House School, 1929) and E.A. and B.H.S. (eds.), *Impressions*.

Lucy and her mother corresponded daily, and sometimes twice daily, through-out the years when they lived apart, and she never ceased to seek her mother's advice at every turn. During her youth her mother was her sole teacher, apart from officiating clergy. Though she later eulogized maternal education, it is interesting to find one letter from the 17-year-old daughter in which she complains of her mother's stifling effect on her own self-expression.[33] The domestic economy was run on a knife-edge, yet with the utmost gentility. Womanly duties were learnt in a household without servants: her mother made a virtue of enforced simplicity whilst continuing to extend maternal care to the local neighbourhood. During an idyllic five years in Salcombe, when Lucy was in her early twenties, her voluntary service included being principal Sunday School teacher, assisting at the village school and at her mother's winter prayer meetings for 'the Mothers of the Valley', and running evening classes for young labourers.[34] Gentility was established not only by such philanthropic, civilizing efforts, but also by methodical household management which enabled the two women to confine their chores to the morning, set out the afternoon tea 'all ready in the dining room, so that when visitors arrive there is no trouble', then devote the afternoon and evening to 'parish', reading, and writing.[35]

Lucy Soulsby was so proud of this virtuous and feminine lifestyle that she wrote about it to the editor of *Work and Leisure*, who was '*very* anxious to be allowed to publish it'.[36] Maternal permission was refused, on grounds of modesty. However, more appropriate publishing opportunities soon offered themselves to both mother and daughter. Mrs Soulsby contributed to Charlotte Yonge's *Monthly Packet*, while Lucy wrote stories and poems for *Work and Leisure* and *The Gatherer*, including one early article expressing her conservative views on the Woman Question.[37] Both women joined an essay society, as Louise Creighton had done earlier. However, like Mary Ward, Louise Creighton, and Elizabeth Wordsworth, Lucy Soulsby must have realized during her twenties that she was capable of benefiting from some more formal extension of her education. In 1876, with her mother's encouragement, she successfully entered the Cambridge external examination for women. A few years later she was expressing interest in university education, 'pumping' her cousin about College life ('he says Oxford is cheaper than Cambridge').[38] Enough money was scraped together to ensure a good education for her younger brother, on whose behalf this enquiry was probably made. Were the delights of home-baking and rustic improvement

---

[33] E.A., B.H.S., and P.H. (eds.), *Letters*, 298.

[34] Ibid. 95–6. Mrs Soulsby commented with unconscious irony: 'Lucy has a great idea that as the time is approaching when every labourer will have the vote, they ought at least to be made a little less ludicrously unfit for it than they are at present'.

[35] Ibid. 83   [36] Ibid. 85.

[37] The Soulsbys engaged in debate over the Woman Question with 'a young lady Professor at Girton' in 1883, in the pages of *The Gatherer*, annual magazine of their essay society: ibid. 98. Lucy's paper titled 'The Salic Law' had been published during the previous year.

[38] Ibid. 16.

beginning to pall? Direct evidence of this would be unlikely to find its way into the commemorative volume of letters. But in 1885 Lucy Soulsby jumped at the chance to undertake some teaching at Cheltenham Ladies College. The distinguished Dorothea Beale recognized her talent, at a time when highly educated women teachers were still in short supply. Two years as a form mistress led on to a successful application for the headship of Oxford High School, and the gates were finally opened to a wider world of women's education and social ideals.

ANOTHER OXFORD MOVEMENT?

Mary Ward, Louise Creighton, Ethel Harrison, Elizabeth Wordsworth, and Lucy Soulsby all had strong Oxford connections. During the 1870s Mary Ward and Louise Creighton lived there as young academic wives, for fourteen and five years respectively. Ethel Harrison became a member of their friendship circle, initially through her husband's frequent scholarly visits to his alma mater.[39] Elizabeth Wordsworth joined the same lively group of self-improving young women, attending Ladies' Lectures during visits to her brother's Oxford home before beginning her lifetime's work at Lady Margaret Hall in 1879. She first met Charlotte Yonge when both women were guests at New College in 1870. Lucy Soulsby's arrival in Oxford in 1887 extended to a ten-year stay, during which she mingled socially with university men and women as well as teaching their daughters. Both Louise Creighton and Lucy Soulsby were members of the Lady Margaret Hall Council in the 1890s and 1900s, while Mary Ward's links to Somerville College extended to 1909 (when her anti-suffragism apparently made her an unwelcome patron).[40]

A certain amount of this female networking depended upon the older web of male connections which Oxford University so effectively promoted. Brian Harrison has depicted the Oxford dimension of male anti-suffrage leadership in diagrammatic form, linking it to the related legal-political and imperial-political networks which flourished within late Victorian London 'Clubland'.[41] No fewer than eighteen out of thirty-three prominent male antis belonged to the Oxford inner circle, including Lord Curzon, President of the National League for Opposing Woman Suffrage from 1912 to 1918 and Chancellor of Oxford University from 1907 to 1925. The web of Oxford-linked women who played a role in organized anti-suffragism was looser and much less visible, but was nevertheless of considerable importance to the ideas and activities of the movement. The university initially brought a significant group of anti-suffragist

---

[39] Ethel Harrison's ashes were eventually to be deposited at Wadham College, Oxford, in an urn shared with her husband and conspicuously displayed in the ante-chapel.
[40] See Sutherland, *Mrs Humphry Ward*, 306.   [41] B. Harrison, *Separate Spheres*, 94–5.

women together through their shared work for the cause of womanly higher education. In later life the social reform and philanthropic dimensions of these women's work continued to reflect their interest in educational issues, and also their exposure to aspects of the philosophical debates which absorbed late Victorian Oxford. During their Oxford years all the women experienced a broadening of intellectual horizons which helped to define and justify their conservative views on gender roles. Their personal and familial experience developed alongside a social life and experience of self-education which were inseparable from the life of the university.

Early developments in women's higher education at Oxford provide an interesting case study of conservative reformism.[42] The personal needs and proclivities of this group of women coincided with a particular period of university history which was conducive to cautious innovation. In the opening chapter of an early history of her college, Elizabeth Wordsworth praised the creative ambience of Oxford in the 1870s, noting 'the opportuneness of the moment in our University, and even our national life, for such an effort as was then made for the Higher Education of Women'.[43] The Tractarian dispute was in abeyance, but Oxford theology was stirred by debates over the historicity of the Bible, and the relationship between divine creation and new scientific evidence concerning both geology and biological evolution. Philosophical controversy included discussion of what later became known as English Hegelianism. T. H. Green was 'the greatest intellectual force' among a group of Balliol scholars who were attempting to draw together religious faith, metaphysical reasoning, and a commitment to social improvement.[44] Arnold Toynbee was among his disciples, and Green's views on the connectedness of the divine and the actual through moral social action eventually inspired male settlement work as well as female maternal reformism.[45] Meanwhile the famous Master of Balliol, Benjamin Jowett, became a cautious supporter of university education for women. Whilst Balliol and Christ Church were generally believed to represent opposing poles of religious and social thought, Keble College was ready to demonstrate that a

---

[42] The most authoritative account is by J. Howarth, in M. Brock and M. Curthoys (eds.), *The History of the University of Oxford, vii. Nineteenth-Century Oxford* (Oxford: Clarendon Press, 2000), ch. 10. See also J. Howarth, in B. Harrison (ed.), *The History of the University of Oxford, viii. Twentieth-Century Oxford* (Oxford: Clarendon Press, 1994), ch. 13. Contemporary accounts are provided by A. Rogers, *Degrees by Degrees* (Oxford: Oxford University Press, 1938) and V. Brittain, *The Women at Oxford: A Fragment of History* (London: George Harrap and Co., 1960), and more recent analysis by S. Leonardi, *Dangerous by Degrees: Women at Oxford and the Somerville College Novelists* (New Brunswick: Rutgers University Press, 1989) and P. Adams, *Somerville for Women: An Oxford Women's College 1879–1973* (Oxford: Oxford University Press, 1996).

[43] E. Wordsworth, in G. Bailey (ed.), *Lady Margaret Hall: A Short History* (London: Oxford University Press, 1923), 7.

[44] Ibid. 10.

[45] See M. Richter, *The Politics of Conscience: T. H. Green and his Age* (Lanham: University Press of America, 1983); E. Anderson, 'The Feminism of T. H. Green: A Late-Victorian Success Story?', *History of Political Thought*, 12/4 (1991), 671–93.

newly launched High Church foundation could move decisively in support of the education of women, linked to a more socially aware Christianity. Further inspiration for the female educational cause was drawn from John Ruskin's presence in Oxford, as Slade Professor of Art. His celebrity status among Oxford women was fully established by the 1870s, though he took some time to warm to the view that their 'queenly powers' would benefit from the advent of women's colleges.[46]

The rich intellectual ferment of the university in this period owed much to earlier reforms of its structure and governance.[47] Though Oxford remained an enclave of the British male elite in the later nineteenth century, most of the colleges were no longer semi-monastic communities which shunned all female presence. Religious tests were modified after a Royal Commission inquiry in the 1850s, then abolished in 1871. College fellows were no longer obliged to take Holy Orders and the teaching of the university gradually broadened to include more study of the natural sciences and the humanities, alongside the traditional academic diet of theology, philosophy, mathematics, and the classics. Growing concern over the relevance and quality of the Oxford curriculum related to the needs of government and the professions, as well as to a movement to broaden the social influence of the university. Women students, as we have seen, were among the early beneficiaries of university extension teaching through lecture programmes and public examinations. They were also prospective marriage partners for adventurous academics pushing the boundaries of the regulations which controlled the matrimonial status of college fellows. The foundation of the first residential women's colleges at Cambridge in 1869 and 1871 completed the encouraging context for Oxford women's education, just as several future anti-suffrage maternal reformers took up their residence in the city.

Mary Ward's *Recollections* provide an even more rosy picture of Oxford life than Elizabeth Wordsworth's glowing account, or the nostalgic personal reminiscences of Louise Creighton. The end of her unhappy schooldays coincided with a period of Anglican career stability for her father, as an Oxford tutor from 1865 to 1876, and the family was reunited in a comfortable North Oxford home. Mary soon developed an ambition to become a scholar as well as a writer, and 'slipped into Oxford life as a fish into water'. She describes herself at 17 as 'keenly alive to the spell of Oxford', experienced first in the study of the Rector of

---

[46] Ruskin was universally admired by the women discussed in this chapter. Elizabeth Wordsworth welcomed him to Lady Margaret Hall in 1884, and expressed her enthusiasm for 'the revered teacher' in *Essays Old and New* (Oxford: Oxford University Press, 1919). As a young woman, Mary Ward copied out passages from Ruskin to carry around with her. Louise Creighton described herself as 'a devout follower' (*Memoir*, 56) and met her future husband at one of his lectures. Ruskin was equally admired by some feminists, though disliked by others. L. Peterson, in D. Birch (ed.), *Ruskin and Gender* (Basingstoke: Palgrave, 2002), challenges the view that Ruskin was unsympathetic to progressive women, whilst also noting the ambiguity of his writings.

[47] See J. Roach, 'Victorian Universities and the National Intelligentsia', *Victorian Studies*, 3:2 (1959), 131–50.

Lincoln, then in the deepest recesses of the Bodleian Library.[48] Research into Spanish history whetted her appetite for more disciplined learning, while the jollities of Oxford summers fed her hunger for fun and romance. At the age of 20 she married Humphry Ward, fellow and tutor of Brasenose College. Louise Creighton arrived in Oxford in the spring of 1871, and within a record period of three weeks had been snapped up by a still more eligible young academic, Mandell Creighton of Merton College. His talents were so admired by his college that he was permitted to retain his fellowship, in the teeth of competition from other would-be-married dons. Louise recorded her husband's enthusiasm for the strong social and academic bonds of his male college community, whilst the couple simultaneously developed a frugal but delightful married lifestyle in the congenial company of the Wards, the Greens, the Harrisons, and other 'new and intimate friends'.[49] Academic development was an integral part of this lifestyle. Soon she too was reading in the Bodleian, translating Ranke with her husband, and writing primers on English History. During Mandell Creighton's lectures, his wife sometimes 'sat secreted in the gallery with one or two others who asked to come with me';[50] she also joined male undergraduates for college seminars on political economy, and arranged a small ladies' Latin class.

It is not surprising, perhaps, that the women were soon planning more extended and appropriate educational experiences for themselves. Mary Ward recorded proudly (though not quite accurately) that 'Mrs Creighton and I . . . were the secretaries and founders of the first organised series of lectures for women in the University town'.[51] Louise Creighton noted their intention of improving upon the academic diet which university extension work offered women elsewhere. Plans were laid in her North Oxford drawing room and round the dining tables of her friends. Her memoirs, alongside those of Mary Ward and Elizabeth Wordsworth, reveal how much the Oxford women enjoyed cultivating their own aesthetic, intellectual social circle, forging lifelong friendships in the process. Early lectures linked the study of English history to the study of the literature of each period, and were given by university men to audiences which included, alongside Mary Ward, Louise Creighton, and Elizabeth Wordsworth, Clara Pater (future tutor at Lady Margaret Hall and Somerville College), Charlotte Green (wife of T. H. Green), Bertha Johnson (future Principal of the Oxford Home Students), Lavinia Talbot (wife of the Warden of Keble), and Georgiana Max Muller (wife of a senior Professor).

In 1875 the university passed a statute which established special examinations for women. Honours tests were provided in fourteen subjects, without the normal university requirements of a period of residence in Oxford, limits on

---

[48] Ward, *Recollections*, 102.   [49] Creighton, *Memoir*, 48.   [50] Ibid. 56.
[51] Ward, *Recollections*, 152. In fact the sister of a Balliol don had already briefly tried the experiment of ladies' lectures in 1865.

length of study, and prerequisite Latin and Greek. With the support of both men and women, the stage had been set for the launch of Oxford's first women's colleges in 1879.[52] As Mary Ward wrote, 'My friends and I were all on fire for women's education, including women's medical education, and very emulous of Cambridge, where the movement was already far advanced'. Writing in 1918, she added that 'hardly any of us were at all on fire for woman suffrage, wherein the Oxford educational movement differed greatly from the Cambridge movement'.[53] The Warden of Keble and his wife apparently took the initiative towards residential women's education after an 1878 visit to Girton, which left them convinced that a more domesticated model of student life was needed for Oxford women. An enlarged Association for the Education of Women was established to organize an academic programme, while funds were raised towards suitable accommodation for the first women students. Typically, religious debate threatened to disrupt progress for a while. The Talbots of Keble viewed the Anglicanism of the enterprise as one of its most important characteristics, whilst others on the committee wished to follow the university's general move towards broader religious inclusion. The solution proved to be the foundation of two colleges rather than one: Lady Margaret Hall, following Anglican tradition though open to non-Anglicans, and Somerville College, to be run on completely non-sectarian lines. Mary Ward, whose religious views were by this time deeply influenced by T. H. Green, became the first volunteer secretary of Somerville College. She later claimed the credit for choosing its name, which commemorated the woman astronomer Mary Somerville. Lady Margaret Hall, meanwhile, furnished a house in North Oxford through the efforts of Lavinia Talbot and Bertha Johnson, and appointed Elizabeth Wordsworth as its Principal.

Elizabeth Wordsworth was an inspired choice for this post. As Edward Talbot commented frankly in 1926, the appointment 'brought us not only the lady's own distinction of intellect and character, but the cachet and warrant of a name second to none in the confidence of English Church people. None could have been a greater protection against any charge of rashness in our attempt'.[54] The new Principal soon proved to have qualities which extended beyond her success as an icon of Anglican respectability. However, her decided opinions on the Christian education of genteel young women did undoubtedly owe much to her religious background. The views of her ecclesiastical male relatives were expressed in her father's published sermon of 1884, titled *Christian Womanhood and Christian Sovreignty*. Dedicated to his 'dear daughter . . . with fervent prayer to God for his blessing on her work', it warned against purely academic or career ambitions, concluding that 'the only true "higher Education of Woman" is that

---

[52] As Janet Howarth points out in Brock and Curthoys (eds.), *History of the University*, vii, the colleges were initially 'societies', taking on formal college titles at later dates.
[53] Ward, *Recollections*, 152.   [54] E. Talbot, in Bailey (ed.), *Lady Margaret Hall*, 22.

which trains her to look upward to God'.[55] By this date Elizabeth Wordsworth had already succeeded in inculcating the first generations of undergraduates with her own views on womanly education. In contrast to Somerville's modern woman scientist, she chose to name the college after Lady Margaret, mother of Henry VII : 'She was a gentlewoman, a scholar, and a saint, and after having been three times married she took a vow of celibacy. What more could be expected of any woman?'[56] Another early adviser was Charlotte Yonge, with whom Elizabeth spent a 'nice long day' talking over her plans six months before the college opened.[57] Charlotte Yonge warned of the dangers of founding a mere boarding house to assist examination successes. At the same time she sketched out an alternative future for the women's college: 'If it were in any way possible to make it in some way an institution dedicated to Heavenly Wisdom, training the daughters of the Church to more perfect cultivation of their talents whether as educators or as mothers of families, then I think there would be such salt of the earth in the College as to make it lasting and beloved and a real blessing in raising the whole ideal and standard of women'.[58]

In practice, these ideals were at least partly reflected in Lady Margaret Hall's academic and domestic arrangements. College policy for many years was supportive towards a differentiated curriculum for women students (in contrast to Girton's egalitarianism). As late as 1895 a majority of the College Council opposed the demand for women's university degrees, though Elizabeth Wordsworth herself had no principled objection providing the university men agreed (which they did not until 1920).[59] Meanwhile she worried about how to protect overworked girls from themselves and their sterner tutors, describing in her correspondence her own motherly interventions to insist upon necessary rest and relaxation. Overwork was a threat not merely to feminine health, but also to the 'family atmosphere' promised in the college prospectus. Encouragement towards womanly behaviour was as important to Elizabeth Wordsworth as academic study, and was promoted through communal rather than individual study space and such details as delaying departure from the breakfast table until every student had finished her meal: 'all these little things seem just to give

---

[55] C. Wordsworth, *Christian Womanhood and Christian Sovereignity* (London: Rivingtons, 1884), 44.

[56] E. Wordsworth, in Bailey (ed.), *Lady Margaret Hall*, 153.

[57] E. Wordsworth to her mother, 20 Mar. 1879, E. Wordsworth papers, box 1, 2.

[58] C. Yonge to E. Wordsworth, 1879, quoted in Battiscombe, *Reluctant Pioneer*, 70.

[59] Bertha Johnson, LMH council member and Principal of Home Students, made a stand against degrees in 1895, though by this date she was an active suffragist. One of the formal proposers of women's admission to degrees, on the other hand, was Professor Dicey, later an ardent anti-suffragist. See Janet Howarth's entry for Bertha Johnson in the *Oxford Dictionary of National Biography* (Oxford: Oxford University Press, 2004) and Rogers, *Degrees by Degrees*. This illustrates the varied ways in which the question of women's education could be evaluated alongside the question of votes for women. The argument was not simply over whether education should be available, but over the suitability and purpose of that education, and over its consequences for women's role in society.

the ladylike tone to a place and to make them less selfish'.[60] In the spirit of maternal guidance, she encouraged students to accompany her on social outings or to Church services and commented on aspects of each girl's appearance and comportment. Moral guardianship was the most important responsibility of all, and Elizabeth took her share of chaperoning duties as well as devoting considerable effort to the religious education of her charges.

Over the following decades accepted standards and attitudes in women's university education gradually changed. Elizabeth Wordsworth remained at the helm of Lady Margaret Hall until 1909, but by this date often found herself fighting a rearguard action in defence of conservative values.[61] The development of the other women's colleges, and of mixed universities beyond Oxbridge, contributed towards changing attitudes. Janet Howarth concludes that some historians have exaggerated the conservatism of Victorian and Edwardian Oxford's gender outlook.[62] A reliable balance sheet is difficult to establish, since the university contained a huge range of opinion at any one period, and opinions on women's education and on the Woman Question were constantly evolving. However, whether or not they carried majority Oxford opinion with them, the conservative first generation of Oxford women educators undoubtedly made important contributions to public discussion over the position of women and their role in civic life. In 1894 Elizabeth Wordsworth was invited to address the annual Church Congress at Exeter on the subject of *First Principles in Women's Education*. Beginning from biblical precepts, she developed the argument that 'in an ideal state of society, we never lose sight of the womanliness of women'. Moreover her Oxford experiences had taught her that 'women can never be properly educated in groups; they must be loved and cared for one by one'. Character-building and religious training were vital for true womanhood, and were potentially threatened if 'the high pressure system of modern education' left girls unable or unwilling to heed maternal wisdom concerning 'the great realities of life': 'For ten years or more of her life, if a girl has always got her head in a book, how are we to expect her when grown up to have a quick eye for the personal well-being of those around her—the old, the hard-worked, the little ones, the sick?'[63]

[60] E. Wordsworth to Susie, 6 Nov. 1879. E. Wordsworth papers, box 1, 14.

[61] In a private letter to 'dearest Chris', dated 7 Feb. 1913, Elizabeth Wordsworth wrote of concerns shared with the Master of Balliol and others over 'the modern spirit of the younger generation' and over the suffrage issue 'which has quite taken hold of the woman of the day': 'it seems really like a kind of mania, and one only hopes their own children or something equally dear to them will not be sacrificed in the struggle'. Despite her horror of militancy, she accepted the inevitability of an eventual female franchise by this date, observing in another letter that 'It is bound to come, and a very good thing too, and the longer it takes about it the better'. E. Wordsworth papers, box 3.

[62] See Howarth, in Brock and Curthoys (eds.), *History of the University*, vii. 301–7.

[63] E. Wordsworth, *First Principles in Women's Education* (Oxford: James Parker and Co., 1894), 6, 17, 10, 11.

A similar message was reinforced in the public utterances of other leading anti-suffragist maternal reformers. In the same year Lucy Soulsby asked a London drawing room meeting: 'Is it certain that the new education has so far made the homes of England any happier?' Published under the title *Home Rule or Daughters of Today*, her talk warned apocalyptically of 'tendencies of the age, outside forces, beating like waves against the door of every happy home in England'. The 'wrong form of independence' would unfit young women for 'real work', whether in the home or in wider society: 'let her be soaked through and through with her mother's ways and beliefs and manners, before she is turned adrift among conflicting, outside influences'.[64] Three years later Lucy decided to give up the headship of her prestigious Oxford school, run under the auspices of the Girls' Public Day School Trust, in order to be free to create a truly maternalist boarding school of her own.[65] The Manor House School at Brondesbury was oversubscribed in its early twentieth century heyday, though by this date it presented a conspicuously extreme model of conservative girls' education. Returning to address the Old Girls of Oxford High School in 1913, Lucy Soulsby demonstrated that she had moved with the times by assuring her listeners that she believed woman's sphere should not be confined to 'her own four walls'. Instead, women should extend their maternal influence across all members of their households, and out into the wider world. Her sphere included '*everything that a woman can do better than a man*, i.e. a lion's share of the Teaching, Economic, Organising, Initiating part of the World's business'. This bold assertion was accompanied by a warning against current 'Woman's Unrest' which promoted selfish individualism, and conflict rather than constructive harmony between the sexes.[66]

Although not a professional educator, Louise Creighton also sustained her enthusiasm for a conservative vision of women's education into the twentieth century. As a leading figure in the National Union of Women Workers, as well as in the Anglican women's movement, her views on this subject probably reached a wider range of women than those of either Elizabeth Wordsworth or Lucy Soulsby. Like them, she urged the supreme importance of women's essentially moral and spiritual domestic role, whilst gradually acknowledging in a more positive spirit the changing nature of many women's lives. At the 1901 conference of the NUWW, she told a mass meeting of young women: 'Your

---

[64] L. Soulsby, *Home Rule or Daughters of Today* (Oxford: James Palmer and Co., 1894), 4, 6–7, 9, 14, 26.

[65] Lucy Soulsby took over the school from a previous headmistress, but set out to refashion it around her own and her mother's maternalist ideals, summarized in *Brondesbury Ways, or Toys Old and New* (privately printed, 1916): 'learning, ambition, public life, success, will always be incidents in a woman's life—her essence lies in motherhood' (quoted in E.A. and B.H.S. (eds.), *Impressions*, 82). Lucy had taken a public stand against the admission of Oxford women to 'men's degrees' in 1895, on the grounds that 'true progress was to be found along lines specially suited to women's special work in the world': L. Soulsby, *The Woman's Kingdom* (London: Longmans, Green and Co., 1910), 5.

[66] L. Soulsby, *A Woman's Movement* (London: Longmans, Green and Co., 1913), 23, 24, 22.

lives are your own now, and you have got to make something worth having out of them', before going on to assert the continuing primacy of marriage. Unmarried women would be 'happier for having some definite work in life', but were warned against over-professionalism: 'Be careful not to forget your *métier de femme*. There are things which the world wants from women for which the loss of which no excellent work, no highly developed capacity, will compensate'.[67]

In a longer lecture on 'Home Life and the Higher Education of Women', published in 1909, Louise developed a more detailed discussion of the competing demands upon educated women. Despite her change of position on the suffrage issue in 1906, her views were unaltered on the primacy of marriage and maternity to women's personal fulfilment, to their central role within the domestic kingdom, and to the development of their capacity for wider social service. She believed that women's higher education must be reconciled with the demands of home life, and adapted in ways which would enhance both private and public maternal roles. Well-trained women's minds might be employed in professional life and community service, but were equally valuable to efficient household management and the thoughtful fulfilment of family duties: 'The highly educated woman must be fit not only to become a high-school teacher, a guardian of the poor, a physician, a member of an education authority, but a wife, a mother, a sister in a religious community, a sick-nurse, a useful daughter at home, even a lady of leisure'. Perhaps with her own mother in mind, Louise urged the necessity for busy middle-class mothers to preserve a space in their lives for ongoing study. With her usual honesty, she admitted the obstacles to this ambition but insisted they could be overcome through careful prioritization and the abandonment of time-wasting social ceremony. The development of high-level courses in domestic science would help some women to combine study with domestic duty. But motherhood depended upon far more than mere practical skills. Mothers were central to 'the atmosphere of the home' and 'the standard of family aspiration', and subject to manifold calls of social duty: 'To fit her for so wide a sphere, no education can be too high; she needs not the higher only but the highest, and she needs, above all, to continue her education through life'.[68]

The continuities in Louise Creighton's educational outlook after her conversion to suffragism seem to demonstrate that the franchise issue was not the fulcrum of her beliefs about women's role in society. For her, the vote was merely one means towards desirable social ends, and by no means the most important one. As the ultra-conservative Lucy Soulsby wrote in 1913: 'Compared with this bed-rock question of the right relations of man and woman, the Vote itself is a mere detail'.[69] All the Oxford maternal reformers remained proud for the

[67] L. Creighton, *A Purpose in Life* (London: Wells Gardner, Darton and Co., 1901), 9, 17.

[68] L. Creighton, 'Home Life and the Higher Education of Women', *The Art of Living* (London: Longmans, Green and Co., 1909), 89, 113–14.

[69] Soulsby, *A Woman's Movement*, 30.

rest of their lives of their educational achievements there, and enthusiastic for further educational reforms which suited the particular demands of middle- and upper-class women's lives. They believed that maternal responsibilities within the family included the all-important duty of educating growing children into a proper awareness of their gendered contributions towards Britain's superior civilization. A daughter's education began at her mother's knee, but it did not end there. Whilst boys moved off into the well-defined masculine spheres of public school and university, girls continued to rely upon maternal guidance as they grew towards womanhood. This might take different forms, ranging from home-teaching to the sheltered environment of a carefully tended boarding school or women's college. Whatever form it took, maternal education would help equip future British mothers for a civic role linking family life to the wider social duties for which both gender and social class had already fitted them. In 1910 Ethel Harrison reminded readers of the *Anti-Suffrage Review* that 'the anti-suffrage woman has a great task before her in endeavouring to raise the standard of women in social and public matters, and in helping the mothers of the race to realise their great privilege of training their sons and daughters to be worthy citizens of our country'.[70]

The educational outlook of the maternal reformers could sometimes, though not always, become an integral part of the case against votes for women. Suffragists made early and persistent attempts to appropriate the advancement of female education to their cause, and were later justifiably proud of their extensive support among the ranks of doctors, teachers, and other university-educated women. However, the conservative educational reformism represented by the women who have been introduced in this chapter was entirely compatible with their opposition to women's suffrage. Their faith in socially responsible, genteel, and highly moral maternal education could as readily be used to strengthen the case for anti-suffragism as for suffragism. It was believed by many conservative suffragists, as well as by many female antis, that thoroughly maternal women would make best use of improved educational opportunities. Louise Creighton wrote soon after her suffrage conversion: 'This generation seems to be realising more fully than ever before, the tremendous responsibility of the mother, and surely it is of vital importance that all her powers should be fully developed, that she should be in every way the best that she is capable of becoming'. Once educated, women must learn to achieve 'the nice balance of duties, often seemingly antagonistic . . . here one thing only can keep us straight, the over-ruling desire to lead a life of service'.[71] Mary Ward, whose opposition to the vote remained steadfast to the end, boasted frequently of her role as an educational reformer. Her daughter, Janet Trevelyan, wrote in her biography that the success of her Oxford educational work 'helped convince Mrs Ward that the right lines

---

[70] E. Harrison, 'The Place of Women in Politics', *Anti-Suffrage Review*, 25 (Dec. 1910), 5.
[71] Creighton, 'Home Life and the Education of Women', 113, 114.

for women's advance lay, not in political agitation for the suffrage, but in the broadening of education, so as to fit her sex for the many tasks which were opening out before it'.[72]

Both Mary Ward and Lord Curzon, Oxford-Chancellor and President of the NLOWS, supported the award of university degrees to women.[73] The *Anti-Suffrage Review* reported the debate over this issue to its largely female readership in 1909, contrasting the desirability of educating women to fulfil their feminine potential with suffragist plans to drag them against their will to the polling stations and into Parliament. As Lord Curzon put it, 'there is all the difference in the world between giving women an opportunity of increasing and improving their natural powers, and granting them a share in political sovreignty'.[74] The following year his speech at the ceremonial opening of Lady Margaret Hall's new buildings commended wider occupational horizons for educated women, while at the same time warning them not to forget that 'the highest ideal and conception of womanhood was after all to be found in the home'.[75] Anti-suffrage support for women's education came from a less expected quarter in 1911 when Edith Havelock Ellis, the wife of the famous sexologist, contributed an article to the *Anti-Suffrage Review* titled 'The Maternal in Politics':

The morality of the future is very largely in the hands of woman, so that she will need all the educative discipline possible to fit her for her responsible work . . . The maternal woman's great desire is not so much to be in evidence as to be herself evidence that a nation inspired by women and governed by men will make cleaner and juster laws than one governed by women in defiance of men . . . The maternal instinct only needs enlargement to be the most effective power of modern times . . . Equal opportunities for political usefulness does not imply equal methods of carrying out the work.[76]

Meanwhile in Oxford a substantial number of the earliest supporters of women's higher education had joined the Victorian anti-suffrage movement. Signatories to the 1889 Appeal Against Women's Suffrage included Mary Ward, Louise Creighton, Ethel Harrison, and Lucy Soulsby, as well as Charlotte Green, Georgiana Max Muller, Lavinia Talbot, Charlotte Toynbee, and eleven students

---

[72] Trevelyan, *Life*, 224.

[73] e.g. in a speech to the AGM of the Irish Central Bureau for the Employment of Women, Feb. 1905, Pusey House Library, Oxford, M. Ward papers 1/1; and in Ward, *Recollections*, 98.

[74] *Anti-Suffrage Review*, 6 (May 1909), 3.

[75] *Anti-Suffrage Review*, 24 (Nov. 1910), 7. This speech was reprinted in full in G. Curzon, *Subjects of the Day* ed. D. M. Chapman-Huston (London: George Allen and Unwin Ltd, 1915).

[76] *Anti-Suffrage Review*, 31 (June 1911), 122. Edith Havelock Ellis's views on maternity are discussed in detail in R. Brandon, *The New Women and the Old Men: Love, Sex and the Woman Question* (London: Flamingo, 1991). She shared her husband's eugenic beliefs and his biological determinism; despite her lesbian affairs, she 'wanted to be properly and totally married' (p. 101) and mourned their joint decision to remain childless (p. 107). 'The normal woman is maternal', she pronounced in the *Review*, before going on to argue that 'it is shortsighted to endeavour to minimise women's most significant warrant for political usefulness'. Though no conventional maternal reformer, she was certainly an anti-suffrage maternalist.

and staff from Lady Margaret Hall.[77] Many of the same women rallied again to the standard of the Women's National Anti-Suffrage League in 1908.[78] Its Oxford branch boasted over three hundred female members and associates in 1910, and was still headed by university wives.[79] More than three thousand Oxford signatures were obtained for the League's anti-suffrage petition to Parliament in 1909. Old friendships and enduring principles combined to ensure that, among women as well as men, anti-suffragism was eventually to be mourned as another of Oxford's lost causes.

[77] 'An Appeal Against Women's Suffrage', *Nineteenth Century*, 25 (1889), 781–8. Signatures were published in *Nineteenth Century*, 26 (1889), 357–84.

[78] Mary Ward and Ethel Harrison were members of the WNASL executive committee. Lucy Soulsby and Georgiana Max Muller lent their names to published WNASL manifestos, and the latter also chaired the Oxford branch of the WNASL in 1909/10. Charlotte Toynbee was an Oxford WNASL committee member in 1909/10. See Bod. *Annual Report of the Women's National Anti-Suffrage League, Oxford Branch, 1909/10.*

[79] These included Edith Massie, wife of John Massie MP of Pembroke College, who became national Treasurer of the WNASL and presented its 1909 petition to Parliament.

3

Maternal Reformers and Social Duty

FROM EDUCATION TO SOCIAL SERVICE

Conservative supporters of female education valued women's wider social duty as an extension of their maternal role, though it must not be allowed to over-shadow home life. The promotion of women's education was itself a social duty, since appropriate educational opportunities enhanced women's powers of motherhood and prepared them for other kinds of social usefulness. Womanly social service could take many different forms. In the late nineteenth century older traditions of individual charity mingled with the more demanding and increasingly professionalized work of organized philanthropy. The collective efforts of philanthropic societies linked in turn to growing female participation in the work of local government. By the end of the century old-fashioned amateurism was inadequate to the scale and scope of the social service which the nation required of its women. Anti-suffrage maternal reformers were to the fore (alongside many suffragists) in urging educated women to prepare them-selves for the challenges of effective community work on behalf of the poor. The 1889 Appeal Against Female Suffrage simultaneously supported women's 'growing opportunities for public usefulness' and 'the great improvements in women's education which have accompanied them'.[1] Two decades later the *Anti-Suffrage Review* was again urging its female readers down the path of social duty through public service. This insistence upon a socially improv-ing anti-suffrage agenda became a point of controversy when the Women's National League Against Women's Suffrage merged with its male equivalent in 1910. Undeterred by their critics, the anti-suffrage maternal reformers con-tinued to press for social action commitments within the National League for Opposing Woman Suffrage. They believed that social service was inte-gral to the cause of essential womanhood, and therefore inseparable from anti-suffragism.

In this chapter the lives of anti-suffrage advocates of women's education are followed through in connection with wider social activism at the end of the nineteenth century. Mary Ward and Louise Creighton left a particularly

---

[1] 'An Appeal Against Female Suffrage', *Nineteenth Century*, 25 (1889), 782.

vivid record of their evolving ideas and experience, related to personal and family life as well as to their participation in large-scale collective endeavours on behalf of maternal reform. These women's close association with suffragist social reformers contrasts with Ethel Harrison's separate development as an anti-suffrage Positivist. Elizabeth Wordsworth and Lucy Soulsby were also committed to wider social improvement, though on a less grand scale than Mary Ward and Louise Creighton. As supporters of the National Union of Women Workers and of the largest Anglican women's organizations, their experience of the organized women's movement intersected with that of thousands of other women anti-suffragists. The chapter goes on to show how the NUWW, the Girls' Friendly Society, and the Mothers' Union embodied late Victorian ideals of maternal reform, and how these organizations accommodated themselves to the pressures of the suffrage campaign. The NUWW played a leading part in developing and expressing such ideals. In the years before the First World War it became the site of angry exchanges between suffragists and anti-suffrage women who, in many other respects, thought very much alike. The proximity of conflicting positions sometimes seemed to intensify rather than reduce controversy, as determined minorities on both sides tried to hitch the maternal reform agenda to the debate over votes for women. In contrast, the Anglican women's organizations successfully avoided being hijacked by the franchise issue. They provided sympathetic territory for anti-suffragism, but no more than that. There was genuine outrage among anti-suffrage women when Anglican suffragists eventually sought alternative avenues of religious influence through Church Congresses and the formation of a Church Suffrage League. These case studies of anti-suffrage ideas and activism within the organized women's movement help to illustrate the scope of women's resistance to the vote, linking individuals' social action to their anti-suffrage beliefs, and showing how anti-suffragism was fostered in contexts more far-reaching and more long-standing than the public forum provided for this direct purpose by the pre-war anti-suffrage Leagues.

As Chapter 2 showed, the educational writings of the Oxford women and other anti-suffrage sympathizers often outlined theoretical connections between womanly qualities, successful mothering, commitment to the wider family of the local community, and the acquisition of appropriate skills and knowledge to make social service effective. The early years of women's higher education at Oxford provide interesting practical examples of individual anti-suffragists' transition from small-scale philanthropy towards larger-scale collective social action. For some of the young women involved, experiences of academic discovery, motherhood, and social service converged in quite demanding ways. During the era of 'Lectures for Women' and the formation of the women's colleges, Mary Ward and Louise Creighton were also starting their own families and taking their first tentative steps into social action on behalf of the poor. The first of seven Creighton babies was passed around the women present at educational planning meetings,[2] and Mary Ward worked against the clock to prepare for Somerville's first students less than four weeks before the birth of her second daughter.[3] Maternity and university life combined to inspire these inexperienced young women with a more confident sense of their public responsibilities, including their social duty towards the less fortunate. Louise took up district visiting in one of the poorer areas of Oxford,[4] while Mary penned a leaflet on the principles of infant feeding only a few weeks after the birth of her first child.[5]

Meanwhile at Lady Margaret Hall, Elizabeth Wordsworth wrestled with her awareness of the inaccessibility of her college to poorer students, while preserving her determination to cultivate its exclusive social 'tone' for the benefit of her surrogate student daughters. Funds were raised for charitable student grants, and in 1886 she philanthropically endowed the future St Hugh's College for the benefit of less wealthy women students.[6] At Lady Margaret Hall, upper middle-class status was associated with frequent exhortations to help the poor. In the early years, its students undertook such charitable tasks as sewing flannel petticoats and stuffing pillows for the destitute, entertaining shop girls at college teas, and singing to hospital patients.[7] Students made a major contribution to the Women's University Settlement, founded in Southwark in 1887, and ten years later the college founded its own London settlement house in nearby Lambeth. As Elizabeth wrote in the first college history, 'The world is full of urgent needs, and we cannot "realise ourselves" without spending and being spent in doing what we can to help those who have had fewer privileges than have fallen to our lot'.[8]

This statement reflected her long-standing admiration for the social philosophy of T. H. Green, as well as her own less troubled Christian faith. Green's influence upon both men and women extended far beyond his own premature death in 1882, and was particularly important in shaping Mary Ward's views.[9] He had been a keen supporter of the education of women since the 1860s, and in the

---

[2] Bailey (ed.), *Lady Margaret Hall*, 26.
[3] Somerville opened to students on 13 Oct. and Janet Ward (later Trevelyan) was born on 6 Nov. 1879.
[4] Creighton, *Memoir*, 57: 'It was a great effort to me to visit my street'.
[5] Quoted in Sutherland, *Mrs Humphry Ward*, 61.
[6] As early as June 1879, Elizabeth Wordsworth welcomed an exhibition gift 'which I hope will enable us to have a deserving *poor* girl' (LMH archives, E. Wordsworth papers, box 1, 6). On 15 May 1886 she wrote of her plans to 'install Annie Moberly and half a dozen really *poor* students next October . . . I do not feel we are doing half enough for the class that really needs our help the most' (box 1, 65).
[7] Battiscombe, *Reluctant Pioneer*, 153.   [8] Bailey (ed.), *Lady Margaret Hall*, 19.
[9] See Ward, *Recollections*, 132–3. For Green's work and influence, see O. Anderson, 'The Feminism of T. H. Green: A Late-Victorian Success Story?', *History of Political Thought*, 12/4 (1991), 671–93; J. Harris, *Private Lives, Public Spirit: 1870–1914* (London: Penguin Books, 1993), 226–30; M. Richter, *The Politics of Conscience: T. H. Green and his Age* (Lanham: University Press of America, 1983).

1870s acted as secretary to the Association for the Education of Women, as well as assisting the formation of the Society of Home Students and contributing to the launch of Oxford High School. His abandonment of belief in the miraculous elements of Christianity was linked to an enhanced belief in social service as a means of realizing God's intentions for human society. Ethical fulfilment depended upon personal service at local level, such as his own involvement in Oxford's municipal government as well as in female education. His disciples included Arnold Toynbee and other well-known Balliol scholars. Toynbee's early death in 1883 was commemorated by the foundation of Toynbee Hall in East London, the model for other late Victorian settlements which enabled university men and women to help the poor by living amongst them. The success of such ventures owed much to the general expansion of both philanthropy and permissive social policy during the same period. However, a direct connection to Oxford idealism can be traced not only through Toynbee Hall, but also through Mary Ward's settlement work from the late 1880s onwards. By this date she had followed her husband's career from Oxford to London, and achieved startling success as a novelist with *Robert Elsmere* (1888). This runaway best-seller followed the anguished career of a doubting Christian who eventually achieved redemption and a new form of faith through his work for the London poor. Mary Ward spent longer writing her first major novel than any succeeding one. This was not only because it called upon new skills, but also because the book represented her own experience of spiritual travail under Green's influence and within a family torn apart by her parents' religious strife. The readership for *Robert Elsmere* was enormous at all levels of literate society, both in Britain and America, showing that she had touched upon a deeply sensitive topic as well as spinning a good tale. The profits went into a more luxurious lifestyle for the Wards, and into Mary's own settlement scheme.[10]

University Hall in Bloomsbury opened to settlers and to the public in 1890, the year after the famous Appeal Against Women's Suffrage. Mary Ward was seeking to demonstrate through social action, as Green had done earlier, that her theoretical stance was capable of being actualized. Her first settlement was intended to provide religious and cultural enrichment for the London poor, and was initially staffed by men under the leadership of 'an ex-Balliol man and pupil of T. H. Green'.[11] During the foundation year Mary Ward's letters to her father record that she read Green's books alongside her planning, and that his initials were carved on the settlement's doorposts. Within a few years Mary had learned from experience that the most important side of settlement work lay in its practical social service rather than in French classes, libraries, and the

[10] Readership and profits were exultantly described in Mary Ward's correspondence with her father in 1888–9: by Nov. 1888 over 100,000 copies had been sold, including around 70,000 in America (letter dated 9 Nov. 1888, Pusey House Library, Oxford, M. Ward papers, 2/2). Gladstone's interest in the novel and its author helped to increase its sales.

[11] M. Ward to T. Ward, Aug. 1890, M. Ward Papers, 2/2.

Jowett lecture programme. Green's ideas on social service and his faith in the social role of educated women soon helped to inspire an even more ambitious enterprise. The Passmore Edwards settlement, opened nearby in 1897, had an active Women's Work committee and drew upon female volunteers to provide innovative social welfare activities.

The most successful of these initiatives were devoted to the needs of working-class children. Seth Koven has described Mary Ward's social action as 'civic maternalism', showing how her child welfare work integrated with her anti-suffrage beliefs rather than contradicting them (as hostile suffragists sometimes claimed).[12] Her belief in the profound difference between male and female social functions had always been coupled with a conviction that women must contribute to public life from within their own sphere of womanly expertise. This was clearly stated in the 1889 Appeal and was to be restated persistently by women members of the Edwardian anti-suffrage Leagues. Meanwhile, Mary went on to achieve impressive results in her chosen areas of maternal social service. The Passmore Edwards Invalid School for Crippled Children opened in 1899, setting important precedents for the London School Board and the London County Council. The Passmore Edwards play-scheme of the same year was still more influential, alongside other efforts to keep children off the streets and out of trouble. In 1904 the London County Council agreed to fund an expansion; the 1907 Education Act empowered all local authorities to fund similar schemes from the rates. By 1912 more than a million London children were benefiting from play-schemes which Mary Ward triumphantly toured in her motor car each summer.[13] Her credibility as an anti-suffragist maternal reformer was now beyond doubt.

Louise Creighton was also successful in making a name for herself as a public figure during the 1890s and 1900s, though she did not set out to court celebrity and probably did not enjoy it as much as her friend.[14] Sharing Mary Ward's basic views on womanly duty, she was also motivated towards social service by her Anglicanism and her status as a clerical wife. In 1875 Mandell Creighton made the bold decision to give up his Merton fellowship for a college living in a distant Northumberland parish. The couple's anxious consultation is recorded in their correspondence. For Louise, the loss of Oxford society and of her new educational ventures would be severe. However, her husband appealed to her social conscience with the comment that it was 'more pleasant to talk over schemes of education in

---

[12] S. Koven, in ead. and S. Michel, *Mothers of a New World: Maternal Politics and the Origins of Welfare States* (London: Routledge, 1993), ch. 2, addresses 'the progressive, conservative, anti-suffragist civic maternalism of Mary (Mrs Humphry) Ward' (p. 96).

[13] See descriptions in Dorothy Ward's diary, e.g. 15 Aug. 1912: 'A tremendous day in the Playgrounds and Vacation School for Mother and me—we left here in the car at 9.25 and got back at 8.45!' UCL Archives, D. Ward papers, MS Add. 202.48.

[14] Though Louise Creighton did not seek fame, she did derive considerable satisfaction from the discovery of her own competence as a speaker and organizer. See Creighton, *Memoir*, 102, 113, 116, 127.

a drawing room than to work them out in a poor parish; and "society" gives you all the advantage of looking very wise and very good without much cost of actual effort'.[15] Fortunately the experiment turned out well. Oxford friends visited in droves each summer, including the Greens, the Wards, the Johnsons, the Talbots, the Paters, and other academic and clerical acquaintances. During the rest of the year the couple devoted their time to historical writing and the careful nurture of an expanding family, while Embleton villagers received unaccustomed levels of parochial care. Louise Creighton enjoyed 'the happiest years of our life' as she joined her husband in developing humbler forms of education and social service.[16] Apart from their joint work in the village school, in district visiting, and in tacking local alcoholism, she undertook the womanly work of organizing mothers' meetings on social purity and forming branches of the newly founded Girls' Friendly Society. Though it was 'not easy work' to get into touch with local working-class girls on such subjects as 'their relations with men', Louise persisted and began to find her true vocation as a maternal reformer organizing and inspiring the work of other middle-class women.[17] She was elected diocesan president of the Girls' Friendly Society, spoke for the first time at a large open-air gathering of its members, and organized a GFS conference in Newcastle.

During the next phase of her life Louise Creighton found herself more and more often chairing meetings, speaking in public, and planning conferences primarily for women. As her husband rose through the Church to become Bishop of Peterborough then Bishop of London, the couple's ambitions towards joint work became subsumed within a companionate marriage where the partners performed separate, complementary roles. Her regrets at this transition are a recurrent theme of her autobiography, which presents an unusually poignant account of the intersection between public and private lives. At Embleton a resident student took over her place in her husband's study; later the study became an inner sanctum for a secretary and for male visitors. 'My great desire was to help Max in every possible way in his work,' she recalled; but he encouraged her to 'lead my own life and do my own work'.[18] During the 1880s and much of the 1890s, that work was dominated by the needs of her large family. Louise Creighton conscientiously breastfed her children for nine months and taught them at home for most of their childhood, in model maternal fashion. At the same time she was trying to continue her literary work and taking on an increasing load of public duties.[19] District visiting in Cambridge, where the Creightons moved after their Embleton interlude, was 'rather a grim proceeding', but more to her taste was a Mothers' Union (for working-class mothers) and a mothers' discussion society which received short papers from 'more educated mothers' on aspects of the education and training of children: 'This speaking

[15] L. Creighton, *Life and Letters of Mandell Creighton* (London: Longman, Green and Co., 1904), 141.
[16] Creighton, *Memoir*, 80.   [17] Ibid. 65.   [18] Ibid. 103.   [19] Ibid. 84.

to mothers and the constant preoccupation with educational questions fitted in naturally with all that I was trying to do with my own children'.[20] Ability to call upon her own motherly status helped to give Louise Creighton the confidence she required as a leading speaker and organizer for the national Mothers' Union, which became fully established during her Peterborough years.

Despite the class-segregated approach to maternal education which she herself adopted in Cambridge, Louise resisted aspects of Mothers' Union policy which distinguished middle-class from working-class women: 'It was my constant desire to feel one with them, one mother amongst others'.[21] Her advocacy of a universal ideal of motherhood was attuned to anti-suffrage maternal reformism. However, the practicalities of organized women's work tended to undermine universalism, and to emphasize the gulf in wealth, education, and opportunity between middle-class or upper-class women and the rest. Louise Creighton was a perceptive commentator upon the dilemmas of organized women's work. Her suffrage views were framed, and then later reframed, from within this context. Amongst the key dilemmas were not only issues of class, but also issues concerning effective collaboration between men and women in public work and in family life. These issues were central to her work as a maternal reformer, whether in the Mothers' Union or in the National Union of Women Workers, of which she became the first president in 1895.

As her children grew up, and especially during her widowhood from 1901 onwards, the scope of her activities broadened out into a huge range of organizations concerned with rescue work, settlements, missionary work, and women's role in the Anglican Church, as well as with education and maternity. Her friendships broadened commensurately and came to include moderate suffragists working in the same areas. Kathleen Lyttelton, befriended in Cambridge during the 1880s, took over the intimacy earlier reserved for Mary Ward and the other Oxford women. The wife of a Bishop herself, she shared many of Louise Creighton's interests; her book on *Women and Their Work* (1901) illustrates very clearly the extensive common ground between two women who were not yet in agreement on the suffrage question.[22] Both women were maternal reformers. Both were deeply preoccupied with gender and class issues, as these affected their personal lives and their work. Their different assessments of the consequences of a female franchise, allied to different life experiences, led them for many years to take up opposing views on votes for women despite reaching similar conclusions on most other matters. Kathleen Lyttelton helped Louise Creighton to make a relatively smooth and easy transition from anti-suffragism to suffragism in 1906, the year of her own sudden death.

---

[20] Ibid. 86.   [21] Ibid. 114.

[22] K. Lyttelton, *Women and their Work* (London: Methuen, 1901). She concluded her chapter on 'The Family' by quoting Louise Creighton's claim that family life was 'first the ideal training ground, and afterwards in many cases the ideal background, for work for society as a whole' (p. 58).

POSITIVISM AND WOMEN'S CITIZENSHIP

Close friendships between suffragists and anti-suffragists tend to suggest the limited ideological distance between these viewpoints, and were particularly common among maternal reformers. Support or opposition to the parliamentary vote was sometimes publicly debated as an issue of high political principle, yet for many women antis the most critical issues concerned broad definitions of gender roles, and the social and national causes which suffrage might help or hinder, rather than the detailed matter of casting votes. Differences of judgement and emphasis, rather than of principle, divided many of the more conservative suffragists from the more progressive anti-suffragists. However, the history of women's anti-suffragism does include episodes of sharp conflict. The evolution of women's philanthropic and religious work in the late nineteenth century brought conservative reformers together, but other aspects of the public debate over gender roles drove them apart. It would be wrong to underestimate the depth of enduring hostility to the female franchise felt by at least a proportion of those women who decided to make their opposition public.

Ethel Harrison was among the women who were most hostile to suffragism. She had long-standing friendship links with Mary Ward and Louise Creighton, but stood somewhat apart from them in her public work and her anti-suffrage beliefs. Her Positivism inclined her to take up rather extreme positions on gender difference. Based upon the theories of the French sociologist Auguste Comte, Positivism attempted to find a scientific basis for a 'religion of Social Service'.[23] Women were assigned an important and distinctive civic role within this philosophy of applied humanism. In return for their acceptance of male rule in the public sphere, they could achieve powerful spiritual authority in the family which, in due course, would spread its influence through the wider world and enable social improvements to be achieved. In a speech to the Positivist Society on civil marriage, Frederic Harrison emphasized that 'the dignity of marriage is impaired when the moral sphere of the woman is confounded with, or surrendered for, the practical sphere of the man'; instead of equality within marriage, woman had 'the incomparable task of being its real Moral Providence'.[24] Ethel Harrison developed this view in her book *The Freedom of Women*: 'It is ideals that rule the world; so it is in no sense because we undervalue the importance of women's contribution to public life that we depreciate and deplore the agitation for the vote: we think women can do

---

[23] F. Harrison, *Memoir and Essays of Ethelbertha Harrison* (Bath: Sir Isaac Pitman and Sons, 1917), 23. See also A. Harrison, *Frederic Harrison: Thoughts and Memories* (London: William Heinemann, 1926), 14; and M. Vogeler, *Frederic Harrison: The Vocations of a Positivist* (Oxford: Clarendon Press, 1984).

[24] F. Harrison, *Marriage: A Discourse to the Positivist Society after the Civil Marriage of Frederick Charles Freeman and Faith Flaxman Wright* (London: Newton Hall, 1887), 26–7.

better for themselves and the world. We need votaries to tend the sacred fire'.[25]
A glimpse of this particular domestic votary in action is provided in Austin
Harrison's memoir of his father. Ethel was 'in a rare sense his friend, counsellor
and companion . . . The creative side of my father's life began with her. It would
hardly have taken the same course without her.' Elsewhere he noted that 'In
moulding her, he fashioned himself, and their two egoisms became as one'.[26]
More prosaically, she devoted herself to the care of their five children and
helped to edit his manuscripts. Beatrice Webb described how Ethel 'listened
with reverence to his words from the lectern of Newton Hall', as well as hosting
agreeable political dinner parties.[27]

The London base of the Positivist Society was the equivalent of a humanist
settlement which attracted (even if it did not convince) many leading reformers,
despite scandalizing others by its challenge to conventional religion. Mary Ward,
as well as Beatrice Webb, took the trouble to study the works of Comte and even
included an unflattering sketch of a Positivist couple in *Robert Elsmere*.[28] Newton
Hall provided Ethel Harrison with an approved platform for extending her social
action beyond the task of inspiring her husband and children. Though she never
became involved in large-scale philanthropic work or in the emergent national
organizations promoting women's work, she did undertake a certain amount of
social service in a spirit of (Positivist) maternal reform. A Women's Guild and a
girls' club tried to broaden the social appeal of Positivism, as well as providing
education and practical support in the neighbourhood. The Newton Hall choir
was under her direction, and she compiled a Positivist hymn book including a
dozen of her own hymns.[29] During the 1890s her own social writings began
to reach publication, not only through the *Positivist Review* but also in more
prominent monthly journals including the *Nineteenth Century*. Increasingly her
writings centred on the position of women in society. An essay titled 'Are Women
Citizens?' provided direct impetus towards her successful anti-suffrage book, as
she concluded that 'citizenship lies, not in the suffrage, but in the participation
of each individual in effort for the good of the Community'.[30] Other essays
in the 1890s expressed her dislike of the New Woman, who had emerged as a
prominent literary and journalistic icon and a favourite target for the opponents
of women's suffrage.

During the Edwardian years Ethel Harrison became a more and more impas-
sioned anti-suffragist, avoiding public speeches but writing effective diatribes

---

[25] E. Harrison, *The Freedom of Women* (London: Watts and Co., 1908), 55.
[26] A. Harrison, *Frederic Harrison*, 196, 41.
[27] B. Webb, *My Apprenticeship* (London: Pelican Books, 1938),169.
[28] The Harrisons were near neighbours of the Wards during their summer visits to a Surrey
farmhouse retreat in the 1880s.
[29] Her husband described *The Service of Man—Hymns and Poems* (1890) as 'the complete
manual of the Religion of Humanity, and as such it has ever since been in use in the gatherings of
Positivists'. F. Harrison, *Memoir*, 14.
[30] E. Harrison, 'Are Women Citizens?', *Positivist Review* (Apr. 1899), 85–6.

on the social danger of women's direct involvement in parliamentary politics. Underlying her anger was her escalating concern over women's abandonment of their true familial role. Whilst 'Victorian Woman' (1905) was gently nostalgic,[31] 'Woman Who Toils in America' (1903) was a broadside against married women's paid employment,[32] and 'Abdication' (1913) was one of the strongest statements ever made of the anti-suffrage maternalist case against the vote.[33] Women were deserting their duties as mothers in order to support a 'destructive campaign'; suffragists were colluding in 'the massacre of infants' by working mothers, while many middle-class homes had become 'mere lodging houses'. Suffragism was 'an anti-social movement', for 'society does not need an inferior race of female men standing beside true men. It needs women in the full sense of that word'. Though the physical care of children was vital to the country's future, Ethel remained true to her Positivist roots by asserting that woman's spiritual influence was still more important: 'At present the pure fount of her influence is dried. Woman has abdicated'.[34]

The bleak pessimism of this article was called forth by the political circumstances of 1913. Extreme revulsion against the suffragette campaign was shared, to some extent, by most anti-suffrage women at this stage of the campaign, but did not necessarily reflect despair for the success of their own counter-propaganda. Ethel joined Mary Ward and other supporters of the forward policy in asserting that a better way lay within the grasp of maternal reformers. By the early 1890s Frederic Harrison had become an alderman on the London County Council. Though he never supported the admission of women to the County Council, he published a lecture in 1891 which (apart from extolling feminine spiritual powers, and attacking working mothers) endorsed the view that women could be useful 'in a thousand ways' within 'more or less public institutions'.[35] During the 1900s Ethel Harrison also commended women's work in local government, claiming in her anti-suffrage book that 'The municipal and educational vote stands upon an entirely different footing. For all schools, poor houses, hospitals, asylums etc, for all that concerns the world of women, she may fairly claim that she not only pays rates and taxes, but that women contribute their labour—women share responsibility with men in these matters'.[36]

Ethel Harrison was also among the first anti-suffragists to introduce the concept of a permanent national women's committee, to be appointed in an advisory capacity alongside the male legislature. If ever the majority of British women should come round to demanding the vote (which seemed to her unlikely, but not impossible), then 'let us trust that it will be in a Diet of Women outside the

[31] Ead., 'The Victorian Woman', *Nineteenth Century*, 59 (1905), 951–7.
[32] Ead., 'The Woman Who Toils in America', *Nineteenth Century*, 55 (1903), 1020–5.
[33] Ead., 'Abdication', *Nineteenth Century*, 74 (1913), 1328–35.
[34] Ibid. 1329, 1330, 1331, 1333, 1334, 1335.
[35] On F. Harrison and local government, see Vogeler, *Frederic Harrison*, 210–11.
[36] E. Harrison, *Freedom of Women*, 29.

Imperial Parliament'.[37] This interesting idea was to be taken up by Mary Ward, Violet Markham, Gertrude Bell, and a number of other prominent supporters of the forward policy after 1908, and will be further discussed in Chapter 9. It reflected the anti-suffrage women's growing recognition, by this date, that social service did indeed depend fundamentally upon the decisions of central government. However unwelcome women's direct involvement in parliamentary politics might be, the Liberal reforms of the Edwardian years had changed the landscape of social welfare. The women's anti-suffrage movement was struggling to keep up with the pace of change, whilst still clinging to its belief in immutable gender differences.

ORGANIZED WOMEN, MATERNALISM, AND SOCIAL REFORM

Women's collaborative work for philanthropic and religious causes was an important preparation for other collective endeavours, including the suffrage and the anti-suffrage movements themselves. The National Union of Women Workers became the scene of heated conflicts over women's suffrage between 1910 and 1913, but it is important to set these events in the context of a longer history of successful cooperation among women. The founders of the NUWW valued gender difference and generally prioritized women's social duties over their political rights, whether or not they supported votes for women. Even at the height of the suffrage debate, women from both camps were anxious to protect their shared work of maternal social reform from short-term political damage. The NUWW provides striking evidence of the extensive overlap between suffrage and anti-suffrage reformist ideals, as well as offering an interesting case study of political conflict within a consciously apolitical women's organization. Louise Creighton, Mary Ward, and Lucy Soulsby all occupied leadership positions in the NUWW. Alongside thousands of other women, their views on womanly work and on the vote were influenced by their experience of its evolving aims and development.

A closer look at the early history of the NUWW helps to explain how this organization became a recruiting ground both for suffragism and for anti-suffragism, yet remained fundamentally committed to tolerance and cooperation among women reformers. Suffragist Kathleen Lyttelton and anti-suffragist Louise Creighton sat side by side in the women's conference in Birmingham which led eventually to the formation of the National Union of Women Workers.[38] Louise

---

[37] Ibid. 29.

[38] On the general history of the NUWW, see D. Glick, *The National Council of Women of Great Britain* (London: National Council of Women, 1995). On the relationship between the NUWW and the suffrage movement, see J. Bush, 'The National Union of Women Workers and Women's Suffrage', in M. Boussahba-Bravard (ed.), *Suffrage Outside Suffragism* (London: Palgrave, 2007).

described the impact of this event in her *Memoir*, in terms which might have been echoed by many other attenders:

It was then a conference of the Association for the care of friendless girls . . . I knew none of the women who were concerned in it, and I was much interested by those I met. It was a great joy and surprise to find amongst this collection of rather ordinary looking middle-aged women so much intelligence, capacity and zeal. My eyes were opened to discovering all the work that was going on. By degrees I got more and more drawn into it; and I discovered a latent power for organisation which I did not know that I possessed.[39]

This first conference enhanced her confidence in herself and her fellow women, expanded her knowledge, and before long offered opportunities to extend her organizational expertise as well. A collective decision was taken to spread these benefits more widely. The NUWW constitution was drawn up and in 1895 Louise Creighton found herself, to her surprise, the first president of a national 'umbrella' organization formed to link together female social work on a continuous basis. Ten vice-presidents were appointed at the official founding conference, including anti-suffrage signatories Lady Frederick Cavendish and Beatrice Webb alongside declared suffragists Lady Laura Ridding and Edith Lyttelton. Millicent Fawcett was among the speakers. The new president cleared up any possible confusion over the class composition of the event by defining 'women workers' as 'women who are engaged in some real work whether it be paid or voluntary and who do that work, not for the sake of their own satisfaction, not for the sake of pay, though some may need some pay, but because they look upon their work as a vocation'.[40] The declared objectives of the NUWW included 'the encouragement of sympathy . . . among the women of Great Britain; the promotion of their social, civil and religious welfare; the gathering and distribution of serviceable information', as well as the creation of a standing national federation of women's organizations and the founding of local branches.[41] Specialist sectional committees formed from 1896 onwards, and the number of regional branches expanded from fifteen in 1895 to around fifty by 1914. More than 150 women's associations, with a collective membership of well over half a million women, were affiliated to the pre-war Union.[42] It had adapted somewhat to changing times, but remained recognizably the same

---

[39] Creighton, *Memoir*, 90.   [40] Glick, *National Council*, 7.   [41] Ibid. 6.

[42] Membership varied from year to year, and is reported rather obscurely in the annual *Handbook and Report of the National Council and Union of Women Workers of Great Britain and Ireland.* Changes in the constitution, and the many different categories of membership, make it very difficult to provide a consistent account of the Union's growth. The 1913 annual conference attempted to clarify the membership categories. The NUWW included individual ordinary members paying 5s. per year, corporate members who were members of local branches subscribing not less than 6d. per member, and members of affiliated societies subscribing 1 guinea annually. The NCW was the 'Governing Body' of the NUWW, composed of members of the executive committee and representatives of local branches, sectional committees, and affiliated societies. *NUWW Handbook and Report 1913–1914* (London: NUWW, 1914), 210.

meeting ground for middle-class, socially concerned ladies—many of whom resented the intrusion of politics into their womanly social work.

Supporters of the NUWW enjoyed referring to its impressive annual conference as the 'Parliament of Women'. It was, perhaps, the nearest thing to the separate women's chamber which some anti-suffragists had begun to hope for. From 1896 onwards a limited number of resolutions on policy matters were submitted to a conference vote. Sectional committees included a Legislation Committee which noted the Bills before Parliament in each session, and sometimes tried to influence legislative outcomes by gathering fresh information through the branches network and sending it forward to government departments or Members of Parliament.[43] In 1897 the NUWW affiliated to the International Council of Women, an organization with strong suffrage links as well as a social reform purpose comparable to that of the British organization. But the programme of NUWW conferences and the composition of its local branches continued to reflect the breadth upon which the organization had always prided itself. Key concerns included the many moral issues which preoccupied women reformers—protection of children, moral training of young women, 'rescue work' among fallen women, guidance for mothers—as well as more down-to-earth matters such as health, the Poor Law, employment issues, and schooling. When the 1912 *NUWW Handbook* listed 'Twelve reasons why every woman should join', the arguments chosen were quite as compatible with anti-suffragism as with any more radical political outlook. Importantly, they included reference to the NUWW's constitutional commitment to organize 'in the interests of no one policy', together with a statement of its intention to promote 'sympathy of thought and harmony of purpose among women workers'. Gendered philanthropy lingered on in the suggestion that women should join up 'because every woman is a "worker", in her own home, if not elsewhere, and by joining you will be enabled to help your less fortunate sisters'.[44] But by this date anti-suffragists had good reasons to fear that the NUWW was in danger of departing from its long-established conservatism and inclusivity.

Throughout its pre-war history, there can be little doubt that many women in the NUWW wanted to turn away from politics and the whole divisive business of parliamentary affairs, including the controversy over women's suffrage. A successful tradition was established of tolerant discussion focused upon the accepted common ground of womanly social service. However, the evolution of social service itself, as well as the gathering pace of the suffrage campaign, gradually called this approach into question. In 1895 a first conference debate was held on women's suffrage. Millicent Fawcett stepped forward to make the case for enfranchisement as an extension of the NUWW's existing work of

---

[43] See Minute Book of the NUWW Legislational [*sic*] Sectional Committee 1906–13, LMA, ACC/3613/01.070.

[44] *NUWW Handbook and Report 1912–1913*, covert.

maternal social reform, but no vote was taken. By 1902 voting on conference resolutions was permitted and the suffrage issue had assumed new urgency. A suffrage resolution was proposed by women concerned over parliamentary erosion of female participation in local government, specifically through their exclusion from the London County Council, and the abolition of London vestries and School Boards. Women's ability to serve their local communities was being undermined, and for this reason the conference quietly endorsed the view that 'without the firm foundation of the Parliamentary Franchise for Women, there is no permanence for any advance gained by them'.[45]

Despite the lack of drama over this resolution, anti-suffragists and some suffragists warned of a divisive threat to the Union's traditionally apolitical stance. The following year Louise Creighton proposed to head off future divisions by ending altogether the practice of passing resolutions at conference. Controversial resolutions were not compatible with the NUWW ideal that 'all should be represented, and all should have the opportunity of meeting, to learn to understand one another, and discover the points on which we agree: that we should be a Union, not a body expressing policy'. Briefly grasping the nettle, she suggested 'we should have if there were such a body . . . even an Anti-Suffrage Society as well as Suffrage Societies affiliated, and so on about all other matters about which there are differing opinions'.[46] Henrietta Barnett, a leading East London settlement worker and tacit suffragist, rose to second the resolution. No women who worked for others should be excluded from the Union's ranks, or discouraged from contributing to its work: 'Our Women Workers entrance cards should be that we are women'.[47] Some women opposed the passing of resolutions on the grounds that the NUWW was a space for thinking and learning, and for cultivation of women's 'subtle spiritual forces'; while others argued for a continuation of voting because 'we shall destroy ourselves if we only come here to talk, and if we never let our talk pass into action'. There was widespread support for the view that conflict should be avoided wherever possible: 'We must look to the wisdom and gentleness of our Executive to carry these things without friction'.[48] In that spirit, a decision was taken to defuse the issue by referring it to the branches for further discussion.

Over the following years Louise Creighton came to accept that anti-suffragists (and opponents of resolutions) were in a minority at the national gatherings of the Union, and made a gradual transition herself to a suffragist position. However, like many speakers in the 1903 debate, she did so without losing faith in the ability of women to run their own organizations in ways which reflected their own distinctive gender characteristics. After announcing her conversion to moderate suffragism at the NUWW's 1906 conference, she continued to exert

---

[45] *Report of the Annual Meeting of the NCW of Great Britain and Ireland, 1902* (London: NUWW, 1902), 66.
[46] Ibid. 118.　　　[47] Ibid. 119.　　　[48] Ibid. 119, 121, 123.

her considerable influence to keep the Union united in the cause of female social service. The Women's National Anti-Suffrage League was duly accepted as an affiliate of the Union, and Mary Ward became one of its vice-presidents. Lucy Soulsby acted as a long-serving member of the Executive Committee. Elizabeth Wordsworth accepted an invitation to speak at the national conference of 1910. Meanwhile the suffrage issue became inescapably prominent in national life, and within the NUWW itself. The suffrage resolution of 1902 was reaffirmed by a conference vote in 1909 and the Executive voted on more than one occasion to give official support to suffragist meetings and demonstrations. In 1907 a single vote divided supporters and opponents when the Executive took one such decision, but the following year the NUWW paraded its banner and organized carriages of supporters at one of the biggest London suffrage processions.[49]

By 1910 Mary Ward and the *Anti-Suffrage Review* had decided to take up cudgels in defence of an inclusive Union untrammelled by suffrage activism. Strong public and private protests were registered against the NUWW's presence at a Trafalgar Square suffrage meeting, and Mary tried to force a conference debate over the principle of allowing NUWW policy commitments which antagonized a substantial minority of members. Agitated correspondence between the two old friends, and informal notes of an Executive discussion, show how hard Louise Creighton worked to prevent a damaging confrontation between suffragists and anti-suffragists within the Union.[50] 'It is horrid about the N.U.W.W.,' wrote Mary privately, 'But I have had many letters appealing to me to take the thing up . . . Why break up one of the few Women's Associations of importance, where Suffragists and Antis can really meet on neutral ground for common objects?'[51] Louise begged her to refrain from making an angry vice-presidential visit to the executive, which could only prove counter-productive. She hoped to carry a compromise proposal to review NUWW procedures for supporting demonstrations in the future, whilst avoiding an open debate at the Executive which 'would only call attention to the fact that it was the suffrage question which was at the bottom, and would invite the small body of the violent to oppose on principle'.[52] In Mary Ward's absence, she told the Executive that 'It is most desirable to retain those who are opposed to the suffrage . . . we do not

---

[49] A letter dated 5 June 1908 gave supporters of the forthcoming demonstration practical information on how to join 'the NUWW group'. For 1s. they could ride in 'a special NUWW brake', though it was hoped that 'members who are able to do so will walk in preference to driving'. Ribbons in the NUWW colours were helpfully provided for coachmen to tie to their whips, or for members to wear in the procession. LMA, ACC/3613/3/1/B.

[50] See NUWW Correspondence re Women's Suffrage, including 'Draft of Rough Notes on Mrs HW's Resolution at EC meeting' (n.d.). Lucy Soulsby backed up Louise Creighton's efforts to keep the conflict out of the forthcoming conference. Louise Creighton undertook to write to the *Anti-Suffrage Review* correcting some details of Mary Ward's published denunciation of NUWW support for the Trafalgar Square suffrage meeting. LMA, ACC/3613/3/1/B.

[51] M. Ward to L. Creighton, 14 Sept. 1910. M. Ward papers, 3/3/1.

[52] L. Creighton to M. Ward, 26 Sept. 1910. M. Word Papers, 6/3.

want to bring the matter to a head, but to deal with it quietly'. Other speakers accepted this position, including Lady Laura Ridding who felt that branches were 'pretty evenly divided on this matter', and that their 'paramount duty' was to preserve the breadth and tolerance which enabled the NUWW to 'excel all other Societies in usefulness'.[53]

Mary Ward believed she had won an important victory as the NUWW drew back from further controversy. Her argument that the suffrage debate would do lasting damage evidently struck home with an executive which was already aware that local opinion did not always mirror that represented by conference resolutions. Limited evidence survives on discussion within local branches, but the minute book of the Bournemouth branch, founded in 1909, makes it clear that both suffragist and anti-suffragist societies were welcomed as affiliates. In 1912 the branch politely declined a renewed attempt by the NUWW's Central Council to test suffrage opinion locally, judging it 'wiser to confine its energies to those matters upon which its members were practically united'.[54] The Peterborough branch had been founded by Louise Creighton herself, and its minutes between 1896 and 1906 suggest that the suffrage issue was regarded as strictly off-limits. Speakers addressed purely social issues, and no suffrage groups were affiliated.[55] In Torquay, on the other hand, the anti-suffragists seem to have been in the ascendant. As early as 1906 the Executive received an indignant letter from Minna Gray, announcing her resignation as local NUWW President on the grounds that the Union sympathized with suffragette methods which were doing 'irreparable damage to the cause of women'. Seventeen out of twenty-two members of her local committee signed the protest resolution which accompanied her letter, including some moderate suffragists and the anti-suffragist writer Christabel Coleridge.[56] Published annual summaries of branch reports from 1912 onwards provide general confirmation both of branch diversity and of members' reluctance to become bogged down in suffrage politics.

The Executive's 1910 compromise over official support for suffragist activity produced only a short-lived truce. During 1912–13 conflict over suffragism reached new heights, and neither Mary Ward nor Louise Creighton was able to prevent an acrimonious debate at national level, followed by recriminations and a substantial number of anti-suffragist resignations. Influenced by current events in Parliament and in the country, an Extraordinary Meeting of the NUWW resolved in November 1912 that no franchise reform should be passed

[53] NUWW, 'Draft of Rough Notes' and written statement from Lady Ridding, n.d. (1910). LMA, ACC/3613/3/1/B.

[54] In 1910 the 14 societies represented included the 'National Anti-Suffrage League' and the NUWSS. Minutes of the 1912 Council recorded the decision against testing local suffrage opinion. Bournemouth NUWW Minutes 1909–22, LMA, ACC/3613/08/069.

[55] Peterborough NUWW Minute Book 1896–1918. LMA, ACC/3613/08/025.

[56] NUWW, 'Correspondence re Women's Suffrage', letter from M. Gray to E. Janes, 13 Nov. 1906, with Protest Resolution from members of the Torquay NUWW branch. The protest was provoked by Millicent Fawcett's public support for early militancy. LMA, ACC/3613/3/1/B.

without 'some measure of Parliamentary Suffrage for Women'.[57] A year later, the NUWW conference rejected final attempts to introduce constitutional reforms which would curb divisive debates over this issue and others.[58] Mary Ward resigned in protest, and turned her full energies towards the task of developing an alternative forum where suffragist and anti-suffragist women could meet to discuss joint social action without political distractions.[59] Once again, open hostilities within a Union which prided itself on its gendered unity of purpose led to both public and private lamentations. 'I hate controversy so much that I perhaps avoid it in almost a cowardly way,' wrote Louise to Mary in December 1913, assuring her rather belatedly that in future 'Whatever happens we won't quarrel publicly, and will discuss our differences, if differences should ever be discussed, in private'.[60] From the platform of the national conference two months earlier, Mary had warned delegates that the NUWW risked losing its many anti-suffragist supporters, and with them its 'unique power and promise'. If conflict continued at local and national levels, 'you will have the ordinary work of the Union devastated by this question, and the real interest of the annual meetings would come to lie, not in what has hitherto made the glory of the Union, the common and disinterested effort it represents, or ought to represent, to bring women of all political and religious opinions together to work for the betterment of life—but in the advance or retrogression of parties, the strengthening or weakening of one political cause'.[61]

Some conclusions can now be drawn about the connections between anti-suffragism, maternal reform, and the social service represented by the NUWW. No other organization could claim to represent such a wide range of women's voluntary work in the late Victorian and Edwardian period. Its affiliates included not only large and small philanthropic associations, but also the main women's religious and educational societies, and increasing numbers of women's societies connected to the work of local government and public administration. If the strength of the Union lay in its breadth, this was perhaps also a weakness. Connections between members, branches, and affiliated bodies needed to be relatively weak in order to be successfully maintained. On the other hand, there is

---

[57] *NUWW Handbook and Report 1912–1913*, 203. The majority was a decisive one: 159 to 59, with 13 abstentions. In the aftermath Mary Ward and Millicent Fawcett debated the past history of the NUWW in the pages of *The Times*. A London protest meeting was organized on 5 Dec. 1912, with both suffragist and anti-suffragist speakers: *The Times*, 29 Nov. 1912, 10.

[58] Lady Laura Ridding proposed to increase the majority required to pass NUWW conference resolutions from two-thirds (agreed in 1910) to three-quarters. Louise Creighton proposed an elaborate scheme of 'alternative resolutions', designed to defuse confrontational debates. *NUWW Handbook and Report 1913–1914*, 168.

[59] Mary Ward considered trying to engineer a formal split in the NUWW, but decided instead to launch the Joint Parliamentary Advisory Committee to promote consultation between MPs and leading suffragist and anti-suffragist women on social reform legislation. Suffrage debate was forbidden on this body. See Ch. 9, below.

[60] L. Creighton to M. Ward, 23 Dec. 1913. M. Ward papers, 6/3.

[61] *NUWW Handbook and Report 1913–1914*, 189.

overwhelming evidence that Union members felt themselves to be united by more important bonds than those of a mere constitutional rule book. The NUWW was pre-eminent as a symbol of 'true' womanhood: the widespread conservative consensus on female gender roles which had been both tested and reinforced by the Victorian Woman Question debate, and was being further tested by the new challenges of the Edwardian suffrage campaign. Both suffragist and anti-suffragist members continued to express their enthusiasm for united, womanly social action. The Union's ideal was 'all-embracing and maternal', designed to 'combat evil' as well as to 'work for the betterment of life'.[62] Introducing the painful suffrage debate of November 1912, the President (Mrs Allan Bright) attempted to defuse latent antagonism by introducing the principal speakers in terms of their maternal role rather than their suffrage politics: Louise Creighton as 'practically the mother of this very large and flourishing Union'; Millicent Fawcett as 'a model in fulfilling those practical obligations of a wife and mother which are the dearest of all ties'; Mary Ward 'who, in addition to the distinction she has earned as an author, has done so much for children'.[63]

Despite so much unanimity on basic ideals, and so much desire to work harmoniously for common ends, the records of the Union also provide evidence of differences of emphasis which could ultimately influence a choice between support for or opposition to votes for women. Whilst anti-suffragists seldom deviated from the shared ground of long-established NUWW ideals, many suffragist speakers emphasized the need for the Union to have more impact upon government, and to be seen to be effective by its members. Younger women, especially, were unlikely to maintain faith in a mere 'talking shop', nor would they accept the prioritization of philanthropy over democratic politics.[64] Whilst anti-suffragists (with some suffragist support) continued to characterize the Union as 'something universal and divine', with important spiritual dimensions, many suffragists placed more emphasis upon its practical policy achievements.[65] Although there was widespread support for a continuing ethos of tolerance within the Union, anti-suffragists were even more eloquent than their opponents in defence of womanly methods of conducting business through discussion, reflection, and emergent consensus. They were also more critical of parliamentary-style, confrontational politics as a dangerous alternative which they believed would defeat the Union's feminine purposes. This was an issue of principle, rather than merely one of organizational style. As one anti-suffragist speaker put it, 'It is what we *are* in this National Council that matters . . . not what we *say*'.[66]

By 1912 the anti-suffragists had come to accept that they were a minority within the Union, at least at leadership level. However, they were a sizeable

---

[62] *NUWW Handbook and Report 1913–1914*, 174, 176.
[63] *NUWW Handbook and Report 1912–1913*, 201–2.
[64] e.g. Margaret Ashton's speech, *NUWW Handbook and Report 1913–1914*, 195.
[65] Mary Ward's speech, *NUWW Handbook and Report 1912–1913*, 213.
[66] Mrs Victor Williams's speech, *NUWW Handbook and Report 1913–1914*, 178.

minority, with well-founded confidence in their wider grass-roots support. The surviving local evidence seems to bear out Laura Ridding's 1910 view that the branches were 'pretty evenly divided' over suffragism, and reluctant to let their divisions impede their joint work for social improvement. Even at the height of the suffrage conflict, this issue was seldom allowed to dominate local agendas, and in many branches was deliberately excluded from discussion. Mary Ward made an understandable, though ill-judged, strategic decision to defend women's anti-suffragism vigorously from within the most broadly representative forum of social maternalism. She regarded the NUWW as a natural recruiting ground, and was as determined as any suffragist to capture its support for her cause. Her comprehensive defeat in 1912–13 should not obscure the continuing existence of anti-suffragism within the NUWW, much of it at a relatively passive level. Anti-suffrage resignations in 1913 did not live up to Mary Ward's expectations.[67] This reflected a predominant wish to avoid a split, rather than unanimous enthusiasm for the parliamentary franchise. The leaders of the NUWW did their best to keep their anti-suffrage members, and Lucy Soulsby was among those who resisted a schism in the ranks. Her letter appealing for unity was read out after the suffrage vote at the 1913 conference. Alongside its formal support for suffragism, the NUWW as a whole remained committed to the wider views of womanly work which the anti-suffragists claimed most truly to represent.

ORGANIZED WOMEN, SOCIAL DUTY, AND THE ANGLICAN CHURCH

The religious dimensions of the women's suffrage campaign surely deserve more attention than they have so far received from most historians of suffragism and anti-suffragism. Jose Harris has described religious bodies as 'the mass media of mid-Victorian Britain';[68] no other institutions were more important in shaping British cultural life and, by extension, public opinion. Between 1870 and 1914 society as a whole became gradually more secular, but this process occurred very unevenly and was accompanied by other changes which enhanced middle-class and upper-class women's involvement in religious life.[69] Anti-suffrage women

[67] Mary Ward to Louise Creighton, 6 and 22 Dec. 1913. M. Ward papers, 3/3/1. Compare with *NUWW Handbook and Report 1914–1915*, 67. Only one local branch and one major organization (the NLOWS) seceded from the NUWW, together with 46 individual resignations over the following months. By the following year the NUWW Annual Report claimed 'increased activity in all departments of its work'.

[68] Harris, *Private Lives, Public Spirit*, 162.

[69] See S. Gill, *Women and the Church of England from the Eighteenth Century to the Present* (London: SPCK, 1994); B. Heeney, *The Women's Movement in the Church of England 1850–1930* (Oxford: Clarendon Press, 1988); R. Mudie Smith, *The Religious Life of London* (London: Hodder and Stoughton, 1904).

were drawn from all denominations, and often made connections between their religious faith and their views on the vote. The *Anti-Suffrage Review* carried several articles on anti-suffragism and Roman Catholicism.[70] At the other end of the spectrum, the distinguished Quaker Caroline Stephen was better known for her religious writing than for her anti-suffragism, but regarded the two subjects as inseparable.[71] In April 1914 the *Anti-Suffrage Review* carried an appeal to Britain's Nonconformist ministers to resist the lures of suffragism, signed by John Massie and fifteen co-religionists.[72] Developments within the Anglican Church in this period were of particular importance to the anti-suffrage movement. At leadership level, the Church made its own interventions into national debate on the Woman Question. According to Brian Heeney, Anglicanism was 'a major centre of resistance to the women's movement generally', using its doctrinal authority to reinforce traditional gender hierarchy and at the same time resisting the democratization of its own institutions.[73] Debates over the admission of the laity (and women) to Church government influenced many participants in the parliamentary suffrage campaign, though connections between the two issues were far from straightforward.[74] Both suffragists and anti-suffragists continued to insist that their faith in the special social value of womanly, maternal qualities was grounded in Christian teaching, without coming closer to consensus over the female franchise. Suffragists also claimed religious sanction, and some clerical support, for the suffrage cause itself. This was not territory which anti-suffragists were prepared to give up lightly. The Church's reluctance to admit women to its own decision-making bodies—let alone to the priesthood—encouraged widespread hope that the Anglican majority would remain staunchly conservative on gender issues, including the disputed parliamentary vote.

Women who were at the forefront of maternal social service were also prominent in Anglican discussions of the nature and duties of women: none more so than Louise Creighton, who during her widowhood earned her reputation

---

[70] e.g. *Anti-Suffrage Review*, 18 (May 1910), 8. Josephine Ward claimed that 'the majority of Catholics, and especially of Catholic women, are strongly opposed to the Suffrage Movement . . . the intrusion of combative political aims and interests into the home is the main danger of the movement'. In Jan. 1913 the *Review* reported on 'the striking series of addresses given by Father Day, S.J., at Manchester', which included an analysis of the dangers of the 'feminist movement'. *Anti-Suffrage Review*, 51 (Jan. 1913), 321–2.

[71] On anti-suffragism and Nonconformity, see L. Lauer, 'Women in British Non-Conformity 1880–1920, with special reference to the Society of Friends, the Baptist Union and the Salvation Army', D. Phil. thesis (Oxford, 1994). Caroline Stephen was influenced by her experience of debates over the admission of women to Quaker business meetings in the 1890s, and by the decision to end separate Women's Meetings by London Yearly Meeting in 1907.

[72] *Anti-Suffrage Review*, 66 (Apr. 1914), 52. Massie was the WNASL and NLOWS Treasurer, and formerly a fellow of the Nonconformist Mansfield College, Oxford.

[73] Heeney, *Women's Movement*, 1.

[74] Some women categorized representation in Church councils as specialized work suitable for women, while other drew parallels between their exclusion from Church government and national government.

as one of the leading women in the Church.[75] Apart from her status as the 'mother' of the NUWW, she held a wide range of responsibilities in Anglican women's organizations and was a leading campaigner for women's representation in Church government, both before and after her conversion to suffragism. Louise refused to join a suffrage association even after she had publicly signalled her support for this cause. She was, however, entirely happy to speak out for the religious dimensions of women's social service and to support the expansion of women's Church work.[76] From the outset she also insisted upon elements of religious observance within the formal agendas of the NUWW, despite its commitment to avoiding denominational controversy.[77]

Like many other socially conservative women, Louise Creighton found another influential and congenial platform at the annual Church Congress. This event, which moved to a different city each year and attracted enormous numbers of lay and clerical attenders, provided unusual opportunities for leading women to address male or mixed audiences containing senior clerical figures, as well as addressing crowded fringe meetings of women and girls. Whilst their views on theology or affairs of state might be dismissed by a male-led Church, their expertise in 'women's work' commanded respect and interest. From the 1860s onwards some women contributed papers which were delivered on their behalf by men; in 1881 Agnes Weston delivered her own address on 'fifteen years personal work among the seamen of our Navy', and the following year Ellice Hopkins spoke on 'Legal and Social Protection of our Girls'.[78] Mary Sumner, founder of the Mothers' Union, was invited to the Church Congress platform in 1885,[79] and Louise Creighton, Lucy Soulsby, and Elizabeth Wordsworth all followed in the 1890s. In a private letter Elizabeth Wordsworth described the crowded Exeter Church Congress of 1894 as 'three of the most fagging days I ever had in my life'. Her own paper on women's higher education had to be given twice, because the Women's Meeting overflowed into a second hall. Unfortunately it coincided with Louise Creighton's address to the Congress, but after lunch she 'hurried off to hear Miss Soulsby read *her* paper at three—a very good one too—and it was pleasant to see the Bishop of London's interest in it'.[80] Audiences at the Church Congress included large numbers of clerical

---

[75] In a letter to her sister (10 Nov. 1907) she described her work for the Pan-Anglican Congress as 'really an opportunity to do what I most want to do, get the work of women for the Church to be more recognised and better done'. Lambeth Palace Library, L. Creighton papers, MSS3678/148.

[76] See e.g. *The Ministry of Women: Its Relation at the Present Time to Work Done by Men* (London: SPCK, 1908), in which she argued for more extensive, better-trained Church work by women, conducted in closer association with men: 'They must meet as equals. This does not mean that they will make the same contribution to the common work' (p. 6).

[77] Glick, *National Council*, 10.   [78] *Church Congress Report 1913*, p. vi.

[79] Anon., *Fifty Years* (London: Mothers' Union, 1926), 6.

[80] Elizabeth Wordsworth to Dora, 11 Oct. 1894. LMH, E. Wordsworth papers, box 1, 97.

wives, for whom the Congress was a combined social and educational event.[81] For this reason it became a reference point in the development of the NUWW. During the 1903 debate over the status of resolutions, Henrietta Barnett used the Church Congress as her example of successful debate organized upon non-voting lines; several other women took up her argument, commenting knowledgeably on its strengths and weaknesses.[82]

Church Congresses continued to provide opportunities for public pronouncements on gender issues during the climactic years of the suffrage campaign. The Pan-Anglican Congress of 1908 brought together churchmen from across the British Empire. Louise Creighton led its Women's Committee, responsible for convening mass meetings at the largest halls in London which were addressed by both male and female speakers. 'We wished on this wonderful occasion to think more deeply than we had ever done before, about what was women's special place in the work, about what was their particular responsibility,' she wrote in her published report: 'Again and again the primary importance of women's work in the home was emphasised, often by definite words, more often by implication. Again and again too, came the call to women to do more active, more efficient work outside the home'.[83] The suffrage issue was studiously avoided by all the women speakers. However, it was present by implication in much of what was said by suffragists and anti-suffragists alike. Elizabeth Burgwin, a distinguished teacher and soon after a prominent member of the Women's National Anti-Suffrage League, criticized state intervention in child welfare as inferior to 'the inestimable blessing of a pure home', urging the need for 'restoring to the mother the sacredness of her vocation'.[84] Lady Acland, another strong anti-suffragist, warned women to keep their public work in due perspective, since 'no amount of attendance at committees, of organising, of bazaar opening, even of such work as district visiting, can make up for a neglected home'; the home was 'a purely Christian institution, because on it rests the position of our women, which is entirely the result of Christian teaching'.[85] Louise Creighton herself called for a balance between maternal and state responsibilities, and between home and public work, asserting that women were 'called upon to be the guardians of Society'. They were also 'the salt which purifies society', a Christian as well as a feminine calling.[86]

Despite sporadic attempts to distance religion from unseemly political conflict, the Church of England became more and more deeply engaged in Edwardian debates over gender roles and suffragism. Anti-suffrage women took comfort from clerical conservatism, while Anglican suffragists formed a Church Suffrage

---

[81] Louise Creighton commented on the fact that she enjoyed the Congresses more than her husband did. Creighton, *Memoir*, 112.

[82] *NUWW Handbook and Report 1903*, 119–23.

[83] *Report of the Women's Meetings held in connection with the Pan-Anglican Congress of 1908* (London: SPKC, 1908), pp. v–vi.

[84] Ibid. 6.   [85] Ibid. 26.   [86] Ibid. 104.

League as well as claiming their share of the Christian territory of maternal social action. Would determined suffragists succeed, as they eventually did within the NUWW, in inserting support for the vote into the policies of the major Anglican women's societies? Would the women antis manage to convert widespread outrage over suffragist tactics into increased support for their own cause?[87] The anti-suffrage response to Church suffragism will be revisited in Chapter 8, but it can be concluded immediately that the anti-suffragists were on much firmer ground in opposing suffragism within the Anglican Church and its affiliated organizations than they were within the NUWW. The existence of a lively, outspoken Church Suffrage League from 1910 onwards did not cancel out deeply entrenched conservatism elsewhere in the Church.[88] Progress towards the inclusion of women in Church lay government remained extremely slow, while the Bible continued to provide theological arguments for lack of franchise reform. Most importantly of all, the tacitly anti-suffragist Anglican women's associations were carrying all before them in terms of membership and influence. These organizations reached out to the mass of unorganized women across the country, helping to consolidate conservative views of womanhood which were readily compatible with indifference or even active opposition to the vote.

During the nineteenth century the Church of England had launched a wide range of philanthropic societies giving religious sanction to women's work for the temperance movement, education, emigration, missionary work, and social purity. By far the largest were the Girls' Friendly Society and the Mothers' Union, both of which concerned themselves closely with the spiritual and social dimensions of the Woman Question.[89] Like the NUWW, to which the GFS and Mothers' Union quickly affiliated, these organizations stood committed to motherly social service mainly on behalf of fellow women and children. They situated their work firmly within the orbit of the Anglican Church, drawing strength from its spiritual authority and its unparalleled framework of diocesan organization. It was inevitable that the GFS and the Mothers' Union would distance themselves from suffragism, given the policies of the Church towards female representation upon its own councils, and given the weight of theological objections to women's further advance into public life. Both societies had

[87] See e.g. Gladys Pott's article, 'A Mockery of the Movement: The Church League and the W.S.P.U.', *Anti-Suffrage Review*, 60 (Oct. 1913), 209.

[88] According to B. Heeney, who discusses the theological context of women's restricted role within the Church, 'Until well into the twentieth century the advocates of subordination dominated the ecclesiastical scene'. His examples of conservative clerics include Bishop (Christopher) Wordsworth. *Women's Movement*, 6–9.

[89] For the GFS, see A. Money, *History of the GFS* (London: GFS, 1913); M. Heath-Stubbs, *Friendship's Highway* (London: GFS, 1926); B. Harrison, 'For Church, Queen and Family: The Girls' Friendly Society 1874–1920', *Past and Present*, 61 (1973), 107–38; J. Bush, *Edwardian Ladies and Imperial Power* (London: Leicester University Press, 2000). For the Mothers' Union, see M. Porter and M. Woodward, *Mary Sumner: Her Life and Work* (Winchester: Mothers' Union, 1921); anon., *Fifty Years* (London: Mothers' Union, 1926).

originated from women's efforts to supply both religious and practical support within their local communities, and the majority of their members remained satisfied to restrict their commitment to such modest bounds. Despite the presence of some declared suffragists among the Anglican women leaders, the most important figures in the GFS and the Mothers' Union stayed resolutely silent on the subject of the vote. The extensive literature produced by the two organizations offers considerable support for the view that they were a source of indirect opposition to suffragism. Undoubtedly they provided strong encouragement to the many thousands of women who remained willing to accept a gendered public role defined by maternalism and social service, as well as circumscribed by feminine religious duty towards home and family.

The Girls' Friendly Society was founded by Mary Townsend in 1874. Her initial aim was to organize moral guidance by middle-class 'associates' for small groups of working-class members, the majority of whom were likely to be employed as domestic servants. Brian Harrison has described this relationship as 'semi-maternal'.[90] The maternal purposes of the GFS became still more evident as its work grew to include a wide range of practical assistance related to employment, emigration, education, health, and recreation whilst never ceasing to emphasize the all-important religious dimension. The imperial work of the GFS assumed major importance from the 1880s onwards. During the Edwardian years the ideals of maternal social care, Christian self-improvement, and imperial opportunity were intimately linked, together offering food for the imagination alongside practical help and spiritual support. By 1900 the GFS claimed 1,361 branches, 32,103 associates, and 152,398 members; ten years later these numbers had risen to 1,653, 38,401, and 191,269.[91] Though the society was stronger in rural than in urban areas, and had to make significant adjustments to its rules in order to expand into Scotland, it could fairly claim to have achieved a truly national scope and to have incorporated poorer, younger women whom no other organization could reach. Its carefully differentiated range of periodicals wielded considerable influence over female public opinion, adapting many of the traits of popular journalism to convey the GFS message.[92] It would be hard to exaggerate the ideological gulf between GFS publications and the more radical forms of suffrage propaganda. The GFS positioned itself at the far end of the spectrum of conservative ideas concerning femininity and social service. Both members and associates were required to display the feminine, Christian virtues of patience, unselfishness, and service to others, allied to sexual purity and faithful religious observance. A cheerful acceptance of one's lot in life required unquestioning acceptance both of the existing social class structure and of conventional gender hierarchy.

---

[90] B. Harrison, 'For Church', 109.   [91] Figures from Money, *History*, pp. xxii, xxix.
[92] *Friendly Leaves* for members, *The Girls' Friendly Society Reporter* for associates, and *Our Letter* for candidates.

Unsurprisingly, the writers and speakers who conveyed these messages to the membership included prominent anti-suffragists. Louise Creighton's earliest public speeches were undertaken on behalf of the GFS, and twenty years later she was still lecturing the GFS annual conference.[93] Lucy Soulsby was a regular contributor to *Friendly Leaves*, the GFS members' main journal and an appropriate vehicle for her ideas on girls' education at humbler social levels than her own school. Charlotte Yonge and Christabel Coleridge were also mainstays of GFS journalism. Though GFS editorial policy strictly forbade any intrusion of politics, the anti-suffrage message was sometimes close to the surface. In 1903 *Friendly Leaves* presented 'A G.F.S. Dialogue', during which Marian successfully persuaded Ethel to join up on the basis of women's special calling to Christian purity and to service: 'First, to God, and then to each other; a service from Woman to women, as a need and an obligation'. Marian outlined her vision of 'Our rights as women to stand firm, as a compact body':

Ethel.—What, to get into Parliament?
Marian.—No; to band ourselves together in a crusade against evil . . . standing shoulder to shoulder, foot to foot, in the effort to raise the standard of our men—brothers, husbands, sons—to a higher level by attaining to it, ourselves.[94]

The theme of womanly social service as primarily a moral, familial duty was frequently reiterated, and more than once juxtaposed with the alternative, more selfish definitions of the 'women's rights' commonly associated with suffragism.[95]

The Mothers' Union had many ideals in common with the GFS and women often moved seamlessly from one organization to the other at the point of marriage. Hampshire clergyman's wife Mary Sumner was its founding figure in 1876; according to an early history, her appearance at the Portsmouth Church Congress was 'a great ordeal for a woman of 57 who had hitherto led the quiet sequestered life of the English gentlewoman of her day'.[96] By 1892 the Mothers' Union had 1,550 branches and over 60,000 members;[97] twenty years later its membership had risen above 300,000.[98] This phenomenal growth owed much to Church support, and also to the widespread contemporary enthusiasm for maternal improvement which was already multiplying smaller-scale, more localized mothers' meetings and conferences before the arrival of a centralized society. The Mothers' Union flourished because it brought greater unity of purpose as well as clerical blessing. Like the GFS, it both drew upon and reinforced conventional expectations of female gender roles, linking these to

---

[93] L. Creighton reported in *Friendly Leaves* (Sept. 1903).   [94] *Friendly Leaves* (Apr. 1903).
[95] e.g. 'A Lovable Woman', in *Friendly Leaves* (Sept. 1899): 'For "Women's Rights" she has no love, beyond her "kingdom"—Home'. In Feb. 1908 *Friendly Leaves* republished 'The Rights of Woman', a popular poem by philanthropist Isabel Reaney: 'The Rights of woman, what are they? | The right to labour, love and pray . . .'.
[96] Anon., *Fifty Years*, 7.   [97] Ibid. 11.
[98] By 1926 the Mothers' Union claimed 490,000 members worldwide. *Fifty Years*, 6.

Christian doctrines and to existing social hierarchy. The Union's objectives were 'To uphold the sanctity of marriage and to awaken in mothers a sense of their great responsibility as mothers in the training of their boys and girls'.[99] From the outset the emphasis was upon individual maternal self-improvement, rather than upon any form of material assistance for mothers. Mothers' Union 'associates', who must be communicant members of the Anglican Church, were encouraged to visit local homes and to organize meetings in support of the founding objectives. Though motherhood needed to be improved at all social levels, the Mothers' Union, like the GFS, rested upon methods arising from social inequality. It also shared the GFS commitment to the moral reform of the nation and the strengthening of the Empire through womanly influence. In a book of Addresses to Members, Mary Sumner expressed her hope that 'even the poorest and hardest worked Mother will remember that her life is of infinite value, not only to her husband and children, but to the nation at large, for the future of England depends greatly upon the home training of the children of today'.[100]

Mothers' Union periodicals conveyed the same patriotic message. The *Mothers' Union Journal*, founded in 1888, relayed Union news, advice articles, prayers, poems, and moral tales to the mass membership, while *Mothers in Council*, founded three years later and initially edited by Charlotte Yonge, advertised itself as 'the Organ, for the Upper Classes, of the Society entitled the Mothers' Union'.[101] Elizabeth Wordsworth contributed during the 1890s, alongside Lucy Soulsby's mother and the anti-suffragist novelist Marie Corelli. Like the tiered journals of the GFS, the Mothers' Union papers enjoyed flourishing sales and claimed influence as well as popularity. Despite official neutrality on the suffrage question, the Mothers' Union gave extensive coverage to the wider Woman Question from the 1890s onwards, especially through *Mothers in Council*. The presence of some acknowledged suffragists among the Mothers' Union leaders[102] did not prevent the majority of articles tending towards a conservative and anti-suffragist standpoint. The first issue carried an article by the Countess of Airlie titled 'Woman's Power': 'Consider what power has been given by God to women, and how far greater it is than any of the powers which man can cede to them. This great work of moulding future generations is the true woman's work, and in this work her future lies'.[103] Several thoughtful articles followed on the impact of women's expanding educational opportunities, generally welcoming improved preparation for womanly duties in life, but emphasizing the need to

---

[99] The objectives were regularly published in *Mothers in Council*. By 1908 the second objective had been subtly altered: 'To awaken in mothers of *all classes* a sense of their great responsibility as mothers in the training of their boys and girls (the future fathers and mothers of the Empire)'.

[100] M. Sumner, *Home Life: Addresses to Members of the Mothers' Union* (London: Wells Gardner, Darton and Co., n.d.), 1.

[101] *Mothers in Council* (Jan. 1891).   [102] Notably, Lady Knightley of Fawsley.

[103] *Mothers in Council* (Jan. 1891).

preserve 'the special impress of our womanhood'.[104] Mothers retained paramount responsibility for all that was most important in girls' education, and it was their duty to defeat 'the terrible evils brought in by the prevailing love of independence, beginning with disobedience, proceeding to licence of speech and thought in moral and religious matters, and ending in licence of action'.[105] Edith Robson warned that 'The world does not want intellectual goddesses, but bright, loving, intelligent women', prepared for their growing sphere of influence, but aware of the dangers of sacrificing their womanly, caring birthright on the altar of "self-development".[106] Meanwhile the *Mothers' Union Journal* carried occasional direct references to the suffrage issue. In 1889, the year of the published Appeal Against Women's Suffrage, a cosy article titled 'A Home at Peace' assured readers that 'Home is the grandest of all institutions', followed by: 'Talk about Parliament! Give me a quiet little parlour. Boast about voting and the Reform Bill if you like, but I go in for weeding the little garden and teaching the children their hymns'.[107]

Both the GFS and the Mothers' Union made some attempt to adjust their methods to changing times during the Edwardian period, despite the fundamental conservatism of their message. Mary Sumner urged her organization to adopt more democratic internal procedures, and to extend its work across a broader social spectrum.[108] However, the GFS proved less adaptable than the Mothers' Union, and its membership suffered accordingly during and after the First World War. The Mothers' Union probably benefited from the more intangible nature of its key message and the relative simplicity of its organizational practices. Changing emphases could be accommodated without any fundamental change of policy and purpose, and gradually the Union became more interested in practical social reforms affecting mothers and the work of local government.[109] The 1909 appearance of Mothers' Union representatives before the Royal Commission on Divorce marked an epoch in terms of engagement with national government, though they did no more than restate the Union's long-established belief in the sanctity of Christian marriage as the foundation for successful motherhood.[110] The imperial work of the Union was popular with members and advancing strongly. The Mothers' Union was also concerned to meet the changing expectations of its working-class membership, and its journals carried self-conscious articles on the most acceptable means of organizing across class

---

[104] Lady Montagu, 'The Worth of Womanhood', *Mothers in Council* (Apr. 1891).
[105] Dowager Marquess of Hertford, 'Parents' Perplexities', *Mothers in Council* (Apr. 1891).
[106] E. Robson, 'University Education', *Mothers in Council* (Jan. 1892).
[107] *Mothers' Union Journal* (July 1889).   [108] See B. Harrison, 'For Church', 135.
[109] *Mothers' Union Journal* (July 1914), included a 'dialogue' on 'The Use of a Vote': explaining the extent of women's local government franchise, and the value of 'women's work' undertaken by County Councils. The journal also carried an increasing number of articles on practical issues such as child health.
[110] See *Fifty Years*, 20–1. Mary Sumner had hoped to rouse public support for the repeal of the existing 1857 Divorce Act, as an affirmation of the sanctity of marriage.

boundaries.[111] Probably the best guarantee of continuing growth for the Anglican women's organizations was their proximity to the Anglican Church itself. Church attendance expanded between the 1880s and 1910, due partly to the church building programme in these years, but also to the connections between religious observance and social aspiration, and to the achievements of the many Anglican auxiliary associations devoted to social service.

The Edwardian suffrage campaign left little direct mark upon the Mothers' Union, as it continued its established work of religious training, maternal education, and maternalist social reform. Beneath the title 'The Old Order Changeth', Mrs Lionel Crawfurd reminded readers of *Mothers in Council* that 'there is no antagonism between home and citizenship'. Skilfully avoiding the quicksands of political controversy, she emphasized women's growing responsibilities for social welfare and the interests which united rather than divided them:

> Surely it is this increased sense of responsibility which is behind all that is good—and so much is good—in the Woman's Movement. Our sympathy may be with the Suffrage or Anti-Suffrage Party, but in convinced supporters of either side one finds there is the same motive at work: each is aiming at the up-lift of national and home life, though each believes it will be achieved through diverse means. It is the mass of indifferent women who are the despair of all who care![112]

She recommended women to engage more fully in the work of local government, concentrating upon their existing, under-used opportunities for public work in the areas which were most directly relevant to motherhood. This recipe for womanly unity closely mirrored the views of most leading women anti-suffragists.

On the eve of the First World War, maternal reformers continued to be found on both sides of the suffrage divide. Women expressed their shared faith in motherhood and in wider social maternalism during the fraught suffrage debates in the NUWW, as well as in the calmer environment of the Mothers' Union. However, elsewhere in public life the common ground among organized philanthropic women was sometimes obscured by polemical debate, as the suffrage campaign assumed a political momentum of its own which inexorably distanced supporters from opponents. The association of suffragists with militancy, and of anti-suffragists with misogyny, drove women apart despite their long-standing commitment to many shared social causes. Disagreements over the parliamentary franchise were real, and deeply felt despite the evident overlap between anti-suffragist and anti-suffragist women's views on gender, education, and social duty. It is necessary to study other dimensions of the women's anti-suffrage movement, and to examine the evolution of the anti-suffrage campaign as a whole, in order to understand the full extent of the conflict among like-minded maternal reformers in the final years before the First World War.

---

[111] e.g. E. Field, 'Working Class Mothers and Modern Problems', *Mothers in Council* (July 1907).
[112] *Mothers in Council* (July 1914).

4

Women Writers

ANTI-SUFFRAGISM AND WOMEN WRITERS

The anti-suffrage cause was extremely fortunate in its women writers. Opponents of votes for women included many of the best-selling female novelists of the day.[1] Some of these felt strongly enough about the suffrage issue to include a measure of anti-suffragism in their fiction, and to address the Woman Question even more vigorously through their journalism and other non-fiction publications. All helped to validate an ideal of womanhood which could be used in support of the anti-suffrage cause. As writers of fiction they were licensed to address delicate and highly important issues of sexuality and human relationships, as well as more easily accessible aspects of the Woman Question. Alongside the novelists, several prominent women writers on social issues made known their opposition to votes for women.[2] Their adherence to anti-suffragism proved more fragile, and was not often declared in their writings. It nevertheless helped the antis' claim to intellectual credibility and encouraged some younger social reformers to join the Edwardian anti-suffrage Leagues.[3] Social reform literature was a minority taste, and its authors' reputations influenced a restricted social sphere. Much more important, in terms of swaying mass public opinion, was the anti-suffrage movement's fairly plausible claim to represent the outlook of 'ordinary' women readers. The outpouring of directly or indirectly supportive novels, articles, and tracts by famous women novelists proved one of the most potent means for anti-suffragism to define its viewpoints and encourage potential supporters. The success of these publications in the late Victorian period meshed with the expansion of female education and the arrival of popular journalism aimed at women readers from all social classes. Women writers were never a unified group, and were usually resistant to working with each other or within any kind of formal anti-suffrage organization. Their collective contribution to anti-suffragism was invaluable, none the less. This chapter will discuss evidence

---

[1] Marie Corelli (1855–1924), Eliza Lynn Linton (1822–98), Ouida (1839–1908), Mary Ward (1851–1920), Ellen Wood (1814–87), Charlotte Yonge (1823–1901).

[2] Florence Bell (1851–1930), Octavia Hill (1838–1912), Beatrice Webb (1858–1943).

[3] Violet Markham notes in her autobiography, 'If I erred, I erred in good company . . . Distinguished women in the vanguard of progress had at one time supported it [anti-suffragism]'. Markham, *Return Passage* (London: Oxford University Press, 1953), 96–7.

of a mass female readership, as well as evaluating the ideas and attitudes of the leading anti-suffrage women authors.

The most prominent woman anti-suffragist, Mary Ward, was a professional writer first and foremost, supporting herself and her family through the power of her pen even at the height of her Edwardian anti-suffrage activism. Her emphatically married status, signified by her authorial title Mrs Humphry Ward, was not typical of successful novelists.[4] However, her financial success was mirrored in the achievements of other women writers who established independent careers on the basis of popular fiction extolling the joys and sorrows of romantic love, marriage, and motherhood. Charlotte Yonge was the archetypal unmarried proponent of matrimony, and of the womanly qualities which it fostered, though she also defended spinsters' equally valid contribution towards socially necessary maternalism. Eliza Lynn Linton, famed both as a novelist and as a polemical journalist, married late and unsuccessfully, living apart from her husband during most of her remaining career. Marie Corelli, whose novels of romance and religious mysticism outsold those of all competitors in the early twentieth century, lived with a woman friend throughout her adult life and failed in her attempted heterosexual relationships. Ouida, as Louise de la Ramée called herself, spent an increasingly lonely and eccentric old age living abroad in the company of her animals, after achieving comparable fame with novels of romantic adventure in an earlier era,[5] and intervening in the New Woman debate of the early 1890s. More minor novelists who publicly pledged themselves to anti-suffragism included Christabel Coleridge,[6] biographer of Charlotte Yonge and her successor in Anglican and Mothers' Union journalism, and the Dartmoor novelist Beatrice Chase[7] (pseudonym for Olive Katharine Parr). These women also remained unmarried and self-supporting, whilst commending feminine dependence and family-centred life to their readership.

In some ways the anti-suffrage novelists seem unlikely champions of conservative womanhood. To a greater or lesser extent, all achieved fame and financial

---

[4] Mrs Henry Wood (Ellen Wood), author of the best-selling *East Lynne* (1861), provides an earlier example. Her novels are not discussed here because they pre-date the main anti-suffrage campaign.

[5] Ouida's novels are not discussed here, because her literary fame mostly pre-dated the anti-suffrage campaign. After her death, Edward Cooper wrote that 'a dozen of her books made gigantic fortunes, and were probably at one time the most popular English books in the world'. *Fortnightly Review*, 83 (1908), 449.

[6] Christabel Coleridge (1843–1921), niece of S. T. Coleridge, wrote 'at least fifteen novels', as well as many religious works. C. Durrant, in *Oxford Dictionary of National Biography* (Oxford: Oxford University Press, 2004). She was also the author of a tract defending conservative middle-class spinsterhood, titled *The Daughters Who Have Not Revolted* (London: Wells Gardner and Co., 1894).

[7] Beatrice Chase (1846–?1942) wrote more than twenty works of fiction and autobiography and launched a Crusade for Moral Living during the First World War. She self-published a pamphlet titled 'Woman's "Emancipation" (By one who does not want it)' (*c*.1912). Women's Library, London.

success by themselves stepping beyond the bounds which they set for other women's behaviour and ambitions. Their lives were sometimes unconventional and their novels often entertained through tales of transgression and the depiction of negative role models, rather than through the more straightforward commendation of conservative values. The apparent dissonance between the lives and the didactic intentions of these authors has led some recent biographers into primarily psychological explanations of the connections between their private and public lives.[8] The anti-suffragism of women writers on social questions can also be related to biography and personal experience, as well as to the social and intellectual context in which they lived. Beatrice Webb's evolving views on the Woman Question were fully documented in her diaries and autobiography, and have been carefully analysed by historians.[9] Jane Lewis has extended her comparative study of female social activists to include Octavia Hill, a very different writer and reformer whose anti-suffragism was largely tacit, but endured and apparently strengthened until her death in 1912.[10] Florence Bell, the author of a classic Edwardian work of social investigation, *At the Works* (1907), has yet to receive analysis as an anti-suffrage sympathizer as well as an influential writer.[11] For the purposes of this book, it is more important to investigate the content and potential influence of women writers' anti-suffrage thinking than to arrive at definite conclusions about the genesis of their opinions. However, it is certainly interesting to try and unravel the reasons why some social activists, as well as many novelists, chose to oppose votes for women. As in the case of the maternal reformers, the lives of the anti-suffrage writers illustrate characteristics and affiliations which linked these exceptional women to their contemporaries, as well as revealing how their unique talent was shaped by individual circumstances.

Unlike the novelists, female social commentators did not often use their literature to make a conscious contribution to the anti-suffrage cause. Their female readers and admirers numbered at the most a few thousand well-educated women, rather than the hundreds of thousands attained by the leading women novelists. For these reasons, successful novelists were incomparably the more useful women writers for the anti-suffrage movement. Contemporary evidence and recent scholarship on Victorian and Edwardian female readers makes it possible to comment upon the potential female audience for anti-suffrage fiction and journalism, before moving on to an analysis of its gender-oriented and

[8] e.g. N. Fix Anderson, *Woman against Women in Victorian England: A Life of Eliza Lynn Linton* (Bloomington: Indiana University Press, 1987). Sutherland, *Mrs Humphry Ward*, also rests heavily upon his interpretation of her relationship with her father.

[9] B. Webb, *My Apprenticeship* (London: Penguin Books, 1938); ead., *Our Partnership* (1948), ed. B. Drake and M. Cole (Cambridge: Cambridge University Press, 1975); ead., *The Diary of Beatrice Webb*, ed. N. and J. MacKenzie, vol. i (London: Virago, 1982). See also B. Caine, 'Beatrice Webb and the "Woman Question"', *History Workshop*, 14 (1982), 23–43; Lewis, *Women and Social Action*, ch. 2.

[10] Lewis, *Women and Social Action*, ch. 1.

[11] F. Bell, *At the Works* (1907; London: Virago Press, 1985).

potentially anti-suffragist content. The more modest contribution of social commentators towards support for anti-suffragism provides a postscript to the chapter.

WOMEN WRITERS AND WOMEN READERS

A number of recent studies have demonstrated how 'the woman reader' became an increasingly important construct in Victorian Britain.[12] She was lavishly provided for by both male and female authors, but women writers played a leading part in supplying their own sex with appropriate literature. They were widely assumed to possess insight into the needs and the particular qualities of women readers, as well as performing a quasi-maternal role as advisers and supporters of women, and especially of young girls. The woman reader was defined both by her innate qualities and by her need for the right kind of feminine socialization. Women were believed to be uniquely susceptible to the influence of literature, due to their emotionality and their limited capacity for critical thought. Middle-class women had leisure time available to devote to reading, while even young working-class girls could be taught to use their limited leisure time more wisely. These characteristics created openings for writers to promote a deeper understanding of women's gendered duties and responsibilities, whether through religious and didactic literature or through fiction and poetry. Victorian writers were unhampered by modern theories concerning reader reception, and manifested an uncomplicated belief in the ability of reading to influence women's lives for good or ill.[13] Though womanly qualities were believed to be linked to the natural biological distinction of the sexes, they required enhancement through careful nurture. The content and the contexts of suitable reading were a vital part of feminine education. Women's education needed to be subtly differentiated in relation to class, age, religious affiliation, locality, and family expectations, but was widely assumed to relate to universal truths about ideal womanly behaviour within the domestic sphere. The woman reader required literature which would inculcate devotion to family life, and cultivate the qualities needed to render it morally improving and

---

[12] See M. Beetham, *A Magazine of her Own? Domesticity and Desire in the Woman's Magazine 1800–1914* (London: Routledge, 1996); K. Flint, *The Woman Reader 1837–1914* (Oxford: Clarendon Press, 1993); J. Rowbotham, *Good Girls make Good Wives: Guidance for Girls in Victorian Fiction* (Oxford: Basil Blackwell, 1989); D. Gorham, 'The Ideology of Femininity and Reading for Girls, 1850–1914', in F. Hunt (ed.), *Lessons for Life: The Schooling of Girls and Women 1850–1950* (Oxford: Basil Blackwell, 1987).

[13] Kate Flint provides an interesting analysis of reading practices, based upon autobiographical evidence. This indicates that reading was indeed a formative influence for many women—but not necessarily in the directions intended by teachers, parents, or authors. The potential gap between authorial intention and reader reception somewhat qualifies the conclusions drawn in this chapter about the anti-suffrage women novelists' significance.

harmonious. These included Christian faith coupled with the feminine virtues of purity, altruism, and motivation towards care for others within the family and beyond, coupled (especially in the case of working-class girls) with the virtues of contentment, honesty, and obedience.

Research into the characteristics of the Victorian woman reader has revealed both the genesis of this construct in early Victorian religious tracts and the ways in which expectations became modified later in the century. The gradual evolution of conventional femininity was both charted and assisted by writers who aimed to provide for 'the woman reader', alongside the part played by general advice literature in prescribing conservative gender roles. Advice manuals for young girls and older women were slow to change with the times, despite the success of fiction and magazine literature which captured the dilemmas and opportunities created by expanding female employment and education, and by the evolution of nation and empire.[14] Other forms of didactic literature ranged from school texts to 'improving' historical works such as assembled biographical studies of great women. *Stories of the Lives of Noble Women*, published in the 1860s, noted that woman's sphere was 'much wider than society sometimes supposes', whilst reminding young readers that 'their true happiness will always lie within the home circle'.[15] Fifty years later *A Book of Noble Women* still dwelt upon models of feminine domestic virtue who possessed the added attraction of being saints, queens, heroines, gifted writers, or artists, but the range had been extended to include Catherine Booth, founder of the Salvation Army, and the educationalist Dorothea Beale.[16] During the nineteenth century the volume of advice on suitable reading for girls and women grew relentlessly. Reading aloud within the family circle was specially commended[17] and Readers' Circles and Essay Societies aimed to spread its benefits more widely.[18] Advice on suitable literature often reflected underlying anxieties over the Woman Question, so it is unsurprising to find anti-suffrage women making their contribution to the debate over 'the woman reader'. Lucy Soulsby published *Stray Thoughts on Reading* (1897), which provided reading lists for the first five years after leaving school and emphasized the value of literary self-improvement for married women. Her pupils were encouraged to categorize their holiday reading into columns headed 'Sunday,

---

[14] Flint, *Woman Reader*, ch. 5.

[15] W. Davenport Adams, *Stories of the Lives of Noble Women* (London: Thomas Nelson and Sons, n.d.), p. v. The book was 'originally issued under the title of "The Sunshine of Domestic Life" and passed through several editions' p. vi. My copy is inscribed 'To Dear Lena with love from her teacher'.

[16] C. Cairns, *A Book of Noble Women* (London: T. C. and E. C. Jack, n.d.), p. vii. Dates of both books have been estimated from contents, typeface, and illustrations.

[17] e.g. by F. B. Low, 'The Reading of the Modern Girl', *Nineteenth Century and After* (1906), 287.

[18] Essay societies were aimed at clever young ladies (such as Mary Ward, Louise Creighton, and Lucy Soulsby), but reading circles were often promoted by middle-and upper-class women to help the less fortunate: e.g. within the GFS.

Sensible, Poetry, Novels, Rubbish'.[19] A limited amount of 'Rubbish' would be tolerated, if recognized as such and counterbalanced by plenty of more improving literature. She supported the right and duty of mothers to censor their daughters' reading but also, less conventionally, listened to the advice of 'daughters' on her own literary work: 'If I wrote a speech for the Church Congress or M.U. Conference, it was sure to be revised by lantern light with a band of officers who ought to have been in bed long ago.'[20] The dangers of unsuitable fiction or drama feature frequently in anti-suffragist laments over moral decadence, often linked in turn to regrets over the decline of home education.[21]

Fiction occupied a prominent place in lists of approved reading for women, but its attractions were themselves a source of danger. An undiluted diet of novels was believed to be bad for any woman, especially if these included large doses of romance and sensationalism and were read in rapid succession. An addiction to exciting novels became a far easier vice to cultivate as the nineteenth century proceeded. Not only were standards of literacy improving across all classes, but simultaneous developments in the printing and publishing industry were making literature of all kinds more accessible to women. By the end of the century costs of paper production, printing, and distribution had fallen significantly, and an enormous market for popular fiction had opened up through the press, magazines, and periodicals, as well as through the publication of cheap editions. Margaret Beetham and Kay Boardman identify no fewer than eight different types of Victorian women's magazines, all of which 'took on, more or less overtly, the task of defining what it meant to be "a woman", or what it meant to be a particular kind of woman'.[22] Between 1880 and 1900 well over a hundred new women's magazines were launched.[23] The front page of the first edition of *Woman* (1890) carried Eliza Lynn Linton's description of the 'ideal' woman; while downmarket versions of the same message were to be found in penny weekly magazines such as *Home Chat* and *Home Notes*.[24] The year 1894 marked an important change for publishers and for women readers, when pressure from the middle-class circulating libraries ended first publication of full-length novels in expensive three-volume editions. Cheaper single volumes became standard, enabling Marie Corelli to achieve higher sales for *The Sorrows of Satan* in 1895 than had been gained by any previous novel written in English.[25] In the same period improving copyright controls made the American mass market more lucrative for British authors, whilst the net book agreement of 1900 permitted earlier, cheaper reprints. Meanwhile the growth

---

[19] L. Soulsby, *Stray Thoughts on Reading* (London: Longman, 1897), 83.   [20] Ibid. 84–5.
[21] e.g. E. Colquhoun, 'Woman and Morality', *Nineteenth Century and After*, 75 (1914), 128–40; H. Hamilton, 'Suffragette Factories', *National Review*, 60 (1912), 591–8.
[22] M. Beetham, and K. Boardman (eds.), *Victorian Women's Magazines* (Manchester: Manchester University Press, 2001), 1.
[23] Beetham, *A Magazine of her Own?*, 122.   [24] Ibid. 180, 191.
[25] T. Ransom, *The Mysterious Miss Marie Corelli* (Stroud: Sutton Publishing, 1999), 81.

of public libraries opened free borrowing opportunities to those who could not afford to subscribe or buy.[26] Women librarians and separate women's reading rooms encouraged the female readership. Florence Bell's survey of working-class reading habits in Middlesborough showed that by 1907 4,500 borrowers were reading mainly fiction from the Free Library. Working-class women devoted less time to reading than men, but were to be found among the enthusiasts for the novels of Marie Corelli and Ellen Wood, preferring 'something about love, with a dash of religion in it'.[27]

As reading opportunities expanded, so also did educated curiosity and concern about their consequences. A number of rather primitive surveys seemed to confirm that women might be reading too much of the wrong sort of fiction. In 1886 Edward Salmon addressed the subject of 'What Girls Read' in the *Nineteenth Century*.[28] He found evidence of working girls' taste for 'love and murder concoctions' in the form of 'decidedly unwholesome' penny novelettes, while the fiction intended for middle-class girls was often decidedly dull.[29] Twenty years later the same journal published further research on women readers.[30] Florence Low asked 'What does the modern girl actually read?', and deduced from her own survey of two hundred schoolgirls that there was much 'desultory, miscellaneous reading' which revealed tastes shifting away from 'standard novels' towards 'stories by tenth rate writers and magazines of all kinds'. Parents and schools were roundly blamed for a decline in standards, and public libraries were 'not such a blessing as some of the admirers of Mr Carnegie would have us believe'.[31] However, Miss Low's bad news appeared to be better news for popular women authors, since the girls' favourites included Marie Corelli, Edna Lyall, L. T. Meade, and Evelyn Green. A survey of 'The Reading of the Colonial Girl' a few months later indicated rather defensively that girls at 'the best Colonial high schools' were still reading classics by male and female authors, as well as historical novels and 'the works of Colonial novelists'.[32] Edna Lyall emerged as the most popular novelist overall, whilst Marie Corelli was the only other woman novelist appearing in both British and Colonial 'top ten' lists. Charlotte Yonge seemed to be holding her own more successfully with young colonial women than with readers in Britain. Alongside their revelation of the issues which troubled contemporary investigators, these surveys confirm

---

[26] See A. Trodd, *Women's Writing in English* (Harlow: Addison Wesley Longman, 1998), ch. 2; Flint, *Woman Reader*, 171–4.

[27] F. Bell, *At the Works*, 162, 167.

[28] E. Salmon, 'What Girls Read', *Nineteenth Century*, 20 (1886), 510–29.

[29] Ibid. 523, 527.

[30] F. B. Low, 'The Reading of the Modern Girl', *Nineteenth Century and After*, 59 (1906), 278–87; C. Barnicoate, 'The Reading of the Colonial Girl', *Nineteenth Century and After*, 60 (1906), 939–50.

[31] Low, 'Reading', 278, 280, 283. The 1901 Census shows that Florence Low lived with her sister, the anti-suffragist Frances Low, who was a founder of the WNASL.

[32] Barnicoate, 'Reading', 939, 943.

both the ubiquity of novel-reading among young women, and the commercial opportunities opened up for women writers of popular fiction aimed primarily at a female readership.

Anti-suffrage writers were among those who stood to benefit, both financially and in terms of potential influence over an expanding audience. Their success, of course, depended upon their ability to reflect as well as to shape the tastes of that audience. In this context, it is worth noting that popular readership surveys did not include the more polemical fiction of the so-called New Woman novelists. The sensation which famous (or notorious) New Woman novels created in the media during the 1890s and 1900s did not translate into the sort of mass sales enjoyed by Marie Corelli. There was, however, a wide readership for more light-hearted fiction including heroines with borrowed characteristics from these novels. Chris Willis identifies L. T. Meade as one of the novelists who successfully packaged the New Woman for mass consumption, by creating heroines who combined strength, independence, and intellectual gifts with strongly accentuated feminine beauty and maternal instinct.[33] However, not all popularizers of the New Woman were sympathetic to the emancipation of women. Grant Allen, author of the highly successful novel *The Woman Who Did* (1895), seems to have been both attracted and repelled by emancipated women. His heroine came to a bad end, along with the majority of other fictional women who failed to reconcile themselves to the joys of subordination within marriage. Millicent Fawcett thought his tale of unmarried motherhood sufficiently threatening to merit a vitriolic review pointing out his fundamental antagonism to the women's cause.[34]

Both suffragist and anti-suffragist commentators were highly conscious of the importance of popular fiction as a vehicle for influencing women's outlook on life and politics. The distinctive role of the New Woman at the turn of the nineteenth century has stimulated considerable research in recent years, much of it sympathetically focused upon the content and style of the leading polemical novels.[35] Recent studies also address issues of readership, and attempt to broaden and contextualize our understanding of contemporary controversies.[36] The fact

[33] C. Willis, in Richardson and Willis (eds.), *New Woman*, ch. 2.

[34] See M. Fawcett, '"The Woman Who Did"', *Contemporary Review*, 47 (1895), 625–31; G. Allen, 'Plain Words on the Woman Question', *Fortnightly Review*, 46 (1889), 448–58.

[35] See e.g. A. Ardis, *New Women, New Novels: Feminism and Early Modernism* (New Brunswick: Rutgers University Press, 1990); J. Eldridge Miller, *Rebel Women: Feminism, Modernism and the Edwardian Novel* (London: Virago, 1994); A. Heilmann, *New Woman Fiction: Women Writing First Wave Feminism* (Basingstoke: Macmillan, 2000); ead., *Feminist Forerunners: Womanism and Feminism in the Early Twentieth Century* (London: Rivers Oram, 2001); ead., *New Woman Strategies: Sarah Grand, Olive Schreiner, Mona Caird* (Manchester: Manchester University Press, 2004); ead. and M. Beetham (eds.), *New Woman Hybridities: Femininity, Feminism and International Consumer Culture, 1880–1930* (London: Routledge, 2004); S. Ledger, *The New Woman: Fiction and Feminism at the Fin de Siecle* (Manchester: Manchester University Press, 1997).

[36] Richardson and Willis (eds.), *New Woman*, includes chapters relating the New Woman to popular fiction, to changing female transport, to Ibsen and the stage, to Hellenism, to medical

that the New Woman became a literary icon, as well as a contested media concept, helps to explain her appeal. She was popular because she was controversial, and controversial because she was believed to be influential. Anti-suffrage women writers were to the fore in shaping responses to the New Woman, both through their fiction and through their journalism. Novel-writing was one form of subjective response to visible social changes which stimulated multiple debates over the Woman Question in the late nineteenth century. This literary response rapidly assumed its own momentum and influence, as those who welcomed and those who feared the evolution of female gender roles fed off each other's ideas and off the widespread public interest.

The New Woman soon became, and has remained, very difficult to define. She was famously named by the anti-suffrage novelist Ouida, in a journalistic clash with the suffragist Sarah Grand in 1894.[37] Both these writers acknowledged their debts to literary antecedents, in Ouida's case including Eliza Lynn Linton. The New Woman of the 1890s also owed much to the furore surrounding Mona Caird's attack upon the inequities suffered by married women, and to the *Daily Telegraph*'s subsequent correspondence on the marriage question which provoked over 26,000 reader responses.[38] By the mid-1890s the New Woman had become a construct possessing multiple identities, most of them hostile.[39] Her qualities were often contradictory, including a threat to marriage derived either from heterosexual promiscuity or alternatively from asexualism or sexual inversion; a threat to motherhood which extended into a wider social threat to British racial qualities, and the stability of nation and empire; and a degree of over-education which threatened the economic interests of men, as well as the established gender order. These characteristics linked her into parallel debates over decadence, socialism, imperialism, modernism, and the growth of mass culture. At all levels, from the works of prominent novelists to the output of many humorists of the age, she proved a spur to argument over the position of women. She also personified the connections between various aspects of the Woman Question, helping to shape the hostile stereotype of feminism which became a favourite anti-suffrage propaganda target. Attacks upon feminism were to become an important component of Edwardian anti-suffragism, effective mainly because of the existing widespread familiarity of negative portrayals of the New Woman. Anti-suffrage women novelists were far from the only source of such portrayals, but their contribution was significant. Through fiction, they

discourse, to colonial discourse, to eugenics, to utopianism, and to aestheticism and decadence. Heilmann and Beetham (eds.), *New Woman Hybridities*, places the New Woman in a transnational context.

[37] Ouida, 'The New Woman', *North American Review*, 158 (1894), 611; S. Grand, 'The New Aspect of the Woman Question', *North American Review*, 158 (1894), 270.

[38] See M. Morganroth Gulette, 'Afterword' to M. Caird, *The Daughters of Danaus* (1894; New York: Feminist Press, 1989), 493–5.

[39] See T. Schiffer, in Richardson and Willis (eds.), *New Woman*, 39.

helped to foster deeply rooted fears about marriage and sexuality among women readers, and simultaneously to put these ideas at the heart of the anti-suffrage campaign.

ANTI-SUFFRAGE NOVELISTS AND FICTION

Whilst the New Woman debate helps to explain contemporary dislike of feminism, it also highlights once again historians' difficulty in drawing clear boundaries between the beliefs of suffragists and anti-suffragists. In adversarial mode, women anti-suffragists stereotypically condemned their opponents' feminism and linked it negatively to their own opposition to votes for women. However, the effectiveness of anti-suffrage fiction, and its literary success, often depended upon less straightforward approaches. The novels of Charlotte Yonge, Eliza Lynn Linton, Mary Ward, and Marie Corelli contain interesting evidence of these writers' varied and fluctuating viewpoints on many aspects of the Woman Question. Each writer was herself an engaged participant in the extended public discussion of gender roles, as well as an influence upon other women's evolving attitudes towards the suffrage and the more profound issues which it seemed to embody. In an important study, Valerie Sanders describes Victorian anti-feminist women novelists as 'self-appointed consciences of a confused and anxious society, reflecting in their complex and self-contradictory explorations of women's lives the wavering direction of public opinion as a whole'.[40] The shared middle ground between suffragist and anti-suffragist maternal reformers has already been discussed in this book; interesting parallels may be drawn with Sanders's view of literary feminism and anti-feminism as 'inchoate groupings of ideas with much in common'.[41] Though women anti-suffrage novelists used the New Woman concept to polarize opinion through their journalism, their novels certainly include many deliberate ambiguities and reflect aspects of an ongoing debate rather than a closed argument. Perhaps for this very reason, they offered multiple points of connection to women readers interested in the wider dimensions of the Woman Question. Anti-suffragism, as has already been suggested, was inseparable from the wider gender debate but connected with it in many different ways. The anti-suffrage novelists themselves illustrate this variety of ideas and motivation, as well as potentially fostering it among their readers of both sexes.[42]

---

[40] V. Sanders, *Eve's Renegade: Victorian Anti-Feminist Women Novelists* (Basingstoke: Macmillan, 1996), 204.

[41] Ibid.

[42] The ambiguities, and possible ambivalence, of anti-feminist women writers have recently been further explored by other authors, notably in N. Thompson (ed.), *Victorian Women Writers and the Woman Question* (Cambridge: Cambridge University Press, 1999) and in the work of Ann Heilmann (see n. 35, above). See also M. Joannou, 'Mary Augusta Ward (Mrs Humphry) and the Opposition to Women's Suffrage', *Women's History Review*, 14/3&4 (2005), 561–80.

In the context of the present book, it is appropriate to restrict the discussion of novels and novelists to a selection of the works which are most directly relevant to anti-suffragism. Chronologically, Charlotte Yonge provides the obvious entry point. Though she lived out almost the whole of a retiring and religious life in her Hampshire village, her status as the leading mid-Victorian woman novelist is borne out in the life histories of younger female antis. Louise Creighton received *The Daisy Chain* as a memorable maternal Christmas present.[43] Mary Ward, who was distantly related to Charlotte, joined the essay-writing circle of 'goslings' nurtured by this distinguished 'Mother Goose'.[44] Lucy Soulsby taught from her texts, and her mother sent her articles.[45] Elizabeth Wordsworth respected her as a literary mentor as well as adult friend.[46] Charlotte Yonge's literary career included a substantial output of educational articles for working-class and middle-class girls, as well as historical texts and religious instruction for older women in the Mothers' Union and elsewhere. Her life, as well as her work, exemplified Anglican feminine virtue in its gentler forms, though her popularity also owed much to her exceptional talent, humour, and steady labour which produced over two hundred works of fiction and non-fiction. Many of her novels were family sagas, illustrating the small-scale tribulations and triumphs of middle-class women's lives. She wrote one strongly worded book summarizing her conservative views on *Womankind*, and taking issue with the social outlook of contemporary suffragists and other female reformers, but undoubtedly her biggest audience was for her popular fiction.[47] Her first biographer, Christabel Coleridge, remarked that her best-selling first novel managed to make 'trying to be very good . . . interesting and romantic to thousands of good girls'.[48] Her influence upon women readers reached across a broad social spectrum. Mary Sumner wrote of her influence upon 'many of our greatest thinkers', while letters from admirers reproduced in the Coleridge biography include fan-mail from several young princesses, alongside that of 'humble admirers'.[49]

Two of Charlotte Yonge's most interesting heroines, from the point of view of a study of anti-suffragism, are Ethel May from *The Daisy Chain* (1856) and Rachel Curtis from *The Clever Woman of the Family* (1865). As the third daughter in a motherless family, and a book-loving girl who preferred Greek grammar alongside her favourite brother to domestic chores and the acquisition of feminine graces, Ethel has a long, hard road to travel before becoming a saintly

---

[43] Creighton, *Memoir*, 15. It was one of 'the books I read over and over again most often'.

[44] C. Coleridge, *Charlotte Mary Yonge: Her Life and Letters* (London: Macmillan, 1903), 201.

[45] E.A., B.H.S., and P.H. (eds.), *Letters*, 96, 110.

[46] Letters between C. Yonge and E. Wordsworth, 1871–7. LMH archives, E. Wordsworth papers, box 1.

[47] C. Yonge, *Womankind* (London: Mozley and Smith, 1876).

[48] Coleridge, *Charlotte Mary Yonge*, 183.

[49] Ibid. 291, 352–3. 'You don't know what an element you have been in the lives of thousands,' wrote one anonymous woman, 'how we have laughed with you, and how little wise sayings have helped in many a difficulty. God bless you, dear friend.'

mother-surrogate at the heart of the home. Charlotte Yonge visualized *The Daisy Chain* initially as a tale of 'aspirations'.[50] Her meandering plot led her eager readers through the mundane dramas of daily life, as Ethel and her ten brothers and sisters learn to overcome their problems and to form their life goals with the help of their family and Anglican faith. This saga of family relationships provides endless opportunities for Ethel to strive and fail, then to strive and succeed in sublimating her personal ambitions through service to God, family, and needy neighbours. Her growing understanding of her responsibility for domestic happiness and the welfare of others is presented as a spiritual journey, dramatized by episodes of danger and temptation. Philanthropic and church-building projects gradually take the place of scholarship in Ethel's imagination, while the ambitions of her elder sister, Flora, provide a counterpoint to Ethel's own experience. This pretty, competent, and somewhat worldly woman makes a calculated marriage to a wealthy neighbour, and soon finds herself aspiring to political success on his behalf at the same time as nurturing a baby daughter. Her mistaken priorities are swiftly punished, when the baby expires at the hands of an ignorant, opium-dosing nurse. Flora is left to reflect that her ambitions have been 'all hollow, for the sake of praise and credit', while Ethel is reinforced in her decision to make home and neighbours her own 'lot in life'.[51]

Similar messages about womanly work and duty emerge from the story of Rachel Curtis's search for happiness through self-fulfilment. A 25-year-old daughter-at-home longs to devote her intelligence to useful work. Rachel's ambitions, fuelled by book-based learning rather than by experience of the world and guidance from her elders, reach beyond the acceptable bounds of female philanthropy. A domestic mission presents itself, in the form of a widowed cousin returning from India with a large family of unruly little boys who require support and education. However, Rachel is heedless of the lessons to be learnt from her own failure to act as the boys' mentor, and rushes recklessly ahead with a dubious scheme to set up a lace school in a neighbouring town. Diphtheria strikes down a girl inmate, and the guilt inspired by this death, combined with the dishonesty and incompetence of others associated with the school, bring Rachel to her knees. Religious faith and the support of wiser friends (including the man she eventually marries) carry her through the crisis, from which she emerges as a more sensible and womanly woman. Unexpected role models emerge, in the form of the widowed Fanny Temple (an unpretentiously perfect mother) and the invalid Ermine Williams (a truly 'clever woman' of saintly temperament combined with well-concealed literary talents). In the final chapters Rachel discovers her maternal vocation and expiates her guilt and grief by caring for an orphaned baby. She also learns to direct her abilities into

---

[50] Battiscombe, *Charlotte M. Yonge*, 94. *Aspirations* was originally an alternative title.
[51] C. Yonge, *The Daisy Chain* (1856; London: Macmillan, 1888), 511, 593.

the more appropriate channels of 'personal and direct labour',[52] with the help of her heroic military husband and his clerical uncle. Rachel has become 'a thorough wife and mother, all the more so for being awake to larger interests, and doing common things better for being the Clever Woman of the family'.[53] The conventional morality and didactic intent of Charlotte Yonge's novels might easily have led them into the deserts of unattractive advice literature, even in an age more receptive to such qualities. However, both Ethel May and Rachel Curtis are rescued for a mass female readership by the fact that they do not find goodness easy. Neither do all the marriages depicted in these novels end as happily as they began. Charlotte sympathized profoundly with middle-class women's struggles to achieve conformity to their gender-defined role in family and public life. Though her novels were being overtaken by more exciting reading matter at the end of the century, she remained an influential advocate for many married and unmarried women's continuing desire to prioritize domesticity, whilst achieving a rewarding balance between family, community, and individual achievement.[54]

Like Charlotte Yonge, Eliza Lynn Linton belonged to the mid-Victorian generation of women writers. However, her career represented a much less steady progression, a different balance between journalism and fiction, and a very different relationship with anti-suffragism.[55] After leaving her Lake District clerical home at the age of 23, she sought fame and independence as a radical writer in London during the 1840s. Modestly successful historical novels reflected her early sympathies with the women's rights movement, while her unusual success as a salaried newspaper correspondent seemed to confirm her choice of an unconventional lifestyle. A disastrous marriage in her late thirties confirmed a growing disillusion with political and gender radicalism, however. As her husband and stepchildren departed in 1864, she set out to regain control over her own life by accentuating the importance of masculine control over other women. Her *Saturday Review* articles on 'The Girl of the Period' and other unpleasant female stereotypes created a sensation in the late 1860s which coincided with the first serious attempts to obtain the parliamentary vote for women. Whilst Charlotte Yonge's mildly self-assertive heroines educated young women through empathetic self-recognition, Eliza's fictional suffragists were designed to shock and amuse. *The Rebel of the Family* (1880) follows the adventures of a discontented daughter, Perdita, who (despite her name) proves capable of redemption and marriage to a good man. With heavy irony, she is

---

[52] Ead., *The Clever Woman of the Family* (1865; London: Virago, 1985), 345.   [53] Ibid. 365.

[54] Soon after her death E. Cooper, 'Charlotte Mary Yonge', *Fortnightly Review*, 64 (1901), 855 contrasted her favourably with New Woman novelists, claiming that 'an immense majority of readers' still preferred her stories to 'sermons on the equality of the sexes'.

[55] See Fix Anderson, *Woman against Women*; G. Layard, *Mrs Lynn Linton: Her Life, Letters and Opinions* (London: Methuen, 1901); H. Van Thal, *Eliza Lynn Linton: The Girl of the Period* (London: George Allen and Unwin, 1979).

described as 'one of that objectionable class—a young person with principles'. However, other family members prove still less attractive, as they scramble for money, status, and matrimony. The reader's sympathy leans towards the principled one, especially as her more feminine traits are thrown into sharp relief by the threatening arrival of Mrs Bel Blount, Lady President of the West Hill Society for Women's Rights, declaring 'Make me your friend . . . I can give you all you want—work, love, freedom—and an object'. Though rejecting Bel's aspirations towards female supremacy, Perdita falls under her influence and that of her same-sex partner, who together embody 'the love between women without the degrading and disturbing influence of men'.[56] Rescue from the stresses of overwork and political indoctrination appears eventually in the shape of a handsome young man. His truly motherly mother takes Perdita under her wing and helps to confirm her growing belief that 'womanly submission (is) so much sweeter than all this egotistical independence!'[57]

Despite its sometimes humorous treatment of issues concerning marriage, work, and suffragism, *The Rebel of the Family* amounted to a serious intervention in the Woman Question debate. It was more favourably received than Eliza's two anti-suffrage and anti-feminist novels of the 1890s. The trajectory of her polemical journalism had taken her, by this date, to such extremes of denunciation that even sympathetic readers had begun to tire of her caricatured arguments. *The One Too Many* (1892) and *In Haste and At Leisure* (1895) sold relatively poorly and probably won few new converts for anti-suffragism. The latter provided a highly coloured account of a marriage destroyed by a young wife's infatuation with the suffragist Excelsior Club, whose sinister coven of female members are 'united as one woman on the great questions of the diabolical nature of husbands; the degrading institution of marriage; the shameful burden of maternity; woman's claim to be a County Councillor, a voter, a lawyer, a judge, an M.P., as well as the usurper of all offices at present filled by men only; the initiation of unmarried girls into all the secrets of life and vice; and the right of the sex in general, whether married or single, to live like men in every particular, if they chose to do so'.[58] This political programme links suffragism to socially and sexually subversive feminism in the plainest possible terms. Phoebe's fall from grace is symbolized by her changed appearance as a suffragist, with 'dark brown hair . . . dyed into a canary-coloured discord', 'inharmonious' painted skin, and a low-cut dress which 'did not leave much to the imagination, and what it did leave was suggestive'.[59] Soon the champions of Women's Rights are actively campaigning to defeat Phoebe's husband in an election. Not surprisingly, his affections begin to stray towards Edith, a neighbouring vicar's daughter. Naturally this paragon of true womanhood is too pure to be tempted into an illicit love affair. Instead, she plays

---

[56] E. Lynn Linton, *The Rebel of the Family* (London: Chatto and Windus, 1888), 5, 30, 35.
[57] Ibid. 128.   [58] Ead., *In Haste and at Leisure*, i (London: William Heinemann, 1895), 70.
[59] Ibid. 129–30.

a role in attempting to reconcile man and wife, after Phoebe has been humbled by political defeat and the loss of her money to a feminist fraudster. Too late, the anti-heroine realizes that she longs for 'someone by whose arms she might be encircled—on whose broad breast she might lay her head'.[60] Her husband cannot learn to love her again, but a neglected little daughter offers the possibility of womanly redemption. On the last page, a penitent Phoebe kisses her 'for the first time in her life. . . with a mother's passion of tenderness and love'.[61]

The heroines of Marie Corelli provide a sharp contrast to those of the polemical Eliza Lynn Linton. Though Marie Corelli also led an independent and somewhat combative personal life, her preferred public persona was one of fragile femininity.[62] The same diminutive figure, blue-eyed and golden-haired, appears regularly in her novels, sometimes in the guise of a modestly feminine authoress. *The Sorrows of Satan* (1895) has been described as 'the first modern best-seller', clearing 50,000 copies within seven weeks and achieving more than sixty editions before its writer's death in 1924.[63] Like most of Corelli's fiction, it mingled religious mysticism with sensational adventure and sexually charged romance. Open didacticism was never her fictional approach, but indirect social commentary was unavoidable and certainly intentional. The targets of her social criticism included profligate, amoral aristocrats, as well as her enemies within a literary world which refused to accept her own estimate of her talents until sales figures forced them to take her seriously. Public admiration was all the sweeter in the face of a critical literary establishment, and was assiduously cultivated through her journalism as well as through a continuous supply of the fiction which her enormous readership so evidently enjoyed. Depictions of gender roles and gender relationships formed an important facet of her social commentary, despite the absence of direct references to suffragism and the Woman Question. In *The Sorrows of Satan* a young male novelist struggles in the toils of a mercenary and corrupt literary world, seduced by an evil aristocratic adviser who proves eventually to be Satan himself. Salvation is fortunately at hand in the form of the fair-haired authoress Mavis Clare, who is 'as unlike the accepted ideal of the female novelist as she can well be'.[64] In a moment of insight, Satan comments that 'A pretty authoress is an offence—an incongruity—a something that neither men nor women care about. Men don't care about her, because, being clever and independent, she does not often care about them—women don't care about her because she has the effrontery to combine attractive looks

---

[60] Ibid. iii. 68.   [61] Ibid. 280.

[62] See A. Federico, *Idol of Suburbia: Marie Corelli and Late Victorian Literary Culture* (Charlottesville: University Press of Virginia, 2000); Ransom, *Miss Marie Corelli*.

[63] Ransom, *Miss Marie Corelli*, 81; Federico, *Idol of Suburbia*, 6–7. Annette Federico suggests that in the early years of the 20th century Marie Corelli was selling an average of 100,000 books each year in Britain, compared with 35,000 for Mary Ward and around 15,000 each for H. G. Wells and A. Conan Doyle.

[64] M. Corelli, *The Sorrows of Satan* (1895; Oxford: Oxford University Press, 1998), 193.

with intelligence, and she makes an awkward rival to those who have only attractive looks without intelligence'.[65] Rather than by joining a women's rights organization, Mavis resolves these potential conflicts by living withdrawn from society, measuring herself against truly feminine ideals of purity and tenderness which are reflected in her work. Towards the end of the book, she reaches out the hand of friendship to the hero. By this stage his tribulations have taught him to rejoice in her success: 'With all my soul I reverenced her genius—with all my heart I honoured her pure womanliness!'[66] This was a tale of womanly victory over male critics and over a society falsely guided towards evil values. As a parable of redemptive womanhood, it probably appealed to anti-suffragists and conservative suffragists alike.

One of her biographers has concluded that Marie Corelli was 'a strong, and often unacknowledged, feminist'.[67] But alongside her defence of talented, independent women, her hostility to the New Woman's excessive independence and loss of femininity is also consistently evident. A much later novel, *Innocent—Her Fancy and His Fact* (1914), introduces an even more extreme example of the fairy-like, ultra-feminine woman writer. Innocent by name, as well as by nature, the heroine rejects an eligible suitor because of her own uncertain origins, and takes her romantic fantasies and mysterious literary talents to London. Her novels of historical romance create a sensation in the literary world, and launch her into a world of high society for which she is singularly ill-equipped. Whereas Mavis Clare triumphed over decadence by withdrawing from society, Innocent soon falls victim to the immoral intentions of a handsome artist. Her natural mother turns out to be a cold-hearted aristocrat whose hypocritical offer to 'adopt' her own daughter is spurned by the young idealist. Instead, when her love affair comes to a one-sided end, she retreats to her rural haven and expires of a broken heart. Her faithful suitor is depicted as a man of sense and loyal sympathy, a model of the supportive masculine qualities which Innocent needs to complete her life, though he is quite without her radiant genius. The flower gardens and dovecotes of Briar Farm, where this improbable couple grew up together, are described in loving detail and represent a lost era of chivalry and natural beauty which is in stark contrast to the false manners and ugly morals of the capital city. Though evidently not a very satisfactory role model, the helpless Innocent is meant to be pitied as a social victim as well as the victim of her own femininity. A purer society, and the protection of a good man, would have allowed her spiritual qualities to blossom for the good of the world.

Women anti-suffragists were frequently confronted by the difficulty of commending gender difference without either overplaying female moral superiority or alternatively accepting an inferior status defined by their own emotionalism

[65] M. Corelli, *The Sorrows of Satan* (1895; Oxford: Oxford University Press, 1998), 194.
[66] Ibid. 387–8.
[67] Ransom, *Miss Marie Corelli*, 222.

and lack of rationality. Novels provided a relatively 'safe' opportunity to explore different models of true womanhood and the opportunities which these offered for achieving (or failing to achieve) a happy, fulfilling life. No novelist made more extensive and varied use of such opportunities than Mary Ward. Like Charlotte Yonge, she wrote with a passionate sense of moral and religious purpose. Like Eliza Lynn Linton, she enjoyed polemical debate and incorporated her views on the Woman Question openly into some of her novels. Like Marie Corelli, she was a professional author who lived by her sales, though in her personal life she strove self-consciously to preserve a feminine self-image (in her case, as wife, mother, and maternal philanthropist rather than as presiding domestic angel). Mary Ward differed from most other women novelists in having serious intellectual aspirations, being well connected in politics and high society, and eventually choosing to devote considerable effort to organized anti-suffragism. Her novels reflected all these enthusiasms, and have consequently received more attention from historians than those of any other anti-suffrage writers.[68] Still more than Corelli, she managed to make her fiction interesting to a remarkable number of leading men as well as to a large, mainly middle-class female readership.[69] The popularity of her novels was extended through skilful use of serialization and other commercial publishing techniques, as well as by literary lecture tours in Britain and America from 1897 onwards. Though she needed good sales to sustain a lifestyle based around her own fondness for country houses and lavish hospitality, Mary was even more of an idealist than a materialist. She consciously planned to use her powers of influence through her novels, so that it is not surprising to find a close correlation between her current 'causes' and her chosen paths in fiction. In 1911 a *Nineteenth Century* article provided an overview of her work which dwelt critically upon the prominence of 'the collision of ideas' within her novels. In the reviewer's opinion 'the publicist in her has bolted, dragging the artist off her feet . . . Her gift has been to interest rather than to move.'[70]

Mary Ward's later novels did sometimes suffer from the pressures of excessive ideological enthusiasm, not to mention the pressures of writing to tight timescales imposed by financial worries and the demands of anti-suffrage activism. Her earlier novels of religious and social conscience included well-developed successes such as *Marcella* (1884) and *Helbeck of Bannisdale* (1898), which already showed her skills in portraying conflicted heroines whose struggles of conscience and

---

[68] e.g. see B. Sutton-Ramspeck, 'Shot Out of the Canon: Mary Ward and the Claims of Conflicting Feminisms', in N. Thompson (ed.), *Victorian Women Writers*; Joannou, 'Mary Augusta Ward'.

[69] See Ward, *Recollections*, 237–40, for a vivid description of her encounters with William Gladstone. Mandell Creighton read and commented upon many of her novels before publication. Pusey House Library, Oxford, M. Ward papers, 3/4.

[70] S. Gwynn, 'Mrs Humphry Ward's Novels', *Nineteenth Century and After*, 70 (1911), 1056–7. Mary Ward was herself aware of these tensions, writing on 31 Jan. 1909 to Louise Creighton about her latest novel (*Daphne*) 'which I am afraid has grown into something of a tract'. M. Ward papers, 3/3.

engagement with ideas and social issues consumed many pages. During the height of her anti-suffrage campaigning, Mary wrote three novels of lesser literary quality, but of even greater interest as evidence of her own thinking and her desire to sway the minds of the reading public. *The Testing of Diana Mallory* (1908) emerged at the same time as the Women's National Anti-Suffrage League. Its heroine is one of Mary's typically spirited, free-standing creations, more akin to Eliza Lynn Linton's Perdita than to Marie Corelli's Innocent, though born into higher social circles and by no means susceptible to suffrage propaganda or New Womanism. After an overseas childhood Diana has developed a 'passion' for the British Empire which provides for lively political discussion with the increasing number of admiring men in her life.[71] Mary Ward was herself enthused by the Empire at this point, having recently joined the imperialist Victoria League. However, the main plot of the novel revolves around the discovery of a scandalous secret in Diana's past—her mother committed unintentional murder—and the impact of this discovery upon the innocent daughter's romance with Oliver Marsham, a promising Liberal Member of Parliament. Oliver is persuaded to end his engagement to Diana, since this scandal threatens his career. Among those who lead him to this decision is his unpleasant sister Isabel, who has 'frequented platforms' in the women's suffrage cause. From her first appearance as 'a lady with red hair and an eye glass', it is apparent that she will act as a foil both to Diana's imperialist politics and to her feminine enchantments.[72] Observing the two women together, a distinguished elder statesman observes that Isabel is 'a type—a strange and modern type—of the feminine fanatic who allows political difference to interfere not only with private friendship but with the nearest and most sacred ties . . . Let a woman talk politics, if she must, like this eager idealist girl—not with the venom and gall of the half-educated politician.'[73] Towards the end of the novel Diana expiates her mother's guilt by tenderly caring for an injured and politically defeated Oliver, thus proving that her womanly qualities are more powerful than her political beliefs.

Diana Mallory was a success on both sides of the Atlantic, but *Daphne* (1909) undoubtedly suffered from haste and over-didacticism. During her American tour in the spring of 1908, Mary Ward was appalled by evidence of American women's growing readiness to turn to divorce in order to escape from unhappy marriages. She turned out a short but lurid novel on the subject, fuelled not only by the divorce question itself but also by the connections she perceived between the suffrage campaign and threats to the institution of marriage.[74] Daphne is an American heiress whose marriage to a considerate English gentleman is soon in

---

[71] M. Ward, *Diana Mallory* (London: Smith, Elder and Co, 1908), 9.   [72] Ibid. 38, 29, 31.
[73] Ibid. 63.
[74] On 23 Aug. 1908 she introduced her new novel to Louise Creighton, explaining that it would 'deal with one of the divorce cases which struck me so much in the States. The whole idea of marriage is becoming radically transformed in that strange nation, and part of the strong opposition to the suffrage comes there from the feeling that it is the suffrage women who are helping on the

difficulties. As she languishes in rural boredom, she begins to ask herself 'Why should a woman of her gifts, of her opportunities, be chained for life to this commonplace man, now that her passion was over?' and reaches the conclusion that 'My first duty is to myself—to my own development!'[75] Divorce follows, leaving her husband deprived of his infant daughter as well as his wife. Roger is soon in a state of mental and physical breakdown, compounded by the death of little Beatty. He is comforted by a friend who combines East End ministrations to the poor (a standard feature in Ward's novels) with happy marriage to another young American woman who is 'the symbol, in her young motherliness, of all that Daphne had denied and forsaken'.[76] Daphne herself seeks solace in feminism (named unusually in this novel, with inverted commas and a capital F). She uses her money to endow a Women's College and an art gallery and, as a 'Feminist', becomes 'particularly associated with those persons in the suffrage camp who stood for broad views on marriage and divorce'.[77] Repentance, inspired by a divorced friend's dying plea, comes too late to save her husband from an early and resentful death. The crudity of the novel's plot was compounded by Mary Ward's rather clumsy (and unsuccessful) attempt to appease her friends by providing some sympathetic American characters and acknowledging the existence of non-'Feminist' suffragism. The novel caused offence and sold poorly.

Delia Blanchflower, Mary's principal novel of the suffrage movement itself, was a far better developed literary tract. Written in 1913–14 and published in 1915, it made little impact upon a wartime readership but gave valuable insight into its author's evolving relationship with suffragism and anti-suffragism. Delia is a wealthy, beautiful orphan who has fallen under the sway of a fanatical suffragette tutor, Gertrude Marvell. Her appointed guardian, Mark Winnington, fulfils her father's dying wish by saving her from the snares of extreme suffragism, but not before she has risked life and reputation at suffragette demonstrations and suffered the guilt of indirect responsibility for a suffragette arson attack which destroys both a Tudor mansion and the life of a crippled child. The Delia who eventually marries her guardian is a sadder, wiser woman. The most obviously new feature of this novel was its direct engagement with the tactics as well as the ideas of the suffrage movement. Although the novel made an unsparing attack upon militancy, it also revealed Mary Ward's awareness of other dimensions of 'feminism' and suffragism.[78] As in her earlier novels, political behaviour and personal life choices were shown to be inextricably linked. Recantation is clearly in prospect when Delia decides to forgo an early return to militant duty on the streets of London so as to care for her seriously ill maid in her country home.

disintegration of the family'. The letter went on to describe Mary's own current anti-suffrage work in Britain. M. Ward papers, 3/3.

[75] M. Ward, *Daphne* (London: Cassell and Co, 1909), 188–9.

[76] Ibid., illustration, 235.   [77] Ibid. 252–3.

[78] As she began writing, Mary Ward told Louise Creighton, 'The new book is going to plunge into "feminism". I don't know what I shall make of it.' 29 July 1913. M. Ward papers, 3/3.

Mark's campaign of political re-education is most effective when he unobtrusively introduces Delia to the joys of womanly local philanthropy, and reveals to her the nature of his own philanthropic work through local government. Gertrude Marvell's politics are linked to a difficult and neglectful relationship with her own mother. Meanwhile more positive female role models are available to Delia in the form of Mark's women friends, some of whom are moderate suffragists. Mark himself is plainly hostile to the suffragettes and to 'feminism', but much less so to the general idea of an enhanced role for women in public affairs. On the final page the author concluded that 'Delia must still wrestle all her life with the meaning of that imperious call to women which this century has sounded . . . the end is not yet. And for that riddle of a changing time, to which Gertrude and her fellows gave the answer of a futile violence, generations more patient and more wise will yet find the fitting key'.[79] For Mary Ward, too, the search continued. Though she was not prepared to embrace any form of suffragism, by this date she was working actively to construct a Joint Advisory Committee linking women's knowledge to the work of a male imperial Parliament. *Delia Blanchflower* was ultimately a novel of the anti-suffrage forward policy, rather than merely a diatribe against suffragism.

Together and separately, the women novelists made a richly diverse contribution to anti-suffragism. To the reassuring family chronicles of Charlotte Yonge, the heavy irony of Eliza Lynn Linton, the mystical dramas of Marie Corelli, and the troubled sagas of Mary Ward must be added the lesser contributions of other late Victorian women novelists who used their fiction to promote their views on the Woman Question. From amongst the diversity, a number of key shared beliefs emerge. Suffragism was closely associated, for all these women, with the deeper, more insidious threats to the social order represented by the New Woman and her imitators. Marriage and motherhood were twin pillars of social solidarity and moral rectitude, offering women the best opportunities to fulfil their special talents as well as to perform their Christian duty and attain personal happiness. Suffragism and feminism together threatened to subvert these fundamental institutions, squandering womanly gifts in their wake. The anti-suffrage movement was generally characterized by sexual reticence, especially among its female proponents. But novelists made the most of their wider licence to explore the sexual politics of suffragism through the medium of fiction, presenting large numbers of women readers with vivid pictures of the perils of gender subversion in both public and private life. What 'ordinary woman' would want to risk being associated with the deviant excesses of Bel Blount, Phoebe Barrington, or Gertrude Marvell, or to risk suffering the self-inflicted sorrows of Charlotte Yonge's Rachel Curtis or Mary Ward's Daphne and Delia? The British social order is shown by all these writers as potentially vulnerable, and becoming more so in later decades. A society in which poverty, moral decadence, and

---

[79] M. Ward, *Delia Blanchflower* (1915; London: Ward Lock and Co, 1917), 411.

social unrest loomed, but imperial glory also beckoned, required the best talents which its men and women could offer. The suffrage issue was viewed by these anti-suffragists as part of a larger challenge to which women should respond by developing their own existing strengths, rather than attempting to usurp those of men.

ANTI-SUFFRAGE NOVELISTS AND JOURNALISM

Women's journalism made a significant contribution to anti-suffragism from the 1880s onwards, through correspondence in the press, articles in magazines and periodicals, and eventually the foundation of the *Anti-Suffrage Review* in 1908. All the novelists discussed in the previous section produced non-fictional declarations of their anti-suffragism, often published first in periodicals then later in book form. Whilst their novels sometimes traded in ambiguity, the novelists' journalistic anti-suffragism was often more akin to straightforward propaganda. In the case of Charlotte Yonge, anti-suffrage beliefs and generally conservative views on the Woman Question steadily permeated a huge output of religious and educational journalism, rarely finding direct expression except in the series of *Monthly Packet* essays which formed the basis of her book *Womankind* (1876). Mary Ward, on the other hand, made consistent and deliberate use of the printed media to spread her views on the issues which most concerned her, including the suffrage debate. Eliza Lynn Linton and Marie Corelli went further still, commandeering press platforms to their own commercial advantage as well as in support of the anti-suffrage cause. This section will comment briefly on the non-fictional anti-suffrage output of these writers, comparing their views and relating them to the development of organized anti-suffragism.

Charlotte Yonge's journalism has already been considered in the maternal reform context of the Girls' Friendly Society and the Mothers' Union. Her potential influence upon women readers as an editor and journalist, as well as a leading novelist, was second to none. However, trenchant propaganda was certainly inimical to her conception of her feminine duty, as well as uncongenial to her personally. Her shyness and antipathy both to controversy and to public platforms were legendary. The decision to publish a substantial and strongly worded book titled *Womankind* in 1876 is therefore striking evidence of the importance which she attached to this particular subject. Its much-quoted opening sentence seemed designed to provoke debate, even in Victorian Britain: 'I have no hesitation in declaring my full belief in the inferiority of woman, nor that she brought it upon herself'. Woman was created as 'a helpmeet to man', and in the Garden of Eden had been 'the first to fail'.[80] Beyond these

---

[80] Yonge, *Womankind*, 1.

crushing biblical certainties, Charlotte offered some encouragement for women who wished to serve God, and through Him a wider society, rather than simply 'some particular man'.[81] Single women, in particular, had need of a vocation and were encouraged to find it within the Anglican Church and its growing panoply of philanthropic and educational activities. Much of the rest of the book was devoted to warnings against unwomanly deviations from domestic duty and feminine behaviour. In home-making and maternity, women could find fulfilment and the joys of truly appropriate service: 'It is not so essential that she should sit on ladies' committees, preside at mothers' meetings, hear lectures, or even attend weekday services, as that she should prevent her husband and sons from being alienated from a fireside with no-one to greet them, or her girls from being formed by stranger hands'.[82] The remaining chapters roamed over different aspects of home-making during different phases of a woman's life. As the usually sycophantic Christabel Coleridge commented, ' "Ladykind" would have better expressed their scope. Even in their own day they only applied to the few'.[83]

Charlotte Yonge's views on women's role in public life were highly restrictive in terms of both class and gender ideology, the more so because of her underpinning religious faith. By the time of her death in 1901, she already seemed to some obituarists to belong to a bygone age. Her reticence in public debate is in marked contrast to the anti-suffrage journalism of other novelists. Mary Ward, like Eliza Lynn Linton and Marie Corelli, enjoyed career success through her journalism until her success as a novelist, combined with a busy social life and the demands of her philanthropic work, reduced its scope. Her knowledge of the London press remained a very useful attribute for a social and political campaigner. The *Anti-Suffrage Review* was originally her brainchild, though it soon fell victim to the other demands upon her time and to the adverse internal politics of the amalgamated National League for Opposing Woman Suffrage. Mary Ward was undoubtedly a sturdy campaigner who enjoyed making her arguments for the anti-suffrage cause in newsprint and upon public platforms, as well as through her novels, but her role as the antis' leading woman organizer set her journalistic contribution apart from that of other writers. Her articles were calculated interventions in a debate where she was among the leading players, with both the influence and the constraints which that role implied. Despite her taste for debate, her journalism never approached the over-extended heights of rhetoric achieved by Marie Corelli and Eliza Lynn Linton. Mary Ward was a more socially refined and intellectually self-aware writer, and also a tactician working alongside other anti-suffrage leaders who would have deplored any such unstatesmanlike excesses. She was probably also inhibited by her closeness on many issues to suffragist fellow-maternal reformers, whom she hoped to

---

[81] Yonge, *Womankind*, 4.   [82] Ibid. 266.
[83] Coleridge, *Charlotte Mary Yonge*, 277.

persuade into the anti-suffrage camp. Perhaps partly because of her leadership responsibilities, as well as because of lack of time, she does not seem to have contemplated publishing her anti-suffrage views in book form. *Delia Blanchflower* was a more congenial and (she vainly hoped) more lucrative way of expressing these views.

Ultimately Mary Ward may simply have preferred the writing of fiction to the toils of repetitive speech-making and journalism.[84] Eliza Lynn Linton, on the other hand, hammered anti-suffrage arguments to death through nearly forty years of vitriolic articles which provided the main basis of her authorial reputation. During her radical youth she had been 'the first woman journalist in England to draw a fixed salary', as a staff member of the *Morning Chronicle* from 1848 to 1851, then a foreign correspondent in Paris for a number of years.[85] Her decisive shift towards social conservatism was linked to the success of her *Saturday Review* articles on modern women published in the late 1860s, after her unhappy marriage. The most famous of these articles, 'The Girl of the Period', attacked the immodesty of fashionable young women's appearance and behaviour in terms associating them with prostitution.[86] Eliza Lynn Linton wrote a total of over a thousand articles on the Woman Question during the remainder of her life, many of them verging on notoriety because of the strength of her language and imagery. She delivered a more sustained, detailed commentary on the sexual politics of suffragism than any other woman writer, in a manner which both shocked and delighted her supporters, whilst dismaying and angering her opponents. Though suffragists did their best to ridicule her increasingly extreme views, her intervention in the debate was an influential one. In contrast to most other women antis, and in a vein which presaged the most strident male anti-suffragism of the suffragette era, she unhesitatingly linked arguments over women's role in public life to discussion of the intimacies of marriage and sexual behaviour. Like so many other journalists, she knew the commercial appeal of openly describing vices in order to condemn them. Her frankness was justified by appeals to science and social science, as well as by stress upon her duty to advise and warn. Friends and admirers included Herbert Spencer and other important male writers,[87] and the

[84] In her correspondence with Louise Creighton she often laments the encroachment of her anti-suffrage work upon her novels, e.g. on 22 Sept. 1909, 4 Aug. 1910, 22 Sept. 1910. M. Ward papers, 3/3.

[85] N. Fix Anderson, 'Eliza Lynn Linton', in *Oxford Dictionary of National Biography*.

[86] E. Lynn Linton, 'The Girl of the Period', *Saturday Review*, 14 Mar. 1868. The ripple effects from this article included the launch of a journal of the same title, together with GOP almanacks and miscellanies and numerous 'caricatures, comedies and farces'. See Layard, *Mrs Lynn Linton*, 143.

[87] Among her friendly correspondents were Thomas Hardy, Walter Besant, Coventry Patmore, and Arthur Balfour. Herbert Spencer asked her to vet the proofs of his *Principles of Ethics* 'against the susceptibilities of the public' (1893); she also wrote a hostile review of one of Spencer's rivals, at his request, in the *Fortnightly Review* (1894). Van Thal, *Eliza Lynn Linton*, 195, 197–8.

willingness of so many editors to continue publishing her lurid denunciations suggests that they found a receptive audience among a section of the reading public.

Despite much repetition in Eliza Lynn Linton's journalism, it is possible to identify gradual changes of emphasis over the decades. During the 1870s she linked wealthy women's fashionable silliness to immorality, mercenary attitudes, and dereliction of feminine home duties. In the early 1880s these articles found new currency, and were republished in book form. At the same time she began a fresh onslaught upon the emancipation of women, ranging over a wider field. A *Fortnightly Review* article of 1886 attacked the higher education of women.[88] In the same year the *National Review* carried a comprehensive attack on women's suffrage, ominously titled 'The Future Supremacy of Women'. Beginning from a standard summary of gender differences, Eliza went on to claim that 'the lines of demarcation between the sexes' were becoming obliterated.[89] After piling up examples of immodest behaviour, and taking a sideswipe at the social purity movement, she turned to the business of condemning feminine ambition towards professional education and employment, and above all political power. Parliamentary suffrage would 'unsex women by enactment'. Not only would it endanger national affairs, but also 'do infinite harm to individuals' by increasing 'that disastrous desire to ape men which is as a canker in the women of today'.[90] With a fine disregard for consistency, Eliza castigated the mannish women who would dominate government and destroy happy homes, while at the same time condemning the specifically feminine vices of women in positions of authority. Alarming predictions of sex war and the inversion of sex roles across all spheres of life received fresh impetus from the New Woman controversies of the 1890s. Eliza Lynn Linton was to the fore in defending marriage and maternity from the threat of female emancipation, with arguments which went far beyond those of the anti-suffrage maternal reformers. Whilst Mary Ward, Louise Creighton, and Ethel Harrison organized their measured Appeal Against Women's Suffrage during 1889, Eliza's simultaneous broadsides proclaimed the emasculation of the British race. Three articles on 'The Wild Women', published in the *Nineteenth Century* during 1891–2, marked the climax of Eliza's anti-suffrage rhetoric.[91] This attempt to develop a crescendo from what was already a fortissimo campaign was perhaps the inevitable consequence of a her desire to remain centre stage after having overused her main arguments. The 'Wild Women' articles reiterated her views on unsexed, masculine women and effeminate men, linking these to a fulsome defence of maternity and a scatter-gun attack upon the 'excrescences

---

[88] E. Lynn Linton, 'The Higher Education of Woman', *Fortnightly Review*, 275 (1886), 498–510.

[89] Ead., 'The Future Supremacy of Women', *National Review*, 43 (1886), 3.   [90] Ibid. 13, 7.

[91] Ead., 'The Wild Women as Politicians', *Nineteenth Century*, 30 (1891), 79–88; 'The Wild Women as Social Insurgents', *Nineteenth Century*, 30 (1891), 596–605; 'The Partisans of the Wild Women', *Nineteenth Century*, 31 (1892), 455–64.

of the times' which she most deplored.[92] Alongside a series of relatively trivial complaints, she repeated that women's emancipation amounted to an attack upon British society and the British Empire, and indeed upon civilization itself.

Eliza Lynn Linton has been described as a misogynist.[93] Undoubtedly she succeeded in alienating many anti-suffrage women, as well as suffragists, with her frank views on women's deficiencies and her condemnation of attempts by women to reform the behaviour of men and improve the morality of public life. Though she signed the 1889 Appeal Against Women's Suffrage, it is interesting to find that leading maternal reformers privately thought her an impossible colleague for any future collaborative work.[94] Her vehement journalism helped to stoke up male opposition to women's suffrage, providing emotive language and images to other speakers and writers. It was probably also enjoyed by the more diehard female supporters of anti-suffragism, some of whom were closer in their beliefs to misogynistic men than they were to progressive maternal reformers like Mary Ward.[95] Eliza herself was a curious mixture of radical independent and extreme reactionary, the latter obviously predominating in her later journalism. Marie Corelli is also somewhat difficult to categorize in relation to the Woman Question, and was equally unlikely to be assimilated into any organization headed by Mary Ward. Like Eliza, she admired the sensational novels and the anti-suffrage rhetoric of the anti-suffragist writer Ouida. Her own journalism on the Woman Question was far smaller in volume than Eliza's, but almost equally exaggerated in tone. She wrote as a professional, as well as a committed polemicist, spreading her articles through American as well as British journals and newspapers. Some of her favourite pieces were collected together into a book titled *Free Opinions Freely Expressed on Certain Phases of Modern Social Life and Conduct* (1905).[96] This volume provides a useful overview of her ideas, illustrating both their more progressive and more conservative aspects.

The range of chapter titles in *Free Opinions* reveals that Marie Corelli had many social concerns apart from the Woman Question. As in her novels, she was deeply critical of what she perceived to be the decadent features of British society, including 'Unchristian Clerics', 'The Vulgarity of Wealth', and 'The Social Blight' of decadent morality, as well as the corrupting influence of a sensation-seeking popular press. Unwelcome changes in women's lives were more a symptom than a cause of decadence, but due attention to restoring appropriate

---

[92] Ead., 'The Wild Women as Social Insurgents', 605.

[93] Fix Anderson, *Woman against Women*, 232.

[94] See Louise Creighton to James Bryce, 30 June 1889, which mentions her exclusion as an act of deliberate policy. Bodl., Bryce papers, B53/129. Ethel Harrison to James Bryce, 26 June 1990, also omits Eliza Lynn Linton from a list of names of prospective anti-suffrage workers. Bryce papers, B77/1.

[95] Protests by some women against the forward policy are discussed in Chs. 7 and 8, below.

[96] M. Corelli, *Free Opinions Freely Expressed on Certain Phases of Modern Social Life and Conduct* (London: Archibald Constable and Co., 1905).

womanly influence could make a major contribution towards strengthening society as a whole. Chapters on 'Coward Adam', 'Accursed Eve', and 'The Decay of Home Life in England' outlined her views on gender difference and the dangers presented by women's neglect of their primary duties. Absolving the poorer classes, she blamed the 'smart set' of women for moral retrogression and neglect of 'the pivot', Home, asserting that 'noble, God-fearing women make a noble, God-fearing people. It is not too much to say that the prosperity or adversity of a nation rests in the hands of its women. They are the mothers of the men—they make and mould the character of their sons'.[97] For all her swingeing criticisms of those who failed to live up to womanly ideals, this passage exemplified the fundamentally positive attitude of Marie Corelli towards her fellow women. In many passages of thinly disguised self-assertion, she praised women's potential powers as well as their domestic virtues. There was much to celebrate in 'The Advance of Woman', as she titled another chapter, and much to ridicule in men's futile attempts to cling to undeserved privileges. The advance of female intellectual and artistic talent was an unalloyed benefit for mankind, as well as for women themselves. Women must be allowed to advance within the professions, to the extent that this could be achieved without turning them into imitations of men. This faith in feminine difference shaped Marie Corelli's view that the profession of politics should remain barred to women. Like the maternal reformers, she believed that women could exert civic influence by more suitable methods. Unlike them, however, she chose to recommend the wiles and stratagems of feminine political influence upon male politicians and voters, rather than contemplating the steady labour of philanthropy and local government. Her views on this matter were sufficiently strong to inspire a forty-page anti-suffrage tract in 1907, dramatically titled *Woman, or Suffragette? A Question of National Choice.* This publication was advertised in the *Anti-Suffrage Review*, and must have pleased many women anti-suffrage leaders with its forceful plea to 'the mothers of the British race' to avoid exchanging 'the birthright of their simple *womanliness* for a political mess of pottage'. However, some would have been less happy with her brazen claim to control 'at least forty or fifty votes' for any male candidate of her choosing, and her interesting assertion that 'man is seldom anything more than a woman's representative'.[98]

Many of Marie Corelli's slightly eccentric opinions were decidedly at odds with the moral seriousness which characterized most female anti-suffragism. Like Eliza Lynn Linton and the somewhat scandalous (though anti-suffrage) Ouida, she sometimes succumbed to the temptation to prioritize her own problematic

---

[97] M. Corelli, *Free Opinions Freely Expressed on Certain Phases of Modern Social Life and Conduct* 212, 182.

[98] Ead., *Woman, or Suffragette? A Question of National Choice* (London: C. Arthur Pearson Ltd, 1907), 4, 15.

identity issues above the general interests of her cause. Perhaps she simply did so more openly than most other men and women engaged in the suffrage debate. Women novelists were not the easiest of colleagues within a collective campaign, and indeed (with the notable exception of Mary Ward) were rarely prepared to contemplate the loss of freedom which joint campaigning required. They compensated with other strengths, and the anti-suffrage cause would have been very much the poorer without their eloquence and the public reach of both their fiction and their journalism.

WOMEN WRITERS, SOCIAL REFORM, AND ANTI-SUFFRAGISM

The final section of this chapter returns briefly to the issues of social service and social reform. Anti-suffrage writers on social issues were sometimes closely linked to civic maternalism, and to the collective work of conservative women's organizations. However, some influential reformers stood aside from such collective women's work and made their impact upon social thinking through their writings, as well as through their own social action. These women included Octavia Hill, Beatrice Webb, and Florence Bell. As has been indicated, their contributions to anti-suffragism were minor, despite the eagerness of other women in the movement to claim the reputation-based benefits of their support. Octavia Hill shunned any public political action, and restricted herself to a single letter to *The Times* in 1910 declaring her opposition to the vote.[99] Beatrice Webb used the same forum to recant her anti-suffragism in 1906, after having been a signatory to the 1889 Appeal Against Women's Suffrage and a collaborator in social service alongside both Octavia Hill and Mary Ward during the 1880s and 1890s.[100] Florence Bell maintained a dignified public silence on the suffrage issue, and may well have been uncomfortably divided between her loyalty to the prominently anti-suffrage views of her husband and stepdaughter, and the suffragism of her literary friends.[101] Despite its limited impact upon the anti-suffrage campaign, the motivation of these women towards even a modest level of support was of some contemporary as well as historical interest. Their reasons for rejecting the parliamentary vote reflected more widely held currents of opinion which favoured female anti-suffragism, as well as encouraging other intelligent, socially concerned women like Violet Markham and Gladys Pott to join the movement.

---

[99] *The Times*, 15 July 1910.   [100] *The Times*, 5 Nov. 1906.

[101] Violet Markham describes Florence Bell as 'less emphatic in her views' than her husband and daughter. Her house in Sloane Street was 'well-known in London society as a meeting place for many distinguished people in the world of politics, literature and art'. Markham, *Return Passage*, 101–2.

The anti-suffragism of Beatrice Webb, for long seen as a curious anomaly, has now been subjected to rigorous analysis.[102] Beatrice herself provided a careful retrospective explanation of this 'false step' in her autobiography.[103] The historians have concluded that she dealt with the issue honestly, if not quite completely. As a wealthy young woman, she battled long and hard to achieve an education and a purpose in life which satisfied both her intellectual appetite and her social conscience, without overstepping deeply internalized barriers surrounding conventional expectations of Victorian womanhood. For several years this attempt directed her energies into work among the poor of East London, first with the Charity Organization Society then also as a visiting rent-collector on one of Octavia Hill's housing schemes. Her support for the 1889 Appeal coincided with the end of this personal social service, the end of her failed romantic relationship with Joseph Chamberlain, and the beginning of her highly successful career as a social investigator of poverty and working-class life, and eventually a Fabian socialist. In personal terms, her public support for anti-suffragism may well have been unconsciously linked to her decision to enter a 'masculine' sphere of work, and her desire to be respected within this new arena rather than merely within female philanthropic circles.[104] In 1888 she turned down a flattering suggestion that she should devote her research skills to a study of female labour, connecting this proposal with the fact that 'I was at that time known to be an anti-feminist'.[105] She determined instead to study the co-operative movement. Despite her dislike of being intellectually labelled as an anti-feminist, she continued to associate with both Louise Creighton and Mary Ward during the 1890s, taking a supportive interest in the latter's University Hall settlement.[106] In 1897 she resigned her membership of the NUWW executive, on the grounds that its Christian prayers detracted from its inclusiveness. However, her membership of NUWW subcommittees continued, her respect for Louise was undimmed, and she remained satisfied that the Union was 'doing good work', including in its resistance to invasion by suffragism.[107] It seems likely that Beatrice's move

---

[102] B. Caine, 'Beatrice Webb and the "Woman Question"', *History Workshop*, 14 (1982), 23–43; J. Lewis, *Women and Social Action in Victorian and Edwardian England* (Stanford: Stanford University Press, 1991).

[103] Webb, *My Apprenticeship*, ii (London: Penguin Books, 1938), 400–2.

[104] Jane Lewis emphasizes this argument, claiming Beatrice had 'decided to give up work that she found dull and increasingly of questionable merit and become one of the boys'. Lewis, *Women*, 99.

[105] Webb, *Apprenticeship*, ii. 400.

[106] Beatrice Webb joined the Council of University Hall. S. Koven and S. Michel, *Mothers of a New World: Maternalist Politics and the Origins of Welfare States* (New York: Routledge, 1993), 131. Mary Ward discussed northern working-class life with Beatrice, in relation to her novel *Sir George Tressady* (1896). Ward, *Recollections*, 307. Mary also followed in Beatrice's footsteps to Bacup for first-hand experience, and described both her own and Beatrice's impressions in a letter to her father. Mary Ward to Thomas Arnold, 20 Sept. 1890. M. Ward papers, 2/2.

[107] Webb, Diary, 5 and 30 Oct. 1897, quoted in Webb, *Our Partnership*, ed. B. Drake and M. Cole (Cambridge: Cambridge University Press), 134–6. Beatrice commented, 'The "screeching

away from philanthropy and into social science did not yet represent a complete break, and that her sympathies with anti-suffragism had not entirely evaporated.

The reasons for supporting the 1889 Appeal which Beatrice herself lists in her autobiography suggest that her longer-term motives were shared with many other women holding conservative gender views, rather than being purely the outcome of her own immediate circumstances and life choices, or the result of uncharacteristic thoughtlessness.[108] The list includes her conservative temperament, her distrust of democracy, her dislike of some suffragists and their methods, and her equal dislike of parliamentary party politics, as well as the fact that she claimed not to have suffered personally from 'the disabilities assumed to arise from my sex'.[109] Beatrice also retained strong convictions about gender difference, fostered by her friendship with Herbert Spencer, which influenced her conscious and unconscious attitudes throughout her life. Her 1906 letter to *The Times* referred to her earlier belief that 'women might well be content to leave the rough and tumble of party politics to their mankind, with the object of concentrating all their own energies on what seemed to me their peculiar social obligations, the bearing of children, the advancement of learning, and the handing on from generation to generation of an appreciation of the spiritual life'. The franchise was required by 1906 to enable women 'more effectually to fulfil their functions by sharing the control of state actions in those directions', since the state had become increasingly interventionist in such matters on behalf of the community as a whole. Beatrice's letter underlined the fact that her suffragism rested upon this pragmatic basis, rather than upon 'a claim to rights or an abandonment of women's particular obligations'.[110]

Octavia Hill belonged to an earlier generation of social reformers, though her life and work overlapped with that of Beatrice Webb. By the turn of the century she was a highly respected figure, in government circles as well as among philanthropists. She became a member of the 1905 Royal Commission on the Poor Law (together with Beatrice Webb), after having been a founding member of the Charity Organization Society (1869) and the National Trust (1896).[111] Her most famous lifelong work was the reform of London working-class housing through the efforts of middle-class female visitors who combined rent collection with 'improving' friendship and advice. By the 1890s she was working closely with the Women's University Settlement in Southwark, and devoting an increasing amount of thought to the training of her workers. Despite her

---

sisterhood" are trying to invade them, but Louise's battalions of hard-working religious and somewhat stupid women will, I think, resist the attack' (p. 136). (Eliza Lynn Linton had invented the 'screeching sisterhood' in her *Saturday Review* articles of the late 1860s.)

[108] The accusation of thoughtlessness is made by Caine, 'Beatrice Webb', 34, and repeated by Lewis, *Women*, 98–9.

[109] Webb, *Apprenticeship*, ii. 2, 402.   [110] Ead., *The Times*, 5 Nov. 1906.

[111] See G. Darley, *Octavia Hill: A Life* (London: Constable, 1990); E. Moberly Bell, *Octavia Hill* (London: Constable, 1942); J. Lewis, *Women*, ch. 1.

training achievements, she had no ambitions towards the establishment of social work as a high-status profession, instead preferring to emphasize the connections between voluntary home-visiting and middle-class women's accepted family duties. Social work was the more effective for being unpaid, 'out-of-sight', and in female hands.[112] Beatrice Webb parted company with Octavia Hill because of her refusal to address the structural causes of poverty and poor housing, and her rejection of state-led solutions. However, the scale and success of her work helped to ensure that it did indeed become a model for others.

Octavia Hill did not set out to develop a reputation as a writer, yet one of the most effective means of spreading her ideas and training her workers was through her privately published 'Letters to Fellow-Workers', and through her articles in periodicals and in the press. Her advocacy did not include any direct reference to the suffrage debate, with the exception of her 1910 letter to *The Times*. But her writings provided indirect support for anti-suffrage maternal reformism through their advocacy of successful social reform by women working outside the frame of parliamentary politics, and on the basis of their own distinctive strengths. In the *Nineteenth Century* in 1893, she described the benefits of home-based training for social work: 'In my experience, those who are deeply imbued with the spirit of family life are those who best help the poor; in this spirit they meet on the great human ground, older than theories of equality, safer than our imaginings of fresh arrangements for the world, and fitter to inspire the noblest and the simplest sense of duty'.[113] Her 1910 anti-suffrage letter revisited familiar territory: 'I believe that men and women help one another because they are different, have different gifts and different spheres . . . Let the woman seek the quiet paths of helpful real work, be set on finding where she is wanted, on her duties, not on her rights . . . let her seek to do her own work steadily and earnestly, looking rather to the out-of-sight, neglected sphere, and she will, to my mind, be fitting the place to which, by God's appointment, she is called'.[114]

Florence Bell did not achieve the distinction of Beatrice Webb or Octavia Hill, either through her social action or through her writing. As the lively, literary wife of the anti-suffrage ironmaster Sir Hugh Bell, and stepmother of Gertrude Bell, she led a busy social life as well as authoring more than forty novels, plays, and children's books. Her theatrical work brought her into close friendship and a working relationship with Elizabeth Robins, leader of the Actresses' Franchise League. Other friends included Mary Ward and Beatrice Webb. Her reputation nowadays rests mainly upon her book of social investigation, *At the Works*, published in 1907. This study of Middlesborough focused on the lives of her husband's employees, and especially on the experiences of their families. Based upon

[112] See O. Hill, 'Our Dealings with the Poor', *Nineteenth Century*, 30 (1891), 161–70.

[113] Ead., 'Trained Workers for the Poor', *Nineteenth Century*, 33 (1893), 37.

[114] *The Times*, 15 July 1910. This letter was reprinted in full in the *Anti-Suffrage Review*, Sept. 1912, after Octavia Hill's death.

many years of home-visiting by Florence, Gertrude, and their women friends, the book presented a detailed, sympathetic discussion of the trials of domestic exis tence alongside descriptions of town and workplace. It was dedicated to Charles Booth, the famous author of a much larger and more systematic study of urban life. References within the book to contemporary studies by Booth and Rowntree suggest that Florence Bell had some ambitions as a social scientist. However, the strengths of her book lay in its anecdotal and observational evidence, rather than in considered methodology or consistent analysis.[115] Two full chapters were devoted to 'The Wives and Daughters of the Ironworkers', beginning with the categorical statement: 'The key to the condition of the workman and his family, the clue, the reason for the possibilities and impossibilities of his existence, is the capacity, the temperament, and, above all, the health of the woman who manages his house; into her hands, sometimes strong and capable, often weak and uncertain, the future of her husband is committed, the burden of the family life is thrust'. Florence went on to link her own study to widespread anxieties over 'the much-discussed deterioration of the race'.[116] Despite her sympathy with the difficulties faced by workers' wives, she had only small-scale local pol icy proposals to offer (provision of wholesome family recreation opportunities, cookery classes, health education), and continued to attach much importance to women's characters and general attitudes towards their home duties. Solutions related to government intervention, and above all solutions related to women's own collective political mobilization, were conspicuously absent from her pro posals. Instead, her book conveyed an overwhelming impression of women's ignorance and largely unavoidable apathy in relation to wider issues beyond their own families and immediate neighbourhood. Working-class women were plainly unqualified to exercise the parliamentary vote, and showed no signs of wanting it.

Florence Bell's book linked the experiences of a working-class community to wider issues of national wealth and power, but she remained satisfied to leave these larger matters in other, masculine hands. The introduction to *At the Works* explained the scope of her investigation. She had 'not attempted to deal with the larger issues connected with the subject, with the great questions involved in the relations between capital and labour, employers and employed'. She wanted her readers, however, to be aware of the economic importance of the iron industry, and therefore of the fact that the living conditions of its workforce were 'of vital moment to the country'.[117] Her book was intended to help readers to grasp the human realities behind the great abstractions of economics and national affairs. Like the work of many women novelists, it successfully put a human face on current political ideas and social ideals. Florence Bell believed

---

[115] See Angela John's introd. to F. Bell, *At the Works*, which comments interestingly on her methodology and intentions.
[116] F. Bell, *At the Works*, 171.   [117] Ibid., pp. xxvii–xxviii.

that women could make their most valuable contribution towards racial health through the homes of Middlesborough, rather than through Parliament. 'The deterioration of the race' recurs as a concern in most social reform literature of the early twentieth century. Social evolutionary concerns over racial health were fundamentally linked to the concerns and hopes embodied in the British Empire, the biggest political abstraction of them all. Anti-suffragism was in many ways an imperialist cause, as the next chapter will demonstrate. There is thus an interesting thread of connection between Gertrude Bell's support for her stepmother's book, her anti-suffragism, and her exploits as one of Britain's most famous women imperialists.

5

Imperial Ladies

CONTEXTS OF EMPIRE

Both suffragists and anti-suffragists laid claim to the mantle of empire. Suffragists welcomed contingents of women from India and from the Dominions to their mass demonstrations, basing arguments for British enfranchisement upon the needs of 'dependent' colonial sisters and the successes of female voters in New Zealand and Australia. But anti-suffragists held some of the trump cards. The National League for Opposing Woman Suffrage was presided over by Lord Cromer and Lord Curzon, two of the most distinguished empire-builders of the age. Lady Jersey simultaneously chaired the Women's National Anti-Suffrage League and the Victoria League, the most prominent female imperialist association. Anti-suffragists claimed that the female franchise would actively threaten Britain's empire. Such claims had widespread resonance in the years which separated the tribulations of the South African War from the outbreak of the First World War. During this period the future development of the Empire was a source of both pride and concern. Its importance to Britain's world power status achieved greater public recognition than ever before, through the combined efforts of the media and entertainment industries as well as those of politicians, academics, educators, and the multiplying imperial propaganda societies. Emigration to the colonies stood at record levels, offering families at all levels of the social hierarchy a sense of personal engagement with the Empire. At the same time as the British public celebrated the constructive possibilities of imperialism, they received regular reminders of external threats to British pre-eminence. Foreign competitors challenged Britain's industrial and financial strength; Germany's naval ambitions caused growing alarm; colonial hot spots in Africa and Asia required constant vigilance; and the unresolved Irish issue threatened conflict on Britain's very doorstep. 'Greater Britain', as the extended family of 'white-settler' colonies became known, was more than a mere sentimental construct. Many believed that it offered the nation's best hope of countering economic competition and potential military and strategic threats from rival powers.

How should Britain make the most of its empire? How could it bind together imperial kith and kin, and wisely rule less civilized peoples? These questions provided an inescapable context for the suffrage debate. They were questions which offered propaganda openings to both sides, and also fed internal discussion within suffragist and anti-suffragist organizations. Imperial issues were not merely useful ammunition. They helped to define the terms of the franchise debate, and to consolidate beliefs around gender roles and their social purposes. As in the case of maternal social reform, suffragist and anti-suffragist women often found themselves drawing opposed political conclusions from broadly similar premisses. Shared womanly work on behalf of Britain's empire sometimes brought together those who hotly contested the franchise issue in other arenas. Yet imperial demands were also regarded by many anti-suffragist women, as well as by most anti-suffragist men, as among the most conclusive reasons why British women should be denied the parliamentary vote. Female deference to the judgement of a male imperial Parliament provided an important unifying belief for anti-suffrage leaders and supporters. This did not preclude women anti-suffragists from developing their own particular emphases when they voiced the imperial case against the vote. As in other areas, they were able to draw upon feminine strengths and experiences in support of their anti-suffrage conclusions. However, they were also to be found admiringly repeating the imperialist arguments developed by the leading anti-suffrage men. The views of Lord Cromer and Lord Curzon on the British Empire were incontrovertible for female followers, even when other aspects of their anti-suffrage leadership proved open to criticism.

The cause of empire was integral to suffragism, and still more so to anti-suffragism. Whilst a number of historians have analysed 'imperial feminism' and its contribution to the discourses of British suffragism,[1] only limited attention has so far been given to the role of empire within the ideas and activism of anti-suffrage women. This chapter will outline the general imperial contours of the Edwardian suffrage debate, before examining in more detail the masculine definition of an imperialist agenda for anti-suffragism. Interactions between imperialist men and women within the anti-suffrage movement provide revealing insights into the motivation of some of the leading women. An analysis is offered of the contrasting relationships to male imperialism of Violet Markham and Gertrude Bell, Margaret Jersey and Ethel Colquhoun, Mary Kingsley and Flora Shaw (Lugard). The more subservient imperialism of other anti-suffragist wives, sisters, and daughters must also be acknowledged; though less prominent in public life, Lady Cromer, Lady Hamilton, the Frere sisters, and Beatrice Chamberlain made notable contributions towards organized anti-suffragism. To a greater or lesser extent, nearly all the leading anti-suffrage women held views on the franchise which were imbued with their loyalty to the Empire. This loyalty sometimes found expression through their parallel membership of societies dedicated to the

---

[1] See esp. A. Burton, *Burdens of History: British Feminists, Indian Women, and Imperial Culture, 1865–1915* (Chapel Hill: University of North Carolina Press, 1994), and I. Grewal, *Home and Harem: Nation, Gender, Empire and Cultures of Travel* (London: Leicester University Press, 1996).

imperial cause. In its final section, the chapter comments on the indirect role of the female imperialist associations in the suffrage campaign. Some parallels exist with other collective women's work which united suffrage opponents around gendered social action, but there was never any prospect of suffragists seizing the high ground within the imperialist associations, as they had done within the more domestic National Union of Women Workers. This was due not only to the strength of anti-suffragism among the Empire enthusiasts, but also to these women's overriding commitment to a higher imperial cause. Anti-suffragism stood to benefit more than suffragism from such an ordering of priorities.

SUFFRAGE OR ANTI-SUFFRAGE: AN IMPERIAL DEBATE

British suffragists based their case for the vote upon the needs of the Empire as well as the capabilities of women. The Empire required the civilizing powers of women, as well as their biological role in reproducing members of the superior, colonizing British race. Clare Midgley has explored early origins of these beliefs among female anti-slavery campaigners, who 'based their own claims to fuller participation in the public life of the British nation upon their feminine roles as moral reformers of empire'.[2] The suffrage campaign of the 1860s drew directly upon the tradition of associating women's emancipation with that of the freed slaves, both in Britain and America. Abolitionism was a crusade which evoked the moral duties of civilized Christian women towards their inferiors, rather than egalitarian sisterhood. In the later nineteenth century, British women's duties of self-emancipation on behalf of oppressed women in distant lands became gradually translated into the 'imperial feminism' explored by Antoinette Burton and other historians. Burton emphasizes the particular importance of downtrodden Indian women to British feminists.[3] Female self-worth could be measured in relation to the backwardness of lesser races, as well as in relation to women's invaluable contribution as mothers, educators, and a source of patriotic inspiration. The enfranchisement of women would enhance British rule across the world, both in terms of practical reforms and in terms of the moral stature of imperial governance. At the same time, maternalist reforms within Britain itself would safeguard the Mother Country against racial degeneration and consequent failure to meet the colonizing, civilizing, and defensive needs of the Empire. The early enfranchisement of women in New Zealand and Australia, as well as in some American states, added strength to British suffragists' arguments,[4] while

---

[2] C. Midgley (ed.), *Gender and Imperialism* (Manchester: Manchester University Press, 1996), 165–6.

[3] Burton, *Burdens*, 7. See also B. Caine, *Bombay to Bloomsbury: A Biography of the Strachey Family* (Oxford: Oxford University Press, 2005), 294–5.

[4] Women were granted the vote in New Zealand in 1893, Australia in 1902, Wyoming in 1869, Utah in 1870, Colorado in 1893, and Idaho in 1896.

the growth of an international women's suffrage movement helped to bring women from British colonies and Dominions together as campaigners for more feminized imperial rule.[5] Suffrage support for the Empire was accentuated during the pre-war years by the need to respond to the active anti-suffragism of Britain's most prestigious male imperialists. However, its roots lay deeper. The wartime imperial patriotism of Millicent Fawcett, Emmeline and Christabel Pankhurst, and many other suffragists was far from an aberration. On the contrary, it was a logical and predictable extension of their pre-war 'imperial feminism'.[6]

Despite some differences of emphasis among the suffragists, the imperialist case for extending the vote to British women can be coherently summarized. Not all suffragists were imperialists, but criticism of imperialism played a very limited public role in their campaign. Imperialist anti-suffrage arguments were also relatively consistent, and met with little or no public criticism from within the anti-suffrage ranks.[7] Any attempt to summarize anti-suffrage imperialism will immediately encounter overlap with suffragist rhetoric on woman's imperial role. Like the suffragists, anti-suffrage men and women declared their respect for distinctive female contributions towards Britain's imperial strength. Womanly imperialism was identified with maternity in all its idealized and symbolic forms, as well as with the practical necessity for successful motherhood to provide rulers and settler populations in an extended Empire.[8] Maternal qualities included moral strength as well as physical nurturing, and extended to the mothering of communities and of lesser imperial races.

However, anti-suffrage believers in this kind of extended maternal reformism drew quite different conclusions about its relevance to women's part in imperial government. Women's very importance to the Empire dictated that they should stand aside from the polluting rigours of parliamentary politics. Their mission as womanly empire-builders required a special status within British society which was protected by their exclusion from the imperial franchise. The precedent set by colonial enfranchisements was dismissed as irrelevant, since the powers of colonial governments were judged to be scarcely greater than those of local government bodies within imperial Britain.[9] British women already possessed powers of intervention in the social and educational areas which most concerned

[5] See C. Daley and M. Nolan (eds.), *Suffrage and Beyond: International Feminist Perspectives* (Auckland: Auckland University Press, 1994); J. Hannam, M. Auchterlonie, and K. Holden, *International Encyclopedia of Women's Suffrage* (Oxford: ABC-Clio, 2000).

[6] See Burton, *Burdens*, 204.

[7] Harrison identifies Frederic Harrison, Lord Weardale, Lord Loreburn, and Henry Labouchere as 'critics of imperialism' amongst the antis: B. Harrison, *Separate Spheres*, 76. However, Ethel Harrison invoked the argument of India in *Anti-Suffrage Review*, 1 (Dec. 1908), with her rhetorical demand 'And what about India? Can we share in the government of India?' (p. 6).

[8] See the pioneering article by A. Davin, 'Imperialism and Motherhood', *History Workshop*, 5 (1978), 9–65, as well as later research on maternalism in Edwardian Britain, and on women and empire.

[9] See M. Ward, 'Minor Parliaments and Woman Suffrage', *The Times*, 15 May 1914, 9.

them, and should focus upon making better use of these existing powers rather than on dangerously misguided claims towards participation in parliamentary government. Simultaneously, they might also make their own, more suitable, contributions towards strengthening the empire.[10] Imperial propaganda and social action through the Victoria League, the Girls' Friendly Society, the Mothers' Union, or the female emigration societies was entirely compatible with gender conservatism and anti-suffragism. So, too, was the informal exercise of female imperialist pressure upon politicians and administrators through time-honoured channels well known to ambitious women of the British ruling class. Leading female anti-suffragists put such methods to good practice during the years when they campaigned most strongly for women's exclusion from the public work of imperial government.[11]

Anti-suffrage imperialist arguments against the vote did not stop at the point of (largely consensual) insistence upon women's importance to the Empire's future. As well as drawing their own conclusions about the damaging impact of the vote upon more appropriate forms of womanly imperialism, many anti-suffrage imperialists emphasized the perils of female interference in the military and administrative affairs of empire.[12] 'Don't make yourselves and your country the *laughing stock of the world*, but keep political power where it ought to be—in your own hands', begged one undated leaflet from the Men's League for Opposing Woman's Suffrage.[13] This argument caused some misgivings among women who wanted to emphasize a more positive anti-suffrage agenda. As we shall see in later chapters, such women often agreed a tacit division of labour within the National League for Opposing Woman's Suffrage, devoting their own speeches to non-imperial matters whilst sharing platforms with male imperialists eager to denounce women's weaknesses.[14] Such denunciations were integral to the imperialist anti-suffrage cause, and were either endured or actively supported by the leading women. The claims of empire, after all, were supreme. It was necessary for selflessly patriotic women to accept that the price of placing the imperial cause at the heart of anti-suffragism included recognition of their own deficiencies,

---

[10] These imperialist anti-suffrage arguments were variously rehearsed by both men and women in speeches and articles throughout the campaign. For well-developed examples of the female version of the imperial anti-suffrage case, see V. Markham, 'The True Foundations of Empire: The Home and the Workshop', *Nineteenth Century and After*, 344 (Oct. 1905), 570–82 and 'A Proposed Women's Council', *National Review*, 55 (1910), 1029–38; also M. Maxse, 'Votes for Women', *National Review*, 52 (1908), 300–3; E. Massie, 'A Woman's Plea Against Women's Suffrage', *National Review*, 52 (1908), 381–5.

[11] See J. Bush, *Edwardian Ladies and Imperial Power* (London: Leicester University Press, 2000).

[12] See anti-suffrage propaganda leaflets in the Women's Library anti-suffrage file, e.g. 'Votes for Women, NEVER!', 'Look Ahead', 'Why I Oppose Woman Suffrage', 'Power and Responsibility: The Just Claims of Men'. All these leaflets were addressed to men, rather than to women supporters.

[13] 'Votes for Women, NEVER!', Women's Library, London. The leaflet concluded by urging men to 'Play up and save your country. Save suffragist women from themselves, and other women from Suffragists'.

[14] e.g. Lord Cromer's meetings alongside Violet Markham and Ethel Colquhoun.

as well as of their particular strengths. Suffragists, on the other hand, could be accused of taking selfish risks on behalf of narrow gender interests. '*Suffragists neglect entirely in their campaign the Imperial affairs which are the peculiar duty and responsibility of this nation,*' claimed *The Anti-Suffrage Handbook* of 1912: 'This is not accidental; it is a true characteristic of the woman suffragist, and it shows an attitude and a type of mind which ought not to be admitted to the franchise of an Imperial nation'.[15]

Meanwhile male and female anti-suffrage imperialists combined happily behind the social evolutionary view that differentiated gender roles were a vital component of British racial superiority. Imperial authority rested upon acceptance by the rulers and the ruled of a gendered racial hierarchy which would be severely undermined by any descent into British 'petticoat government'. It appeared self-evident to Edwardian anti-suffragists that the Empire had been won by masculine strength and masculine enterprise, and that it must be held through the unfettered exercise of these same qualities. The 'physical force' argument was important to anti-suffragists from the 1880s onwards, and became ever more so as it was increasingly linked to imperial rule.[16] 'Physical force' referred to more than the armed force ultimately needed to ensure public order and obedience to the British government. Anti-suffragists related such collective, state-sanctioned manifestations of force to the inherent differences between individual men and individual women. The average man was physically stronger and more aggressive than the average woman, as well as possessing calmer, more objective powers of judgement. Such differences were natural, but required fostering through wise government in order for British imperial civilization to achieve its full, beneficent potential. Thus the maintenance of clear distinctions between male and female roles in state and society was seen as a matter of high imperial principle, and integral to masculine self-respect, as well as scientifically sound and pragmatically necessary to guarantee the Empire's future.

LEADING MEN, ANTI-SUFFRAGISM, AND EMPIRE

Edwardian supporters of votes for women included some prominent male imperialists. Lord Selborne, Governor General of South Africa from 1906 to

[15] NLOWS, *The Anti-Suffrage Handbook of Facts, Statistics and Quotations for the Use of Speakers* (London: National Press Agency, 1912), 55–6. The main author was Gladys Pott, the highly competent NLOWS secretary in 1912–13.

[16] Women were 'incapacitated from discharging the ultimate obligations of citizenship', according to Lord Curzon: 'No precedent exists for giving women as a class an active share in the Government of a great Country or Empire, and it is not for Great Britain, whose stake is the greatest, and in whose case the results of failure would be most tremendous, to make the experiment.' Leaflet, 'Lord Curzon's Fifteen Good Reasons Against the Grant of Female Suffrage', NLOWS, n.d. Women's Library, London.

1912, actively assisted his wife's suffrage campaigns after his return to Britain. Alfred Lyttelton, Colonial Secretary from 1903 to 1906, overcame personal doubts to lend support to his suffragist wife. Lord Haldane, Secretary of State for War (1905–9), and Sir Edward Grey, Foreign Secretary (1905–16), were also suffrage sympathizers with suffragist female relatives. However, these supporters paled into insignificance alongside the phalanx of prestigious male imperialists who were more or less active in the anti-suffrage cause. Lord Cromer and Lord Curzon were the most respected imperial administrators of their day, having governed Egypt and India respectively before presiding over the National League for Opposing Woman's Suffrage. Lord Milner, recently returned from governing South Africa, completed a trio of imperial proconsuls active in Edwardian politics and opposed to women's suffrage, though he chose not to join the organized opposition. Joseph Chamberlain, as Colonial Secretary from 1895 to 1903, was one of the principal architects of turn-of-the-century imperialism, and a well-known anti-suffragist. A stroke brought his political career to a premature close in 1906, but both his imperialism and his anti-suffragism were represented through his daughter's executive membership of the anti-suffrage Leagues and his sons' support for the NLOWS. Another executive member was Lady George Hamilton, whose anti-suffrage husband had been Secretary of State for India from 1895 to 1903. Sir Alfred Lyall's Indian administrative and literary career extended as far back as the 1857 Mutiny, and underpinned both his own anti-suffragism and that of women admirers who included Gertrude Bell, Violet Markham, and Mary Ward.

The anti-suffrage movement benefited enormously from its close links to the national press, through anti-suffrage and imperialist editors as well as many journalists. Moberly Bell of *The Times*, St Loe Strachey of the *Spectator*, James Knowles of the *Nineteenth Century*, and Leo Maxse of the *National Review* were all stalwart supporters, and friendly with leading anti-suffrage women. The same was true of the anti-suffrage academic A. V. Dicey, though misogynist imperialists such as Sir Almroth Wright and Harold Owen caused some female offence. More influential than any of these authors were the leading Edwardian male exponents of popular imperialism who were also known to be forthright anti-suffragists: writers Rudyard Kipling and Henry Newbolt; musician Edward Elgar; geographer and educator Halford Mackinder. Kipling and Mackinder gave active assistance to organized anti-suffragism, and their public association with the movement helped substantiate its claims to be a truly imperial cause.

An extensive historical literature now exists on ideologies of empire, on the lives and beliefs of individual male imperialists, and on the mediation of imperialist ideas into British popular culture during the late nineteenth and early twentieth centuries.[17] However, few authors have addressed these issues in an anti-suffrage

---

[17] For the impact of empire upon British popular culture, see esp. J. Mackenzie, *Propaganda and Empire: The Manipulation of British Public Opinion, 1880–1960* (Manchester: Manchester

context, and still fewer from the perspective of anti-suffrage women.[18] Despite the efforts of 'imperial feminists', it was plausible for Edwardian anti-suffragists to claim widespread support for the view that suffragism was potentially unpatriotic. The British public's fondness for imperial glory, and growing faith in empire as a solution to looming national and international problems, helped to bolster popular anti-suffragism at a time when its more traditional gender-difference arguments were being steadily undermined by social change. Male imperialists led the way in establishing anti-suffragism's strong imperialist credentials with the general public. They also controlled the imperialist agenda within the mixed-sex National League for Opposing Woman Suffrage. It is therefore necessary to provide a more detailed introduction to the most famous and influential male imperialist antis, before turning to examine their relationship with the leading women.

The stature of Lord Cromer and Lord Curzon within the Edwardian anti-suffrage movement is self-evident. However, the ideas of Joseph Chamberlain[19] and Lord Milner[20] also require attention, for these men provided equally important inspiration to women imperialists and anti-suffragists. Unlike Cromer and Curzon, Chamberlain and Milner did not publish lengthy public explanations of their anti-suffragism and its imperial dimensions. However, their views on gender roles were part of a wider world view in which empire clearly predominated. Joseph Chamberlain's political career was founded on successes in business and in civic government, both of which had fuelled his interest in social policy and social class relationships. In the early 1880s he gained a reputation for radicalism, due to his support for domestic reforms and an expanded male franchise, but was already engaging with Britain's imperial role in relation to Ireland and South Africa. He played a key role in the Home Rule crisis of 1886, and during the following decade helped cement links between Liberal Unionists and the Conservative party through his growing enthusiasm for constructive imperialism. As Colonial Secretary in the 1890s, he took the lead in rousing public enthusiasm for empire as well as taking practical steps to consolidate British power in Africa and to link together the future 'white' Dominions.

University Press, 1986) and ead. (ed.), *Imperialism and Popular Culture* (Manchester: Manchester University Press, 1986), as well as other volumes in the Manchester University Press *Studies in Imperialism* series. For the impact of empire on British political opinion, see A. Thompson, *Imperial Britain: The Empire in British Politics c.1880–1932* (Harlow: Pearson Education Limited, 2000).

[18] B. Harrison, *Separate Spheres,* ch. 4, gives a cogent summary of the imperialist content of anti-suffrage beliefs, but with limited reference to women leaders and supporters.

[19] For Chamberlain's life and ideas, see P. Marsh, *Joseph Chamberlain, Entrepreneur in Politics* (New Haven: Yale University Press, 1994); C. Boyd (ed.), *Mr Chamberlain's Speeches* (London: Constable, 1914).

[20] For Milner's life and ideas, see A. Gollin, *Proconsul in Politics* (London: Anthony Blond, 1964); J. Marlowe, *Milner, Apostle of Empire* (London: Hamish Hamilton, 1976); F. Halperin, *Lord Milner and the Empire: The Evolution of British Imperialism* (London: Odhams Press, 1952); A. Milner, *The Nation and the Empire* (London: Constable, 1913).

Colonial backing for the South African War of 1898–1902 seemed to justify his confidence in closer imperial federation; a year later he split his party by declaring support for the tariff reforms he believed necessary to seal imperial unity.

Never less than a controversial figure, Chamberlain succeeded in projecting an inspiring vision of racially based and socially beneficial imperialism to the broadest possible audiences in Britain and the Dominions. His partnership with Alfred Milner in South African affairs was an appropriate one, for the two men arrived at a generally shared view of Britain's imperial future despite their different starting points and contrasting public styles. Milner's brilliant Oxford career in the 1870s coincided with the influence of T. H. Green and Arnold Toynbee, and his first public work outside the university was related to social service and the founding of Toynbee Hall as a London settlement. Following Chamberlain into the Unionist camp, he spent three years in Egypt working under the Governorship of Sir Evelyn Baring (Lord Cromer). This experience fuelled his enthusiasm for effective, reforming British imperialism, and he eagerly accepted the post of British High Commissioner in South Africa in 1897. The war which followed was at least partly of Milner's making. After several strenuous years of post-war reconstruction, he returned to Britain in 1906 to face Liberal censure, but with continued ambitions towards large-scale empire-building through imperial federation. Like Chamberlain, he saw the British Empire in visionary as well as practical terms. Both men had been influenced by current social evolutionary thought and believed imperialism to be a combined racial mission and social duty. While Chamberlain voiced his beliefs mainly through populist speeches, Milner's imperialist faith was expounded in depth and detail through his writings. He believed that public opinion would give the necessary impetus to imperial union, whilst parliamentary politics merely raised false obstacles. Britain's material interests were bound up in imperial success, but 'deeper, stronger, more primordial than these material ties is the bond of common blood'.[21]

Chamberlain and Milner did not descend from the heights of imperial rhetoric to address the women's suffrage issue directly in their public utterances. However, both men contributed indirectly to the anti-suffrage cause by their emphasis upon the need for selfless service on behalf of a united empire, and by their insistence upon the importance of racial duty. Possibly the suffrage campaign simply failed to engage Milner's interest, alongside grander priorities. It seems probable that he was a tacit anti-suffragist, given his close links to the leading ladies of the Victoria League and to the anti-suffragist press, as well as his rather dismissive views on parliamentary and party politics. Chamberlain's views on womanhood are most fully recorded in relation to his failed romance with Beatrice Potter in the 1880s.[22] Despite her anti-suffragism at this time, she was unable to reconcile

---

[21] Milner, *Nation*, pp. xxv, xxxiii, xxxv.
[22] See *The Diary of Beatrice Webb*, i, ed. N. and J. MacKenzie (London: Virago, 1982); B. Caine, 'Beatrice Webb and the "Woman Question"', *History Workshop*, 14 (1982), 23–43.

her passion for this powerful man with her intuitive grasp of his dislike of strong-minded women. She had been introduced to Chamberlain by his eldest daughter. Beatrice Chamberlain's social work in Birmingham and in London schools was extensive enough to call into question the view that she was merely a pallid cipher, but she certainly prided herself on prolonging the influence of her father's beliefs during his declining years.[23] Her work for the Women's National Anti-Suffrage League was on his behalf as well as her own, and was valued as such by other leading women. As late as 1917, three years after her father's death, she was still addressing schoolboys on 'Mr Joseph Chamberlain's Ideals of Empire'.[24] Meanwhile Chamberlain had enjoyed a happy third marriage to a beautiful and submissive American, whose charms included a willingness to 'obey': 'a pretty and simple expression of the natural relationship of the woman to him who ought to be her guide and counsellor'.[25]

Lord Cromer was another imperialist who preferred on principle to keep his domestic life and his female friendships apart from his public duties.[26] However, his role as the first president of the National League for Opposing Woman Suffrage inevitably required public statements of his reasons for rejecting the female franchise. Cromer's engagement with anti-suffragism came in the final years of a spectacular imperial career. After military training and several years of duty in India, he spent more than two decades consolidating British power in Egypt and the Sudan. By his retirement in 1907, Cromer had stamped his authority on Egypt as a powerful reformer whose beliefs in British moral and intellectual superiority seemed to have been translated into imperial peace and prosperity. Lord Curzon later eulogized him as 'the saviour and regenerator of modern Egypt', claiming that he had 'left a name as an administrator second to none among those who, by their services, have glorified the British race'.[27]

Cromer's return to England coincided with the most active phase of organized anti-suffragism. Alongside his work for this cause, he continued to engage with imperial affairs through opposition to Irish Home Rule, support for imperial unity

---

[23] Beatrice Webb described Beatrice Chamberlain as 'a quiet, genuine woman not attractive or interesting in person or intellect' (*Diary*, i. 94: Sept. 1883). Peter Marsh seems to share this unflattering view, describing her as 'drained of opinions of her own' when in her father's presence (*Entrepreneur*, 141 and 320–1). However, her papers show that she held a number of public appointments (University of Birmingham Library). Apart from membership of the executive of the WNASL, she was active in the Women's Tariff Reform Association and worked for twenty-eight years on behalf of the South Fulham Group of Special Schools. Obituaries described her as 'an attractive and convincing speaker' (*Birmingham Daily Post*, 20 Nov. 1918) and even praised 'her vivid personality, her brilliant intellect, her sense of humour', as well as her loyalty to her father and to the empire—'the passion of her life' (*The Times*, 22 Nov. 1918).

[24] *The Times*, 26 Mar. 1917.

[25] J. Chamberlain to M. Chamberlain, 1888, quoted in Marsh, *Entrepreneur*, 302.

[26] For Cromer's life and ideas, see R. Owen, *Lord Cromer: Victorian Imperialist, Edwardian Proconsul* (Oxford: Oxford University Press, 2004); L. Dundas, *Lord Cromer* (London: Hodder and Stoughton, 1932); Earl of Cromer, *Modern Egypt* (London: Macmillan, 1908).

[27] G. Curzon, in *Memorial to the late Earl of Cromer* (London: H. R. Stokes, 1920), 8, 12.

and national defence, and extensive writing. *Modern Egypt* (1908) was a testament not only to his own achievements, but also to his faith in essential principles of British imperial rule over Eastern peoples. Like Milner and Chamberlain, he believed that Britain's moral duty to 'control and guide'[28] alien races rested upon natural superiority, as well as upon the competitively established hierarchy of nation states. Gender relations were an index of civilization and Cromer contrasted the deficiencies of Islamic social customs related to women with the role of Christianity in upholding their status.[29] His anti-suffrage speeches and articles laid heavy emphasis upon the threat to the Empire posed by the female franchise, as well as reiterating his veneration for 'the sacred and all-important functions of motherhood': 'Nature has pointed out with no faltering or erring hand that the functions and spheres of action of men and women, though equally important, are widely different'.[30] His presidency of the National League for Opposing Woman Suffrage lent the full weight of imperial authority to such commonplace assertions.

Both Cromer and Curzon shared Milner's distrust of democracy and impatience with the distracting divisions of party politics. These attitudes were tied to faith in Britain's exalted imperial destiny, and provided helpful reinforcement to the anti-suffrage campaign. Curzon also shared Cromer's particular fascination with 'the illogical and picturesque East'.[31] The duties and demands of ruling lesser races were believed by both men to lie at the heart of successful imperial rule, and their focus on India and Egypt stood in contrast to the imperial federalists' obsession with the future of the 'white-settler' Dominions. Lord Curzon's public career began, like Milner's, at Oxford.[32] He entered Parliament as a Conservative in 1886, but spent much of the following decade travelling and studying Asian affairs. A spell in the Foreign Office was followed by his despatch to India as Viceroy in 1899, and soon he was engaged on a programme of administrative, economic, and educational reforms no less challenging than that of Cromer in Egypt. The Delhi durbar of 1903 was a moment of glory for Curzon. This triumphant celebration of the coronation of a new British emperor was witnessed at first hand by a number of the women who became leading anti-suffragists, including Margaret Jersey and Gertrude Bell. It successfully imprinted the splendours of British India on the public imagination at home, but was followed by a period of political conflict over military management which ended in Curzon's disgruntled departure for England in 1905. During the

---

[28] Cromer, *Modern Egypt*, 5.   [29] Ibid. 539.

[30] Cromer, 'Speech at 2nd Annual Council Meeting of Women's National Anti-Suffrage League—28.6.1910'. National Archives, Cromer papers, FO633/127.

[31] Cromer, *Modern Egypt*, 7.

[32] For Curzon's life and ideas, see D. Gilmour, *Curzon* (London: John Murray, 1994); K. Rose, *Curzon: A Most Superior Person* (London: Macmillan, 1985 edn.); *Subjects of the Day, Being a Selection of Speeches and Writings of Earl Curzon of Kedleston*, ed. D. Chapman-Huston (London: George Allen and Unwin, 1915).

pre-war years his parliamentary career gradually revived. Despite his aloofness from party politics, his ambitions towards high office were undimmed, and his commitments to the anti-suffrage movement were squeezed alongside a heavy schedule of parliamentary and other responsibilities.

The Empire remained at the forefront of Curzon's political beliefs. He delivered a fuller public explanation of his imperialism than any of the other proconsuls, as well as lengthily expounding his anti-suffragism through speeches and publications which gave due weight to its imperial dimensions. Introducing a collection of Curzon's speeches, Lord Cromer described him as 'by far the most eloquent exponent of that sane Imperialism to which this country is wedded as a necessity of its existence'.[33] The volume included Curzon's grandiloquent toast at a dinner in Milner's honour, where he lauded the British Empire as 'part of the dispensation of a higher Power which for some good purpose—it cannot possibly be for an evil one—has committed the fortunes of all these hundreds of millions of human beings to the custody of a single branch of the human family'.[34] Oxford's contribution to the Empire was the subject of a speech to the Imperial Press Conference of 1909, whilst the mainly female annual general meeting of the Victoria League in 1914 was honoured with an address titled 'The Cement of Empire'. Family metaphors were again to the fore as Curzon urged his audience to contribute towards 'a wall of human hearts built round our Empire, a wall which, when all other defences crumble and give way, will perhaps avail to keep it safe'.[35] Curzon's views on womanhood and higher education were noted in Chapter 2. His major anti-suffrage speeches ranged broadly over political and moral issues linked to the franchise question, but were deeply infused with his corresponding views on womanhood and empire. Whilst publicly honouring women's abilities, he dreaded their misapplication. To a mixed audience in Glasgow in 1912, he confided his fear that 'if the vote were extended to the women of this country . . . our hold upon India would not be strengthened, but would be sensibly weakened'. Nevertheless, women might contribute towards Britain's imperial heritage 'by fostering the ideals upon which Empire alone can exist with advantage. In this way women wield a power, all the stronger because it is not written in the Statute Book . . . You do not require the vote to defend the share in Empire which women already own'.[36]

The anti-suffragism of male imperialists was fully integrated with their ideology of empire, rather than standing as a matter apart. Despite some differences over imperial policy, Chamberlain, Milner, Cromer, and Curzon were united behind a creed of patriotic imperialism which laid heavy emphasis upon British racial superiority. For these imperial leaders, 'race' was defined in both biological and cultural terms. British women were its natural defenders, capable of enhancing British civilization by their womanly patriotism just as surely as they were capable of threatening it by greedy encroachment upon the masculine tasks of imperial rule.

---

[33] Curzon, *Subjects*, p. xv.   [34] Ibid. 5.   [35] Ibid. 21.   [36] Ibid. 303, 304, 305.

WOMEN IMPERIALISTS AND THE ANTI-SUFFRAGE CAUSE

Leading male imperialists reinforced each others' ideas and often assisted each others' careers. Brian Harrison's study of anti-suffragism emphasized the importance of male networking through the friendship circles of 'Clubland', showing how contacts extended across the elite institutions of Oxford, politics, and the legal profession, as well as reaching out into the press and the social worlds of Edwardian London and the British Empire overseas.[37] Women were excluded both by law and by social custom from many of the venues and activities which drew male anti-suffragists and imperialists into close association. Nevertheless, leading anti-suffrage women could draw upon their own significant female networks, as we have seen in the case of their philanthropic and educational work. Imperialist ladies constructed social and political networks in Edwardian London through the female imperialist associations as well as through more informal social contacts among upper-class and upper-middle-class women. Many of the most active anti-suffrage women were also keen imperialists, and their enthusiasm for the Empire sometimes led them into close relationships with the leading imperialist men. Their efforts to advance imperialism, while simultaneously promoting the anti-suffrage cause, often began from such personal contacts. Before turning to the role of anti-suffragism within the female imperialist associations, this personal aspect of anti-suffrage motivation deserves closer investigation. Individual examples reveal that some women approached imperialist anti-suffragism through youthful hero worship; some married into roles of imperial responsibility; while a few made their imperial reputations more independently, at least for part of their lives. The anti-suffrage women imperialists discussed below have been tentatively grouped into three categories, each defined by a different relationship to male imperialism.

Imperial Acolytes: Violet Markham and Gertrude Bell

Violet Markham[38] and Gertrude Bell[39] were probably the anti-suffrage movement's most talented women supporters. Both came from wealthy northern

---

[37] B. Harrison, *Separate Spheres*, ch. 5.

[38] For Violet Markham's life and ideas, see V. Markham, *Return Passage* (London: Oxford University Press, 1953); H. Jones (ed.), *Duty and Citizenship: The Correspondence and Papers of Violet Markham, 1896–1953)* (London: Historians' Press, 1994); J. Lewis, *Women and Social Action in Victorian and Edwardian England* (Stanford: Stanford University Press, 1991).

[39] For Gertrude Bell's life and ideas, see *The Letters of Gertrude Bell*, ed. Lady F. Bell (London: Ernest Benn Ltd, 1927); *The Earlier Letters of Gertrude Bell*, ed. E. Richmond (London: Ernest Benn Ltd, 1937); E. Burgoyne, *Gertrude Bell from her Personal Papers 1889–1914* (London: Ernest Benn Ltd, 1958); S. Goodman, *Gertrude Bell* (Leamington Spa: Berg, 1985); J. Wallach, *Desert Queen*

industrial families, and social contact led to a friendship based upon shared political beliefs. Both developed an interest in social reform issues, and both later became highly committed imperialists with a strong admiration for individual empire-builders as well as a wider circle of male and female imperialist friends. They also shared the experience of living relatively independent lives as unmarried women, despite their conventional views on the centrality of marriage and motherhood to female happiness and the social good. Violet's late marriage during the First World War made little impact upon her public work, whilst Gertrude's failed love affairs may have helped to propel her further into a life of constant travel and continuous intellectual and political commitment. Friendships were important to both women, both at an emotional level and in relation to their public work. Though their lives and work also diverged in significant ways, there are interesting similarities between these women's development of an imperialist faith influenced by hero-worshipping contact with leading imperialist men.

Violet Markham grew up in Chesterfield, where she had the usual rather limited education of an upper middle-class girl, and found early openings for her abilities in local philanthropy and educational work. A family visit to Egypt in 1895 proved a life-changing experience, for it brought her into contact with 'the world of British administration shepherding a backward oriental land into paths of righteousness for which many of its people had little taste'. She discovered that 'a handful of able, disinterested men were working miracles'. Her admiration for Lord Cromer knew no bounds, while Milner's book *England in Egypt* 'shook me away from my Liberal moorings and made me for a long time a convinced Imperialist'.[40] Four years later, she arrived in Milner's South Africa on the eve of the war. Her visit laid the foundations of a lifelong devotion to Milner, and parallel friendships with members of his 'kindergarten' of imperial administrators. Strolling in the gardens of a Cape Town hotel, the High Commissioner used their first encounter to open up his political heart to her (a ploy he was subsequently to repeat with several other potentially influential female visitors). She spent the following weeks gathering materials for a propaganda onslaught on behalf of 'Milner's War', which began immediately after her return to Britain. Her first book, *South Africa Past and Present*, made the case for defending British South Africa: 'The great question at issue has been this: shall we or the Dutch rule South Africa? It is a game for empire which is being played out, and the stake is a continent'. She described 'the federated empire of our dreams' in Milnerite terms as 'but the association of different members of the same family, who have drawn closer together existing natural ties because they feel that as men of one blood and one race the pillars of their house must stand or fall together'. Racial hierarchy drew her particular attention, as she applied 'the principle of natural selection' to explain

(London: Weidenfeld and Nicholson, 1996); H. Winstone, *Gertrude Bell* (London: Jonathan Cape, 1978).

40 Markham, *Return Passage*, 46, 47, 4.

that 'It is not only our task to conquer the Boers; it is our task, if possible to raise them in the scale of existence'.[41] Beyond the Boers lurked the greater long-term racial threat of black domination, a spectre which seems to have alarmed Violet Markham rather more than it did Milner himself. Violet soon received the rewards of imperial admiration in the form of flattering comments from the great man himself, who wrote that he had found 'some portions of your book quite excellent and the whole a *tour de force* . . . I feel "the cause" is very safe in your hands'.[42]

A second book followed in 1904, when Milner's reconstruction policies required another urgent defence.[43] A year later Violet made an imperialist pilgrimage to Canada, and added Lord Grey, the charismatic Governor General, to her pantheon of imperial heroes. His daughter became a close friend, and Grey himself seems to have reciprocated her admiration, to the extent of including her in his later fulsome and opinionated correspondence on imperial affairs.[44] Like Milner, he valued her abilities as an imperial propagandist, and also hoped that she would intercede privately with her political friends on behalf of causes they both held dear. Grey's protégé Mackenzie King was another influential new friend who shared the Milnerite view of empire, and (like Violet Markham and Milner himself) linked it to a commitment to domestic social reforms. A forty-year friendship was to last throughout King's long Canadian premiership until his death in 1945.[45]

However, Alfred Milner remained at the centre of her political firmament. Their correspondence during the 1900s reveals interesting new dimensions of political intimacy as Milner began privately to draw upon her financial resources in support of his own small-scale South African projects. 'I *just jump* at your most generous gift,' he wrote in November 1902, '. . . I have before now been able to do an enormous amount of good with a few thousands which friends gave me for *purposes outside those to which definite public funds are applicable*'.[46] In September 1903 he acknowledged a 'further contribution to our many needs', offering to meet Violet in London the following month.[47] During the Chinese labour crisis of 1906, Milner actively sought her help as a Liberal lobbyist, but also continued to request her money for imperial purposes. 'I shall grow shy of "bleeding" you if you always give me more than I ask', he wrote after she sent a private £100 donation to support Sir Frederick Pollock's work for the forthcoming Colonial Conference.[48] A year later his approach to her finances, and also to general issues of democracy, was spelt out even more directly as he boldly suggested an

[41] V. Markham, *South Africa, Past and Present* (London: Smith, Elder and Co., 1900), 208, 144, 224, 220.

[42] Alfred Milner to Violet Markham, n.d. 1900. BLPES, LSE, Markham papers, 25/56.

[43] V. Markham, *The New Era in South Africa* (London: Smith Elder and Co., 1904).

[44] See Lord Grey to Violet Markham. Markham papers, 25/33.

[45] See Markham, *Return Passage*, 82–4.

[46] Milner to V. Markham, 15 Nov. 1902. Markham papers, 25/56.

[47] Ibid., 25 Sept. 1903. Markham papers, 25/56.

[48] Ibid., 12 Apr. 1906. Markham papers, 25/56.

alternative to her proffered gift to the Empire Education Fund: 'I must own that, if possible, I would rather have what you are able and kind enough to give me for "secret services" purposes when they arise. One can generally do more good with £100 of which one has absolute control than with £1000, the use of which has to be decided by a committee and publicly advertised'.[49]

It is apparent that Milner trusted Violet Markham and respected her abilities, while she supported his imperialist vision and revelled in their friendship. Their relationship should perhaps be understood as a modernized and less patrician version of the kind of discreet political friendships between upper-class men and women which had played such an important role in the political lives of earlier generations, and were still current in Edwardian Britain. Violet offered talent and political contacts, as well as money and, though hardly a fully fledged political hostess, seems to have enjoyed her small share of female power-broking. Meanwhile her views on empire were further consolidated by her experiences of social work, and intertwined with her long-standing anti-suffragism. As well as establishing her own settlement in Chesterfield, and contributing to the Personal Service Association, she devoted much time to the Victoria League, attempting to steer its ladylike imperial service in the direction of working-class needs at home and overseas. In a *Nineteenth Century* article titled 'The True Foundations of Empire: The Home and the Workshop', she made the imperialist case for improved legislation to protect children and married women workers: 'The foundations of Empire are at stake in this matter, the Empire whose purple is a mockery unless it prove a symbol of the strength and righteousness of its people'.[50] The health and welfare of children depended upon creation of the necessary conditions for successful motherhood. The most sacred of womanly duties eluded Violet Markham herself, but this in no way lessened her strong conviction of its importance both to British society and to the Empire. She was the most sought-after of the female anti-suffrage speakers, alongside Mary Ward, due to her thoughtful synthesis of many of the most important aspects of the antis' cause as well as to her appealing platform persona.

Violet Markham's anti-suffrage campaigning after 1909 brought her for the first time into close contact with Lord Cromer. Another admiring friendship was soon established, providing further imperialist reinforcement for her views on womanhood and the franchise. Violet's correspondence with Cromer was frank enough to give us important insights into some of the more problematic aspects of the anti-suffrage movement, which will be discussed in later chapters. However, she always maintained a highly deferential stance towards this senior proconsul which was much less apparent in her relationships with Milner and Grey. A

---

[49] Milner to V. Markham, n.d. 1907. Markham papers, 25/56.

[50] V. Markham, 'The True Foundations of Empire: The Home and the Workshop', *Nineteenth Century and After*, 344 (1905), 580. She also claimed that 'the greatness of any nation is proportionate to the strength of its family life . . . Empires are not built up on the offspring of denaturalised parents'. Ibid. 575.

more intimate connection had meanwhile developed between Lord Cromer and Gertrude Bell. Their shared enthusiasm for the Middle East provided a promising basis for a friendship which was to be consolidated by shared opinions on many other matters, including votes for women. Though Gertrude Bell was the first secretary of the Women's National Anti-Suffrage League, and remained sporadically active in anti-suffragism throughout the pre-war years, her main energies in this period were devoted to her extensive travels and to her writings about Middle Eastern countries whose control was gradually slipping from the Turks towards imperial Britain and rival European powers. Her status as a gifted linguist and historian enabled her to take up an unofficial intelligence role even before the First World War granted her official recognition in that capacity, culminating in a diplomatic job in post-war Iraq. Gertrude's later career, and especially her well-publicized achievements as a traveller and archaeologist in harshly remote places, have been portrayed by some historians as seriously at odds with her anti-suffragism. However, her earlier life provides adequate evidence of the reasons for her choice.

Like Violet Markham, Gertrude Bell was influenced by her parents' views on womanhood. The devoted daughter of a devoted father and stepmother, she was fortunate enough to be allowed considerable personal freedom, including the opportunity of an Oxford education at Lady Margaret Hall where she met other intellectual women with conservative gender views. Over the following years she joined in Florence Bell's philanthropic social work, as well as making influential friendships through the London social scene and beginning her adventures abroad. Both her academic and social skills stood her in good stead when she joined her uncle's diplomatic household in Roumania then in Persia, befriended Valentine Chirol (later foreign editor of *The Times*), and learnt to enjoy back-scene politics as well as to admire the work of indirect British imperialism. The suffrage campaign offered few attractions to a woman whose family and friends opposed it, and who had found her own route into a fulfilling engagement with the politics of empire. Again like Violet Markham, Gertrude Bell had conventional aspirations towards a happy, companionate marriage, and throughout her life valued feminine pursuits such childcare, gardening, and elaborate dress.

Gertrude's first contact with Lord Cromer seems to have occurred when both she and her stepmother wrote him adulatory letters praising *Modern Egypt*.[51] By 1908 she was already familiar with Persia, Turkey, Syria, and Asia Minor, so was well placed to test Cromer's views on Oriental government alongside her own. Her account of her Syrian expedition, published the same year, was dedicated to the Indian imperialist Sir Alfred Lyall. In the preface she lamented

[51] Florence Bell to Cromer, 23 Mar. 1908; Gertrude Bell to Cromer, 8 Mar. 1908: 'I cannot hold myself back from telling you how far beyond all praise it seems to me to be. Reading it is like turning over the pages of the Recording Angel'. Cromer papers, FO633/12/121 and 97.

loss of 'English' influence in Turkish territories, suggesting that 'it should not be impossible to recapture the place we have lost'.[52] Her next major work, *Amurath to Amurath* (1911), was dedicated to Cromer himself. Travelling from Aleppo to Baghdad, she observed the current politics of the region as closely as its ancient monuments, attempting to weigh up the outcomes of the recent Turkish revolution and its significance for British interests. A dedicatory preface noted that 'the return of prosperity to the peoples of the Near East began with your administration in Egypt', before invoking his sympathetic understanding for her attempt to 'record the daily life and speech of those who had inherited the empty ground whereon empires had risen and expired . . . you, with your profound experience of the East, have learnt to reckon with the unbroken continuity of its history'.[53]

Essentialized Oriental and British characteristics stand out almost as clearly from Gertrude Bell's pages as from those of *Modern Egypt*. In 1910 Cromer sent her his 'essay on Imperialism', which she acknowledged as 'specially welcome in the middle of an election, a moment when all really important things are apt to be forgotten. Your words set me thinking about the future of a democratic empire . . . the incompatible ideals are extremely striking'.[54] Gertrude continued to correspond regularly with Cromer, exchanging political and travel news from distant places in far greater depth and detail than she devoted to the anti-suffrage organization in which they both held leadership positions. Her dismissive attitude to elections echoed his own non-partisan and anti-democratic view of politics; suffragism needed to be opposed because it threatened to interfere with more important imperial matters. Cromer's first comments on the book she dedicated to him contained much jovial praise ('How well you know your East and your Eastern!'), together with a sideswipe at the suffragettes and a semi-serious warning against dangerous Mesopotamian river crossings: 'I should not mind Mrs Pankhurst and some of her militant friends sailing out into the British Channel on these frail craft, but you are really too valuable'.[55]

By 1912 she had become 'My dear Gertrude', and in the last two years before the war the correspondence on both sides ranged between lengthy, serious exchanges on political and imperial affairs, and more frivolous comments on personal matters. 'My very dear Lord . . .', wrote Gertrude from Baghdad in March 1914, 'I love your most characteristic observations on flirting, and fully agree with them. Your account of Miss Durham is disconcerting. No stays! tut, tut! (We won't dwell on what I've worn in Arabia)'. In the same long letter she dwelt in more sombre mood on the disappointments of her latest travels, and (most unusually, for her) on the disadvantages of being a woman traveller: 'on the

[52] G. Bell, *Syria: The Desert and the Sown* (London: Heinemann, 1908), p. xii.
[53] G. Bell, *Amurath to Amurath* (London: Heinemann, 1911), pp. ix, vii.
[54] G. Bell to Cromer, 23 Jan. 1910. Cromer papers, FO 633/30/246.
[55] Cromer to G. Bell, 14 Jan. 1911. Cromer papers, FO633/20/160.

whole it's a drawback being a woman on such adventures as these. One cannot do them as well, nor as swiftly, nor as easily as a man'.[56] Was this a calculated appeal to Cromer's gender prejudices? It seems more likely to have been a sincere comment revealing both her innermost self-doubts and her trust in her established mentor. By this date Cromer was occasionally forwarding Gertrude's news and views to Violet Markham, herself touring the Far East, thus providing an extra dimension of imperialist, anti-suffragist networking. Though Violet also became somewhat confiding towards Cromer during this period, she remained 'Miss Markham' and never enjoyed the same relationship of shared expertise which Gertrude Bell had established with Cromer through her travels and her academic studies. The warmth of their friendship is apparent. But platonic male–female networking had its limits, as an ingredient of anti-suffrage organization. It is interesting to find a spiteful aside on Gertrude's poor judgement, coupled to the comment that she was 'an extremely clever woman', in a very private letter from Cromer to Curzon written at the height of gender-related conflict within the NLOWS in 1912.[57] Despite some respect and even affection for their female acolytes, neither Milner nor Cromer accepted them as equal colleagues. Their views on different gender roles, as much as their own public stature, made that impossible.

Imperial Wives: Margaret Jersey and Ethel Colquhoun

A number of leading anti-suffragist women acquired an enthusiasm for the British Empire as a result of the imperial service of their male relatives. David Cannadine has vividly portrayed imperial proconsuls at work and at play from the 1880s onwards, under the borrowed soubriquet 'Great Ornamentals'.[58] Though ceremonial duties and the parade of British aristocratic values played an important part in sustaining a particular form of British imperialist rule during the pre-war decades, the Empire offered varied work at different levels of the imperial ruling class hierarchy. Even at the top of the imperial tree, the wives and other female relatives of Governor Generals, Viceroys, and High Commissioners generally supported their leading men in more than purely ornamental duties. Amanda Andrew has recently analysed a category of 'new viceregal women' who successfully linked aspects of their imperial roles with some of the more assertive, independent characteristics of Edwardian new womanhood.[59] Such women were greatly in demand as figureheads and activists within the collective associations

---

[56] G. Bell to Cromer, 26 Mar. 1914. Cromer papers, FO633/23/24 and 27.

[57] Cromer to Curzon, 23 Feb. 1912: 'She has not got much judgement and has a tongue'. BL, Curzon papers, MSS Eur F112/35.

[58] D. Cannadine, *The Decline and Fall of the British Aristocracy* (London: Macmillan, 1996 edn.), 588–602. See also id., *Aspects of Aristocracy* (London: Penguin, 1995).

[59] See A. Andrew, 'The Great Ornamentals: New Viceregal Women and their Imperial Work 1884–1914', D.Phil. thesis (University of Western Sydney, 2004).

of female imperialism, both in Britain and overseas. Shirley Ardener's concept of 'incorporated wives' remains useful as a means of examining female dependence on male career patterns, including in colonial contexts.[60] However, those who found themselves involuntarily committed to female imperial work sometimes developed into its leading experts and keenest advocates. There was evident scope for an extension of maternal social and educational reform into colonial settings. For many British women, whether active at viceregal or at more humble levels, there was the additional, more exalted satisfaction of helping to consolidate an empire believed to be founded on racial superiority and racial duty.

A number of the leading viceregal ladies were known to be supporters of women's suffrage, and manifested genteel support for the movement after their return to Britain. Of these, Lady Selborne, Lady Dufferin, and Lady Aberdeen were the most prominent. However, many other imperial wives, sisters, and daughters joined the opposition, and became advocates of anti-suffragism alongside husbands, brothers, fathers, and the large number of other well-known imperialist men. Some may have done so purely out of a sense of 'incorporated' wifely duty. Lady Cromer, for example, took on the presidency of a branch of the NLOWS but apparently disliked the work, judging from Cromer's complaint to Curzon about its stressfulness.[61] Others became active imperialists but tacit anti-suffragists, such as Lady Edward Cecil (sister of Leo Maxse and later Milner's wife). However, Beatrice Chamberlain and Lady George Hamilton seem to have been enthusiastic members of the executive of the WNASL, and Georgina and Lily Frere (daughters of former South African Governor Sir Bartle Frere) were supportive participants at anti-suffrage meetings. The most conspicuously imperial lady of the anti-suffrage movement was undoubtedly Lady Jersey,[62] who served first as Chairman of the Women's League, then as Vice-President to Cromer within the National League. Another very active imperialist wife was Ethel Colquhoun,[63] whose anti-suffrage speeches and journalism were inspired and reinforced by her Empire travels and her links to the Royal Colonial Institute.

Margaret Jersey was a powerful woman in her own right, and a great traveller even before her husband became Governor General of New South Wales from 1891 to 1893. Eldest daughter of an aristocratic family related to the wealthy Grosvenors, she was known as 'Head Girl' by close relatives. After marriage to the Earl of Jersey in 1872 she found a managerial role as mistress of a large

---

[60] See H. Callan and S. Ardener (eds.), *The Incorporated Wife* (London: Croom Helm, 1984).

[61] Cromer to Curzon, 4 Nov. 1910. Curzon papers, MSS Eur F112/33B. Lady Cromer had accepted the Presidency of the Marylebone branch of the NLOWS 'on the distinct understanding that she was not to be bothered', only to find herself caught up in the disagreements between other women committee members.

[62] On the life and ideas of Margaret Jersey, see M. Villiers, Countess of Jersey, *Fifty-One Years of Victorian Life* (London: John Murray, 1922); V. Powell, *Margaret, Countess of Jersey* (London: Heinemann, 1978).

[63] On the life and ideas of Ethel Colquhoun, see D. Lowry, in I. Fletcher, L. Nym Mayhall, and P. Levine (eds.), *Women's Suffragism in the British Empire* (London: Routledge, 2000), ch. 11.

estate and leader of a political and literary salon at Osterley House, conveniently close to the London parliamentary and social scene. An opportunity existed to step into the shoes of the mid-Victorian Lady Jersey, an arch-practitioner of the politics of female influence. However, Lord Jersey's own ambitions were relatively modest, and his wife turned instead to the public welfare activities which were burgeoning in the late nineteenth century, graciously acting as 'Lady Bountiful' on her own estate and presiding over the Children's Happy Evenings Association as well as taking up a leading role in the Ladies' Grand Council of the Primrose League. Her literary aspirations found an outlet in children's stories and accounts of her own travels. A journey to India in 1888 was a more serious undertaking, and was followed by a *Nineteenth Century* article which caught Queen Victoria's attention. Margaret Jersey had met Indian rulers and noted gratifying veneration of the Queen-Empress. Soon after, she visited Egypt, befriending male imperialists who included Colonel Kitchener (future commander in the Sudan, South Africa, and India) and the African explorer Henry Stanley. The Jerseys' Australian sojourn extended her imperial education into a close-up view of imperial government, as well as offering travels which took in New Zealand, Samoa, and the Far East. Margaret Jersey was born into a Liberal family, but by this date had become a Conservative and a convinced imperialist. Her *Nineteenth Century* articles of the 1890s suggest a rather lofty confidence that all would be well with imperial Britain, providing racial hierarchy was preserved in the colonies and female gender role adjustment sensibly managed at home.[64] The presidency of the Victoria League, from 1901 onwards, enabled her to contribute towards both these desirable outcomes. So too did her work for the anti-suffrage movement.

The writings of Margaret Jersey reveal much less about her ideas than do those of Violet Markham and Gertrude Bell. Her autobiography, articles, and published speeches suggest a slightly ponderous sense of humour, and a determination to entertain her readers which often crowded out expression of her personal opinions. She was more complimented for her silvery tones than for the content of her speeches. Possibly this reflects aristocratic and feminine discretion, or merely a lack of the moral earnestness which characterized so many other leading women in public life. The extent and nature of her public commitments nevertheless suggests strongly held views about both womanhood and empire. Her *National Review* article on the work of the Victoria League described the solemn beginnings of this organization, under the shadow of the South African War and the recent death of the Queen.[65] Englishwomen obeyed 'the impulse of their race' as they gathered together feeling that 'war had drawn together the Empire as never before . . . a thrill of Imperial sentiment was flashing from land

[64] See M. Jersey, 'Ourselves and Our Foremothers', *Nineteenth Century*, 27 (1890), 56–64; 'White Slaves: A True Tale', *Nineteenth Century*, 43 (1898), 417–30.
[65] M. Jersey, 'The Victoria League', *National Review*, 51 (1907), 317–26.

to land, and from sea to sea'. Much of the article was devoted to a summary of the League's practical work for imperial education and social welfare, but Lady Jersey also took care to explain its attitudes to the inclusion of men and to party politics. Male collaboration had always been welcome, but there was a special role for 'the wives and sisters of prominent statesman' who 'could devote the time and thought necessary to formulating the work and setting it on foot'.

Efforts had been made to ensure that the League was broadly representative of the main political parties. Though there was to be no 'colourless abstention from politics', its work stood above the party conflicts of the parliamentary system: 'in all maintaining the personal sympathy so much more easily promoted by individual effort than by legislation however wise, or Governments however beneficent'.[66] When the *Anti-Suffrage Review* celebrated Lady Jersey's achievements in a front-page article in 1910, it noted both her philanthropic and her 'Imperial' successes in 'that work which it is her faith to declare the especial privilege of her sex. As President of the Victoria League, she has shown women where their Imperial duties lie, irrespective of party politics'.[67] The anti-suffrage implications of such statements would have been obvious to readers of the *Anti-Suffrage Review*, however hard the Victoria League tried to insist upon its own suffrage neutrality.

Margaret Jersey's marriage opened up unique opportunities for an imperial education, and gave the anti-suffrage Leagues the benefit of her extensive friendships among leading male empire-builders. The formative influence of marriage is still more evident in the case of Ethel Colquhoun. Starting from a much less privileged family background, she became a worldwide traveller and an influential figure at the Royal Colonial Institute. After her first husband's death in 1914 she expanded her journalistic achievements by taking over his editorship of the Institute's monthly journal. After her second marriage she emigrated to Rhodesia, eventually becoming (ironically enough, for a leading anti-suffragist) the first woman elected to membership of a colonial legislature. Ethel was a doctor's daughter who spent her youth developing her artistic talents at the Slade School of Art and doing voluntary social work in South and East London. In 1900 she was swept off her feet into a romantic marriage to a man more than twice her age. Archibald Colquhoun, 'powerfully built, with a walrus moustache and a fondness for champagne',[68] was already a well-known and much-published explorer and colonial administrator. His experiences had included an unsuccessful South African episode as Cecil Rhodes's first Mashonaland administrator, as well as projects in Asia and South America. Ethel's first, self-illustrated book, *Two On Their Travels*, gave a light-hearted account of their prolonged honeymoon voyage, during which she honed both her grasp of racial stereotypes and her views

---

[66] M. Jersey, 'The Victoria League', *National Review*, 317, 318–19, 323.

[67] *Anti-Suffrage Review*, 17 (Apr. 1910), 1.

[68] D. Lowry, 'Archibald and Ethel Colquhoun', in *Oxford Dictionary of National Biography*.

on femininity. Her husband's influence was apparent on every page, even before she included a helpful description of his habit of looking over her shoulder and commenting as she wrote.[69]

Soon Ethel was developing a more serious analysis of womanhood, closely related to their shared hopes for the imperial future. Her Royal Colonial Institute paper on 'Women and the Colonies' was given in 1904 to an audience containing representatives of all the leading female imperialist associations as well as male imperialists.[70] This did not inhibit her from expressing criticisms of the unrealistic aspirations of emigration societies which were over-preoccupied with women's selfish ambitions for economic benefits and professional employment. The true need of the colonies was for simple, homely girls who 'would become a valuable centre of sweetness and light in the new communities'. The true motive for successful female emigration should be patriotic service, rather than merely self-interest: 'many of us must play our parts in narrow circles here at home, but can we not rise beyond our environment to the conception that we are but a tiny speck in a great Empire?' She proceeded to set forth a vision of imperial education which would enable women to contribute towards 'this great question of the Federation of the Empire': 'it is worthwhile for the mothers of England to rouse themselves from an apathy which is undeniable. I do not want to see more so-called "political" women . . . But Imperialism need not be confined to the sterner sex . . . it appeals peculiarly to women because it affects so strongly the home, not only of the present but of the future'.[71] Despite her critical tone on this occasion, Ethel eventually became active in the British Women's Emigration Association as well as in the Imperial Maritime League, the National Service League, and the Women's Unionist Association. She did not herself achieve the much-longed-for prize of imperial motherhood, but continued to exhort other women to treasure its importance rather than succumbing to the selfish lures of university education and careerism.

A series of articles in the *Nineteenth Century* and the *Quarterly Review* provided the anti-suffrage movement with some of its strongest statements of principle.[72] Ethel Colquhoun believed that 'it is evident to women who know their own sex that the demand for the parliamentary franchise is symptomatic of a far deeper and more fundamental discontent than can be met by the mere granting of votes to women'.[73] Her book *The Vocation of Women* (1913) attempted a full-scale analysis of the social evils which were so dangerously undermining established

[69] E. Colquhoun, *Two on Their Travels* (London: William Heinemann, 1902).

[70] Ead., 'Women and the Colonies', *Royal Colonial Society Proceedings*, 35 (1903–4), 326–38.

[71] Ibid. 336, 337, 338.

[72] See ead., 'Modern Feminism and Sex Antagonism', *Quarterly Review*, 219 (1913), 143–66; 'Quo Vadis, Femina?', *Nineteenth Century and After*, 73 (1913), 517–27; 'Woman and Morality', *Nineteenth Century and After*, 75 (1914), 128–40; 'The Superfluous Woman: Her Cause and Cure', *Nineteenth Century and After*, 75 (1914), 563–73.

[73] Ead., *The Vocation of Woman* (London: Macmillan, 1913), 10.

gender roles, and with them the stability and happiness of Britain and its empire. Addressed primarily to women, her book relentlessly exposed the deeper threats which social change posed to marriage and the home. 'Feminism', rather than suffragism, was the real danger. Only one chapter in a long book was dedicated directly to 'Woman and the Empire', and another to the suffrage issue itself: however, Lord Cromer was her preferred reviewer. She sent the book to him with a letter claiming it to be 'the first Anti-Feminist book by a woman and . . . a very serious and earnest attempt to get to the bottom of the extraordinary state of affairs prevailing in the ranks of my sex today'.[74] He responded positively, not only reviewing her book favourably in the *Spectator* but also associating it with his own current study of 'Feminism in France', published almost simultaneously in the *National Review*.[75] The anti-suffrage onslaught on 'feminism' was closely linked to current alarm over the implications of suffragism for sexual behaviour, marriage, and divorce.[76] Ethel had moved into this difficult territory without in any way abandoning her views on the centrality of the Empire to Britain's future. However, she had concluded that imperial arguments alone were not enough to deter women from suffragism, nor a sufficient explanation of its dangers. Evidently she was by now a formidable polemicist in her own right, rather than merely a compliant imperial wife.

Imperial Celebrities: Mary Kingsley and Flora Shaw

The final pair of influential imperialist women will be considered more briefly. They were not active campaigners for the anti-suffrage cause, though they made clear their support for it. This indirect support was useful, for both women were distinguished writers and travellers with an unusually high public profile. Their achievements provided rather extreme examples of what women were capable of, and were widely admired. It did anti-suffragism no harm to be associated with female achievement, especially when (as in this case) it was coupled with feminine deference to male imperial authority upon the domestic scene. Mary Kingsley[77] died as an imperial heroine performing feminine nursing duties during the South African War. Flora Shaw[78] successfully made the transition from imperial celebrity to imperial wife, when she abandoned her own public career in 1902 to marry Frederick Lugard, Britain's leading proconsul in West Africa.

---

[74] E. Colquhoun to Cromer, 30 Oct. 1913. Cromer papers, FO633/22/165.

[75] E. Colquhoun to Cromer, 5 Nov. 1913. Cromer papers, FO633/22/165–6. 'Feminism in France' was published in the *National Review*, 62 (1913–14).

[76] See Ch. 9, below.

[77] For Mary Kingsley's life and ideas, see D. Birkett, *Mary Kingsley, Imperial Adventuress* (London: Macmillan, 1992). Mary Kingsley and Flora Shaw are compared in J. Schneer, *London 1900: The Imperial Metropolis* (New Haven: Yale University Press, 1999), ch. 6.

[78] For Flora Shaw's life and ideas, see E. Moberly Bell, *Flora Shaw* (London: Constable, 1947); H. Callaway and D. Helly, 'Crusader for Empire', in N. Chaudhuri and M. Strobel (eds.), *Western Women and Imperialism: Complicity and Resistance* (Bloomington: Indiana University Press, 1992).

Mary Kingsley's biographer, Dea Birkett, has developed an interesting general explanation of the connection between Victorian women's adventurous travels and their rather emphatically feminine behaviour in British public life. In her view, there was an inverse relationship between adventurousness and support for women's social and political reforms.[79] Anti-suffrage travellers, including Mary Kingsley, Gertrude Bell, and Marianne North, were among the most adventurous women of their age, and were committed to pushing the boundaries of female achievement in distant, dangerous places. Birkett concludes that their travels were undertaken for 'essentially selfish' reasons, and that their conventional femininity in Britain was necessary to counter accusations of impropriety and to secure male professional and political support.[80] There is certainly evidence which suggests that disassociation from female reform movements fulfilled these women's personal needs and served their careers, but it is also necessary to set their choice in the context of their views on British imperialism. Mary Kingsley adopted more than one persona as she embarked upon her West African adventures. After many claustrophobic years as a dutiful daughter to her ill-matched parents, she was released by their deaths in 1892 to travel to Africa in the next two years as an explorer and collector of biological specimens. During the rest of the decade she wrote her books, gave public lectures, and developed her controversial opinions on ethnography and the nature of British imperial intervention in Africa. She demonstrated an unusual appreciation and sympathy for the African people she had met on her travels. This led her to argue against attempts by missionaries and others to 'civilize' West Africa, and to introduce direct British administration and political control which would undermine indigenous culture. Instead, she believed that Britain could reap the benefits of empire through indirect economic control exercised by traders rather than government officials.

Mary Kingsley developed her imperial views through contact with old empire hands in Africa and in Britain, as well as on the basis of her own observations and experience. She formed an 'unrequited attachment' to Matthew Nathan, who became Acting Governor of Sierra Leone,[81] and corresponded with Joseph Chamberlain over the imposition of a hut tax in West Africa and other colonial matters. Her links with male imperialism extended in the late 1890s to include George Goldie of the Royal Niger Company and Frederick Lugard, whose interventionist trade policies and prospective governorship of Nigeria roused her strong opposition. Her friends included the Liverpool trader John Holt and the explorer Henry Stanley, and she had also made friendly contact with Sir Alfred Lyall. Though death prevented the full development of her schemes for West Africa, it is clear that Mary Kingsley was using the stratagems of female influence to advance her own imperialist agenda. She had very little sympathy

---

[79] D. Birkett, *Spinsters Abroad: Victorian Lady Explorers* (Stroud: Sutton Publishing, 2004 edn.), 199–200.
[80] Ibid. 199.   [81] D. Birkett, 'Mary Kingsley', in *Oxford Dictionary of National Biography*.

for imperial maternal reformism, nor was she among the uncritical admirers of Rhodes, Chamberlain, and Milner. However, her views on empire, race, and gender were also being developed in close, if largely untheorized, connection, and under the powerful influence of leading male imperialists. Imperialism helped to create opportunities and a public platform for her. A wide British readership at the turn of the century was made aware of her womanly reticence concerning the franchise and female entry to learned societies, as well as being invited to admire her bravery and to share her knowledge of Africa.[82] It seems probable that Mary Kingsley, like the other women imperialists discussed in this chapter, saw little or no contradiction between these different sides of her outlook and achievement.

In comparison with Mary Kingsley, Flora Shaw was a rather conventional imperialist, though another bold traveller who roused the admiration and astonishment of her contemporaries. After limited education in a large military family, she wrote fiction and undertook charitable work before turning to journalism as a career. As a correspondent for the *Pall Mall Gazette*, she visited Cromer's Egypt in 1889 and reported favourably on his achievements. She began a decade of work for *The Times* soon after, travelling to South Africa, Australia, New Zealand, and Canada to gather material for her fortnightly column on 'The Colonies', and in 1893 was promoted to the position of colonial editor. This unprecedented achievement was followed by another in 1894, when she became the first woman to speak at the Royal Colonial Institute, as well as addressing the Scottish Geographical Society and the Royal Society of Arts. 'She is imbued with the modern form of imperialism,' wrote Mary Kingsley rather sourly; 'It is her religion'.[83] Certainly Flora Shaw proved more than willing to fall under the spell of masculine imperialism. This played an important part in her journalistic success, as she became a trusted aide and confidante to Rhodes, Chamberlain, and Milner in South Africa, as well as later to Goldie and Lugard in West Africa. Her *Letters from South Africa* were reprinted in book form in 1893, 'at the request of several of the most important public men in South Africa', for the purpose of informing British public opinion on South African affairs.[84] An embarrassing episode followed, as *The Times* and its correspondent appeared to be directly implicated in the failed Jameson raid of 1896. However, Flora extricated herself with sufficient reputation to take up the cause of West African development. She supported orthodox colonization and trade controls, in opposition to Mary Kingsley but in agreement with Lugard, whom she married in 1902.

---

[82] Mary Kingsley put across her views in public lectures as well as through her publications and journalism. She distanced herself from New Womanhood by her dress and behaviour, and also by refusing to support the entry of women to the Royal Geographical Society, as well as to Parliament.

[83] M. Kingsley to J. Holt, 20 Feb. 1899, in Birkett, 'Mary Kingsley'. Mary Kingsley's hostility is analysed by Schneer, *London 1900* and by Callaway and Helly, 'Crusader for Empire'. She may have felt some jealousy, but there were also substantive differences between the two women's views on West African imperialism.

[84] F. Shaw, *Letters from South Africa* (London: *The Times*, 1893).

Thereafter her activities were mainly restricted to wifely imperialist lobbying on his behalf. Though she no longer acted as an independent professional, there were obvious continuities with her earlier journalism undertaken in support of male imperialist heroes, and also some parallels with Violet Markham's voluntary propaganda work on behalf of Alfred Milner. Letters to her husband in 1904 reveal that Flora thought of her journalism retrospectively as 'active politics without the fame'; she also confided to him that she 'liked being nothing while the work remained'.[85] She had in fact succeeded in establishing a role for herself which was both powerful and acceptably feminine, in her own eyes and presumably in his. After marriage her public work included membership of the conventionally maternal Victoria League. Her anti-suffragism remained muted, but had always been implicit in her satisfaction with her own behind-the-scenes role in politics, as well as in her affirmation of feminine boundaries to the widespread entry of women into public life. In July 1910 she was among the signatories of a published statement announcing the formation of the NLOWS.[86] Like Mary Kingsley, Flora Shaw made her friends and wider public aware that she had no aspirations to become a 'feminist' role model. Her consistency on this point suggests genuine conviction, rather than merely an instrumental tactic to open career opportunities for herself within a male-ruled empire.

FEMALE IMPERIALIST ASSOCIATIONS AND THE VOTE

Edwardian Britain was crowded with Leagues and other associations advocating patriotic imperialism. Most were male-led and, if they admitted women at all, did so on terms which signified their subordinate status. The Royal Colonial Institute created a category of lady associates in 1910, allowing them limited privileges in return for lower subscriptions. Navy League women paid half the male subscription, while the British Empire League formed separate female branches. Even the Women's Tariff Reform Association, which provided substantial support to the campaign for imperialist trade policies, was merely an auxiliary of the male Tariff Reform League. However upper-class and upper-middle-class women took the lead within their own organizations, including some which had been formed around other objectives but became steadily more committed to the British imperialist project after the turn of the century.[87] The origins of the Girls' Friendly Society and the Mothers' Union were described in Chapter

---

[85] F. Lugard to her husband, 1904, quoted in Schneer, *London 1900*, 144, 145. Callaway and Helly suggest Flora Shaw had a 'double consciousness', deliberately combining feminine decorum with 'masculine' work, and protesting her reticence while priding herself on her exercise of power. 'Crusader for Empire', 80–1.

[86] *The Times*, 21 July 1910, 9.

[87] For analysis of the imperial work of the GFS, the British Women's Emigration Society, the Primrose League, and the Victoria League, see Bush, *Edwardian Ladies and Imperial Power*.

3. The size and geographical range of these Anglican women's societies made them an especially important source of influence upon female public opinion. Though their attitudes towards suffragism remained deliberately veiled, feminine commitment to the Empire gradually became a very prominent part of their maternal and religious social service amongst women and girls. The British Women's Emigration Society and its affiliates provided further active support for womanly imperialism. Founded in 1884, its roots extended back to the mid-century Langham Place circle and its support for emigration as an opportunity for impoverished gentlewomen. By the early twentieth century, emigration was seen as an imperialist cause, tied to the needs of the Empire as much as to those of the emigrants themselves. The Primrose League's origins in 1883 lay within the development of the Conservative party, and its desire to reinforce the social hierarchy and social cohesion potentially threatened by advancing democracy. Again, imperialism provided useful extra impetus to an existing cause. Primrose Dames were as enthusiastic as the organization's male leaders in pressing imperial glory to the forefront of propaganda and public events in the 1900s. The Victoria League stands apart as an organization founded at a later date, and with the explicit, sole purpose of developing women's work on behalf of the British Empire. Its activities ranged from the care of South African war graves to support for patriotic colonial education and provision of upper-class British hospitality for colonial visitors, allied to imperialist propaganda at home and in the Dominions.

There were evidently abundant opportunities in Edwardian Britain for imperialist women to undertake collective social work and exert collective political pressure. The female imperialist associations, like the National Union of Women Workers, were a site for discussion and collaboration among like-minded women. Like the NUWW, they were dedicated to work which stood somewhat apart from the question of votes for women. However, in contrast to the NUWW, they succeeded in maintaining unity around their chosen priorities, despite the presence of both suffragists and anti-suffragists within their ranks. The achievements of the female imperialist associations have been analysed in *Edwardian Ladies and Imperial Power*. Their relationship to feminism was discussed in the same book, leading to the conclusion that they formed part of a broadly defined women's movement which was far from being entirely feminist, though it contained both feminists and suffragists.[88] For present purposes, it is only necessary to revisit those aspects of that discussion which are most relevant to female anti-suffragism. How did the women imperialists handle the potentially divisive suffrage debate? Did the women antis attempt to make political capital out of organized female imperialism, and did they succeed? Were there other ways in which the engagement of some women in simultaneous anti-suffrage and imperialist campaigning affected the anti-suffrage movement? The answers to these questions help us to

[88] Bush, *Edwardian Ladies and Imperial Power*. ch. 10.

understand the motivation of leading women anti-suffragists, and also suggest possible reasons why a wider female public offered their tacit or active support to anti-suffragism.

Neutrality on the suffrage issue was the chosen public stance of all the female imperialist organizations. This choice has been weighed up in relation to the main Anglican women's organizations in Chapter 3. It did not prevent the Girls' Friendly Society and the Mothers' Union from propagating conservative gender roles, and making occasional critical references to suffragism in their literature. The women's emigration associations seem to have been particularly successful in excluding even indirect references to the suffrage issue from their records, despite occasional direct invitations to return to their suffragist roots. Perhaps the existence of a feminist past made abstention from suffrage debate all the more necessary; or perhaps the female emigrators were influenced by the dangers of a political divide between their President, the suffragist Louisa Knightley, and their Organizing Secretary, the highly conservative Ellen Joyce (who was proudly related by marriage to Margaret Jersey). The Primrose League took a more relaxed attitude to the issue, despite the evident divisions within its own ranks. Discussion of votes for women was permitted, but not encouraged, within its branches and publications. Louisa Knightley reappears presiding over a Towcester Habitation meeting in 1901 which voted in favour of women's suffrage; while Betty Balfour indignantly resigned from her Woking Habitation when the local Conservative candidate fought an anti-suffrage campaign in 1910.[89]

The Victoria League, on the other hand, took a clear-cut decision to exclude the franchise issue from its meetings. This was linked to its general determination to rise above parliamentary party divisions, as well as to the obvious potential for conflict within an organization which was presided over by Lady Jersey yet included leading moderate suffragists such as Maud Selborne, Edith Lyttelton, and the ubiquitous Louisa Knightley. An interesting situation arose when Nina Boyle, a member of the suffragist Women's Freedom League, decided to challenge the Victoria League's suffrage neutrality. After a spell as a South African journalist, she offered strong support for the League's imperial work at its annual conference in June 1911, 'appealing to educated women for Imperial Service'. Even on this occasion, her 'vigour and earnestness' apparently jarred with the ladylike calm which normally prevailed at the League's meetings: the *Victoria League Notes* commented, 'perhaps Miss Boyle forgot that for the moment she was addressing a meeting of the converted'.[90] Five months later she wrote to 'withdraw her connection with the League owing to the President's action in regard to the Anti-Suffrage movement'. Peace was restored as the Victoria League's suffragist

---

[89] See Louisa Knightley's journal, 21 Apr. 1901 (Northamptonshire Record Office) and the *Primrose League Gazette*, 1 Sept 1910.

[90] *Victoria League Notes*, June 1911.

secretary replied 'calling the writer's attention to the support given to the League by those holding opposite opinions on controversial questions'.[91]

Margaret Jersey was only the most obvious symbol of anti-suffragism's support among the female imperialists. She had earlier been Vice-Chairman of the Primrose League's Ladies' Grand Council, and was determined to continue her Victoria League Presidency whilst acting as Chairman of the Women's National Anti-Suffrage League, then Vice-President to Cromer in the National League for Opposing Woman Suffrage. In all these organizations she found herself in familiar company. Anti-suffragists in the Victoria League included Violet Cecil, Beatrice and Mary Chamberlain, Mary Curzon, Georgina and Lily Frere, Mary Harcourt, Theresa Londonderry, Flora Lugard, Susan Malmesbury, Violet Markham, Harriet Wantage, and Mary Ward. Support from active male antis included the extensive Victoria League committee work of Halford Mackinder, as well as the formal vice-presidencies of Lord Cromer, Lord Milner, Leo Maxse, and Rudyard Kipling. Mary Ward's contributions to the Victoria League seem to have been limited to small-scale financial support and offers of hospitality to colonial visitors, but Violet Markham chose to devote a considerable amount of her time to this female-led body, despite her evident ability to hold her own in any mixed-sex imperialist organization.[92] From 1907 onwards she seems to have squared her social conscience with her enjoyment of Osterley House hospitality by making efforts to steer the Victoria League out of a narrowly elitist approach to its work. As secretary to the League's Industrial Sub-Committee, she produced a handbook on 'The Factory and Shop Acts of the British Dominions' which detailed industrial legislation across the 'self-governing Colonies' for the benefit of imperial employers and prospective emigrants.[93] She was also to the fore in persuading the League's executive to sponsor 'extension' work: imperial propaganda to working-class audiences in British industrial cities. In 1913 the Victoria League's Annual Report claimed considerable success for its 'pioneer work' in such adventurous locations as Newcastle, Sheffield, and Liverpool.[94]

Anti-suffragists played a particularly important role in the Victoria League, as well as contributing to other female imperialist associations. There were few overt departures from these organizations' policy of suffrage neutrality, but the importance of the empire to both sides in the suffrage campaign meant that all concerned hoped to benefit indirectly from women's growing interest in imperialism. The responsibilities of empire were regularly invoked by the *Anti-Suffrage Review* and at anti-suffrage meetings. Claims and counter-claims were traded over the 'practical' issues which absorbed the female imperialist

[91] Victoria League Executive Committee minutes, 26 Oct. 1911. London, Victoria League archive.

[92] For details of these anti-suffragists' Victoria League involvement, see Victoria League Annual Reports and *Victoria League Notes*. Victoria League archive.

[93] Victoria League Sixth Annual Report (1908), Industrial Sub-Committee report, 27.

[94] Victoria League Eleventh Annual Report (1913), 5.

organizations, such as the conditions of motherhood in the Dominions, rather than over the strategic questions of imperial development which preoccupied male imperialists. Maude Selborne was a particularly persistent advocate of the benefits of enfranchisement for Australian and New Zealand mothers.[95] Her statements provoked heated refutations from the female antis, who claimed that any improvements were due to evolving social conditions rather than to political action.

Female imperialists and women anti-suffragists frequently drew upon each other's support and arguments, despite the official separateness of these two campaigns. There were some less predictable outcomes from the proximity between organized female imperialism and anti-suffragism. Women who shared imperial work were able to engage in friendly dialogue with their franchise opponents as well as supporters. The evidence of such dialogue has sometimes survived, for example in the extended correspondence between Maud Selborne and Violet Markham conducted during 1913. The surviving letters show that both these Victoria League members were earnestly searching for common ground between their conflicting views on the vote. Maud Selbourne was prepared to accept criticism of the 'wildly absurd' hopes of suffragists for a transformed world, and to agree that 'sound public opinion does more than voting power to improve things'. She also accepted the need to avoid 'sex antagonism' in politics, and recognized the value of womanly political influence (in which she was herself a practised expert). Her suffragist counter-arguments went no further than the assertion that 'men and women work together very well and do each other good, and this is just as true in politics as it is in home life'; she believed that 'influence and the vote would be more effective' than influence alone. Violet Markham must have appreciated her view that 'It is really the end we have in view which is the important thing', followed by a familiar litany of necessary improvement in women's lives.[96] The upshot of the correspondence was an agreement to cooperate in investigating the impact of women's enfranchisement in several American states. Other examples of cooperation between suffragists and anti-suffrage women appear in the history of organized anti-suffragism, for example the successful launch of Mary Ward's Joint Parliamentary Advisory Committee in 1914 in the wake of the NUWW suffrage split. Maud Selborne and other imperial suffragists were prominent in this venture, alongside a majority of anti-suffragists.[97] It seems very likely that their joint work for the female imperialist associations had helped to oil the wheels.

Many anti-suffrage women felt that the collective activities of female imperialism reflected their most fundamental beliefs. Imperial social action drew upon the well springs of maternal care, and bestowed an exalted public status upon the

---

[95] See e.g. M. Selborne, 'Imperialism and Motherhood', *National Review*, 63 (1914), 984–8.
[96] M. Selborne to V. Markham, 27 Feb., 1 Mar. and 11 July 1913. Markham papers, 26/30.
[97] See Ch. 9, below.

tasks of motherhood and cultural transmission which elevated these womanly responsibilities alongside the masculine achievements of empire. Imperialism combined gender difference and gender complementarity, enabling women to demonstrate both their feminine strengths and their interdependence with men in the performance of moral and racial duty. The issue of votes for women could sometimes seem trivial within this worldwide context. But more often the female franchise was viewed as a serious threat to the Empire, so that the cause of empire became a central motivating force within the anti-suffrage movement for both men and women. Female imperialist associations leant towards maternal education and reform, as they practised philanthropy on a worldwide scale. As this chapter has demonstrated, masculine authority was assumed to have forged the Empire, and most anti-suffragist women were content to operate under its shadow and its inspiration. Their pride in imperial achievement was linked to still greater hopes for the united British Empire of the future. No doubt these outstanding women consciously or unconsciously pursued personal fulfilment as they served the Empire, but the compatibility of their personal and imperial ambitions provided anti-suffragism with some of its finest leadership. In the heat of imperial enthusiasm, there seemed no reason to doubt that men and women were destined to work smoothly together to defeat the threatened imposition of votes for women. Both male and female leaders believed that there were good prospects of rallying wider public support for anti-suffragism on the strength of the imperial cause. The following chapters will investigate the extent to which such hopes were fulfilled, before being ultimately frustrated by the suffrage victory.

PART II
WOMEN'S ANTI-SUFFRAGISM IN ACTION

6

The Women's Appeal and After

ORIGINS OF THE 1889 APPEAL

Organized opposition to women's suffrage lasted almost as long as the suffrage movement itself, from the first collective attempts to rally parliamentary opponents in the 1870s through to the final days of debate over the Representation of the People Bill in 1918. By definition, anti-suffragism was a reactive movement which waxed and waned in response to the successes and failures of the suffrage campaign. But the organized opposition was also founded upon widely held gender beliefs which had developed over time and in broader social and political contexts, and therefore did not simply disappear during the periods when collective campaigning became dormant. Previous historical narratives have recounted the successful defeat of the first parliamentary suffrage efforts of the late 1860s and early 1870s, followed by an anti-suffrage revival linked to the extra-parliamentary Women's Appeal of 1889, then (after a mysterious gap) the climax of organized opposition through the anti-suffrage Leagues of 1908 and 1910.[1] The present study revisits these events from the perspective of women participants, whose major involvement began in the late 1880s and continued directly or indirectly throughout the following three decades. The high-water marks of 1889, 1908, 1910, and 1917–18 continue to define the landscape of anti-suffrage activism, but in this account the emphasis is upon the continuous contours of extra-parliamentary opposition rather than upon its episodic nature. Various ideological and associational continuities have already been suggested through an exploration of the provenance of women's anti-suffrage views. In the chapters which follow, many of the same women will reappear as committed organizers and supporters of the extra-parliamentary campaign against the vote.

The continuities which link together the organizational milestones of anti-suffragism include a number of recurrent problems, as perplexing at the end as at the beginning of the campaign. How could an extra-parliamentary movement make its impact felt upon parliamentary decision-makers? How could women supporters exert their influence without contradicting their own abstentionist

---

[1] See B. Harrison, *Separate Spheres: The Opposition to Women's Suffrage in Britain* (London: Croom Helm, 1978); M. Pugh, *The March of the Women* (Oxford: Oxford University Press, 2000); C. Rover, *Women's Suffrage and Party Politics in Britain* (London: Routledge and Kegan Paul, 1967).

beliefs? Above all, how should women leaders exemplify their own deep-seated faith in complementary gender roles during an organized campaign against the vote? The relations between anti-suffrage men and women were seldom straightforward. At every stage the demands of collective action revealed the tensions integral to a delicate balancing of gender roles within the opposition campaign. The history of organized anti-suffragism was characterized by ongoing and dynamic negotiations over the practice as well as the theory of gender difference. Both in terms of its ideas and its chosen paths of action, female anti-suffragism developed its own emphases from the 1880s onwards. At the same time women anti-suffragists remained fully committed to collaboration with men, as well as conscious that the outcome of their campaign rested in the hands of male politicians. The relationship between these diverse aspects of anti-suffragism will be investigated throughout the history of extra-parliamentary activism which began to unfurl in 1889: the year in which women anti-suffragists first voiced their collective viewpoint, and stood up to be publicly counted.

The Appeal Against Female Suffrage, published in the *Nineteenth Century* journal in June 1889, is generally acknowledged as the first key event of the anti-suffrage campaign. Its significance was greatly enhanced by the fact that the Appeal was supported by 104 well-known women, while the accompanying 'Women's Protest' eventually attracted over two thousand more female signatures.[2] Despite the unanimity among the historians over the Appeal's importance, there remains a need to reassess its meanings. Were women simply mobilized on this occasion to support a male anti-suffrage cause? This has been too readily assumed by many previous historians. A careful investigation of the organization, authorship, published support, and political aftermath of the 1889 Appeal suggests otherwise, and provides an appropriate backdrop to the revisionist account of the Edwardian anti-suffrage campaign which follows. This chapter will consider the parliamentary and extra-parliamentary contexts of the 1889 Appeal, before proceeding to a discussion of its arguments, its publicly declared female support, and its short-term and longer-term aftermath.

The origins of the 1889 Appeal can be found in many places. From the point of view of its female authors, women's maternal reformism and their related public service had already provided a seedbed for ideas about female citizenship, and a motivating influence towards collective action. The parallel development of suffragism owed much to the same source, offering an alternative strategic direction to the British women's movement as well as an influential tactical model. The Appeal was part of an ongoing debate, following suffragist precedents at the same time as marking a novel departure for the conservative opposition. By the late 1880s the New Woman had begun to make her disturbing presence felt within contemporary debates over gender roles. Meanwhile the accelerating

---

[2] 'An Appeal Against Women's Suffrage' was published in *Nineteenth Century*, 25 (1889), 781–8. Mass signatures followed in *Nineteenth Century*, 26 (1889), 353–84.

advance of 'civilizing' British imperialism was beginning to impinge upon the Woman Question as well as upon many other social and political dilemmas, adding an extra dimension of concern over national strength and moral worth to the multifaceted suffrage debate. Alongside these general contexts, it is necessary to note some relevant aspects of contemporary British politics and government. Though anti-suffragism was always more than a political cause, it was also just that: the timing of anti-suffrage peaks and troughs was inescapably tied to events in Parliament, as well as to suffrage campaigning and to the continuous evolution of conservative gender ideals in other arenas of national life.

In the early 1880s, both male and female anti-suffragists had considerable grounds for political optimism. Far from being a foregone conclusion, parliamentary assent to the enfranchisement of women seemed unlikely for the foreseeable future. After the first flurry of hopeful suffragist activity in the late 1860s and early 1870s, the anti-suffragists had achieved substantial success both in marshalling the parliamentary opposition and in giving public voice to weighty counter-arguments.[3] By the late 1870s some of the most frequently rehearsed Edwardian arguments against female suffrage were already becoming widely familiar.[4] Combined with party political pragmatism, they ensured that successive suffrage Bills went down to defeat throughout the 1870s and 1880s. Parliamentary reform legislation in 1884–5 further dashed suffragist hopes of seizing the democratic momentum, as Gladstone led his government into declared opposition to female suffrage whilst doubling the size of the male electorate. Soon after, the Home Rule crisis merely confirmed suffragism's lowly status in the order of parliamentary and party political priorities. In these promising political circumstances, no extra-parliamentary campaign against the vote seemed necessary.

There were various grounds for renewed anxiety and renewed anti-suffrage activism by the beginning of 1889. The creation of an enlarged electorate, combined with recent anti-corruption legislation, was accelerating the growth of party organization in the country; in turn, this depended on the electoral efforts of volunteers who included increasing numbers of women. The Conservative ladies of the Primrose League mostly saw themselves as exercising old-fashioned 'influence' rather than preparing the way for parliamentary votes for women, but the Women's Liberal Federation was being rapidly taken over by suffragists.[5] The reform of local government had enabled some women to vote in borough council elections, as well as to stand for election to School Boards and as Poor Law guardians. A much more significant slice of local government was now offered to women through the establishment of County Councils in 1888. Anti-suffrage women used local enfranchisement as an argument against the parliamentary

---

[3] B. Harrison, *Separate Spheres*, 114–15.

[4] e.g. the 'physical force' argument and the case for gender complementarity, rather than equality, were set out in J. Fitzjames Stephen, *Liberty, Equality, Fraternity* (London: Smith Elder and Co., 1873).

[5] The Primrose League was founded in 1883 and the Women's Liberal Federation in 1887.

vote, but the nominally apolitical Women's Local Government Society was another magnet for suffragists.[6] Meanwhile the late 1880s were also marked by growing public concern over levels of urban poverty, infant mortality, and maternal ignorance, as well as by dawning fears of the power of organized labour and the threat of socialism: 1889 was the year of the Great Dock Strike, as well as of the Appeal Against Female Suffrage. From a position of some complacency at the start of the decade, anti-suffragists both inside and outside Parliament found themselves moving towards an uncertain future. The threat of votes for women was inseparable from other social and political anxieties, and short-term political circumstances seemed suddenly to be moving in its favour.

Political expediency, rather than the efforts of organized suffragism or the more general advance of democracy, appeared to pave the way for a possible suffrage breakthrough in early 1889. The fifth franchise attempt in three years was before the House of Commons in April 1889, and Lord Salisbury was known to be taking discreet soundings over the electoral advantages of enfranchising an elite body of wealthy, Conservative-leaning women voters. It seems certain that this short-term political threat determined the eventual timing of the 1889 Appeal Against Female Suffrage. In April 1889 Frederick Harrison, soon to be a prime mover in the Appeal campaign, privately denounced 'that scoundrel S.' to a Liberal confidant, as well as admitting that 'the true cause is in great danger'.[7] Meanwhile James Knowles, anti-suffragist editor of the *Nineteenth Century* and Harrison's friend and publisher, was weighing up the journalistic as well as the political advantages of a bold intervention in the debate. Laurel Brakes has recently analysed the media history context which produced the 1889 Appeal and an accompanying spate of periodical articles on gender roles and the suffrage issue.[8] Clearly there were commercial as well as political incentives to publish, reflecting the rivalry among editors and the progression towards more popular and interactive forms of journalism in this period. However, the necessity for male support and the existence of masculine opportunism should not be allowed to obscure the proactive role played by women anti-suffragists in the 1889 controversy. Women, as well as men, feared the consequences of a female electorate in a period of social unease, expanding democracy, and fractured party politics.

Turning to the detailed evidence of women's involvement in the 1889 Appeal, we find Mary Ward already talking over the topic with James Knowles at a dinner party at the French Embassy in January 1889. A letter to Louise Creighton, dated 24 January 1889, provides the first intriguing glimpse of a joint male and female conspiracy. The dinner companions discussed the possibility of 'a

---

[6] The Women's Local Government Society originated as the Society for Promoting Women as County Councillors in 1888; it became the WLGS in 1893.

[7] F. Harrison to J. Morley, 13 Apr. 1889, BLPES, LSE, F. Harrison papers, 1/68.

[8] L. Brake, in A. Heilmann and M. Beetham (eds.), *New Woman Hybridities: Femininity, Feminism and International Consumer Culture, 1880–1930* (London: Routledge, 2004), ch. 3.

Manifesto against Women's Suffrage. He is very anxious for it, but thinks it must not be done except at exactly the right moment. He is to keep it in mind and communicate with me. Meanwhile he suggests that you and I should keep our eyes and ears open, and note down the names of as many sympathisers as we can. So please keep a little book, as I mean to do!'[9] A letter to her father, written two days earlier, tilted the balance of initiative slightly more in Mary's direction by implying joint decision-making over both production and publication: 'It was a large and amusing dinner. . . The Lord Justice was delightful, and Mr K. was entertaining. He and I concocted a women's manifesto against women's suffrage which we mean to launch when the critical moment comes!'[10] Neither letter proves conclusively who first proposed the 'manifesto'. Mary was at this time at the height of her early fame as the author of a controversial, best-selling novel. In January 1889 she was busy researching her *Nineteenth Century* response to Gladstone's critical commentary on *Robert Elsmere*, a task which gave her personal confidence and status in dealing with the journal's editor as well as demonstrating her willingness to engage in public debate.

Whether or not she originated the 1889 manifesto, Mary's later correspondence shows clearly enough how ready she was to seize the initiative as well as to collaborate. This point is worth emphasizing, for too many historians have assumed she was merely the instrument of her male anti-suffragist friends[11] and in some cases this conclusion has been extrapolated into a more general view of female anti-suffragism as sycophantic and devoid of independent ideas. Naturally suffragists enjoyed portraying the female opposition as tools of the male antis, but surviving contemporary evidence suggests a different balance. James Knowles offered an important publication opportunity and helped to organize the collection of mass signatures through his journal. Publication occurred in the context of male-dominated journalism and in relation to debates within an all-male Parliament. Yet the text of the original Appeal was primarily the work of women authors who wished to develop and share their own ideas, as well as to publicize the arguments of leading anti-suffrage men. A first planning meeting took place at Frederick Harrison's house. Ethel Harrison and her Positivist friend Emily Beesly were drawn into the inner circle of women signature-gatherers, but authorship rested mainly with Mary Ward and Louise Creighton. On 18 April Mary invited Louise to send 'a few notes of what you want said . . . I will add

---

[9] M. Ward to L. Creighton, 24 Jan. 1889. Pusey House Library, Oxford, M. Ward papers, 3/3.

[10] M. Ward to T. Arnold, 22 Jan. 1889. M. Ward papers, 2/2.

[11] See e.g. John Sutherland's account description of the Appeal as the 'brainchild' of male antis, and Mary Ward as their 'catspaw', in J. Sutherland, *Mrs Humphry Ward: Eminent Victorian, Pre-Eminent Edwardian* (Oxford: Oxford University Press, 1991), 199. Barbara Caine claims that 'Frederic Harrison organised Mrs Humphry Ward and others' into support for an Appeal 'ostensibly written and signed by women', in B. Caine, *Destined to be Wives: The Sisters of Beatrice Webb* (Oxford: Clarendon Press, 1986), 167. Martin Pugh describes a 'flattered' Mary Ward as an evident asset to male antis 'in connection with the petition of 1889 which they published under her name'. See Pugh, *March of the Women*, 149.

anything of my own that occurs to me, will do my best, and send the result back to you for criticism.' In the same letter she confided that 'I am not so sure that I see the matter quite as Mr Harrison does.' She did not 'altogether share' his 'semi-religious beliefs on the natural and necessary position of women', preferring to emphasize 'state expediency', or 'the probable public loss or gain' from women's suffrage.[12] Louise Creighton, with her devout Anglican faith, undoubtedly shared this distrust of Positivism, however sincere her own beliefs in special womanly qualities. In a letter to her sister on 23 May, she further complicates the evidence on authorship by claiming a leading role for herself in a mainly female enterprise:

One or two of my friends and I started the idea of organising an opposition to the extension of the suffrage to women. I have always been opposed to it, but I did not regard it as deserving serious attention until lately when various circumstances have combined to make it seem likely that Parliament might suddenly pass a bill granting female suffrage. I felt that we women who do not want it ought to speak out. So I set to work writing to people and consulting with them and as a result we have drawn up a sort of protest against female suffrage which is to appear in the *Nineteeth Century* journal for June . . . [13]

Mary Ward's more anxious correspondence probably conveys the most accurate picture of the Appeal's composition. On 18 April she contemplated the need for 'mutual accommodation' with the Positivists, but anticipated full agreement over the Appeal's content between herself and Louise Creighton. By 1 May she was struggling with a painful hand, as well as with difficult ideas: 'However I have written something but it is too long and too much in the style of an article'.[14] No further mention was made of the need for compromises, so it seems likely that the male sponsors of this venture happily accepted a version put together by the two leading women. The actions of Frederick Harrison and James Knowles in the aftermath of the Appeal show their awareness of the tactical advantages of an independent and distinctive women's anti-suffragism: it seems likely that they were prepared to relinquish a measure of editorial control in order to achieve it.

The preparation of the Appeal was incomplete until an impressive array of women could be persuaded to add their signatures. This was no straightforward matter. Surviving correspondence indicates that the delicate task of persuasion was left very much in the women's own hands. A formal committee for the purpose seems to have been considered, but rejected in favour of an informal division of canvassing among the leading women. 'The difficulty about names is indeed most serious', wrote Mary Ward to Frederick Harrison on 20 May.[15] In a separate letter to Ethel Harrison the same day, she confessed herself

---

[12] M. Ward to L. Creighton, 18 Apr. 1889. M. Ward papers, 3/3.

[13] L. Creighton to I. Koch, 23 May 1889. Lambeth Palace Library, London, L. Creighton papers, MSS3678/47.

[14] M. Ward to L. Creighton, 1 May 1889. M. Ward papers, 3/3.

[15] M. Ward to F. Harrison, 20 May 1889. F. Harrison papers, 1/113.

'much disheartened' before proceeding to a detailed discussion of individual signatories and a further allocation of canvassing duties.[16] Each woman was busy approaching her own friends as well as a selection of other women believed to be sympathetic. Wherever possible, personal networking was called into action, for example through Mary Ward's Oxford friends, Louise Creighton's Cambridge and Church connections, and the Positivists' more radical acquaintances. 'I have no better report to give than yours just received,' wrote Emily Beesly to Ethel Harrison, also on 20 May; 'It is extraordinary how timid people are—the men quite as bad as the women'.[17] However, Louise Creighton's report the following day was a little more encouraging: 'Here are the names I have got so far . . . Some people have been very tiresome, but on the whole they have been very cordial'.[18]

As with most such attempts, success depended upon achieving enough influential early signatures to encourage the reluctant to join a moving bandwagon. Lady Stanley of Alderley, as a pioneer of women's education as well as a senior aristocrat, gave much-needed impetus when she changed her initial refusal into an agreement to sign. Florence Nightingale's refusal, on the other hand, was a severe and unexpected disappointment. The women's correspondence presents clear enough evidence of the obstacles to signing, many of which had little to do with dissent from the Appeal's anti-suffragist views. Lady Arthur Russsell and Lady Grant Duff were 'afraid of embarrassing the Government'; Lady Hayter was 'afraid of making a split in the W(omen's)L(iberal)F(ederation)'; Lady Knutsford wrote 'clearly sympathising but Lord K. thinks it would not do for her to sign'.[19] As Ethel Harrison wrote retrospectively, 'the political ladies' were particularly 'shy of us when we made our little effort'.[20] Other women feared upsetting friends, or were inhibited by unexpressed fears of overstepping the bounds of feminine propriety. 'At first it looked as if we should get hardly anybody,' reported Mary Ward to her father: 'Everybody agreed but for various cross reasons wouldn't sign'.[21] Louise Creighton supported this picture of widespread, obstinately silent support with her claim that 'we could get any number more [names] if there was no need to think about the possible fame of their owners'.[22]

Because of the large number of refusals, it would be wrong to assume that the 104 women whose signatures were eventually published alongside the Women's Appeal were necessarily all first-choice candidates. The organizers seem to have been aiming for 'political ladies', and others bearing well-known names associated with social status or their husbands' achievements, as well as for a minority of

[16] M. Ward to E. Harrison, 20 May 1889. BLPES, LSE, E. Harrison papers, 3/1.
[17] E. Beesly to E. Harrison, 20 May 1889. E. Harrison papers, 3/1.
[18] L. Creighton to E. Harrison, 21 May 1889. E. Harrison papers, 3/1.
[19] M. Ward to E. Harrison, 20 May 1889. E. Harrison papers, 3/1.
[20] E. Harrison to J. Bryce, 26 June 1890. Bodl. Bryce papers, 8/26 B77.
[21] M. Ward to T. Arnold, 2 June 1889. M. Ward papers, 2/2.
[22] L. Creighton to E. Harrison, 21 May 1889. E. Harrison papers, 3/1.

women whose own achievements had brought fame and social recognition. Both Millicent Fawcett and Emily Davies later sneered at this emphasis upon 'wives of famous men'.[23] However, it was consistent with anti-suffragist beliefs about women's role within marriage to attribute weight to such signatures. Female distinction should not necessarily be construed individually, but could also be achieved through successful complementarity within marriage. A wife providing feminine support to a distinguished husband rightfully shared in his distinction and social status. Certainly the aim was to attract 'women whose names are likely to carry weight', as Louise Creighton put it.[24] One willing signatory wrote approvingly to Ethel Harrison: 'No-one can feel more strongly than I do the importance of letting it be known that a certain number of cultivated, intelligent, active-minded gentlewomen feel the utter inadvisability of extending the franchise to women . . . One wants a strong, rather than a numerous, list of signatures, I think'.[25]

Similar emphases upon social hierarchy, indirect female political influence, and the status conferred by successful matrimony continued to characterize female anti-suffragism into the twentieth century. So, too, did the 1889 Appeal's reliance upon women's existing social networks as a source of organized support. The Oxbridge connection helped to supply Mary and Louise with the signatures of Charlotte Green (wife of T. H. Green), Georgina Max Muller, Alice Green (wife of J. R. Green), Charlotte Toynbee and Lucy Soulsby, as well as Mary Seeley and four other Cambridge ladies. Louise's contingent of 'Church women' (as Mary Ward described them to Ethel Harrison) included Mrs Boyle of The Deanery, Salisbury, and Mrs Church, of The Deanery, St Paul's, as well as Lavinia Talbot and several leading women from Worcester, where Mandell Creighton was a Cathedral canon. The Positivists' labour movement connections presumably helped to bring in Mrs Henry Broadhust, wife of the trade union leader. Beatrice Potter's reasons for signing the Appeal have been discussed in Chapter 4, and may well have included her friendship with both the Harrisons. Family groups were a particularly useful source of networked support for the anti-suffrage cause. Mary Ward rejoiced in the signatures of Churchill wives, whose opposition was bound to weigh with Lord Salisbury as well as lending social prestige to the Appeal. Lady Frederick Cavendish was another prestigious recruit, alongside her sisters Meriel and Lavinia Talbot, and her sister-in-law Lady Louisa Egerton. Sisters Louisa Baldwin (wife of the future Prime Minister) and Agnes Poynter (wife of the society artist Edward Poynter) signed, along with Miss Frances Poynter and the wife of another well-known artist, Laura Alma-Tadema. Mary Ward's own

---

[23] See E. Davies, quoted in B. Stephen, *Emily Davies and Girton College* (London: Constable, 1927), 348; M. Fawcett, 'Women's Suffrage: A Reply', *Fortnightly Review*, 46 (1889), 126: 'The names of very many are chiefly known through those of the distinguished men who have fought the battle of life for them'.

[24] L. Creighton to I. Koch, 23 May 1889. L. Creighton papers, MSS3678/47.

[25] J. Ilbert to E. Harrison, 20 May 1889. E. Harrison papers, 3/1.

family stood divided on the suffrage issue, but she was able to produce signatures from her aunts, Mrs W. E. Forster and Mrs Matthew Arnold.

Evidently the process of composing the Appeal and gathering the necessary public display of female support was time-consuming and difficult. The organizers' correspondence shows that it made heavy demands upon them, sometimes requiring repeated personal visits rather than merely persuasive letters. Refusals to sign were often due to extraneous causes, but presumably all the women who made the more difficult choice of adding their signatures to the Appeal were genuinely committed to supporting its anti-suffrage message. The female relatives of some well-known male antis participated, though many did not. It certainly seems to have been easier for socially conservative women to refuse rather than to agree to join in this rather novel form of protest. Yet ultimately many women did sign. It is therefore worth examining the Appeal's message in some detail, since it provides both direct and indirect evidence of the political outlook of its women authors and of their first wave of women supporters.

WHAT THE APPEAL SAID

The Appeal Against Female Suffrage consisted of a five-page reasoned statement of opposition, followed by the names and short addresses of the 104 signatories. It was accompanied by an invitation from the Editor to women readers to sign and return a separate sheet headed 'Female Suffrage: A Women's Protest'. The Protest, which elicited two thousand more signatures published in the August edition of the *Nineteenth Century*, summarized female suffrage as 'a measure distasteful to the great majority of the women of the country—unnecessary—and mischievous both to themselves and to the State'. In this message of his own—a mere postscript to the main Appeal—James Knowles attempted to lure his women readers with a combination of alarmism and exaggerated sympathy for their feminine reticence. Silence might be interpreted as 'indifference or consent', thus inadvertently contributing to the 'public danger' of a female franchise. Therefore even those who 'entirely object to mixing themselves up in the coarsening struggles of party political life' must step forward 'for once, and in order to save the quiet of Home life from total disappearance'.[26]

This mixture of threats and blandishments is in interesting contrast to the more dignified tone of the Appeal authored by Mary Ward and Louise Creighton. In 1889 Mary was not only enjoying the literary and financial success of *Robert Elsmere*, but was also attempting to follow through the religious and social principles explored in her novel. Letters to her father during the year of the Women's Appeal reveal that her current preoccupations ranged from the

---

[26] J. Knowles, introductory paragraph to 'Female Suffrage: A Women's Protest', *Nineteenth Century*, 25 (1889), 788.

demands of her busy social life to her reflections on the nature of social service and its relationship to religion. In the spring of 1889 she was researching biblical criticism for the *Nineteenth Century* whilst simultaneously planning towards a new novel of social concern; within a year her response took the more practical form of plans for her University Hall settlement. Louise Creighton, her closest collaborator in the authorship of the Appeal, was also becoming steadily more involved in various forms of social action during this period, alongside the demands of family life. It is not surprising to find that the text of the Appeal reflected these women's commitment to female social service, rather than merely echoing the negative arguments of leading male anti-suffragists.

The first section of the Appeal opened with an immediately positive assertion: 'Whilst desiring the fullest possible development of the powers, energies, and education of women, we believe that their work for the State, and their responsibilities towards it, must always differ essentially from those of men'. The case for equal political rights for women was then dismissed. On the one hand, women were excluded by natural disability, 'or by strong formations of custom and habit resting ultimately upon physical difference', from 'the hard and exhausting labour' of national government, foreign affairs, military action, and industrial production. Women's indirect interest in such matters was already proportionately reflected in their indirect political influence, which would enlarge 'more and more as the education of women advances'. On the other hand, 'we are heartily in sympathy with all the recent efforts which have been made to give women a more important part in those affairs of the community where their interest and those of men are equally concerned'. Women were able to exercise 'judgement . . . weighted by a true responsibility' as voters and members of local bodies responsible for the sick, the insane, the treatment of the poor, the education of children, and other matters: 'To sum up: we would give them their full share in the State of social effort and social mechanism; we look for their increasing activity in that higher State which rests on thought, conscience and moral influence; but we protest against their admission to direct power in that State which *does* rest upon force'.[27] Never had the 'physical force' argument been expressed in more attractive terms to a female audience, with only a brief mention of women's inferiority in unsuitable roles, but an abundance of encouragement to develop more appropriate and character-forming 'public usefulness'.

The next section of the Appeal juxtaposed these rosy prospects with the threats which the parliamentary suffrage posed to women's moral influence. Inherently feminine qualities of sympathy and disinterestedness would be 'seriously impaired by their admission to the turmoil of active political life'. Qualities which constituted 'the peculiar excellencies of women', when employed to influence politics indirectly, might lead towards 'a national calamity' if given free rein within the parliamentary political arena. Political partisanship 'would

[27] 'An Appeal' (1889), 781–2.

tend to blunt the special moral qualities of women, and so to lessen the national reserves of moral force'. Women's patriotism must seek appropriate expression through other channels than those of party politics and parliamentary government. The Appeal set out in the clearest possible terms its authors' conviction that women's importance to national life was not thereby diminished: 'Citizenship lies in the participation of each individual in effort for the good of the community. And we believe that women will be more valuable citizens, will contribute more precious elements to the national life without the vote than with it.' The section which followed explained the damage which a female franchise would inflict upon the nation and upon women themselves. The issue of enfranchising married women presented 'grave practical difficulties'. Their exclusion would admit only those women less versed in 'the practical experiences of life', among them some 'leading immoral lives'. Their inclusion, on the other hand, threatened to challenge 'the English conception of the household', posing a wholly disproportionate threat to family life and the nation which depended upon its success.[28] Readers of the Appeal were left in no doubt where patriotic as well as domestic duty lay.

The fourth section addressed 'the manner in which this proposal has won its way into practical politics'. A momentous social change was being proposed for quite the wrong reasons, and on the basis of insufficient knowledge. In the first place, 'the mass of those immediately concerned in it are notoriously indifferent; there has been no serious and general demand for it'. Public debate had been inadequate, and many pledges of support had been given for the sake of short-term political advantage; all this, at a time when 'masses of new electors' had not yet been fully assimilated and trained to exercise their votes. The Appeal played cleverly upon fears of advancing democracy, linking this widely shared concern to a plea for stability in political and family life as well as to shaming references to party political opportunism. In 1889, the lack of 'serious and general demand' for female suffrage seemed incontrovertible.

The final section of the manifesto moved on to address the suffragists' claim that the female franchise was essential to the redress of women's legal disabilities: 'We reply that during the past half century all the principal injustices of the law towards women have been amended by means of the existing constitutional machinery'. This process of successful reform had been undertaken by a male Parliament acting under womanly influence, which in turn had been enhanced by 'those advances made by women in education, and the best kind of social influence, which we have already noticed and welcomed'. No doubt the Appeal's authors were referring mainly to middle-class voluntary work in philanthropy and public administration at this point, as well as perhaps to extra-parliamentary influence upon such legislation as the 1882 Married Women's Property Act and the 1883 Repeal of the Contagious Diseases Acts. There was also a fleeting

[28] Ibid. 783–4.

reference to the needs of working-class women in the same paragraph. Parliament could be relied upon to listen to the needs of all women, but in relation to 'the business or trade interests of women' it would be 'safer and wiser to trust to organisation and self-help on their own part, and to the growth of a better public opinion among the men workers'.[29] This somewhat optimistic prescription represented a coded message to those suffragists who distrusted trade unionism and opposed restrictive industrial legislation apparently designed to protect male jobs rather than women workers' welfare.

The concluding paragraph returned to the Appeal's most fundamental message: 'Nothing can be further from our minds than to seek to depreciate the position or the importance of women. It is because we are keenly alive to the enormous value of their special contribution to the community, that we oppose what seems to us to endanger that contribution'. The Appeal condemned 'mere outward equality with men' as thoroughly bad for women themselves, leading to 'a total misconception of woman's true dignity and special mission'. In place of 'struggle and rivalry', women and men should combine to contribute 'the best gifts of each to the common stock'.[30] The more progressive arguments of female anti-suffragism were succinctly summarized here. Male anti-suffragists had played a central part in framing the case for the constitutional defence of gender 'difference' during the 1870s and 1880s, often overshadowing praise for women's 'special mission' with an extended analysis of their political deficits. But in 1889 Mary Ward and her colleagues adjusted the emphasis of familiar anti-suffrage arguments by drawing upon their own experiences of the 'special mission' in action. Through expanding education and womanly work in the community, as well as in the realms of middle-class family life, women were proving themselves more valuable to British society than ever before. An alternative, truly feminine citizenship beckoned, offering all the rewards of appropriate patriotic service without the divisive social dangers threatened by female suffrage.

FOR AND AGAINST THE APPEAL

The publication of the Women's Appeal in June 1889 produced a flurry of activity among both its supporters and its opponents. 'It is extraordinary how little people have really thought the matter out,' Louise Creighton wrote to her sister a few weeks earlier; '. . . I hope that we may at least succeed in making them think'. She also commented apprehensively that she was expecting 'a perfect storm of opposition' and 'much abuse after the appearance of our manifesto'—some of it from her many suffragist friends.[31] At this stage she probably did not anticipate being at the forefront of the second round of public debate.

---

[29] 'An Appeal' (1889), 784–5.   [30] Ibid. 785.
[31] L. Creighton to I. Koch, 23 May 1889. L. Creighton papers, MSS3678/47.

Predictably, the leading suffragists were quick off the mark in responding publicly to the Appeal. Millicent Fawcett and Emilia Dilke wrote their 'Reply' for the July edition of the *Nineteenth Century* journal.[32] Their vehemence suggests that the original article had caused some alarm in suffrage circles, raising serious concerns over its possible impact upon politicians and the wider public. Both women placed heavy emphasis upon their own faith in female 'difference'. 'We cannot as a nation allow such a potent moral influence as that of women to lie fallow', wrote Emilia Dilke.[33] Millicent Fawcett protested still more strongly: 'We do not want women to be bad imitations of men; we neither deny nor minimise the differences between men and women. The claim of women to representation depends to a large extent on those differences. Women bring something to the service of the State different from that which can be brought by men'. Her alignment of suffragist and anti-suffragist ideas ended at this point. For she not only insisted that effective representation of female difference must include direct parliamentary representation, but also indulged in an ill-tempered attack upon the 'condescension' of the Appeal and the credentials of its signatories. Most of those who had signed were 'ladies to whom the lines of life have fallen in pleasant places'. They were not qualified to speak for those who 'earn their living by daily hard work'; and, equally important in view of the Appeal's welcome for recent reforms, neither were they amongst those who had 'moved purse, tongue or pen in support of those changes before they became accomplished facts'. The majority of social reformers and supporters of women's education were to be found in the suffrage camp. More temperately, Mrs Fawcett conceded that political opportunism should not be allowed to determine the question of votes for women, but otherwise ridiculed the view that women needed to be spared from the 'turmoil of political life'. Another point of concession was her admission that the question of married women's suffrage was a divisive one. She herself was opposed to this step, in deference to traditional views on marriage as well as because of its numerical impact. Perhaps unintentionally, she made clear her own distrust of the new mass electorate through her comments on the anti-suffragist signatories as 'employers of labour': 'It cannot be seriously argued that the means of making an intelligent choice between voting for this candidate or that, is not as much within the reach of women of education and property as within that of their footmen, ploughman or other employés'.[34]

A second, more detailed suffragist onslaught upon the Appeal appeared in the *Fortnightly Review* a few weeks later, accompanied by a triumphant list of more than five hundred suffragist signatures (out of two thousand received). Though unsigned, this article's acerbic tone and close similarity of argument

[32] M. Fawcett and E. Dilke, 'The Appeal Against Women's Suffrage: A Reply', *Nineteenth Century*, 26 (1889), 86–96 and 97–103.
[33] Ibid. 101.   [34] Ibid. 88, 89, 96.

suggest that Millicent Fawcett was again the key author. Every claim in the Women's Appeal was forensically dissected, further ridicule heaped upon its authors, and further protestations made of the suffragists' dedication to womanly 'difference'. The heavyweight suffragist response clearly called for self-defensive measures from the Appeal's supporters. Eliza Lynn Linton published one of her familiar broadsides in the *National Review* of July 1889,[35] but Frederick Harrison and James Knowles turned to Beatrice Potter as the female anti-suffragist most likely to produce a truly effective counterblast. Their role as sponsors, rather than authors, of the Appeal is underlined by Harrison's letter to Beatrice, which included veiled criticism of its content: 'There is needed something more full, more sympathetic and more definite than the Appeal'. To their disappointment, she turned them down, citing her wish to 'keep out of the controversy' and uncertainties over her own status and grounds of argument.[36] Louise Creighton soon proved a powerful replacement. Again at the request of Harrison and Knowles, she interrupted her family holiday to write a full-length 'Rejoinder' for the August edition of the *Nineteenth Century*.[37] A letter to her sister proves that she did so single-handed: 'It was very tiresome for I had [been] so out of it all being away and time was so short that I wrote my article in one day. However Mr Harrison is most tremendously delighted with it, so I can feel rewarded for the effort I made'.[38]

There were grounds for his delight, both in her deft response to key suffragist arguments and in her fuller exposition of women's special qualities in private and public life. Louise Creighton turned criticism of the relative 'obscurity' of the Appeal's signatories on its head by claiming that it made them more representative of British womanhood as a whole than suffragism's distinguished supporters. Anti-suffragism celebrated those women who provided 'service to society' in humbler ways, through quiet reforms, practical effort, and the raising of families; their views were as valid as those of a suffragist movement in which 'none but the accredited leaders may speak'. Despite the credentials of the suffragists, female suffrage was by no means synonymous with female education: 'it is possible that a more healthful stimulus to women's education might be given by a larger conception of their duties to society and to the State than is involved in giving them the franchise'. Women did not require the vote in order to fulfil their wide range of existing responsibilities, which included public service in local government, as well as participation in trade unions and the co-operative

---

[35] E. L. Linton, 'The Threatened Abdication of Man', *National Review*, 13 (1889), 577–92.

[36] See B. Webb, *My Apprenticeship*, ii (London: Pelican Books, 1938), 401.

[37] L. Creighton, 'The Appeal Against Female Suffrage: A Rejoinder', *Nineteenth Century*, 26 (1889), 347–54. I have found no evidence to support John Sutherland's claim that 'Using Louise Creighton as her front-woman, Mrs Ward delivered a hammer-blow "Rejoinder" ', Sutherland, *Mrs Humphry Ward*, 198. The timescale seems to preclude this, and moreover the emphases of the article are entirely consonant with Louise Creighton's own views on womanhood, as expressed in her other publications.

[38] L. Creighton to I. Koch, 4 Aug. 1889. L. Creighton papers, MSS3678/48.

movement: 'The present organisation of society offers an abundant field for the energies of women. The fields are white for the harvest and the reapers are few'. Moreover, prioritization of female suffrage offered 'a wrong ideal to women'. The enfranchisement solely of unmarried women would reinforce the dangerous idea that marriage was an obstacle to 'the real work for their sex and for society at large'. The alternative was for women to 'be content to continue working side by side with men, possessing their own duties and their own opportunities . . . The present need is that women should do their own work better'. Reprovingly, Louise hoped suffragists would 'believe that we value as much as they do the true progress of women'. Finally, she returned to the issue of womanly influence. Women were responsible for 'the keeping of a pure tone in society, of a high standard in morality, of a lofty devotion to duty in public life', and these must not be risked for the sake of the 'wild will-o'-the wisp of political power'. Taking up Emilia Dilke's metaphor of voteless women as eager listeners excluded from a concert hall, Louise concluded by asserting that 'women who, not content with what they have, still demand the franchise, are like those who . . . stand within the concert hall but cannot hear the music'.[39]

Louise Creighton's article was fully consonant with the original Appeal, but more polemical in tone. It combined defence of feminine reticence in parliamentary politics with the strongest possible assertion of women's worth and potential in public as well as private life. Still less than the original Appeal did it dwell upon women's weaknesses and inadequacies as parliamentary voters. Despite their delight at this highly persuasive outcome, it seems inconceivable that Harrison and Knowles would themselves have led the argument in quite the same direction. The impact of the article was increased by the fact that it appeared in August 1889 alongside publication of the two thousand signatures collected in response to the June Appeal and Protest. These signatures offer an interesting contrast to the suffragist list published in the *Fortnightly Review* the previous month.[40] Whilst the suffragists presented a well-marshalled list, grouped under different categories of supporter and with professional, high-achieving women to the fore, the anti-suffrage list was apparently unedited, apart from the prioritization of titled ladies (in order of aristocratic precedence). The 'obscure' of all ranks certainly predominated.

It is apparent that the anti-suffrage list was the outcome of a request for postal signatures, rather than of targeted canvassing. Yet local canvassing had certainly taken place, judging from the large number of signatures clustered by location. This seems to indicate that a proportion of the anti-suffragist women felt strongly enough to make an effort to rouse the support of friends,

---

[39] Creighton, 'A Rejoinder', 347, 348, 349, 352, 353, 354.

[40] *Fortnightly Review*, 46 (1889), 132–9. The suffragist list included ten separate categories of signatories, beginning with a General List (headed by titled ladies and including Mary Ward's sister, Ethel Arnold) and concluding with Working Women (amongst them 65 pit-brow women, famous for their well-publicized resistance to protective legislation).

family, neighbours, and, in some cases, female servants. Thirteen Somerset signatures are listed together; nineteen from Windermere; twenty-six from Cheltenham; eighteen from Ventnor, Isle of Wight; thirteen from Fulneck, Leeds; seventeen from St Leonards on Sea (including six from Pevensey Road). Mrs Sydney Buxton of 15 Eaton Place signed ahead of four untitled women with different surnames at the same prestigious address, presumably her female workforce. Central and suburban London produced large numbers of signatures, but so too did many small town and villages. Large industrial cities were represented, but not numerously. There is no evidence of any substantial, independent representation of working-class women. A promising sign for the eventual organization of local anti-suffragist support on a national basis was the wide geographical spread of the signatories. Though southern England predominated overall (as it did within the later anti-suffrage Leagues), there were signatures from most parts of England and also some from Scotland and a few from Wales and Ireland, as well as a sprinkling from Europe and even India. Identification of educational or occupational status was not sought for the anti-suffragist list, but was sometimes implied by addresses. Clerical wives were present in noticeable force; many Board School and some High School teachers chose to identify themselves; and Lady Margaret Hall, Oxford and Girton College, Cambridge were represented by eleven and twelve signatures respectively.

The breadth of support for the 1889 Women's Appeal was striking, both at the time and in retrospect. The fact that it was not immediately followed by the launch of a continuous organization dedicated to the defeat of women's suffrage should not surprise us, however. The somewhat random manner in which the signatures were assembled reflected not merely the lack of a pre-existing anti-suffrage association, but also the uncertainty and political inexperience of the oppositionists. As well as being inexperienced, most had no desire to engage in any kind of organization for political ends. To a greater or lesser extent, they shared the anti-suffragist women leaders' vision of existing womanly work and influence which would be undermined by competing priorities. As Louise Creighton explained in her eloquent article, 'The influence which we value in women could not be organised, and it is being put into action every day'.[41]

THE AFTERMATH OF THE WOMEN'S APPEAL

The immediate aftermath of the Appeal suggests that it had struck home successfully. As early as 2 June, Mary Ward reported triumphantly to her father that 'for this Parliament I believe the matter is settled'. The basis for her optimism

---

[41] Creighton, 'A Rejoinder', 354.

was the eventual strength of the first list of published signatures, including as it did both leading Conservative and leading Liberal wives as well as many other 'good names'.[42] The strength of the suffragist response was further evidence of a job well done. Millicent Fawcett later claimed that 'The anti-suffrage protest of 1889 had the effect which similar protests have ever since had of adding to the numbers and the activity of the suffragists'.[43] But Ray Strachey's sympathetic history of suffragism tells a different story: 'the damage had been done, and a new argument was presented to the other side. "Women themselves don't want the vote," they could now say; unfortunately it was partly true.'[44]

The Appeal's arguments, as much as the subsequent evidence of its mass support, represented a very significant intervention in the parliamentary and public debate over suffragism. As well as drawing upon earlier writings and debate, its authors had succeeded in inflecting anti-suffragism with new, more positive emphases designed especially to appeal to female public opinion. The Appeal helped to motivate Millicent Fawcett's insistent efforts to appropriate female 'difference' to the suffrage cause from the late 1880s onwards,[45] as well as being directly referred to by many distinguished male antis in their speeches and writings.[46] It also found an echo in Gladstone's important anti-suffrage statement of April 1892. In a published letter, the Prime Minister noted that 'in addition to widespread indifference, there is on the part of large numbers of women who have considered the matter for themselves, the most positive objection and strong disapprobation', before proceeding to weigh up female competence and the potentially damaging effects of women's suffrage upon 'the relations of domestic life'.[47]

The language of the Appeal resonated through the suffrage debates of the following two decades, providing a link with the organized anti-suffrage movement which developed from 1907 onwards. The Women's National Anti-Suffrage League was launched in 1908 with the help of a retrospective *Nineteenth Century* commentary from Mary Ward on change and continuity since 1889.[48] However, there is no evidence that she even considered leading an extended anti-suffrage campaign in the 1890s. Her commitments to writing and to social

---

[42] M. Ward to T. Arnold, 2 June 1889. M. Ward papers, 2/2.

[43] M. Fawcett, *Women's Suffrage* (London: T. C. and E. C. Jack, 1912), 46.

[44] R. Strachey, *The Cause* (1928; London: Virago, 1978 edn.), 285.

[45] See B. Caine, *Victorian Feminists* (Oxford: Oxford University Press, 1992), 222; also S. Holton, *Feminism and Democracy* (Cambridge: Cambridge University Press, 1986), 13–15.

[46] e.g. G. Smith, 'Woman's Place in the State', *The Forum*, 8 (1890), 515: 'A protest from some of the foremost women of England . . . relieves a male writer of the fear that he may be actuated by selfishness of sex in arguing against a female claim'. Goldwin Smith had been an important anti-suffrage writer since the 1870s.

[47] 'Female suffrage: a letter to Samuel Smith MP, 11 April 1892', reprod. in J. Lewis, *Before the Vote Was Won: Arguments For and Against Women's Suffrage 1864–1896* (London: Routledge and Kegan Paul, 1987), 444, 446.

[48] M. Ward, 'The Women's Anti-Suffrage Movement', *Nineteenth Century and After* (1908), 343–52.

action were all-absorbing, while further campaigning did not yet seem necessary. Paradoxically, new proposals for extra-parliamentary organization seem to have come mainly from male supporters of the Appeal who had far less faith than its female authors in the collective power of women. The leading women's responses provide further evidence of the interplay of male and female agency. During the signatures campaign, Frederic Harrison had tentatively proposed a standing committee of anti-suffragists. Mary Ward reacted cautiously, suggesting that an ad hoc committee with a paid secretary would have more success in attracting 'a good many people we may still get . . . without being deterred by the prospect of having to do much personal work afterwards'. She felt that success depended upon having 'at least 20 or 25 good and representative names';[49] and eventually, as we have seen, the idea was shelved in favour of a more informal approach drawing upon existing female social networks.

Soon after, another male anti-suffragist took up the idea of an anti-suffrage organization. James Bryce was a well-known figure in academic and political life: an Oxford Professor of Civil Law from 1870 till 1893 and a Liberal MP from 1880 onwards, as well as holding Cabinet office under Gladstone in the 1890s and later becoming British ambassador in Washington. His extensive correspondence included most of the male and female leaders of anti-suffragism, including Louise Creighton and Ethel Harrison from 1889 onwards, and Mary Ward from 1893 until the conclusion of the campaign. Undoubtedly these women were flattered by his interest in their cause, and anxious to cooperate with a distinguished and friendly politician who valued their role within anti-suffragism. However, their response to his organizational suggestions was distinctly lukewarm. On 30 June 1889, Louise Creighton wrote that 'It has seemed for some time as if we should be obliged to contemplate some such organisation as you propose'; she was 'ready to do my part', but expected the work to centre on London and not begin until the autumn. The *Nineteenth Century* organizers and signatories were a starting point, and her experience in Cambridge and Worcester suggested widespread support from 'very many obscure people'. Yet there would be advantages in a fresh start, since 'we should certainly do better without two members . . . namely Mrs Stuart Glennie and Mrs Lynn Linton'.[50] Ethel Harrison was only slightly more enthusiastic when the proposal for a women's committee was revived by James Bryce a year later. She sent him an annotated list of possible names, accompanied by a summary of the problems encountered during the previous summer's campaign: 'It is very difficult to move in the matter. But as I said I will help you as much as

---

[49] M. Ward to F. Harrison, 20 May 1889. F. Harrison papers, 1/113.

[50] L. Creighton to J. Bryce, 30 June 1889. Bryce papers, 8/20 B53. Mr Stuart Glennie was the author of a vituperative anti-suffrage letter published in the *Fortnightly Review* in Apr. 1889, and his wife may have shared his negative views.

I can'. She felt that a drawing room meeting offered the best opening gambit, 'at your own home—or in some other well-known drawing room'. But again there was a caveat. Ethel felt that 'It would be well to begin by finding out how many of the original protesters would join a society'; her own preference was for a fresh start inspired by 'a good article . . . from a man political or otherwise'.[51]

Louise Creighton's correspondence with Bryce in the summer of 1890 offers a rather different perspective on the situation. A letter written on 25 July suggests that she herself was beginning to take up active organization, just as his interest in an anti-suffrage society was waning. 'Would you be willing to allow the first drawing room meeting about the Anti F. Suffrage Ass. [*sic*] to take place in your house?' she enquired, suggesting early November as 'the right time to meet'. Hoping for a decision before his imminent departure for America, she sketched the probability of a 'comparatively small and informal' gathering, and urged him to 'put down the names of any persons whom you think should be asked to this meeting; we ought to have men as well as women'.[52] The tried and tested technique of personal invitations to friends and acquaintances would be used to bring the gathering together. Louise cannot have been happy with James Bryce's response, for only three days later she wrote again protesting that 'it will not do to have this preliminary meeting about an Anti Female Suffrage League without you'. Those present would want to hear from him 'how such a League has worked in America' (an interesting first reference to the transatlantic influences which later helped to shape Edwardian anti-suffrage organization). Moreover women would only support the new initiative if it was demonstrably needed to 'strengthen the hands of the politicians'. The remainder of her letter outlined other doubts and uncertainties, which were rapidly sapping her own enthusiasm for the scheme. Mary Ward was unavailable, while Ethel Harrison was 'not at all keen about the League'. Louise Creighton was determined to avoid meeting at the Harrisons' house again in any case, because to do so meant 'the world might say we were inspired by the positivists'. Convinced that success depended upon a degree of male advice and support, she was nevertheless convinced that 'if the League is to be started it must be a woman's league and be managed by women'. Its launch would be an uphill effort, since 'In itself I should think it must be hateful to most of us, as it offers no inducements to those women who love agitating; for to agitate against a change has no charm'. She described her own position as unpromising, since she was 'in no sense political, and have my hands full of other things'.[53] Evidently the necessary reassurances were not forthcoming, for this was her last letter to Bryce on the subject.

[51] E. Harrison to J. Bryce, 26 June 1890. Bryce papers, 8/26 B77.
[52] L. Creighton to J. Bryce, 25 July 1890. Bryce papers, 8/20 B53.
[53] Ibid. 28 July 1890. Bryce papers, 8/20 B53.

It seems likely that most women anti-suffragists of this period shared Louise Creighton's mixed feelings about the desirability of an extra-parliamentary campaign. Despite widespread opposition to the vote, there were divisions among the leading women. Despite these women's proven willingness to voice their own views, and some initial success in using existing female social networks to mobilize support for anti-suffragism, there remained an acknowledged and willing dependence upon male collaborators. Working alongside like-minded men was an issue of anti-suffrage principle, as well as a matter of practical necessity in a campaign which aimed to influence the decisions of Parliament. Yet even the most sympathetic male collaborators were already proving unreliable allies. There was also the perennial problem of a logical distaste among conservative women for any form of collective action on behalf of a parliamentary cause. More progressive anti-suffragists, on the other hand, were deterred by the campaign's apparent negativity. Only extreme political urgency could ignite enough enthusiasm to overcome these varied obstacles; yet in the early 1890s the suffragist threat in Parliament once more appeared to be receding. For the Appeal's women supporters, the time had not yet come when anti-suffrage committee work deserved priority over more rewarding and constructive activities.

The years between the 1889 Appeal and the launch of the Women's National Anti-Suffrage League in 1908 were nevertheless marked by other kinds of anti-suffrage continuity. There were persistent parliamentary attempts to introduce female suffrage legislation, despite Government apathy or opposition. An unexpected Commons majority for a Private Member's Bill in 1897 provided the most visible warning since 1870 of slowly shifting political opinion. Mary Ward roundly condemned MPs' opportunism on this occasion in a letter to her father, but remained optimistic over the lack of genuine parliamentary support for suffragism.[54] Meanwhile the suffrage campaign in the country provided constant reminders of the issues involved, as it made slow but steady headway during the 1890s. Equally important, from the perspective of anti-suffragism, was the public prominence of the wider Woman Question throughout this period. Though they did not form an anti-suffrage League in response, the women who had led the 1889 Appeal remained active commentators upon the changing position of women and the nature of female citizenship. Their views can be read in various publications of the period, as we have seen in earlier chapters, and were also manifested through their public service. It would certainly be surprising to find a complete absence of continuity in the development and expression of female anti-suffragism, given the growth of suffrage organizations, the extensive literary and media interest in the New Woman, and the gradual acceleration of social and political changes affecting women's lives as the century ended. Historians have reached varying conclusions about the strength of the suffrage

---

[54] M. Ward to T. Arnold, 7 Feb. 1897. M. Ward papers, 2/2.

cause during the 1890s. Ray Strachey's depiction of 'the phase of discouragement'[55] influenced several later accounts,[56] but has since been substantially revised by David Rubinstein's lively account of women's history *Before the Suffragettes*,[57] as well as by Jill Liddington and Jill Norris's research into the origins of radical suffragism among women textile workers.[58] Martin Pugh's detailed analysis of parliamentary progress led him to conclude that the 1890s were 'the decade of breakthrough for the suffragists'.[59] There is certainly clear evidence of a regrouping and strengthening of extra-parliamentary suffrage support from 1897 onwards, preceding the launch of the Pankhursts' campaign in 1903.[60] The leading anti-suffrage women may have been largely unaware of the details of suffrage activism, but they moved in circles where the position of women was under continuous debate. Without forming a specific organization for the purpose, many anti-suffrage women remained stalwart defenders of traditional womanhood in a variety of public and private contexts throughout the 1890s and early 1900s.

The closing years of the nineteenth century provided spectacular evidence of the growing significance of empire to Britain's future prospects in the world. Here was another arena of public debate where supporters and opponents of votes for women refined their own views and sought to influence their contemporaries. Though the suffrage issue did not predominate within the discourse of women imperialists, strongly held views on gender roles permeated both male and female visions of the imperial future. Meanwhile the womanly work of family duty and social action in the community remained the universal pole of respectable middle-class femininity, and an influential ideal across the entire social spectrum. Anti-suffragists and the more conservative suffragists equally recognized its importance to their cause, and from 1895 onwards the suffrage issue was periodically debated within the NUWW. At the turn of the century women experienced both a broadening of opportunities for voluntary social service, and the advance of new economic and educational openings which would eventually compete with voluntarism for their time and commitment. Local government expanded, while national government began to encompass legislation which would determine the future contours of social welfare. Anti-suffragists who had supported the 1889 Appeal slowly adjusted their political outlook in response to these changes. Some women, including Louise Creighton and Beatrice Webb, made a gradual, reluctant transition towards acceptance of the parliamentary

[55] Strachey, *The Cause*, 285.

[56] e.g. A. Rosen, *Rise Up Women! The Militant Campaign of the Women's Social and Political Union 1903–1914* (London: Routledge, 1978).

[57] D. Rubinstein, *Before the Suffragettes: Women's Emancipation in the 1890s* (Brighton: Harvester Press, 1986).

[58] J. Liddington and J. Norris, *One Hand Tied Behind Us: The Rise of the Women's Suffrage Movement* (London: Virago, 1978).

[59] Pugh, *March of the Women*, 3.   [60] e.g. the launch of the NUWSS in 1897.

franchise as a necessary precondition for an enhanced female involvement in public life.[61] Others, including Mary Ward and Ethel Harrison, found their anti-suffrage views strengthened by social and political change. It took the arrival of a reforming Liberal government, and the associated phenomenon of suffragette militancy, to end the dormant period of anti-suffrage organization and to bring these women's deeply felt convictions back to the centre stage of British politics.

---

[61] Louise Creighton explained her 'conversion' (announced to the NUWW in 1906) as related to her growing recognition that women were becoming increasingly sucked into party politics without 'the responsibility of the vote'. Creighton, *Memoir of a Victorian Woman*, ed. J. Covert (Bloomington: Indiana University Press, 1994), 146. Beatrice Webb wrote a public letter to Millicent Fawcett in Nov. 1906, explaining that she now accepted the unavoidable and ever-increasing overlap between women's social obligations and the work of government. Webb, *Our Partnership* (1948; (Cambridge: Cambridge University Press, 1975), 363).

7

The Women's National Anti-Suffrage League

A WOMEN'S LEAGUE

The Women's National Anti-Suffrage League was launched in July 1908 to counter a new and highly credible threat of imminent female enfranchisement. Led by women acting in consultation with anti-suffrage parliamentarians, it existed independently for only two years before announcing its prospective merger with the Men's League for Opposing Woman's Suffrage in August 1910. By this date the WNASL had formed over a hundred local branches, published leaflets and a monthly journal, and assembled hundreds of thousands of signatures for an anti-suffrage petition to Parliament. A sympathetic Prime Minister had recently opened his doors to its representatives and encouraged them to continue voicing women's opposition to the vote. By the summer of 1910 the League was also beginning to organize its own local government activities so as to underline the existence of positive alternatives to the parliamentary franchise. There can be little doubt that the WNASL entered the 1910 merger from a position of some strength, despite its growing financial problems and a pressing need for stronger parliamentary influence. Men were never entirely excluded, but its female leaders and members had largely succeeded in creating an organization in their own image. The WNASL developed upon the basis of anti-suffrage views and traditions of female activism which extended back to the 1889 Appeal, and was closely integrated with flourishing networks established through conservative women's work for other causes. Tensions between male and female anti-suffrage leaders during and after the 1910 merger show the importance of understanding the WNASL as a women's organization, before weighing up the successes and failures of the merged National League for Opposing Woman Suffrage between 1910 and 1918. Its short history exemplifies the aims and methods which women later tried so hard to transfer into the larger, mixed-sex League.

When Mary Ward steeled herself to take up the tasks of mass campaigning once again, her confidence rested upon past experience as well as the urgency of the present moment. She believed that her long-established anti-suffrage arguments were more relevant than ever and had high hopes of galvanizing old friends as well as drawing in new women supporters. Yet she was also aware of social and political changes which had driven some of her former colleagues into the opposing camp, as well as creating a situation where the threat of a suffragist victory was more immediate than ever before. Her continuing hopes for an anti-suffrage victory rested upon her conviction that most women were unconvinced on the franchise issue, and under-informed about its threat to traditional gender roles. She was also heartened by the support of a new generation of women leaders, alongside members of the 1889 old guard. Almost all the female leaders of Edwardian anti-suffragism were mobilized by the WNASL, and most were more active during the two years of its existence than they were within the successor League presided over by Lord Cromer and Lord Curzon.

The new generation of antis included enthusiastic imperialists as well as social reformers, and many women who combined both these motivations with their dislike of suffragism and their defence of womanly difference. Some women supported Mary Ward's aim to set the more progressive and constructive aspects of anti-suffragism within a broader programme of female public service. They believed women's social usefulness could be enhanced through their growing role in local government and perhaps also through future constitutional innovations granting them an expert role in public affairs whilst safeguarding them from damaging involvement in party politics. The most adventurous thinking within the WNASL was to be devoted to these possibilities. However, the League also had its female reactionaries who baulked at any proposals extending beyond direct opposition to women's suffrage. The policy disputes which later developed within the NLOWS had their origins within its predecessor, and cannot simply be attributed to unsympathetic male leadership. A study of the WNASL should evaluate its organizational tactics as a manifestation of women's political thinking as well as a reflection of current social and political circumstances. But first, the scene must be set for the resumption of anti-suffrage collective action in 1908.

NEW BEGINNINGS, 1906–1908

In 1908, as in 1889, the women's decision to act related to their fear that Parliament was lurching carelessly towards an irrevocable commitment to the female franchise. An unexpectedly large pro-suffrage vote by the House of Commons in 1897 was privately condemned by Mary Ward as 'disgraceful', 'ridiculous', and 'the most cynical thing you ever heard';[1] but it angered rather than alarmed her, since she put the result down to pure opportunism and believed good sense would rapidly reassert itself. There were no other suffrage majorities during the period from 1870 to 1904, despite persistent efforts from both Houses of Parliament.[2] Nevertheless, with hindsight it appears that the parliamentary

---

[1] Mary Ward to Thomas Arnold, 7 Feb. 1897. Pusey House Library, Oxford, M. Ward papers, 2/2.
[2] See Rover, *Women's Suffrage*, 218–23 (Chart of Major Parliamentary Events). In 1884 a vote on whether leave should be given to bring in a suffrage bill was won, with a majority of 21.

progress of suffragism was continuous. Following strong support for Sir Charles McLaren's suffrage resolution in 1904, there were seven further attempts to commit Parliament to the principle of women's suffrage over the next three years, culminating in an alarming majority of 179 for a second reading in February 1908. Moreover, as Brian Harrison demonstrates, the turnout of Members for suffrage debates began to rise from 1904 onwards, signifying that the issue was moving up the parliamentary agenda; the suffragist proportion of the total vote had been slowly rising since the 1870s.[3] Martin Pugh further develops the case for a long-term growth of parliamentary support, but also highlights the impact of the 1906 Liberal election victory.[4] A built-in majority for female suffrage existed in the House of Commons from this point onwards, while the new cabinet included several members strongly committed to suffragism. Even the replacement of the suffrage-leaning Campbell-Bannerman by the decidedly hostile Asquith in 1907 provided little comfort for the antis, for the new Prime Minister hinted at the possibility of a general electoral reform bill including a women's suffrage amendment even as he refused government support for the 1908 proposals.[5]

A period of alternating hope and frustration opened for the supporters of women's suffrage. No stronger incentive could have existed for active extra-parliamentary protest to force the issue. The improving parliamentary prospects for suffragism were one major reason for the formation of the WNASL, but contemporary developments in the extra-parliamentary suffrage movement were almost equally important. The National Union of Women's Suffrage Societies had been joined in 1903 by the Women's Social and Political Union, with its charismatic Pankhurst leadership and headline-grabbing tactics of militant protest. As the first suffragettes went to prison in 1905 and 1906, Millicent Fawcett hailed their courage and paid tribute to their political impact.[6] Before long, moderate suffragists were making their own public mark, with a large-scale Wimbledon by-election campaign in April 1907 and mass demonstrations in February and October. A colourful procession of 25,000 women made its well-publicized way through the London streets in June 1908, drawing together contingents from multiple professions, from working-class women's organizations, and even from the staid National Union of Women Workers, as well as from political and suffrage societies from across Britain and beyond.[7] In 1903 the National Union of Women's Suffrage Societies had twenty-five affiliated societies; by 1908 this had risen to sixty-four, with approximately 8,000 members. These totals more than doubled during the two years of the Women's League's independent existence.[8] The escalation of militancy during 1908–9 eventually distanced the Pankhurst and Fawcett leaderships from each

---

[3] B. Harrison, *Separate Spheres*, 118.   [4] Pugh, *March of the Women*, 3, 152.
[5] Rover, *Women's Suffrage*, 64, 193–4.
[6] See M. Fawcett, *What I Remember* (London: T. Fisher Unwin, 1924), 184–8.
[7] NUWSS leaflet, 1913. LMA, NUWW papers, ACC/3613/3/1/B.
[8] Pugh, *March of the Women*, 254.

other, at the same time rousing unprecedented levels of indignation among anti-suffragist women. Meanwhile the fact that moderate suffragism was also benefiting from hugely increased media coverage provided an additional source of anger and alarm. It was inevitable that women antis would try to emulate their opponents' successes, as well as to tar all suffragists with the militant brush. The WNASL represented a determined attempt to move beyond private lobbying and published protest out into the propaganda mainstream. A mass assault on public opinion over the suffrage question was already under way, and there was no time to be lost.

Despite the urgency of the anti-suffrage cause by this date, it remained very difficult for the anti-suffrage women to opt for collective commitment to a public campaign. Problems which had been raised in 1889 and 1890 still held sway in the Edwardian years. Many conservative women felt a genuine aversion to public speaking and to public protest of any kind, whilst others feared upsetting friends and relatives, or their husbands' careers. Even those active within social or educational reform, or the related work of constructive imperialism, had often internalized a commitment to female reticence and female altruism which rested uneasily alongside their growing confidence in women's gendered public work. The anti-suffrage campaign demanded uncomfortable levels of self-assertion and the diversion of personal effort away from more conventional duties. It is perhaps not surprising to find that the WNASL had a relatively slow take-off, and that a number of less demanding alternatives were explored by anti-suffrage women during the two years preceding its launch. This period of nascent campaigning is of some historical interest as it introduces us to a wider circle of the women who eventually joined the League, as well as illustrating the hesitancy even of such veterans as Mary Ward and Ethel Harrison. It also reintroduces the complicated subject of relations between leading men and leading women within organized anti-suffragism. As in 1889, supportive men had an important role to play in encouraging women to organize public opposition to the vote. But the anti-suffrage women expressed their own beliefs and often preferred to make their own organizational decisions.

The pre-history of the WNASL began with an escalation of well-established anti-suffrage activities. For example, there had been sporadic debate on the suffrage issue within the National Union of Women Workers at least since 1895, when the first (non-voting) conference discussion took place.[9] During the Union's 1906 conference, when Louise Creighton joined with Millicent Fawcett and Kathleen Lyttelton in support for maternalist suffragism, other members of the anti-suffrage minority spoke up with renewed energy for their cause. Lucy Soulsby demanded to know 'why women should be taken away from their present

---

[9] See Ch. 3, above, and *Women Workers: The Official Report of the Conference held at Nottingham, 1895* (Nottingham: James Bell, 1895). Anti-suffrage speakers in the 1895 debate included Mrs Henry Sandford (an 1889 Protest signatory), Louise Creighton, and Frances Low.

very important work to go out and to vote', while Mrs Cohen pointed out that 'they might, without votes, apply themselves to the discovery and application of the laws governing philanthropy'.[10] The public expression of opposing views was already becoming an increasingly pressing obligation for anti-suffragists as well as suffragists, and during the next two years several women took to print in a renewed effort to put their case across. Marie Corelli's *Woman, or Suffragette? A Question of National Choice* (1907) demanded vehemently 'Shall we sacrifice Womanhood to Politics? . . . Surely the best and bravest of us will answer No!—ten thousand times no!'[11] This patriotic defence of feminine moral influence and vigorous condemnation of the suffragettes was soon to be advertised from the pages of the *Anti-Suffrage Review*. Meanwhile a concerned male supporter of women's suffrage wrote privately to the secretary of the London Women's Suffrage Society urging a riposte, since 'Marie Corelli . . . is very much somebody as a *writer*, who is *read*, and she has received considerable attention from the critics'. Soon after, he noted that 'The pamphlet is simply littered all over London, and I know not elsewhere . . . no such hostile effort as that by MC should be allowed to circulate by hundreds of thousands and to pass, unchallenged'.[12]

In April 1908 Emily Simon, of Birmingham, published a more reflective anti-suffrage pamphlet under the title *Positive Principles for Anti-Suffragists*, drawing direct contrasts between the suffragists' emphasis upon political power and the anti-suffragist emphasis upon 'the extension of women's influence and activity in all those departments of social and national life where there is a real need for it'. Her conclusions were a call to arms for those women who soon after became supporters of the WNASL and its forward policy.[13] Ethel Harrison, whose ill health reinforced her reluctance to engage in organized activism, also set pen to paper during 1908 with a comprehensive restatement of her anti-suffrage views which emphasized the national importance of women's domestic duties and supported their extended service within local communities. Her book, provocatively titled *The Freedom of Women*, led with the argument that women's mass opposition to the vote must be brought to the foreground of the debate. Suffragists had hitherto 'made the capital blunder of despising the opinions of the women who are against them. For it is these women who hold the fort, who refuse the vote, and block the way.'[14]

The adoption of military metaphors by anti-suffragist women writers revealed their growing sense of the dangers of ladylike abstention from the fray. Other

---

[10] *Handbook and Report of the NUWW of Great Britain and Ireland* (London: NUWW, 1906).

[11] M. Corelli, *Woman or Suffragette? A Question of National Choice* (London: C. Arthur Pearson, 1907), 3.

[12] Ernest Pack to Secretary, Women's Suffrage Association (NUWSS), 19 Apr. and n.d. 1907 Women's Library, London Society for Women's Suffrage papers, 298/3.

[13] E. M. Simon, *Positive Principles for Anti-Suffragists* (Birmingham: Cornish Brothers, 1908), 12. Mrs Simon wrote at least two other anti-suffrage pamphlets in 1907–8.

[14] E. Harrison, *Freedom of Women*, 8.

women sent their views to the national press. The Woman Question had seldom been absent from the monthly literary journals during the previous two decades, but in 1907 two significant new contributors appeared. Caroline Stephen, a well-known religious writer and philanthropist, and one of a family of distinguished scholars, published an anti-suffrage manifesto in the *Nineteenth Century and After*, 'on behalf of a great though silent multitude of women'. She argued that women could no longer avoid the suffrage controversy with its inseparable links to 'the much larger and deeper problem of the right general position of women'.[15] Her advocacy of women's maternal attributes was expressed in familiar terms, but strengthened by her fervent insistence upon the importance of harnessing the finest womanly attributes to the service of the nation. By January 1909, she was proposing the creation of a Women's Council from the pages of the *Anti-Suffrage Review*.[16] Early in 1908 Edith Massie published 'A Woman's Plea against Woman Suffrage' in the *National Review*. Though a much less weighty piece, it is of interest as a woman's summary of less flattering reasons why women should not be given the vote. Both physique and temperament disqualified them from the responsibilities of imperial rule: 'In the distribution of the world's work it is an intelligible and consistent principle that public concerns should be directed by men and domestic concerns by women'.[17] Edith was the wife of John Massie, the Mansfield College theologian and Liberal MP who soon after became Treasurer of the WNASL. Her article provided an appropriate supplement to his House of Commons speech in March 1907, later published as an anti-suffrage leaflet, which advocated women's self-organization against the imposition of the franchise.

Meanwhile a sequence of newspaper letters had begun to prepare the way for the Women's League in more concrete terms. On 29 October 1906 Edith Milner wrote to *The Times* expressing her outrage at suffragette militancy: 'I feel that I am voicing the sentiments of many hundreds of thousands when I say I am satisfied with my present position, and with my almost unlimited powers of usefulness, and that I have no need of a solitary vote, and should not use it if I had it'. This forthright Yorkshirewoman was a mainstay of both the Charity Organization Society and the Primrose League, and highly conscious of her class as well as her gender duty.[18] Two months later an anti-suffrage letter from Frances Low set out the case for women's principled opposition to the vote, which she contrasted favourably with 'apathetic indifference'.[19] Her confidence in the shared interests of men and women was strengthened by her fears of sex antagonism, her awareness of women's powers of influence, and her distrust

---

[15] C. Stephen, 'Women and Politics', *Nineteenth Century and After*, 61 (1907), 227, 228. See Ch. 2, above, for further comment on her maternalism.

[16] *Anti-Suffrage Review*, 2 (Jan. 1909), 7–8. See Ch. 9, below, for further discussion of this proposal.

[17] E. Massie, 'A Woman's Plea Against Woman Suffrage', *National Review*, 63 (1908), 383.

[18] *The Times*, 29 Oct. 1906, 10.   [19] *The Times*, 27 Dec. 1906, 9.

of widespread female ignorance. As a professional journalist, she had already condemned female meddling in public affairs in an excoriating review of the International Council of Women's 'Talking Congress of Ladies', published in 1899.[20] Her intemperate language on this occasion and others related to her own difficult personal circumstances. The 1901 census reveals a servant-less spinster household in London, shared with her schoolteacher sister,[21] and Frances's subsequent anti-suffrage writings make clear her bitter resentment of a life of enforced wage labour, which she juxtaposed with frivolous suffragist aspirations towards a life beyond domestic confines.[22] Within the WNASL, she soon became an outspoken critic of the forward policy. However, her 1906 letter to *The Times* had positive results, for it prompted responses from three other women which eventually paved the way for the largest anti-suffrage women's petition since the famous 1889 Appeal and Protest.

First Beatrice Duff endorsed 'every word', suggesting that 'if a paper embodying the sentiments thus put forth was sent round the country, it would be signed by hundreds and hundreds of the best and most intelligent women'.[23] 'A Woman Graduate' forecast on the same day that female suffrage would soon lead to a majority female electorate and women's entry to Parliament; faced with this alarming prospect, opposition was widespread 'not only . . . amongst stupid, ill-educated, ultra-domestic, or obstinately conservative women, but also amongst those who take a deep and practical interest in the future welfare both of their own sex and of the community in general'.[24] Soon after, a more influential voice was added, as Sophia Lonsdale joined the discussion. The unmarried middle-aged daughter of a canon of Lichfield cathedral, and an active philanthropist, educator, and Poor Law guardian, she possessed the resources and self-confidence which Frances Low lacked.[25] 'I am quite sure that we are in an overwhelming majority,' she wrote; 'I have lived in this small town for forty years and I believe I know every woman of education in the place, and I hardly know one who is in favour of women's suffrage'. She then ventured to propose 'a short petition to the Prime Minister', to be 'circulated for signature all over the Kingdom . . . I would gladly subscribe to the expense of getting this done.'[26] Five weeks later Sophia announced that 'a small committee of ladies' had drawn up their anti-suffrage

[20] F. Low, 'A Woman's Criticism of the Women's Congress', *Nineteenth Century*, 46 (1899), 192–202

[21] Her sister was Florence Low, author of the 'The Reading of the Modern Girl' (see Ch. 4, above).

[22] See F. Low, 'Principal Childs on Woman Suffrage: a Rejoinder', *The Hibbert Journal* (Oct. 1910), 163–8; also *Press Work for Women: A Textbook for Young Women Journalists* (London: L. Upcott Gill, 1904).

[23] *The Times*, 11 Jan. 1907, 6.   [24] Ibid.

[25] See V. Martineau, *Recollections of Sophia Lonsdale* (London: John Murray, 1936), and S. Lonsdale, *The English Poor Laws: Their History, Principles and Administration* (London: P. S. King and Son, 1897).

[26] *The Times*, 15 Jan. 1907, 11.

petition and appointed a secretary. Their intention was 'to collect, in the quietest and speediest manner possible, the signatures of the many women whom they believe to be in sympathy with them'. Having decided against holding unladylike public meetings, they were heavily reliant upon the combined influence of newspaper publicity and women's existing social networks. At the launch of the WNASL the following year Lady Haversham reported that an impressive 37,000 signatures were assembled by these methods within the following fortnight: an achievement which dwarfed support for the 1889 Appeal and Protest.[27]

Suffragists were amongst those impressed by the revival of organized female opposition. The archives of the London Women's Suffrage Association include some rather anxious correspondence between Edith Harrison, Frederic Harrison's suffragist sister, and Miss Sterling at the suffragists' headquarters. In response to a direct enquiry, Miss Harrison reported a conversation with her anti-suffragist sister-in-law, who had naturally been invited to sign the petition, adding reassuringly that Ethel 'does not seem to anticipate much success for the anti-suffrage cause, because "people are so supine!"'[28] However, amongst those who had already been roused to protest was the key figure of Mary Ward. During the petition campaign *The Times* published the first of what later became a flood of anti-suffrage letters from this source. Addressed to Ermine Taylor, 'hon. secretary of the Women's Anti-Suffrage Movement', her letter was prefaced by an explanation of her own reluctance to take action. Only the urgency of the situation had driven her to write. In the next paragraph she set out her record of support for the advance of women in higher education, professional training, and local government—'I can hardly be thought to be expressing mere old-fashioned prejudice'—before arguing the case for a distinction between women's roles in local and imperial government. In the former, women were 'fully competent to take a practical part'; in the latter, 'this is not so, simply because women are women, and their work in the world is different from that of men'. Apart from making this familiar case and adding equally familiar warnings against adult suffrage, Mary Ward went on to suggest that working-class women would be particular victims of female suffrage since democracy would threaten protective industrial legislation without any compensating impact upon wages. More original, and less purely reactive, were her comments on two other issues which eventually loomed large within the history of the WNASL. Without making any definite proposals at this stage, she asked whether women might find alternative, more effective channels of communication with Parliament in the future without joining in the masculine business of voting: could the Parliamentary committee system be adapted, or could 'some way be devised' to give female local government representatives a stronger constitutional voice? In

[27] *The Times*, 22 July 1908, 14.
[28] E. I. Harrison to Miss Sterling, 20 Feb. 1907. London Society for Women's Suffrage papers, 298/3.

her concluding paragraph, Mary drew attention to the achievements of American anti-suffragism, soon to become her key exemplar of conservative success: 'In America, I believe, as soon as the women's suffrage movement became dangerous, the common sense of the community practically put an end to it'.[29]

The hesitancy of Ethel Harrison and Mary Ward to lend their experienced support to the fledgling anti-suffrage organization was understandable enough, and certainly shared by the women who had initiated the 1907 petition. Already a variegated mix of extreme traditionalists and idealistic reformers, they had plenty of more congenial occupations and no clear campaign strategy. It seems likely that three main factors eventually propelled them towards the launch of the Women's League the following year. In the first place, there is some evidence of masculine encouragement, including the parliamentary encouragement which of course was a vital ingredient of worthwhile anti-suffrage organization. A number of leading editors were enthusiastic antis, privately consulting with the anti-suffrage women as well as publishing their letters. These included Moberly Bell of *The Times*, whose widow eventually served for a period as secretary of the National League for Opposing Woman Suffrage; St Loe Strachey of the *Spectator* (a friend of Violet Markham and Gertrude Bell); and Leo Maxse of the *National Review*, an influential imperialist whose wife was active in the WNASL, and who himself spoke at several of its meetings. Apart from John Massie, sympathetic politicians included the veteran Lord James of Hereford, who had helped to formulate the case against women's suffrage in the 1870s, and a group of Conservative MPs (among them, Michael Hicks-Beach and Ivor Guest). As early as April 1907, Edith Milner claimed confidently, in a letter defending the anti-suffrage petition, that 'the matter is now in the hands of a more experienced committee, including men as well as women'.[30] However, progress still seems to have been slow. In February 1908 a further series of letters from Frances Low appeared in the *Spectator*, emphasizing the need for stronger female leadership.[31] By the early summer of 1908, according to Lady Haversham's account, a ladies' anti-suffrage committee had been formed with the direct encouragement of the parliamentary antis.[32] A 'confidential' proposal to form a 'National Women's-Anti-Suffrage Association' was next prepared, supported by a combined list of male and female signatories. The names of four peers and seven MPs lent ballast to the proposal, but the text of this document suggests considerable female input. The usual insistence upon womanly difference was accompanied by a paragraph on the 'admirable work' of women in local government, as well as by emphasis upon 'the importance of the sphere which specially calls for the care and devotion of a woman, namely, the home'.[33] The twenty women who signed the document

---

[29] *The Times*, 8 Mar. 1907, 11.   [30] *The Times*, 13 Apr. 1907, 8.
[31] *Spectator*, 1, 8, 15 Feb. 1908.   [32] *The Times*, 22 July 1908, 14.
[33] 'National Women's-Anti-Suffrage Association' undated circular to 'Dear Sir, or Madam' (marked by an archivist 1907–8). Women's Library, WNASL, 2/WNA 281.

were the leading female activists at this stage: alongside Miss Low, Miss Milner, Miss Lonsdale, Miss Taylor, and Mrs Simon, there appeared the names of Mrs Humphry Ward and two of her Oxford friends, and (a significant gain for the movement) those of Lady Jersey and a group of her fellow Conservatives and fellow imperialists.

A combined effort was now underway to form an anti-suffrage organization which would marshal women's large-scale opposition to the vote. This first document of the future WNASL promised 'to counteract the pretensions of a particular section of women to speak for their sex . . . to organise local branches affiliated to the central organisation, and to counter-balance the one-sided pressure of the suffragist party upon parliamentary candidates'.[34] Obviously such ambitions must be seen as a reciprocal response to the current advances in the British suffrage campaign. Suffragists were on the march, and Asquith had recently declared that he would have no principled objection to women's suffrage should it be proven that women themselves desired it. However, a third key influence upon the early history of the Women's League can be detected in the increasingly frequent contemporary references to American anti-suffragism.[35]

It is no coincidence that Mary Ward's first visit to America, from March to June 1908, immediately preceded her decision to commit fully to the work of the League. One of her letters home from Boston records, with tantalizing brevity, that she had 'tea with the anti-suffragists', as well as two encounters with Julia Ward Howe, a national leader of American suffragism.[36] It seems likely that Mary had many other opportunities for reflection upon the tactics as well as the principles of anti-suffragism, as she travelled through the cities of the eastern seaboard, then on through Canada to Vancouver and back. Her journey was framed around a schedule of lucrative public lectures on literary themes (profits to be devoted to her favourite philanthropic causes); but she was also eager for new knowledge and fresh inspiration, and returned full of both, as well as with her self-confidence bolstered by adulatory receptions and the attentions of leading figures in government and academia. Within weeks of her return she had completed *Diana Mallory* and embarked upon her anti-suffrage and anti-divorce novel *Daphne*, to be followed by the imperialist *Canadian Born*. However, the impact of her transatlantic experiences upon her political activity was still more immediate. She believed that in America a truly effective anti-suffrage campaign stood fully revealed and ripe for imitation: an organized

---

[34] 'National Women's-Anti-Suffrage Association'.

[35] Mary Ward was not alone in recognizing the potential relevance of American anti-suffragism to the British suffrage debate. Louise Creighton had noted the value of the American example as early as 1890 (in a letter to James Bryce, 28 July 1890, Bodl., Bryce papers, 53/133–5); John Massie invoked America in his Mar. 1907 anti-suffrage speech to the House of Commons; Mary Ward quoted from F. Foxcroft, 'The Check to Woman Suffrage in the United States', *Nineteenth Century and After*, 56 (1904), 833–41.

[36] Mary Ward to Humphry Ward, 28 and 30 Apr. 1908. M. Ward papers, 2/5.

movement led by educated, philanthropic ladies; using tried and tested ways of influencing politicians; boasting anti-suffrage journals and public propaganda; and promoting suffrage referenda which successfully demonstrated the true strength of male and female opposition. The launch of the WNASL was to be strongly coloured by Mary Ward's belief in the potential for similar activities in Britain. At last the women anti-suffragists seemed about to acquire the female leadership they needed.

THE LAUNCH OF THE WOMEN'S LEAGUE

On 12 June 1908 *The Times* reported with satisfaction that 'a counter-movement of considerable force' was being organized. A circular introducing a National Women's Anti-Suffrage Association had been composed by women 'entitled to speak by their knowledge of the wishes and capacities of their sex', and thousands of copies were being circulated 'chiefly among women'.[37] Mary Ward arrived back in Britain a few days later. Though she did not yet anticipate the full scale of her future commitment, she certainly lost no time in moving to the forefront of the new organization. On 28 June she wrote to her son, the Unionist MP Arnold Ward, 'Today I have been writing an Anti-Suffrage Manifesto!—and entertaining many people at tea'.[38] Two days later she was meeting with other anti-suffrage leaders at Lady Haversham's house,[39] and on the same day an important letter appeared in *The Times* summarizing the lessons she had learnt from American anti-suffragism. Challenging the view that success for the British suffrage movement was 'inevitable', Mary Ward claimed that 'the woman suffrage demand, which during the second third of the 19th century was active throughout the United States . . . is now in the process of defeat and extinction—and that not at the hands of men, but at the hands of women themselves'. Quoting from a recently received American account, she gave a reprise of women's organized anti-suffragism since the early 1880s. Grass-roots support was being mobilized by women 'of high character, often including some of the ablest and most influential in their section of the country'. She went on to summarize recent suffrage setbacks, concluding that 'the women of America . . . have defeated the woman suffrage movement. The same result has now to be achieved in England, and can be achieved, if only the women of this country will rouse themselves to the danger before us.' With typical boldness, she also asserted that the defeat of parliamentary suffrage should be accompanied by a strengthening of women's 'legitimate demand for such a share as rightly belongs to them in the public work and life of England': perhaps through a permanent committee of women on local

---

[37] *The Times*, 12 June 1908, 12.
[38] Mary Ward to Arnold Ward, 28 June 1908. M. Ward papers, 2/9.
[39] Ibid., 30 June 1908. M. Ward papers, 2/9.

bodies 'placed in some consultative relation with the Home Office and the Local Government Board'.[40]

The outlines of a constructive female anti-suffrage organization were already clear within Mary Ward's own mind, but to what extent would she succeed in spreading her vision among the other leaders of the WNASL, and thence to its rank-and-file supporters? On 21 July 1908 Margaret Jersey presided over a crowded launch meeting at the Westminster Palace Hotel. Lady Haversham's account of the League's origins explained that its 'moving spirit' had been suffragist pretensions to speak on behalf of the majority of women, together with 'the challenge from the Prime Minister calling upon women to show whether or not there was a demand for the franchise'.[41] Lady Jersey proposed and Ethel Harrison seconded the League's constitution. But the main speech of the day belonged to Mary Ward, who was responsible for introducing a Manifesto which she had also played a major part in writing. This document repeated the main points of the 1889 Appeal, but supplemented them with some new emphases and a call to action. The threat of 'a momentous revolution, both social and political' was countered by the possibility of repeating American anti-suffrage successes. A summary of reasons for opposing enfranchisement listed hardy perennials such as fundamental gender difference, 'physical force', the effectiveness of female 'influence', and the practical objections to various suffrage proposals. Supplementary arguments aimed at a mainly female audience outlined the enlarged sphere of public work already 'within their powers'; the possibility of strengthening this sphere through a 'closer consultative relation' between representative women and government departments; and redoubled emphasis upon the danger which women voters posed to the imperial nation state.

This speech was one of Mary Ward's most striking pieces of oratory. A torrent of emotion, as well as of well-marshalled argument, lent warmth and colour to the case set forth in the Manifesto and showed her awareness that the renewed campaign would be of a different character from the restrained intervention of 1889. Both her literary talents and her experience of large audiences in America stood her in good stead as she denounced suffragette law-breakers, exhorted anti-suffragists to devote 'Time, money, zeal' to the new movement, and denounced the threat to 'this "dear land of England"' of proposals to 'to embark alone of civilised States of the first rank, on the strange seas of Woman Suffrage'. Alongside the arguments of nation and empire, other causes particularly dear to Mary Ward made their way to the heart of her speech. Drawing upon her own experience of London schools and play-schemes, as well as upon an ideal vision of caring, maternal social influence, she declared that 'all sorts of powers are lying unused under the hands of women . . . meanwhile good brains and skilled

---

[40] *The Times*, 30 June 1908, 9.
[41] *The Times*, 22 July 1908, 14. Henrietta Haversham had chaired the original Women's Anti-Suffrage committee, prior to Margaret Jersey's assumption of office at the end of June.

hands are being diverted from women's real tasks to this barren agitation for equal rights with men . . . this sex rivalry, which has too often masqueraded as reform'.[42] Many aspects of the speech would certainly have won the unanimous support of both male and female anti-suffragists. Mary Ward had not only given new force to well-worn arguments, but also used her rhetorical powers to invoke her audience's underlying fears of gender subversion. Her sense of national threat connected with deeper contemporary anxieties than those provoked merely by suffragette militancy.

However, other aspects of her speech were less well attuned to the sympathies of the more conservative members of her audience. Her insistence that 'No member joining this League should be an idle member' would have jarred a little with those who retained a large measure of ladylike inhibition. As *The Times* commented in its supportive editorial on the launch meeting, 'The women who are opposed to the extension of the suffrage to their sex are by tradition and temperament particularly disinclined to make themselves prominent in a political cause'.[43] More fundamentally, a substantial number of the new League's leaders and supporters were unimpressed by Mary Ward's insistence upon the need for feminine public service within elected local authorities, and by her extension of this view into proposals for an enhanced advisory role for women within central government. A fault-line on these issues was already beginning to open up, dividing anti-suffrage women over an issue of principle as well as of tactics. Should the Women's League concentrate upon single-minded opposition to suffragism, or did it also represent the kernel of innovatory alternatives to the female franchise? How important was women's public work, as opposed to their domestic duties and private influence upon public affairs? Could hard and fast distinctions really be maintained, and in the future reinforced, between women's (suitable) community service within locally elected authorities and their (unsuitable) engagement with party politics and the business of national government?

Margaret Jersey's advantages as chair of the Women's League lay in her considerable social prestige and experience of women's organizations, but also in her ability to hold together potentially competing factions. Engaged herself in philanthropic and imperial social action, she was respected by the progressive supporters of what later became known as the forward policy. At the same time she was thoroughly at home in the inner circles of the Conservative party, and amongst its most conservative women. Lady Jersey's role as an intermediary is confirmed by two surviving, very private letters. In January 1909 Lord Cromer made one of his earliest contacts with the WNASL when he wrote to her confirming a Claridge's luncheon, arranged at his request, so that he could

---

[42] Mary Ward's speech was printed as a WNASL leaflet and within 'The Women's Anti-Suffrage Movement', *Nineteenth Century and After*, 64 (1908), 343–52.
[43] *The Times*, 22 July 1908, 13.

learn more about the internal affairs of the League before addressing one of its meetings. 'I had a glimmering of a split among the "antis"', he wrote, 'and that is one of the reasons why I should like to have a talk with you before I speak'. With a blithe confidence soon to be undermined by even more severe problems within the mixed-sex NLOWS, he added that, 'Personally I am rather in favour of encouraging women's works on municipal councils . . . On the other hand, "la vérité n'est pas toujours à dire", and I particularly want to say nothing to widen the split'. More ominously, 'so far as I can understand some of the Progressives . . . appear to me to have some rather wild ideas. We will talk it all over.'[44]

Later in the same year Margaret Jersey responded in a friendly manner to a suggestion from Violet Markham that the Women's League should commit more strongly to appropriate kinds of female public service. Despite the fact that Violet had already begun to speak from anti-suffrage platforms, she does not seem to have been closely involved in policy-making at this stage. Lady Jersey felt it necessary to inform her that 'Unfortunately from the very first . . . this question of a "Forward Policy" has been a bone of contention!' A number of leading members were already 'strongly in favour of some such policy as you describe. On the other hand Lady Haversham and Mrs Clarendon Hyde and others have been equal[ly] strong against anything of the kind.' She went on to confide:

Between ourselves one main reason which forced me into the Chairmanship—the last thing I desired—was the wish to keep the peace between these views, and to get the thing started *somehow*. If you will look at Constitution you will see that 1(b) *very* vaguely shadows forth some sense of an active as against a purely negative policy—this was the most which the 'negatives' would concede. I have refrained from taking sides as being the only method of keeping things going.[45]

The disputed second objective of the Women's League committed it to maintaining 'the principle of the representation of women on Municipal and other bodies concerned with the domestic and social affairs of the community'.[46] No doubt Mary Ward would have preferred a more specific commitment, but Margaret Jersey's explanatory letter makes it clear that the 'negatives' had successfully blocked further progress down this road during the first year of the League's existence.

Instead, the WNASL turned with considerable enthusiasm to the pursuit of its first objective, the defeat of female suffrage. The launch meeting in July 1908 was followed by a surge of positive press publicity. Escalating suffragette militancy soon lent further impetus, and during its first months

---

[44] Lord Cromer to Margaret Jersey, 11 Jan. 1910. LMA, Jersey papers, LMA/4195/001.

[45] Margaret Jersey to Violet Markham, 23 Sept. ?1909. BLPES, LSE, Markham papers, 26/30. The date of this letter is indecipherable, but the inclusion of a reference to Mrs Somervell as 'the present Hon. Sec.' indicates 1909.

[46] The objectives of the WNASL were reproduced in various official documents, and also in the *Anti-Suffrage Review*.

it seemed truly possible that the League would rouse anti-suffrage women in sufficient numbers to turn back the tide of suffragism. A combined sense of impending crisis and of positive achievement helped at first to hold together anti-suffrage women of diverse opinions, but the League's ultimate success depended upon its ability to mobilize a still more diverse female public. Before turning from planning to performance, and from leaders to followers, the history of the WNASL launch must be completed by a review of its first executive committee.[47] Clearly Mary Ward, the chief visionary of the anti-suffrage movement, was not going to be allowed to carry all before her. The committee's composition also suggests that it was unlikely to become merely an obedient tool of the male parliamentary antis. Its members included women of high ability and strong views, several of whom had already acquired experience of debating policy and practice within other women's organizations. Others had developed a confidence in their own opinions which derived from their privileged social status and (in some cases) from their husbands' membership of the political elite.

Margaret Jersey was a former president of the Ladies Grand Council of the Primrose League as well as current president of the imperialist Victoria League, and a leading society hostess.[48] Edith Massie, who became vice-chairman, was closely associated with her husband's career as a Nonconformist Oxford academic as well as a Liberal MP. Lady Haversham and Lady Weardale were the wives of undistinguished peers who supported the male anti-suffrage movement. Maud Hamilton was married to a distinguished Conservative politician who had been secretary of state for India from 1895 to 1903. Beatrice Chamberlain was another enthusiastic imperialist, a prominent figure in the Women's Tariff Reform Association as well as a mainstay of her brother's election campaigns and an active worker in philanthropy and education.[49] Ellen Countess of Desart, Mrs Simon, Nina Kay Shuttleworth, and Sophia Lonsdale were all active in philanthropy and attended the conferences of the National Union of Women Workers. Frances Low and Ermine Taylor had been leading figures in the 1907 anti-suffrage petition campaign. Mary Ward and Ethel Harrison need no further introduction. Elizabeth Burgwin had collaborated closely with Mary Ward in her work for London schoolchildren, and represented a genuinely strong link to local government. She had been the first woman executive member of the National Union of Teachers and was currently the first superintendent of London's special schools.[50] Gertrude Bell joined the executive alongside her old Oxford friend

---

[47] The names of the first executive committee were listed in *The Times*, 22 July 1908, and (with slight adjustments) in the *Anti-Suffrage Review*, 1 (Dec. 1908).

[48] See Ch. 5, above.

[49] Ibid. Her activities are considerably understated in P. Marsh, *Joseph Chamberlain: Entrepreneur in Politics* (Yale: Yale University Press, 1994).

[50] See R. Betts, 'Included or Excluded? Elizabeth Burgwin on the NUET/NUT Executive 1885–1896', *Journal of Educational Administration and History*, 34/2 (2002), 106–14; P. Horn,

and fellow student Janet Hogarth. Rather surprisingly, given the extent of her scholarly activities and her frequent world travels, she became its first secretary.[51] Her tenure of this post lasted for six months, after which she handed over to Edith Somervell, an 'educationist' and wife of a successful musician.[52] The executive was completed by the 'negative' Mrs Clarendon Hyde wife of a Liberal MP, and by John Massie in the traditionally male office of treasurer.[53] Whilst this array of executive members scarcely matched up to the subsequent fame of their suffrage equivalents, it would have been viewed by contemporaries as impressive in terms of breadth and reputation. It remained to be seen whether all the members would pull their weight, and whether they would pull in the same direction.

WOMEN LEADERS IN ACTION

The documents which introduced the Women's National Anti-Suffrage League to its potential supporters described how the new organization would be built. The League's preliminary statement proposed to 'organise local branches affiliated to the central organisation' and to counter suffrage pressure upon parliamentary candidates.[54] The launch manifesto confined itself to restating the anti-suffrage case, but Mary Ward's accompanying speech promised 'an efficient Central Office', 'a good and active Publication Committee', and 'branches throughout the country, who will take up with energy the work of local persuasion'.[55] MPs and the general public equally needed to be rescued from the snares of suffrage propaganda. Women's widespread opposition to the vote required an influential collective voice which would be supplemented by male opposition at the polls. The organization of male voters was largely a matter for men, while the work of branch-building and of counter-propaganda lay pre-eminently with the Women's League.

The inspiring transatlantic example of anti-suffrage leadership in action was never far from Mary Ward's thoughts. Referring to the women petitioners of 1889 in the American style as 'remonstrants', she insisted that more extensive and varied activity was now needed. Beyond the exercise of local pressure upon parliamentary candidates, the League had no immediate plans to shore up anti-suffragism in Parliament. Like their American equivalents, its leaders tended to underestimate the relative independence of central government between general

'Elizabeth Burgwin', in *Oxford Dictionary of National Biography* (Oxford: Oxford University Press, 2004).

    51 See Ch. 5, above.
    52 See J. Dibble, 'Sir Arthur Somervell', in *Oxford Dictionary of National Biography*, (2004).
    53 See I. Machin, 'John Massie', ibid.
    54 'National Women's Anti-Suffrage Association' (1907–8).
    55 Ward, 'The Women's Anti-Suffrage Movement', 347.

elections, and to overestimate the power of public opinion. The American anti-suffragists seemed to be holding back the tide within individual states mainly through the mobilization of mass public opposition.[56] Local 'influence', rather than the targeted lobbying of legislators, was seen as the primary task of the new British organisation. Though the leaders of the League were confident of latent mass support, its manifestation could not be left entirely to local effort. The notorious reluctance of anti-suffrage women to step forward into the political limelight needed to be countered by WNASL leadership initiatives, including a new national petition, a press campaign, publications, large-scale London meetings, and the missionary work of organizers despatched from headquarters to work up the movement in the provinces.

A very considerable effort was now required from the national leaders, if these tactics were to make the necessary impact within a short timescale. From the outset it was clear that the services of paid staff would be necessary, alongside the voluntary work of the executive committee and others. Ethel Harrison informed *The Times* on 15 August 1908 that 'our secretaries . . . are working until 11 o'clock at night to deal with the mass of correspondence that pours in upon us, asking for advice, offering help and money'.[57] Within weeks the League had six organizers at work in the regions, and a head office at Caxton House, Westminster. Gertrude Bell was only too willing to delegate her duties as honorary secretary, a role which she described to her stepmother as 'most horrible'.[58] Though she had been happy to attend three anti-suffrage gatherings in one day during the exciting early days of the League,[59] her main interests lay elsewhere and she was reluctant to speak in public. In early October 1908 she wrote home: 'I went straight to the office and had an interview with a very capable, bespectacled lady who used to be the organising secretary of one of the Suffrage societies and has seen the error of her ways and wants to work with us'.[60] Ermine Taylor returned to the League's service as coordinator of the new petition, while Lucy Terry Lewis was recruited as an able and popular coordinator of local branch workers.

In Edith Somervell, from January 1909, the League found an honorary secretary who bridged the gap between paid professional workers and genteel volunteers. During the following year she threw herself enthusiastically into the work of organization, travelling the country to speak at a record number of meetings as well as contributing to the press campaign and directing the head

---

[56] See J. Camhi, *Women Against Women: American Anti-Suffragism 1880–1920* (New York: Carlson, 1994); T. Jablonsky, *The Home, Heaven and Motherhood Party: Female Anti-Suffragism in the United States, 1868–1920* (New York: Carlson, 1994); S. Marshall, *Splintered Sisterhood: Gender and Class in the Campaign Against Woman Suffrage* (Wisconsin: University of Wisconsin Press, 1997).

[57] *The Times*, 15 Aug. 1908, 14.

[58] G. Bell to F. Bell, ? Oct. 1908. University of Newcastle upon Tyne, Gertrude Bell letters (http://www.gerty.ncl.ac.uk/letters/1908.htm).

[59] G. Bell to H. Bell, 21 June 1908. Ibid.   [60] G. Bell to F. Bell, 5 Oct. 1908. Ibid.

office.[61] Her summary of the League's work to date was distributed at a Queen's Hall 'demonstration' addressed by Lord Cromer on 26 March 1909. Nearly a quarter of a million signatures had been obtained for 'our great Petition', and over eighty branches 'actually started', while another thirty were 'just forming, and almost ready to come into existence'. The impact of national leadership upon these achievements was illustrated by Edith's description of 'systematic Petition work' and by her appeal for voluntary workers 'to go with one of our organizers to new districts for a week or a fortnight, at their own expense, to help in the formation of new Branches'. Her own forthcoming tour of northern cities had been prepared for by 'three girls . . . doing voluntary spadework for weeks', while 'Two ladies, who do not care for speaking, are going with us at their own expense to help during the week'. The lack of speakers, even from amongst the executive committee, was already a problem for the League. As Edith put it, perhaps with a hint of desperation, 'We could employ 20 more speakers tomorrow if we had them; many amongst you would find you could speak, if you would only try and begin'. An accompanying appeal for finance showed her sensitivity to the gender and social class sensibilities of her readers. Proposed fund-raisers included such philanthropic staples as penny readings, concerts, dances, and garden parties, whilst 'One member is making us a beautiful calendar, the profits of which will go to the League'. She acknowledged that 'most of us have charities and friends less well off than ourselves upon whom, as a rule, we should prefer to spend our efforts'. An uneasy combination of campaigning fervour, reassuring gentility, and somewhat feeble, ladylike humour characterized her four-page report as a whole, providing unintentional insight into the League's campaigning weaknesses.[62]

One gauge of WNASL effectiveness is to be found in suffragist reactions to its work. Alongside ritual scorn in speeches and publications, suffragists took seriously the task of countering anti-suffragist arguments through the national and provincial press. In turn, the anti-suffrage women admitted their willingness to imitate some aspects of suffrage publicity-seeking. 'If there is nothing else to learn from those who are in the other camp, we can at least learn how to "play the game"', wrote Edith Somervell.[63] Leading women were often more willing to write to newspapers than to speak from platforms or to engage in the minutiae of organization. *The Times* remained a favourite haunt of anti-suffrage letter-writers, and their contributions sometimes led to vigorous two-way exchanges with their opponents. Mary Ward's invocation of the American example was particularly galling to suffragists on both sides of the Atlantic. From July to October 1908 debate raged over the impact of American opposition upon the suffrage cause,

---

[61] Edith Somervell spoke at 73 meetings in twelve months, according to the *Anti-Suffrage Review*, 20 (July 1910), 7. Her health apparently broke down under the strain, and her role as national secretary of the WNASL lasted only one year.

[62] 'Queen's Hall Demonstration March 26th 1909', 1–4, Women's Library, WNASL, 2/WNA 281.

[63] Ibid. 2.

and over the transferability or otherwise of its lessons to the British campaign.[64] Mary was forced to gather fresh evidence in support of her arguments, and in the process cemented a relationship with American anti-suffragism which was soon to be reflected in the *Anti-Suffrage Review* and its equivalents in Boston and New York, as well as in her own elevation to an honorary vice-presidential post within the American anti-suffragist National League for the Civic Education of Women.[65] The attractions of American anti-suffragism included not only its spectacular success in mobilizing opposition voters, but also its faith in upper middle-class philanthropy and educational reform as integral to the defence of conservative social values.

During 1909 Mary began a series of press confrontations with Millicent Fawcett. These redoubled in energy after her humiliating defeat at a public debate between the two women at the Passmore Edwards settlement, and included a vigorous spat over her involvement in her son's 1910 election campaign.[66] Other leading members of the Women's League joined her on *The Times* letters page. In August 1908 Edith Milner crossed swords with the distinguished New Woman novelist Mona Caird, accusing her of doing her best 'to set sex against sex . . . daily arousing a feeling of contempt and antagonism, especially amongst the lower classes, that it will be very hard to counteract'.[67] Gertrude Bell scoffed at the suffragist 'territorial army of Amazons',[68] whilst Ethel Harrison supported Edith Milner's attack on the emancipatory views of Mona Caird.[69] Edith Somervell's letters to *The Times* during 1909 directly condemned suffragette militancy and debated the 'facts' of suffrage and anti-suffrage support.[70] Though the quality of anti-suffrage women's letters was variable, they manifested a confident determination to be heard by the public, as well as to hold their own against the suffragist publicity machine.

Favourable press publicity for the League included coverage of its major national meetings, especially when distinguished men graced the platform. *The Times* published the full-length speeches given by Lord Cromer and Mary Ward at the Queen's Hall rally of March 1909, but the first Annual Council meeting of the League, with speeches from Margaret Jersey and Edith Somervell, was more briefly reported.[71] It was the task of the *Anti-Suffrage Review*, launched through Mary Ward's efforts in December 1908, to ensure that League members received the fullest possible national news, as well as information about the development of branches. The first edition denounced the suffragette 'rush' on Parliament which had roused 'a shock of repulsion—a wave of angry laughter—through England . . . bringing recruits from all sides

---

[64] See letters in *The Times* on 10 and 25 July, 1 and 14 Sept., 1 and 10 Oct. 1908.
[65] See Jablonsky, *Home, Heaven and Motherhood*, 78.
[66] *The Times*, 20 June 1910, 10.   [67] *The Times*, 13 Aug. 1908, 8.
[68] *The Times*, 20 Aug. 1908, 6.   [69] *The Times*, 15 Aug. 1908, 14.
[70] *The Times*, 1 July 1909, 16; 15 Oct. 1909, 10.
[71] *The Times*, 27 Mar. 1909, 10; 29 June 1909, 9.

to the Anti-Suffrage League'.[72] Within, the anti-suffrage 'Meeting of Council' was reported, including Lady Jersey's appeal to women to play their part in opposition: 'Let us all have the courage of our convictions, and resist this effort to break up our homes and families, and thereby place ourselves in the proud position of being able to do the utmost for our homes, for our surroundings, and for the Empire at large'.[73]

The executive committee's reception for members in December 1909 was also reported in full detail, and appears to have been a thoroughly feminized political event: 'Caxton Hall was bright with masses of white chrysanthemums and pink begonias . . . the festoons of evergreens and wreaths of flowers on platform and balcony were beautifully arranged by Miss Ermine Taylor, Miss Hyde, and a band of lady helpers, who had spent many hours over them.' The committee was described as 'At Home' to the membership, and 'the scene was rendered all the prettier by the fact that many of the ladies present wore gowns and hats which repeated the colours of the League, and rose, black and white favours were also widely worn'.[74] Many anti-suffrage women were happier to participate in and report upon such a reassuring scene than they were to engage in more confrontational activities, including polemical journalism. Mary Ward found herself writing far more of the *Review* than she had intended when she first lent it her financial and literary support.[75] Well before the merger of 1910, male authors were relied upon for many of the main feature articles, as well as for their lengthy published speeches. Even the letters column suffered from a dearth of female contributors, and members' lack of collective ownership of their monthly paper was implied by Janet Hogarth's urgent appeal for more subscribers at the first Annual Council meeting. Branch news provided the most reliable content, but this detailed evidence of local activism may have had limited readership appeal.

Alongside the *Anti-Suffrage Review*, the national leadership promoted a range of other anti-suffrage publications. There existed a proven demand for published counter-propaganda which the League attempted to meet with its own series of leaflets as well as by publicizing books and pamphlets. Most of the League's leaflets were anonymous, but some women authors identified themselves and collectively the surviving leaflets represent an interesting contrast in style and tone to those published by the Men's League for Opposing Woman's Suffrage. Propaganda leaflets aimed at a female readership spoke mainly of women's existing responsibilities and capabilities, arguing that women's suffrage would threaten these: 'Women cannot be spared for political life, not only because they are incapable of doing men's work (for they could do it in some fashion),

---

[72] *Anti-Suffrage Review*, 1 (Dec. 1908), 1.   [73] Ibid. 5.
[74] *Anti-Suffrage Review*, 13 (Dec. 1909), 8.
[75] A front-page biographical tribute in July 1910 acknowledged that 'It is to Mrs Ward that our *Review* owes its existence'. *Anti-Suffrage Review*, 20 (July 1910), 1.

but because men are similarly incapable of doing women's work'.[76] The sole Women's League leaflet by an acknowledged male author, 'Nature's Reason Against Woman Suffrage', set out the physical force argument in a measured fashion, arguing that the significance of voting would be reduced if women insisted upon participating in elections without the power to enforce their decisions.[77] The wider threat to national and imperial interests received some attention in many leaflets, especially in the context of arguments against adult suffrage. So, too, did the anti-suffragists' firm conviction that they represented majority female opinion. 'Women's Suffrage and the National Welfare' argued that 'Each sex has a sphere as important as the other', and deplored a recent tendency 'to underestimate the importance of the sphere which specially calls for the care and devotion of a woman, namely, the home'.[78] Mary Ward's two leaflets reproduced her speech at the League's launch and her letter to *The Times* denying that women's suffrage was 'inevitable';[79] both pieces stressed her confidence in women's own ability to defeat suffragism, drawing on the American example. Other leaflets attempted, rather clumsily, to provide versions of the same arguments which would appeal to working-class women.[80]

In comparison, Men's League leaflets of the same period offered few blandishments to women, and were often far more aggressive in tone. In a vigorously masculine and populist style, one warned that 'WOMAN SUFFRAGE means sooner or later GOVERNMENT BY WOMEN': '*Men of England*, your interests and the welfare of the country are in danger. Rally to prevent it . . . Don't make yourselves and your country the *laughing stock of the world.*'[81] Another leaflet accused suffragists of 'lowering the rate of wages for men and women by forcing crowds of females into industrial pursuits, teaching them to despise home duties and to shun domestic service'.[82] The Men's League sometimes counterbalanced its apparent hostility towards encroaching women with an appeal to men's chivalrous values. The active anti-suffragism of 'the men of England' was required 'Because the right-minded and womanly women, through the very fact that they are sensitive, gentle, and engrossed in numberless home duties, are unable to meet the bullying, violent suffragette women in boisterous argument'.[83] Such propaganda seemed more likely to divide the male and female supporters of anti-suffragism from each other than to encourage joint campaigning. Both Leagues supposedly believed in the complementary nature of the sexes and deplored 'sex antagonism', but

[76] 'Why Women Should Not Vote', WNASL leaflet no. 12, Women's Library 2/WNA 281.

[77] H. Hart, 'Nature's Reason Against Woman Suffrage', WNASL leaflet no. 6.

[78] 'Women's Suffrage and the National Welfare', WNASL leaflet no. 8.

[79] WNASL leaflets nos. 3 and 5.

[80] e.g. 'What Women's Suffrage Means', WNASL leaflet no. 7; 'Votes and Wages', WNASL leaflet no. 15.

[81] Anti-Suffrage Campaign, 'Votes for Women, Never!' (n.d., address of Men's League for Opposing Women's Suffrage below), Women's Library, 2/WNA 281.

[82] Barlow, 'Why I Oppose Woman Suffrage' (London: Unwin Brothers Ltd., n.d.).

[83] Ibid.

the leaders of the WNASL clearly had far greater faith in women's strengths. It was already evident that complementarity implied difference of approach, and that gender differences might therefore prove difficult to accommodate within a single organization. The merger of 1910 was by no means a foregone conclusion.

BUILDING THE BRANCHES

The Women's League regarded branch-building as central to its success. The branches were to be a vehicle for propaganda among women and for pressure upon male voters and parliamentary candidates, as well as a living exemplar to Parliament of women's mass concern over the suffrage issue. Supporters of the forward policy also hoped that female anti-suffragists would translate their cause into stronger aspirations towards public service in local government, alongside suitably gendered forms of national representation. Motivation was therefore high when the leaders of the Women's League began their campaign for wider support in the autumn of 1908. Early successes exceeded all expectations, as branches in the West End of London benefited from the proximity of experienced speakers and the support of high society. An inaugural meeting of the Kensington branch on 5 November filled the Queen's Gate Hall and overflowed into a second hall: 'several hundred people had to be turned away, as both halls were full to overflowing before the hour fixed for its opening'.[84] Mary Countess of Ilchester presided, alongside Violet Markham, Edith Somervell, Leo Maxse of the *National Review*, and two anti-suffrage Members of Parliament. Announcing that the branch had already enrolled 217 members, the Countess reminded her audience of the defeat of the Gunpowder Plot: another failed conspiracy against the community by an even more dangerous minority.[85] In December Edith Somervell addressed an all-female drawing room gathering in Kensington, claiming suffragism 'struck at everything that made for the sane, wholesome, and continuous life of the State, because it involved the marriage laws and the family and home life'. Despite her alarmist rhetoric, she spoke more in sorrow than in anger. Accusing the suffragists of erroneous judgement rather than evil intentions, she stated that she 'did not feel that the suffragists were really in the opposite camp to them, with few exceptions'; the womanly work they aspired to achieve through Parliament was 'no nobler than that in which they had already been engaged'.[86] By March 1909 the nominal Kensington membership had risen to over 900 and women were busily canvassing the neighbourhood on behalf of the League and its anti-suffrage petition.[87]

[84] *Anti-Suffrage Review*, 1 (Dec. 1908), 2.   [85] *The Times*, 6 Nov. 1908, 9.
[86] *The Times*, 4 Dec. 1908, 10.
[87] *Anti-Suffrage Review*, 3 (Feb. 1909), 4, records that Ethel Colquhoun had become secretary of the South Kensington branch.

The Westminster branch had equally prestigious support at its first reported meeting, which took place 'at Lady Wantage's residence in Carlton Gardens'. Speakers included Lady Desart, Lady Wynne, and Mr St Loe Strachey of the *Spectator*, and 'a resolution was unanimously adopted which declared that the concession of woman suffrage was a danger to the State, and would tend to diminish the influence of women in social work'.[88] The Paddington branch was also addressed in January 1909 by the ubiquitous Edith Somervell and by Frances Low, who declared (in a rare foray into public speaking) that women's 'influence on society and on children was infinitely more important than any amount of political voting. Woman could make her influence felt in moral questions today and had a thousand ways of expressing herself.'[89] Local meetings followed during the spring of 1909 in Chelsea, West Marylebone, Hampstead, Hampton, and Kew; by the April 1910 there were around twenty branches in the capital and its suburbs, concentrated in wealthy areas and conspicuously headed by London's female social elite.

Most of the upper-class leaders of the Women's League had homes in the country as well as in London, and their social prestige soon helped branches to fan out into the English provinces. Ethel Harrison claimed the honour of having founded the first provincial branch, from her home in Kent. She wrote to *The Times* on 15 August 1908, describing a full range of local activities which included meetings in her own drawing room and garden as well as (more democratically) 'in the town hall after the hop-picking'. Her Hawkhurst village branch was soon to be joined by another in Maidstone.[90] An Oxford branch was inevitable and was formally inaugurated in February 1909 with 95 members, under the chairmanship of Georgiana Max Muller and Edith Massie. By the following year there were 148 members (paying 5s.) and 147 associates (paying 1s.). Oxford assembled over 3,000 signatures for the national petition, as well as holding meetings well patronized by sympathetic University men.[91] A crowded meeting at the Corn Exchange attracted suffragist hecklers as well as Professor Dicey, the Warden of Wadham College, and the Rector of Exeter College, but Lady Jersey successfully moved a resolution opposing the female franchise 'while maintaining the principle that the work of women on local authorities concerned with the social and domestic affairs of the community was of great and increasing value'.[92] In Oxford, as in London, the principles of the forward policy were prominent within the leading women's anti-suffrage propaganda. Suffragist press criticism and the presence of combative suffragists at many public meetings gave an added incentive to those who were anxious to explain that anti-suffragism was supportive of women's work and appreciative of their special strengths.

[88] *The Times*, 20 Mar. 1909, 8.   [89] *Anti-Suffrage Review*, 2 (Jan. 1909), 5.
[90] *The Times*, 15 Aug. 1908, 14.
[91] *Annual Report of the Women's National Anti-Suffrage League, Oxford Branch 1909–1910*, Bodl. See also Ch. 2, above.
[92] *The Times*, 9 Feb. 1909, 10.

Lady Wantage and Lady Haversham were meanwhile constructing branches in Berkshire. This county soon became another stronghold of female anti-suffragism, partly through the organizational talents of Gladys Pott, a future national secretary of the National League for Opposing Woman Suffrage and secretary of the North Berkshire branch by June 1909. At the launch meeting of the Reading branch, speeches reflected the more conservative stance of Lady Haversham and Lord Weardale. The former praised male achievements—'It was the men who designed, built and manned the *Dreadnoughts*, the men who defended our homes, the men who had built up the Empire'—while the latter commended the chivalry of confining women to their home duties: 'women must be restricted to that part of life which was especially theirs, and . . . it was the office of men to conduct the affairs of the Empire, to fight for it, and to preserve, if necessary by brute force, the sanction and the authority of law'.[93] Local patronage of a different kind was meanwhile at work in Birmingham, where the Chamberlain family had swung behind the anti-suffrage movement. In February 1909 the *Anti-Suffrage Review* reported that a shop in New Street had been rented for the past three months 'for the sale of the literature issued by the League, and for obtaining signatures to the petition forms'. Meetings were being held, house-to-house canvassing for signatures was proceeding, and voluntary effort was being supplemented by the work of 'a paid lady secretary'.[94] The home of caucus politics was no stranger to well-organized attempts to sway public opinion.

Bristol provided even more impressive evidence of local support for the Women's League, apparently mobilized through the organizational skills of the honorary secretary, Edith Long Fox, rather than as an outcome of social deference or wealthy patronage. Mary Ward was the main speaker at a meeting of 'more than fourteen hundred people' in January 1909.[95] Afterwards she wrote to Louise Creighton wishing that she and other suffragists had been present to observe the 'seriousness of feeling', the broad representation of political parties and religious denominations, and 'the number of excellent women doing excellent work who were there'.[96] Still larger audiences awaited Mary when she joined Edith Somervell on an anti-suffrage northern tour in September. At the Annual Council meeting in the summer Edith admitted that the task of proselytizing in 'the enormous industrial towns in the North' had not been accomplished 'in anything like an adequate manner during this first year of the life of our infant League'.[97] She did not add that the suffragists were already formidably well organized in many cities, and successfully embedded within the local labour movement.

---

[93] *Anti-Suffrage Review*, 7 (June 1909), 5.

[94] *Anti-Suffrage Review*, 3 (Feb. 1909), 4. Beatrice Chamberlain and Emily Simon were Vice-Presidents of the Birmingham branch.

[95] Ibid., 6. The Bristol branch prided itself on its political and religious inclusiveness, illustrated by a detailed analysis of the platform party at its Jan. 1909 meeting.

[96] M. Ward to L. Creighton, 31 Jan. 1909. M. Ward papers, 3/3/1.

[97] *Anti-Suffrage Review*, 8 (July 1909), 2.

The surviving records of the Manchester anti-suffrage organization suggest that it faced an uphill struggle both before and after amalgamation into the National League.[98] The first organizing secretary reported that 'her first meetings were practically broken up, and the rowdiest and rudest of the "suffragettes", men and women, together with their usual allies, the less well-educated Socialists, assiduously attended and disturbed all meetings'.[99] Smaller, semi-private meetings in the spring of 1909 were followed by an autumn campaign featuring a suffrage debate before an audience of several thousands in the Manchester Free Trade Hall. Mary Ward reported to Louise Creighton that the suffragettes had 'packed the galleries with young girls, who rose en bloc against the Resolution. But the body of the hall was very evenly divided, the newspaper reports were extremely good, and altogether we felt we hadn't done badly'.[100] In an article in the *Anti-Suffrage Review* she had the last word against the arguments of the suffragists who had defeated her.[101] Sheffield offered a more positive experience, with an anti-suffrage majority at a large public meeting. In the same month an anti-suffrage motor tour by Mr and Mrs Norris and Mr Maconochie provided a more populist test of northern opinion. Only one out of twelve local meetings (including five outdoor meetings) failed to produce a majority against votes for women. The expedition reported itself satisfied that the British public, both male and female, was 'dead against the whole thing'; however, in terms which echoed Men's League propaganda, Mr Maconochie also drew strong conclusions about the need to spare women from the rigours of democratic campaigning in the future.[102] During the following year the Manchester branch made very limited progress, and the Liverpool branch even less. Organized anti-suffragism remained far stronger in the south and west throughout the League's existence, though it had achieved some visible presence in most counties of England by the summer of 1910.[103]

The Women's League was relentlessly English, in most of its published self-expression as well as in its core organization. This reflected the political and social status of metropolitan London, as well as the anglocentrism of British imperialism and its propagandists. In the face of a strong English bias, some branch-building successes were nevertheless reported from Scotland, Wales, and even Ireland. Mary Ward's most enjoyable experience in September 1909 was at a Scottish meeting: 'Nearly 2000 Edinburgh electors and their wives, solidly with us, and a year ago we could hardly get up a meeting at all'. According to the

---

[98] Records of the Manchester League for Opposing Women's Suffrage. Manchester Central Library, M131.

[99] *Anti-Suffrage Review*, 5 (Apr. 1909), 5.

[100] M. Ward to L. Creighton, 11 Nov. 1909. M. Ward papers, 3/3/1.

[101] *Anti-Suffrage Review*, 12 (Nov. 1909), 12.

[102] *Anti-Suffrage Review*, 11 (Oct. 1909), 6; *The Times*, 8 Dec. 1909, 7; *Anti-Suffrage Review*, 13 (Dec. 1909), 7.

[103] See Brian Harrison's composite chart of WNASL/NLOWS branches, *Separate Spheres*, 122.

same (less than impartial) source, Edith Somervell enjoyed a debating triumph over Christabel Pankhurst in Edinburgh: 'That young lady floundered from one mistake to another, while Mrs S quoted Blue Books, and an astonished meeting looked on'. Subsequent Scottish meetings were reported as 'most excellent and enthusiastic'.[104]

The following spring the Duchess of Montrose assumed the presidency of the Scottish Women's National Anti-Suffrage League, which in May 1910 progressed from being an informal federation of four Scottish WNASL branches to become a semi-independent affiliate of the English organization.[105] With Lady Lovat presiding in Inverness, the Duchess of Hamilton in Glasgow, and the Marchioness of Tweedale in Edinburgh, there was no lack of prestigious female leadership in Scotland even before the Marchioness of Tullibardine (later the Duchess of Atholl) came to the forefront of the National League for Opposing Woman Suffrage two years later. From November 1910 the *Anti-Suffrage Review* listed five Scottish branches (Edinburgh, Glasgow, St Andrews, Berwickshire, Inverness and Nairn) under the heading 'Scottish National Anti-Suffrage League', a title which persisted until the spring of 1913 when 'Scottish League for Opposing Woman Suffrage' was adopted in deference to the NLOWS. A 'Welsh campaign' was reported by the *Anti-Suffrage Review* in May 1909. Edith Colquhoun addressed an audience of 1600 in Newport—where 'the overwhelming majority was with us'[106]—and by February 1910 branches were also active in Cardiff and North Wales. According to the League's first Annual Report, 'From Dublin we received most urgent requests to send speakers to hold meetings, and it was impossible to turn a deaf ear in spite of the overwhelming demands nearer home'. A 'strong branch' and an 'influential' committee followed; a year later the Annual Council was informed (rather vaguely) that 'the question of Woman Suffrage is arousing great interest and enthusiasm all over Ireland'.[107]

SOME CONCLUSIONS

What conclusions can be drawn from all this variegated activity? Had the WNASL been successful in creating a national organization and local branches

---

[104] M. Ward to L. Creighton, 11 Nov. 1909, M. Ward papers, 3/3/1; *Anti-Suffrage Review*, 12 (Nov. 1909), 2.

[105] *Anti-Suffrage Review*, 19, (June 1910), 4. A Scottish Council was established, but 'though the Scottish Council feels that the scope of Anti-Suffrage work in Scotland will be much enlarged by the formation of a Council and Constitution of its own, the Council members have expressed a wish to affiliate their League with the Women's National Anti-Suffrage League, for which they have a already done such splendid work and sent generous help' (Ibid.). The Duchess of Montrose was a speaker at the WNASL Annual Council in July 1910; conversely, the Scottish organization remained heavily dependent on English speakers and organizers, and its numbers were usually included within WNASL (and then NLOWS) membership totals.

[106] *Anti-Suffrage Review*, 6 (May 1909), 7; 8 (July 1909), 3.

[107] Ibid., 8 (July 1909), 3.

which proved beyond all doubt the depth and breadth of female opposition to the vote? 'Great progress and increased energy is seen throughout the League,' reported Lucy Terry Lewis to the second Annual Council Meeting in 1910; '. . . We have nearly doubled our membership in the past twelve months.'[108] By the date of its merger, the League as a whole had between 15,000 and 20,000 members, gathered within a few large branches in the south of England as well as scattered across dozens of small branches elsewhere; 104 branches were claimed in total, representing very varied levels of local activity. Whilst the founding initiative had often come from leading women, and branches remained worryingly dependent upon head office for speakers, many obscure female antis had been motivated to attend local meetings, join committees, and canvass their friends and neighbours in the anti-suffrage cause. This was a not inconsiderable achievement, given that the militant Women's Social and Political Union had a core membership of around 5,000 and the long-established National Union of Women's Suffrage Societies only around 25,000 in the autumn of 1910.[109] Suffrage organizers were justified in asserting that their membership count was more rigorous, their members more active, and their network of affiliated societies much wider than that represented by the anti-suffragists; but the WNASL had certainly achieved enough to impress male sympathizers and even some Members of Parliament. Substantial local effort had gone into swelling the anti-suffrage parliamentary petition, which totalled 337,018 signatures when it was presented to the House of Commons in March 1909, and over 420,000 by the end of the year. In July 1910, petitions were 'still being signed all over the country', and plans were being developed for a systematic canvass of women electors in local government to reinforce this evidence of female opinion.[110] The League had proven numerical support, and it had also succeeded in the important aim of recruiting most of its supporters from amongst women. The silent female majority was being drawn into the suffrage fray in greater numbers than ever before.

Support was uneven geographically, and patently even more so in terms of social class. Ideally, the WNASL leaders wished to attract the broadest possible range of women, both to counter suffrage propaganda among the working-classes and in order to uphold anti-suffrage arguments based upon the universality of woman's role in the family. However, there was never any realistic prospect of a mass recruitment of working-class women as League members, let alone as leaders. One of the most important strands of anti-suffrage propaganda depended upon emphasizing the dangers of democracy, and especially of the female 'ignorance vote'. Even the most progressive anti-suffragists, and those most committed to

---

[108] *Anti-Suffrage Review*, 20 (July 1910), 8. Edith Somervell reported 'about 9,000 members' in *Anti-Suffrage Review*, 8 (July 1909), 2.

[109] See Martin Pugh's commentary on WSPU and NUWSS membership, *March of the Women*, 210–11, 254–5.

[110] *Anti-Suffrage Review*, 20 (July 1910), 8.

social action on behalf of working-class women and children, were convinced that universal adult suffrage would be disastrous mainly because of the political ignorance of poorer women. Mary Ward explained her views on this subject in some detail during her published correspondence with Millicent Fawcett in 1910. Throughout the childbearing years, 'the thoughts of a normal woman are turned inwards and concentrated on her home, her family, her own health, and the physical needs of children'; this was 'infinitely more true of the bulk of the women of the nation, the women of the industrial class' than of 'the women of leisure and wealth'. Despite the fact that such women were 'accomplishing something for the nation of infinite value', they were prevented both by their maternal duties and their poverty from gaining political knowledge comparable to that of their husbands.[111]

Working-class women remained a philanthropic cause, rather than potential partners in the anti-suffrage campaign. When working-class women's anti-suffragism was referred to in speeches or in the *Anti-Suffrage Review*, it was usually in terms which illustrated the social gulf between these good-hearted, simple souls and the more enlightened speaker (or author). For example, Edith Somervell's anecdotes in her pamphlet for the Queen's Hall meeting of March 1909 included 'A Story with an Obvious Moral': upon being canvassed by a suffragist, 'a poor working woman of Canning Town' responded with 'keen sympathy written on her toil-worn face, "*What* did you say they were suffering from, Mam?"' Another anecdote told of a working-class woman who boasted simultaneously of her suffragism and of having 'just come out of a lunatic asylum'; this woman's fellow workers at a steam laundry were, encouragingly, 'eager partisans of Anti-Suffrage'.[112] Ethel Harrison claimed, when collecting petition signatures in Kent, to have found 'all the working women on our side';[113] a claim repeated by canvassers elsewhere, and reinforced in general terms at most major anti-suffrage meetings. A WNASL leaflet titled 'Votes and Wages' linked the truism that working-class women did not want to vote with a refutation of suffragist claims that the vote would bring higher wages and better working conditions.[114] Anti-suffrage ladies were confident that they spoke for anti-suffrage women too. There was no particularly urgent incentive to engage with the working classes more directly, since their passive support for the cause was of limited value and could be complacently assumed.

Despite its lack of social inclusivity, in other respects the Women's League certainly lived up to its title. The League's executive was almost entirely female,

---

[111] *The Times*, 11 July 1910, 11.   [112] 'Queen's Hall Demonstration', 3.
[113] *The Times*, 15 Aug. 1908, 14.
[114] 'Votes and Wages', WNASL leaflet no. 15, Women's Library, 2/WNA 281. Probably written by Ethel Harrison, this leaflet consisted of a rather unlikely dialogue between a self-respecting working-class anti-suffragist and her suffragist friend. It concluded with the anti-suffragist's comments on voting: 'A man can do that sort of thing. My work isn't so easy to put on one side. There's a many more important things than that for *me* to see to.'

and so were nearly all its paid staff. A large majority of the named leaders in local branches up and down the country were also women, though this was much less true of platform speakers at both national and local levels. The presence of male speakers upon WNASL platforms was publicly presented as evidence of the League's successful collaboration with men, providing a welcome contrast to the 'sex antagonism' of suffrage campaign. The contributions of male anti-suffragists to the organization and published propaganda of the Women's League were viewed by anti-suffrage women in the same positive light, rather than as evidence that a female anti-suffrage organization was unable to win its cause without male guidance. Despite private concerns over the shortage of women speakers, and an uncomfortable awareness of financial limitations, many leaders of the League consciously prided themselves upon its achievements as a female organization. In Britain, as in America, it was possible for organized women's anti-suffragism to benefit from its proximity to other women's causes. Mary Ward's insistence upon anti-suffrage affiliation to the NUWW and to the Women's Local Government Society was a matter of principle as well as of tactics. Together with other supporters of positive anti-suffragism, she sought to prevent the takeover of mainstream women's organizations by what she believed to be a suffragist minority. Advocacy of the forward policy became highly contentious within the mixed-sex NLOWS, partly because it was seen as a female stratagem associated more closely with other sectors of the women's movement than with anti-suffragism.

Within the WNASL of 1908–10, the problem of ideological and tactical divisions was already present. The contrasting views of 'forward' and 'negative' anti-suffrage women were reflected in their published speeches and writings, as well as commented upon in Lady Jersey's correspondence. But there is no evidence that divergent views represented a serious threat to organized anti-suffragism at this stage. On the contrary, the 'forward' women demonstrated their willingness to compromise for the sake of unity. The opening manifesto of the League seemed to promise action in support of the organization's second objective: the maintenance of the principle of women's participation in local government, and its possible extension into new forms of national representation for women's interests. Yet action was slow to follow. The first edition of the *Anti-Suffrage Review* also promised more than the League was eventually able to deliver for progressive anti-suffragism. Claiming that 'the members of the new League are no mere advocates of things as they are', Mary Ward wrote that 'Our columns will always be open to the signed advocacy and discussion of reforms concerning the life and work of women. We shall support their present privileges and powers in local government with all our strength'. A meeting was promised of 'women engaged in social and educational work' to consider how to advance local government work and also to find 'means of securing the permanent representation of the opinion of women on questions immediately concerning them'.[115] However, despite several didactic articles on local government, supplemented by exhortations to women readers to participate in local elections, no further collective policy was made on these issues until the summer of 1910. The belated convening of an anti-suffrage women's local government committee in July 1910 eventually coincided with proposals to establish a single, mixed-sex anti-suffrage League. This committee's establishment was to become a focus for more general concerns over the status of women, and of women's ideas, within the new organization.

It seems clear, in retrospect, that the NLOWS inherited a number of unresolved problems from the WNASL. Although the achievements of the League had met some of its founders' expectations, the path ahead was far from certain. The suffrage movement had not been defeated. On the contrary, the House of Commons had voted in favour of women's enfranchisement in successive years between 1908 and 1910, and it seemed more than ever likely that the Liberal government would eventually decide to allow legislation to proceed. The Prime Minister confirmed his personal sympathies with anti-suffragism when he received a joint delegation from the WNASL and the Men's League on 21 June 1910. On this occasion Margaret Jersey and Elizabeth Burgwin advanced the general views of their League on women's social duties in relation to national and imperial interests, while male speakers delivered arguments concerning the current suffrage bill, the state of parliamentary opinion, the responsibilities of an imperial Parliament, and the outcomes of the recent election. Asquith's response mirrored these political preoccupations, and served to underline the fact that the franchise issue would be decided by government and by Parliament, rather than by public opinion as such. To succeed in its primary objective, the WNASL needed to achieve greater direct influence in the political arena. Merely in order to continue its existing work of propaganda and branch-building, the League badly needed an injection of the funding and prestige which seemed likely to accompany closer collaboration with organized male anti-suffragism and its powerful imperialist leaders. The task of mobilizing mass female support for anti-suffragism was far from complete. The task of developing positive alternatives to women's parliamentary suffrage had barely begun, and was already a source of disagreement and division. The merger of the male and female anti-suffrage organizations held obvious attractions for the WNASL, but was soon to create a set of unforeseen problems to set alongside these existing ones.

[115] *Anti-Suffrage Review*, 1 (Dec. 1908), 2 and 4.

8

Working with Men

THE MEN'S VIEW

The Men's League for Opposing Woman's Suffrage has left only a shadowy record of its existence between December 1908 and August 1910. Its slight historical reputation suffers further from comparison with the achievements of the Women's League in the same period. The mildly disparaging attitude of the WNASL towards its partner organization was evident in the *Anti-Suffrage Review*, which noted in its first issue that 'men are at last starting an anti-suffrage movement of their own'.[1] Contact details for the Men's League were published in subsequent issues, but a report of its first annual dinner in May 1909 was accompanied by the half-joking comment: 'We have heard, not perhaps without some natural self-approbation, that in point of activity that body cannot be compared with our own'. The 'vigour and determination' of its leaders, on the other hand, was judged 'beyond all praise'; their after-dinner speeches were 'models of concise and weighty reasoning'.[2] Lord Cromer, president of the Men's League, was privately critical of his own organization during the amalgamation process in 1910. Writing to Lord Curzon, he described it as 'a perfectly useless body' which 'did very little work, much less than that of the women'. Cromer had consequently 'squashed out the Men's League' at the earliest possible opportunity,[3] though his decisive action became a matter for some regret as the negotiations hit difficulties and a bargaining counter appeared to have been prematurely sacrificed.

Meanwhile the fact that the elimination of the Men's League did not go uncontested reveals that some of its members held their own, separate opinions on anti-suffrage tactics and strategy, and more specifically on the subject of working alongside female colleagues. Press reports of the League's limited activities, and surviving examples of its propaganda, suggest that it was founded to promote the free expression of distinctively masculine viewpoints, as well as offering congenial male social gatherings. It was by no means obvious that such benefits could be reproduced within a mixed-sex organization. The doubts and concerns of male anti-suffragists, including the Men's League's distinguished

---

[1] *Anti-Suffrage Review*, 1 (Dec. 1908), 8.   [2] *Anti-Suffrage Review*, 7 (June 1909), 2.
[3] Lord Cromer to Lord Curzon, 13 Oct. 1910. BL, Curzon papers, MSS Eur F112/33B.

leaders, need to be weighed in the balance alongside other factors which finally persuaded majorities from both the male and female Leagues to support the launch of the National League for Opposing Woman's Suffrage (NLOWS).

The Men's League was founded by the same men who had assisted the revival of organized female anti-suffragism in the spring and summer of 1908. *The Times* reported in January 1909 that a Men's Committee formed the previous month had 'grown with such rapidity that it has been found necessary to enlarge it into a league'.[4] Lord Cromer's acceptance of the presidency greatly strengthened its prospects of wider support. In his 'unavoidable absence', John Massie chaired the launch meeting and Heber Hart (the only other male member of the Women's League executive) proposed adoption of the Men's League constitution. His proposal was seconded by Ivor Guest MP, the contact person for the 'National Women's-Anti-Suffrage Association' during its 'confidential' appeal the previous year.[5] A substantial list of honorary vice-presidents included other male signatories of that appeal, alongside such well-known anti-suffrage stalwarts as Rudyard Kipling, Sir Alfred Lyall, 'the Poet Laureate' (Alfred Austin, former editor of the *National Review*), Lord Pembroke, and Lord Weardale. Several vice-presidents were close relatives of leaders of the Women's League: Sir Hugh Bell (father of Gertrude Bell), Austen Chamberlain (brother of Beatrice Chamberlain), Lord George Hamilton (husband of Maud Hamilton), Lord Haversham (husband of Henrietta Haversham), and the Duke of Montrose (husband of Violet Montrose). These family ties seem to reduce the possibility that the two Leagues had been established on rival platforms; however, the decision to found a second, all-male anti-suffrage organization does suggest the desirability of separate agendas and separate tactics. An executive committee agreed to prepare 'plans for future action . . . forthwith', but not much effort was expended to bring any plans to fruition. Most of the Men's League leaders belonged to more important organizations, including Parliament itself, and continued to voice their opposition to women's suffrage through other channels. Their busy schedules of work and leisure had little space for the time-consuming chores of propaganda and local organization which were being simultaneously undertaken by the WNASL. As Lord Cromer's tactics within the amalgamated NLOWS soon proved, he attached far less importance to the rousing of public opinion than female colleagues who were more distant from the seat of political power. Organizational apathy, linked to political complacency, soon afflicted the Men's League. When its views found distinct expression, they were usually those of the organization's distinguished president, suitably modified and abbreviated for the purposes of populist propaganda directed at male audiences.

In May 1909 Lord Curzon joined Lord Cromer in addressing the Men's League dinner guests, and from this point onwards his reputation and eloquence

4 *The Times*, 19 Jan. 1909, 10.
5 See 'National Women's-Anti-Suffrage Association', Women's Library, 2/WNA 281.

reinforced its strongly imperialist message. In Curzon's view, the key questions posed by women's suffrage were 'would the Empire be less safe than it was at present? Would it, in fact, be safe at all?' His catastrophist prediction that 'on the day that adult suffrage was carried they might put up the shutters of the British Empire' was linked to commendation of 'the time-honoured and irrefutable argument of the home and the natural division of the functions of men and women'. This familiar argument, heard from every Women's League platform, was enlivened for a male audience by less respectful references to the suffragettes as 'female howling dervishes'.[6] Cromer made further humorous political capital from his recent 'sparkling' encounter with militant hecklers at the Queen's Hall. Curzon's speech mentioned '15 strong, valid and incontrovertible arguments which could be advanced against women's suffrage', soon to be published in leaflet form. Three of his reasons related directly to the Empire and another to the physical force argument, whilst others referred to women's lack of 'calmness of temperament' and 'balance of mind', especially 'in emergencies or on occasions of emotional excitement'.[7] Both Cromer and Curzon reinforced anti-suffragist belief in women's unfitness for political responsibility, linking this prejudice to men's chivalric responsibilities towards the weaker sex. Similar emphases appeared in Men's League leaflets, and in the speeches of its lesser speakers. Suffragism was represented first and foremost as 'a National Danger'; men were invited to 'Play up and save your country. Save suffragist women from themselves, and other women from Suffragists'.[8]

Despite the considerable overlap between male and female propaganda, the Men's League undoubtedly gave freer rein to these less woman-friendly aspects of the anti-suffrage cause. Use of sporting and military metaphors, and of facetious humour, underlined the different tastes of masculine audiences. These characteristics were also clearly on view at the series of open-air meetings which the Men's League organized in London during the summer of 1910. *The Times* reported approvingly on 'a forward movement by the younger and more ardent members of a society which has been in existence for a considerable time', and hoped that suffrage demonstrations would in future be less one-sided.[9] On 14 July the Men's League mounted no fewer than five platforms in Trafalgar Square, addressing a mixed audience of male and female supporters and opponents. Messages of support were read out from leaders too lofty to engage with the populus, but willing enough to cater for their assumed tastes. Frederic Harrison's message bluntly echoed the League's leaflets: 'Women's franchise will make England the laughing-stock of Europe. It will bring misery on our homes and ruin on our Empire'.[10] Mary Ward offered a solitary message of female support,

6 *The Times*, 19 May 1909, 8.   7 Ibid.
8 Men's League leaflets, Women's Library, 2/LSW 298/3.
9 *The Times*, 18 July 1910, 9; also reported in *Anti-Suffrage Review*, 21 (Sept. 1910).
10 *The Times*, 15 July 1910, 9.

isolated by its content as well as by her gender. Urging 'men electors in particular' to oppose the female franchise 'in the highest interest of women themselves, first and foremost', she equally exhorted men to 'uphold and encourage the legitimate work of women in local government—in that enlarged housekeeping of the nation . . . to which the nation has already ungrudgingly called them'.[11] With hindsight, it is clear enough that some of the leading figures of the Men's League and of the Women's League were already facing in different directions. However, by July 1910 Cromer and Curzon had concluded that neither men nor women could succeed alone in opposing women's suffrage with the vigour which the parliamentary situation now demanded. A joint effort was needed, through which men and women would pursue their complementary roles side by side, providing a model of collaborative effort which would highlight the folly and dangers of 'sex antagonism'.

Successful collaboration was presaged by several joint endeavours by leaders of the existing anti-suffrage Leagues. On 14 June a letter opposing the Conciliation Bill appeared in *The Times* from Margaret Jersey, Henrietta Haversham, Violet Montrose, Lord Cromer, and John Massie, on behalf of the Women's League, the Men's League, and the Scottish Women's League.[12] On 21 June the three Leagues sent a deputation of ten men and ten women to visit the Prime Minister. A week later Cromer addressed the Annual Council Meeting of the WNASL in complimentary terms.[13] He felt he understood both the achievements and the weaknesses of the women's organization and, under the influence of the growing parliamentary threat and the provocations of militancy, was confident that a seamless transition towards a stronger, unified league could be achieved upon his own terms. On 21 July *The Times* published a weighty 'Anti Woman-Suffrage Appeal', summarizing current suffrage threats and prospective measures to oppose them: 'Our idea is to form a large and comprehensive league, in which men and women will be equally represented, possessing central offices in London and branches in all parts of the United Kingdom, exclusively devoted to the propagation of this cause'.[14] The list of signatories provoked an admiring editorial from *The Times* the following day, commenting both on their 'intellectual distinction' and 'the wide catholicity of the interests they represent'; they ranged from variegated politicians to 'prominent representatives of literature, the Church, academic life, the Army, business, science, philanthropy, and the stage . . . The ladies who have signed the appeal, though fewer in numbers, are in no respect less representative'.[15]

Cromer's personal decision in favour of a united campaign was the crucial cause of the amalgamation. By this date he and Curzon were both heavily engaged in a systematic fund-raising effort which promised to set organized anti-suffragism

---

[11] *The Times*, 14 July 1910, 9.   [12] Ibid. 10.
[13] *Anti-Suffrage Review*, 20 (July 1910), 3–6 and 7–10.
[14] *The Times*, 21 July 1910, 9.   [15] *The Times*, 22 July 1910, 11.

upon a completely different footing. Caught up in the momentum of their own campaign, they were prepared to undertake whatever action was needed to secure its success. Amalgamation with the Women's League was viewed in this light: as a necessary tactic, rather than a central objective of their campaign. Their publicly stated reasons for opposing the female franchise had much in common with those of other leading anti-suffragists, but the energy which both men devoted to their cause derived also from their personal circumstances, and especially their experience of commanding the Empire.[16] Lord Cromer had retired as Consul-General of Egypt in May 1907. His long period as one of the Empire's most successful proxy rulers ended on a low note, and for a brief period he found himself somewhat under-employed as well as ill and depressed. The success of *Modern Egypt*, his apologia for imperial rule published the following year, restored his fortunes and health. By 1910 he had embarked upon a varied and formidable schedule of public work, preferring to expend his efforts upon causes beyond party politics and often beyond the immediate environs of Parliament itself.[17] His anti-suffrage activities, including his close collaboration with Curzon in the launch of the NLOWS, need to be viewed in this context. As an imperial proconsul, he was used to being obeyed and thoroughly familiar with the power-broking ways of the British government, the City, and the upper-class London social scene. The same was true of Lord Curzon. After seven years as Viceroy of India, he returned to Britain at the end of 1905 a disappointed man, having lost his contest with Lord Kitchener over the management of Indian military affairs. Famed for his love of imperial pomp, as well as for his diplomatic and administrative achievements, he too had little inclination to bow to the discipline of party politics and for a period found himself somewhat at a loose end. His appointment as Oxford's Chancellor in 1907, and his elevation to the House of Lords the following year, helped revive his public career, and by 1910 he was heavily involved in current debates over budgetary reform and the status of the House of Lords, as well as engaged in many extra-parliamentary causes.[18]

The commitment of two such heavyweight imperialists to the success of a renewed anti-suffrage campaign was likely to brook few obstacles. Cromer and Curzon were able to draw substantially upon their existing reserves of knowledge and personal influence, as they privately raised over £20,000 from their anti-suffragist friends and sympathizers in advance of the amalgamation and

---

[16] See also Ch. 5, above.

[17] See Cromer's Memorandum, summarizing his public work 1907–11 (dated 2 May 1911). National Archives, Cromer papers, FO 633/28. His other public work included the posts of President of the Classical Association, President of the Research Defence Society (opposing the anti-vivisection movement), Chair of the Entomological Research Committee, member of the Council of the Zoological Society.

[18] Curzon's other work included being President of the Royal Geographical Society and a trustee of the National Gallery, as well as a keen conserver of historic buildings.

launch of the National League.[19] Their outlook on the amalgamation process was inevitably coloured by this success, as well as by their general consciousness of masculine power and prestige. Despite the fact that Curzon lacked Cromer's personal affability, the two men rapidly established a close working partnership founded upon their fundamentally similar outlook and experience as well as their shared anti-suffragism. Their views were inseparable from their methods. In neither respect were they inclined towards deference to female colleagues. Nor were they prepared to accept the full consequences of equal gender representation at the heart of an organization which was founded upon women's support, as well as men's money.

AMALGAMATION

The formation of the NLOWS was not completed until 6 December 1910, more than four months after its official announcement to the general public. At this stage in the history of anti-suffragism, an important new source of evidence comes to the fore. Cromer and Curzon exchanged almost daily letters on organizational matters, never more so than during the amalgamation discussions. Curzon carefully preserved his correspondence, on a selective basis which helped reinforce his own preferred version of the League's history.[20] Women's voices are scarcer than they should be in this archive; it is apparent that many women's letters were sacrificed to Curzon's review of his anti-suffrage papers after the cause had been lost. Nevertheless enough correspondence survives to convey a vivid picture of the obstacles to amalgamation, and of other problems experienced by the NLOWS during the pre-war years. Despite the eventual success of male leaders in dominating policy-making, women remained prominent at every level of the new League and provided the vast majority of its members. Alongside the Curzon and Cromer archives, evidence of their ideas and actions survives in the private papers of Mary and Dorothy Ward, Violet Markham, Ethel Harrison, and Gertrude Bell, as well as in published women's writings and the weekly reports of the *Anti-Suffrage Review*.

The summer of 1910 was a fraught and exciting period for women anti-suffragists, as they dreaded the passage of suffrage legislation, denounced impressive suffrage propaganda, and at the same time exulted in the potential strength of a mixed-sex League sponsored and funded by leading male

---

[19] See detailed correspondence on fund-raising, including letters from anti-suffrage donors, in Curzon papers, MSS Eur F112/33A.

[20] Curzon recorded his decision to edit his own anti-suffrage archive, in Curzon papers, MSS Eur F112/37: 'In October 1918 after the final determination of the Woman Suffrage struggle and the victory of the Suffragists I went through the whole of the vast correspondence that I had accumulated . . . and decided that there was no object in keeping it since it would never interest anyone and the cause had been lost.' There are a number of internal references in the correspondence to women's letters which did not survive this cull.

imperialists. As the Men's League embarked upon its open-air campaign, the Women's League was also re-evaluating its tactics. On 4 August Mary Ward wrote to her friend Louise Creighton: 'These weeks since the middle of June have been unusually strenuous for me. Anti-suffragism has been a heavy burden, especially the effort to give the movement a more constructive and positive side.'[21] During June, Cromer and Curzon began their fund-raising drive. Though there is no record of the date when their amalgamation plans were first unveiled to the existing Leagues, it seems probable that renewed efforts to embed 'positive' local government work within the Women's League were influenced by forthcoming negotiations over the purposes of the new, united organization. The July edition of the *Anti-Suffrage Review* carried an article titled 'The Principles of Our League', which reported support for the local government initiative from the executive committee and the recent Annual Council Meeting of the League. In response to proposals from Mary Ward and Janet Hogarth, the executive had resolved to promote women's understanding of their existing powers in local government, to support anti-suffrage women's representation upon public committees, and to appoint a Local Government Sub-Committee. The WNASL Council meeting in the same month gave 'all but unanimous' support to a resolution along similar lines, after speeches from Edith Somervell, Violet Montrose, and others. In every case, the women advocating the forward policy emphasized that it represented important principles, rather than merely a short-term shift in tactics. Elizabeth Burgwin's speech during the July deputation to the Prime Minister carried a similar emphasis. Mary Ward was clearly far from alone in believing that the time had come for 'a certain new and definite stage in the progress of our League', to be marked by advances in policy as well as the promise of extra funding and the arrival of male colleagues. Such advances would benefit organized anti-suffragism through the support of 'thousands of women, anti-Suffragist at heart, or still undecided, who may be attracted to a positive and alternative programme'; most importantly, it would benefit 'the nation also'.[22]

During the autumn of 1910, as amalgamation talks proceeded, the principled advocacy of a forward policy gathered further momentum. Cromer's intention that the NLOWS should work exclusively in the cause of opposition to women's suffrage was eventually modified into an uneasy acceptance that 'clause b' (the local government objective from the WNASL constitution) must be put to a membership vote at the official launch meeting. Deeply rooted in the maternal reformism of so many women anti-suffragists, the forward policy held little appeal for the new masculine leadership. Instead, the debate over 'clause b' was seen as merely another in a growing list of obstacles which needed to be swept aside before the NLOWS could begin its real work. Cromer's correspondence

[21] Mary Ward to Louise Creighton, 4 Aug. 1910. Pusey House Library, Oxford, M. Ward papers, 3/3/1.

[22] *Anti-Suffrage Review*, 20 (July 1910), 2.

with Curzon during this period provides an exceptionally intimate account of the frustration felt by both men, as they gradually came to terms with the fact that the Women's League was an organization of women with ideas of their own. The July announcement of amalgamation in *The Times* had appeared above the names of 105 men and only 20 women.[23] Despite the combined weight of distinguished male signatories, and the extent of their financial support to the unified League, the fact remained that organized anti-suffragism in the country was currently a product of the WNASL. Without these women's support, the NLOWS would lack all patriotic and political credibility. Unwelcome compromises became inevitable, and with them a deterioration of gender relations which was never fully repaired during the rest of the amalgamated League's history.

It is interesting to compare Cromer and Curzon's confident, somewhat technical approach to the amalgamation process with the responses of women leaders who were eager to demonstrate successful feminine collaboration as well as to achieve acceptable outcomes. Shared underlying preoccupation over the definition of appropriate gender roles did not necessarily smooth the path of negotiations. In the first stages of the National League, Cromer and Curzon provided a model of strong leadership, ignoring the sensibilities of the Women's League in their single-minded pursuit of masculine wealth. The man-to-man correspondence which accompanied early donations served to underline their access to social circles, and to frank expressions of opinion, which would never have been open to anti-suffrage women. £100,000 was the target sum, and the financial outcome of direct requests by powerful men stood in stark contrast to the Women's League's philanthropic fund-raising through press appeals, sales of work, penny readings, and garden parties. On the crest of this financial success, Cromer and Curzon at first took an equally high-handed approach to the task of determining the new League's constitution and office arrangements. Early drafts of the NLOWS constitution, amended by each of the proconsuls, show that they were concerned from the outset to establish male authority. Curzon proposed twelve men and six women on the executive committee, while Cromer sought to reinforce the powers of the (male) Organizing Agent over local branch agents ('otherwise they will refuse to obey him and will be always appealing to the EC over his head').[24] The first printed announcement of the new organization was apparently sent out to newspaper editors without consultation with the women leaders. Cromer informed Curzon on 15 July that he had written to Lady Jersey and to Mrs HW 'with apologies for not consulting her on the draft'.[25] The following day Mary Ward telephoned him to object to the unfortunate title of

---

[23] *The Times*, 21 July 1910, 9; repr. in *Anti-Suffrage Review*, 21 (Aug. 1910), 2.
[24] Draft constitution, with marginal amendments from Curzon and notes from Cromer. Curzon papers, MSS Eur F112/33A.
[25] Cromer to Curzon, 15 July 1910. Curzon papers, MSS Eur F112/33A.

the printed document: 'Anti-Woman Suffrage Appeal'.[26] Cromer conceded the point, and by 21 July *The Times* had shifted a hyphen to spare female sensibilities.

This minor contretemps presaged later disagreements, but was counterbalanced by the somewhat obsequious response of other leading women to the proconsuls' amalgamation drive. Harriet Wantage, one of the Women's League's most generous and enthusiastic supporters, wrote to Cromer on 13 July: 'Forgive my troubling you with a letter . . . as you are about to organise a Committee, I am desirous to draw your attention to Miss Gladys Pott . . . I can bear testimony to her remarkable ability and organising capacity — and to her powers of speaking'.[27] Lucy Terry Lewis responded eagerly to Curzon's rather surprising enquiry about the existence or otherwise of a WNASL journal. As well as despatching all the 1910 copies of the *Anti-Suffrage Review*, she requested his biographical information for inclusion in the *Review*'s gallery of front-page leadership portraits: would he wish her to approach his secretary, 'or shall I have it prepared here in the office and sent to you for revision?'[28] The August edition of the *Review* reminded women readers of 'the immense access of strength brought to us by the foundation of the new National League due to the efforts of Lord Cromer and Lord Curzon';[29] their portraits duly graced the front page in 1910 and 1911, together with those of ten other male leaders.

At one level, leading women anti-suffragists regarded the grateful acceptance of male leadership as highly desirable in itself, as well as necessary for the success of the amalgamated League. However, they were also proud of their own organization's achievements, and concerned that its broader policies should not be eclipsed within a single-minded and purely negative campaign. As the weeks passed, mildly critical comments hardened into stubborn resistance to some aspects of the two proconsuls' plans. The issue of 'clause b' was inseparable from anxieties over the status of women within the National League, and over male anti-suffragist attitudes to women's role in public life generally. The Cromer–Curzon correspondence indicates that these fears were well founded. On 18 July Cromer observed condescendingly: 'It is important to keep the Women's Association in a good temper . . . I have told Lady Jersey that I hope she will remain on the Committee. We want her name. We shall have to add other women, even if we go beyond the number of 12 on the Committee. It is very improbable they will all attend at once.'[30] By August the gender balance within the new League's office had become the subject of what was to prove a long-running and acrimonious debate: 'MPs and others who call for information will, as you very rightly say, expect to find a man . . . I gather from various indications that if the staff is made purely feminine a good deal of resentment

[26] Cromer to Curzon, 16 July 1910. Curzon papers, MSS Eur F112/33A.
[27] Lady Wantage to Curzon, 13 July 1913. Curzon papers, MSS Eur F112/33A.
[28] Lucy Terry Lewis to Curzon, 14 July 1910. Curzon papers, MSS Eur F112/33A.
[29] *Anti-Suffrage Review*, 21 (Aug. 1910), 3.
[30] Cromer to Curzon, 18 July 1910. Curzon papers, MSS Eur F112/33A.

will be caused.'[31] Parallel discussions over female committee representation and female staffing continued over the next two months, growing steadily more heated. On 13 August Cromer made the ominous private comment: 'There is a good deal of truth in what you say, namely that the women may perhaps be unconsciously adopting the principle of amalgamation without carrying it out fully in practice'.[32] Office politics continued to feature prominently in his letters, as Lucy Terry Lewis clung to her existing responsibilities and proved 'very jealous of male interference'.[33]

The issue of committee membership was a still more delicate one, since it involved relations between social equals as well as between men and women. From her holiday home in Italy, Margaret Jersey eventually delivered a strongly worded intervention which attempted to break the deadlock without conceding points of principle. Like Cromer and Curzon, she believed that practicality and principle went hand in hand, and that settlement of organizational difficulties on her own terms would contribute to the long-term political success of the League. After listing the outstanding problems, she went to the gendered heart of the matter by stating that 'In an ordinary way in a joint organisation of men and women we anti-suffragists should be perfectly content to leave the hegemony to the men and to act as auxiliaries behind the scenes—but here, since the main object is to convince the country at large and Parliament in particular that the majority of women do not want the franchise, it would appear absolutely necessary to give women at least an equal place with men in the League'.[34] In deference to the proconsuls' fund-raising success, Lady Jersey was prepared to concede financial authority to a separate male Finance Committee, but the constitution of the NLOWS executive was a different matter. The WNASL was governed by a Council of branch representatives and guinea subscribers, and its elected executive could not be summarily dismissed, as had already happened in the case of the Men's League. The new League's executive must be formally approved by the WNASL Council, on the recommendation of its executive: 'If this is not carried out with the goodwill of both bodies we shall seriously damp the enthusiasm of our supporters who are working hard throughout the UK and money will not win the day apart from enthusiasm.'

Touching upon an even more sensitive issue, Lady Jersey continued: 'I observe that Lord Cromer's name already appears on the stationery of the new League as "President". No doubt everyone will agree to his assuming this Office but it must be regularised by his name being submitted to the Council. The Chairman of the Executive must presumably be appointed by the Executive and probably should be a woman if the President is a man'. On the subject of office arrangements,

[31] Cromer to Curzon, 11 Aug. 1910. Curzon papers, MSS Eur F112/33B.
[32] Cromer to Curzon, 13 Aug. 1910. Curzon papers, MSS Eur F112/33B.
[33] Cromer to Curzon, 11 Sept. 1910. Curzon papers, MSS Eur F112/33B.
[34] Margaret Jersey to Curzon, 21 Sept. 1910. Curzon papers, MSS Eur F112/33B.

she proposed a clear division of labour between Miss Terry Lewis's role as Office Secretary and the new male role of Organizing Secretary, adding the prescient comment that 'It is always most difficult to get a first-rate *man* for these positions . . . whereas, anyhow at present, the most capable women are generally available. A first class man may be better than a first class woman—but a first class woman is better than a second class man!'[35] Cromer and Curzon apparently consulted together before replying to this letter. The office proposals were immediately accepted, but other issues remained problematic. Both men were determined that Cromer should chair the executive as well as presiding over the League, and remained suspicious of elective office. They hoped to appease the women leaders generally, as well as Lady Jersey personally, by granting her 'some special position'. Cromer felt that the vice-chairmanship of the executive could safely be conceded without loss of masculine authority: 'I do not think that much harm would be done, for certainly, so long as I am President, I will take very good care that I am always present at the meetings of the Committee, so as to take the Chair.'[36]

By October Margaret Jersey was back in London, and persisting in the defence of the WNASL through a subtle insistence upon her own difficulty in convincing others to accept necessary change. Lord Cromer found her 'perfectly reasonable, but she is evidently greatly exercised at the trouble she is likely to have with her Committee and Council of Women, who are rather a difficult team to drive. More especially she wants to bring on to the new Committee a larger number of the women who are already on her existing Committee.' Swallowing the elective principle, he accepted the need to 'get out of the idea, which would be largely entertained by many of the members, that anyone is being crammed down their throats'. Even if the constitution neutrally specified a President and Deputy President, 'Without doubt, in practice, the President would always be a man and the Deputy President a woman'.[37] However, a couple of days later hostilities were resumed, as Cromer criticized Lady Jersey's attitude ('unfriendly, not to say aggressive'), and supported Curzon's view that 'there must be some limit to these sacrifices'. Observing that 'the Women's League rather have the whip hand of us', he appears briefly to have contemplated re-establishing a separate Men's League, and indefinitely postponing amalgamation.[38] Other correspondence suggests that by this date the anti-suffrage women were successfully enlisting some male supporters to their side of the debate.[39] With the help of persuasion, threats, and arguments, compromise solutions were finally agreed which conceded most of

[35] Ibid. [36] Cromer to Curzon, 26 and 29 Sept. 1910. Curzon papers, MSS Eur F112/33B.
[37] Cromer to Curzon, 10 Oct. 1910. Curzon papers, MSS Eur F112/33B.
[38] Cromer to Curzon, 13 Oct. 1913. Curzon papers, MSS Eur F112/33B.
[39] On 16 Oct. 1910 John Massie forwarded to Cromer a letter from R. C. Lehmann MP which stated categorically, 'My opinion from the very beginning of this agitation has been that the best method of countering and crushing the suffrage movement is to let the anti-suffrage women lead the fight'. Curzon papers, MSS Eur F112/33B.

the women's constitutional demands on the basis that, in practice, the leading men could continue to organize things in their own way. At the beginning of November the WNASL executive approved the new constitution, after insisting upon a change of name to the National League for Opposing Woman Suffrage. The women had remained adamant upon the inclusion of 'clause b', committing the NLOWS 'To maintain the principle of the representation of women on Municipal and other bodies concerned with the domestic and social affairs of the community'. Gertrude Bell reported the executive meeting to Violet Markham, observing that 'We carried Clause B . . . There was a debate over it, more of a debate than I had anticipated. But we were in a majority all the time and I knew that we must win.'[40]

The formal adoption of this clause provided the only discordant note at the December launch meeting. By this date Cromer had been convinced by Margaret Jersey, Mary Ward, Gertrude Bell, Violet Markham, and others that the forward policy was supported by a majority of women members who might defect from a League which rejected their priorities. Cromer himself was not unfriendly to the idea of women in local government, but was opposed to what he regarded as an unnecessary distraction from the League's primary purpose. A membership vote at the first NLOWS Council meeting was intended to legitimate the inclusion of an unwelcome clause, and also to reassure the women that their views were being heeded. Cromer's conversion to this necessary compromise is recorded not only in his disgruntled correspondence with Curzon, but also in his more respectful exchange of letters during October and November with several of the leading women. To Mary Ward he wrote reassuringly about the future independence of existing women's branches and about his hopes for the future of the *Anti-Suffrage Review*, as well as acknowledging her concerns over local government work.[41] To Gertrude Bell, he confessed frankly that his views were being influenced by the threat of 'a very large defection from the Women's League'.[42] Her own personal support for 'clause b' had been expressed in an earlier letter.[43] On 6 December 1910 the WNASL Council finally approved the constitution, before joining with the male anti-suffragists to complete the formal process of amalgamation through the election of Cromer as President, Lady Jersey as Vice-President, and a new executive of seven men and seven women (Elizabeth Burgwin, Maud Hamilton, Ethel Harrison, Edith Massie, Catherine Robson, Edith Somervell, and Mary Ward).[44]

Three letters received (and carefully preserved) by Lord Curzon in the days after the launch bear out the view that the WNASL's own divisions over the

---

[40] Gertrude Bell to Violet Markham, n.d. (Nov. 1910). BLPES, LSE, Markham papers, 25/12.
[41] Cromer to Mary Ward, 10 Oct. 1910. Cromer papers, FO633/19.
[42] Cromer to Gertrude Bell, 2 Nov. 1910. Cromer papers, FO633/19.
[43] Cromer sent Gertrude Bell's letter of support for 'clause b' on to Curzon on 3 Nov. 1910, with the cryptic comment that she was 'about the cleverest, most sensible and, I may add, the most friendly among the women'. Curzon papers, MSS Eur F112/33B. Curzon did not keep her letter.
[44] *Anti-Suffrage Review*, 26 (Jan. 1911), 10.

forward policy were still very much alive, and had probably been underestimated by Lord Cromer. Jeanie Ross, assistant secretary of the large Kensington branch of the WNASL, claimed that the women's vote on the local government clause had been 'hurriedly taken, without discussion, without understanding of the issue'; Curzon's criticisms during the second meeting 'convinced a very large number, if not the majority, of the women present that their vote had been a mistake . . . Clause B may be prized by a few advocates of a Woman's Parliament, such as Mrs Somervell, but for the great body of our supporters it may be said to be non-existent.'[45] Mrs Burdon Muller, of Bracknell, ingratiatingly praised the 'strength and vigour' of the meeting led by men, adding, 'As to that B clause, of course you are right . . . those women who want it included are as bad as those who want the vote'.[46] Agnes Hills, a delegate from the West Sussex branch, lengthily explained her reasons for voting against the disputed clause, claiming that its inclusion reflected women's general lack of political sense: 'it might slip into first place with those of our supporters who are ardent "social reformers", and, before we know where we are, we might even find ourselves as a League apparently associated with some of the hare-brained schemes of so-called "Social Reform"—socialistic or other, which are so rife in these days'.[47] No doubt these letters were kept by Curzon as ammunition for possible future debates within the NLOWS. Within fourteen months the male leaders had in fact succeeded in reversing the League's initial decision to back the forward policy. The value of women's support to the NLOWS was not open to challenge, but their influence within its leadership remained a contested area as the newly constituted League tried to refocus its energies upon the tasks of direct opposition to the suffrage movement.

A JOINT CAMPAIGN

The conflicts within the NLOWS shed revealing light upon its internal gender relations and the varied outlook of anti-suffrage women. However, due attention must also be given to the League's achievements as a mixed-sex organization. In the years before the war it fulfilled some, though not all, of the hopes of its creators. By 1914 the NLOWS claimed over 50,000 adherents, many of them women who had played little or no previous part in active politics. Organized anti-suffragism was an acknowledged part of the suffrage debate by this date, both outside and inside Parliament. Joint campaigning by men and women had become a reality and was symbolized by the collaboration of male and female speakers on public platforms, as well as within the NLOWS executive. Gender

45 Jeanie Ross to Curzon, 7 Dec. 1910. Curzon papers, MSS Eur F112/33B.
46 Mrs Burdon Muller to Curzon, 7 Dec. 1910. Curzon papers, MSS Eur F112/33B.
47 Agnes Hills to Curzon, 12 Dec. 1910. Curzon papers, MSS Eur F112/33B.

collaboration behind the scenes often required negotiation and compromise, but was not without its successes.

Mass meetings were a staple of all campaigns to sway public opinion in this period, benefiting often from overflowing attendances and extensive reporting in the local and national press. The WNASL had been severely handicapped by its lack of confident female speakers, and the women antis must have been relieved to realize that an amalgamated League guaranteed more men upon platforms as well as in anti-suffrage audiences. The distinct yet complementary roles of men and women in public life could be particularly well illustrated by the right line-up of speakers. Considerable effort usually went into achieving a satisfactory gender balance, whether in terms of platform presence, audience composition, or the content of speeches. This point is well illustrated by letters between Violet Markham and Lord Cromer before their joint appearance at the Manchester Free Trade Hall on 28 October 1910. The two had corresponded during the summer over her published suggestion of a national, consultative Women's Council. Though Cromer was dismissive of her idea, Violet remained flattered by his detailed interest. In August she wrote contrasting his eminence with her own 'ordinariness'; she hoped that 'there are many compensations given you in the faith and enthusiasm and reverence of us younger folk in the rank and file, who tread our little paths more cheerfully for the vision vouchsafed us'.[48] It was hard at this stage to imagine a partnership of equals upon the NLOWS platform a few months later. However, Cromer, still in the throes of the amalgamation negotiations, made the gracious gesture of sending her an advance copy of his Manchester speech, and inviting her comments. Taking him at his word, though 'with some diffidence', she promptly suggested that he should modify a passage which 'might, I think, be seized on as representing women too exclusively as men's possessions. I take it that our position is that women are citizens as much as men, only their citizenship is different in kind and quality'.[49] Cromer may well have been surprised to receive a lesson in progressive anti-suffragism from this source; however, the speeches reported by the *Anti-Suffrage Review* represented a scrupulous division of labour between his own lengthy oration upon 'manly' rule of the empire and Violet Markham's brief disquisition upon the functions of men and women in relation to 'the management of the State'. Both speakers emphasized innate gender characteristics. Violet enlivened a serious point about 'natural' difference with the slightly skittish remark that 'I regard women as superior to men, and therefore I don't like to see them trying to become men's equals'. Cromer, on the other hand, delivered his views on feminine weaknesses as an obstacle to imperial rule with masculine gravitas. The *Review* noted that

---

[48] Violet Markham to Cromer, 12 Aug. 1910. Cromer papers, FO633/19.
[49] Violet Markham to Cromer, 24 Oct. 1910. She prefaced her criticism with the comment that his speech was '*quite admirable*—so moderate and all the more convincing for that fact'. Cromer papers, FO633/19.

'Women were not admitted to the body of the hall, as Lord Cromer wished to make a special appeal to the electorate. There were, however, several ladies on the platform.'[50]

As President of the NLOWS, and one of the most sought-after anti-suffrage speakers, Cromer became familiar with the demands of speaking successfully alongside women antis. His speeches were reported in full by the *Anti-Suffrage Review*, while those of women speakers were often abbreviated. At Cambridge, speaking alongside Ethel Colquhoun, he drew upon his own imperial authority to endorse social evolutionary views on gender roles and the suffrage issue, telling his audience that 'the advance of civilisation, far from obliterating sex distinctions, as we are sometimes invited to believe . . . accentuates those differences by the refinement which it brings in its train. There is much more difference, both physically and morally, between an educated European man and woman than there is between a negro and a negress belonging to some savage Central African tribe.'[51] Alongside such weighty male expertise, and before male audiences, women speakers usually sounded rather shallow, and tended to exaggerate their feminine qualities by concentrating upon their own 'expert' areas of womanly work and womanly social influence. Whether consciously or unconsciously, they were fulfilling the expectations set out in the speeches of male anti-suffragists. Mrs Colquhoun, who in other circumstances was certainly capable of a full-length and closely argued speech, confined herself on this occasion to some ironical comments on modern developments in 'feminism', and a commendation of women's alternative roles in public life. Cromer was once again the main speaker at the NLOWS Annual Council in July 1911. Departing from the imperial theme, he told his (mostly female) audience that their influence upon male relatives was the most important service they could render. Ultimately the suffrage issue must be decided by a male electorate and a male Parliament, so he believed the NLOWS should concentrate upon stirring up male public opinion in the country. This unanswerable argument was paralleled, rather than complemented, by Mary Ward's accompanying speech on her favourite theme of the forward policy.[52]

The most successful public meetings ever organized by the NLOWS were held after the first flush of enthusiasm for the united League had worn off. Though branches were expanding, and renewed militancy was winning recruits to anti-suffrage cause, by late 1911 there was an uneasy recognition that suffragism was continuing to make ground while the NLOWS headquarters remained plagued by doubts and divisions. The leadership response was to plan large-scale, prestigious demonstrations of opposition to the vote in both England and Scotland. The Royal Albert Hall was filled to its 9,000 capacity on 28 February 1912, after

[50] *Anti-Suffrage Review*, 24 (Nov. 1910), 9.
[51] *Anti-Suffrage Review*, 29 (Apr. 1911), 72.
[52] *Anti-Suffrage Review*, 33 (Aug. 1911), 167.

20,000 ticket applications had been received. On 1 November in the same year, St Andrew's Hall, Glasgow attracted an audience of over 6,000. The proconsuls were in their element, as they pulled strings and called in favours to attract the largest possible number of Cabinet ministers and other worthies as speakers or well-publicized attenders. Though men and women were present in roughly equal numbers, there was an evident danger that these high-profile gatherings would be entirely dominated by male speakers and masculine priorities. In the weeks before the London meeting, Cromer's attention was entirely focused upon the political complexion of a platform line-up which eventually included senior Liberals as well as Unionists. A phalanx of other distinguished men surrounded them, and it was not until late January that Cromer turned his mind to the question of a lady speaker and the design of platform seating arrangements which would demonstrate the mixed-sex (as well as cross-party) nature of anti-suffrage support.[53]

Violet Markham accepted Cromer's belated invitation, and (to the delight of many fellow women) proceeded to deliver the outstanding speech of the evening.[54] Her skilfully worded defence of the forward policy did much to heal an uncomfortable gender rift within the League which will be further investigated in Chapter 9. Inspired by her success, the organizers of the Glasgow meeting allowed more generous space to their lady speakers, the Duchess of Montrose and the Marchioness of Tullibardine. In his Glasgow speech, Curzon delivered one of his most rotund denunciations of female suffrage from a masculine viewpoint, noting that women's perspectives would be separately addressed by a speaker 'infinitely better qualified to deal with the matter than any man can be'. The Marchioness of Tullibardine, like Violet Markham before her, kept largely to the limited brief assigned her as a representative of her sex, but successfully transformed its narrow boundaries into a passionate defence of the values of the forward movement.[55]

The NLOWS ran most smoothly as a mixed-sex organization when its women leaders were prepared to accept a restricted organizational role defined by conservative gender views. Women activists were a necessary part of the NLOWS, but the Cromer–Curzon leadership expected them to practise what the League preached in terms of differentiated gender behaviour. As the male leaders asserted their authority over policy and organization, some of the most talented women leaders gradually accepted a more back-seat role within the League than had seemed likely in the combative early stages of amalgamation. By 1914 Margaret Jersey was devoting far less time to the anti-suffrage cause; Violet Markham had withdrawn as a public speaker, only partly for personal

---

[53] Cromer to Curzon, 23 Jan. 1912. Curzon papers, MSS Eur 112/35.

[54] Her success is evidenced in press reports and in correspondence she received after the meeting. See 'Albert Hall letters'. Markham papers, 26/30.

[55] *Anti-Suffrage Review*, 49 (Dec. 1912), 293–4.

reasons; Edith Somervell and Ethel Harrison had also virtually retired, claiming health grounds; while Gertrude Bell had moved on to wider arenas. Only Ethel Colquhoun, the leading Scottish ladies, and a small number of less prestigious women speakers such as Gwladys Gladstone Solomon and Helena Norris were still taking to national platforms alongside the dominant males of the NLOWS. Mary Ward, the most formidable of the anti-suffrage women, was as active as ever, but her anti-suffragism was divergent and vigorous enough to prove more of a problem than a support to the male leadership. Gladys Pott, on other hand, provides the intriguing case of a woman leader who worked productively with Curzon and Cromer, whilst also maintaining her forward views and her friendship with Mary Ward. Her full-scale commitment to the League was rather sporadic, being governed by unspecified family commitments.[56] During the difficult period of 1912–13 she spent more than a year as the salaried secretary of the NLOWS, in addition to voluntary activity in Berkshire and in London. More than any other leading woman, she won the undiluted respect of Cromer and Curzon, both because of her evident administrative talent and because of the strength of her anti-suffrage commitment. Her supreme tact was perhaps as important to her success as either of these attributes. It governed her relations with the proconsuls and enabled her to follow through many of her own key tactical ideas, often through collaborative action behind the scenes rather than through public campaigning alongside the leading men.

One of the aspects of the suffrage campaign which most concerned Gladys Pott was the development of the Church Suffrage League. As an Archdeacon's daughter and a devout Anglican, she deeply resented this apparent attempt to appropriate religious sanction to one side of the suffrage argument. As well as venting her annoyance in letters to the press and articles in the *Anti-Suffrage Review*, she achieved a notably successful collaboration with Lord Curzon which helped to curb the Anglican Church Congress's engagement with suffragism during 1912–13. Emanating from the NLOWS headquarters, anti-suffrage lobbying contributed towards modification of the programmes of two successive Congresses. Favourable publicity opportunities were denied to the suffragists, while the anti-suffrage correspondence between Lord Curzon and the Bishop of Winchester appeared prominently in *The Times*.[57] Gertrude Bell was Curzon's other chief informant during this controversy. Though she shared little or none of Gladys Pott's religious faith, Gertrude was well connected in Church circles

---

[56] Gladys Pott's resignation in Oct. 1913 was accompanied by a private explanation of the links between her anti-suffragism and her devotion to family duty: 'We women have so often to make the choice between doing the details of home efficiently or leaving them to chance and devoting all our energy to outside work. It is a very difficult choice, but I should not be as strong an anti-suffragist as I am did I not feel certain that the most monotonous attention to detail is as important a labour as the more notorious public work.' Gladys Pott to Curzon, 21 Oct. 1913. Curzon papers, MSS Eur F112/36.

[57] *The Times*, 16 June 1913, 6.

and supported the view that the NLOWS should take up active resistance to encroaching Anglican suffragism. Like Gladys Pott, she preferred to work on this issue in collaboration with the leading men of the League, and attributed their joint successes to anti-suffrage methods of tactful partnership between men and women. Before the 1912 Church Congress, held on her home ground in Middlesborough, Gertrude exerted her private influence through the Archbishop of York to restrain suffrage interventions.[58]

In 1913 the threat of suffrage opportunism was strongly revived, for the Congress was billed to include a session on 'The Woman's Movement', and to be presided over by a suffrage-friendly Bishop. Gladys Pott raised the alarm in a long letter to Curzon, including details of the proposed programme and of her own correspondence with anti-suffrage clergy, as well as providing extensive information on suffragist religious tactics.[59] After consulting with the anti-suffragist Dean of Westminster (to whom he forwarded Gladys Pott's letter), Curzon agreed to intervene as she had requested. The ensuing correspondence between Curzon and the Bishop of Winchester rested heavily upon her research into Anglican suffragism. In early June Gladys Pott wrote to Curzon: 'I have sketched out a rough suggestion of a reply to him, knowing that you will reframe the matter if you desire to use it. I have actual documentary evidence for each point mentioned.'[60] This dependable but self-effacing approach must have been irresistible to the busy President. The Congress session on 'the Woman's Movement' eventually went ahead, but with the guarantee of a more balanced platform as the Bishop invited Curzon to nominate an anti-suffrage speaker. Lucy Soulsby attended the Congress, in the absence of the requested Violet Markham. Though pleased by this outcome, and well satisfied with her own role in promoting it, Gladys Pott was deeply disappointed not to be invited to speak at the Congress herself. With typical thoroughness, she had sought Curzon's permission to put the whole issue before the NLOWS executive, and extended her own and Gertrude Bell's lobbying to other friendly clerics. As a consequence, there was the consolation of an anti-suffrage fringe meeting alongside the Congress: the Dean of Durham 'took exactly the line that I think all ecclesiastics ought to take in the matter'.[61]

Gladys Pott's skills in backroom persuasion were soon needed in other departments of the League's work. Perhaps most significantly, she sought to improve collaboration between the NLOWS and its supporters in Parliament. A closer working relationship with Parliament had been one of the main WNASL ambitions at the point of amalgamation. A complementary balance was envisaged between male parliamentary anti-suffragism and women's mobilization

---

[58] Gertrude Bell to Curzon, 10 June 1913. Curzon papers, MSS Eur F112/36.
[59] Gladys Pott to Curzon, 16 March 1913. Curzon papers, MSS Eur F112/36.
[60] Gladys Pott to Curzon, 'Thursday' ?June 1913. Curzon papers, MSS Eur F112/36.
[61] Gladys Pott to Curzon, 8 Sept. 1913. Curzon papers, MSS Eur F112/36. See also her diatribe against Church suffragism in the *Anti-Suffrage Review*, 60 (Oct. 1913), 209–10.

of female opinion in the country. But in practice, the direct activities of the League within Parliament soon proved a disappointment. Though the NLOWS boasted a Parliamentary Committee (listed prominently on its headed notepaper), this group of anti-suffrage MPs appears to have undertaken very little concerted activity. Cromer and Curzon were important parliamentary figures, but absent from the Commons; their association with Unionism helped to distance most Liberals from organized anti-suffragism, while their publicly-declared distrust of party political machinations did little to endear them to Conservative colleagues. Arnold Ward's presence in the Commons from January 1910 onwards delighted his mother, without contributing much to the painstaking work of consolidating anti-suffragism's parliamentary forces. During 1912–13 Gladys Pott became increasingly conscious of the League's parliamentary deficiencies. Though successive Conciliation Bills went down to defeat in 1911 and 1912, there was every prospect of a future revival of the parliamentary cause, and also the dangerous prospect of the moderate suffragists' new-found alliance with the Labour party.

Parliamentary anti-suffragism lay very definitely within the masculine sphere of the NLOWS, but Gladys Pott found many opportunities to exercise her own considerable powers of persuasion and organization. During the critical period of the Dickinson Bill (May 1913), her correspondence with Lord Curzon reveals her increasingly desperate attempts to compensate for Arnold Ward's weaknesses as the League's parliamentary coordinator. In April she privately warned her chief that 'Mr Ward is a very busy man and unable to spare much time for interviews and I think at present we are in need of alternative sources of Parliamentary information'.[62] On 1 May she bluntly informed Curzon that 'no help of any kind has been afforded us by our Unionist members of Committee'; instead, she had taken matters into her own hands by sending MPs her own circular letters on behalf of the NLOWS, including one giving the results of women's anti-suffrage canvassing in the constituencies and another (reassuringly) 'upon the lines of your letter to me'.[63] The following day, the situation escalated further. Gladys Pott reported that she had been forced to put aside her researches on Church suffragism since she had been 'hard at work all day preparing notes for Mr Ward and others for speeches in the House on Monday . . . Mr Ward is to move the rejection of the Bill and tells me he finds it very difficult to get people to speak'.[64] The joint anti-suffrage campaigning of men and women appears at this point to have been moving into uncharted territory. Whether or not Gladys Pott realized the full irony of her actions, given successive Presidents' insistence upon masculine authority within the NLOWS, it is to her credit that she successfully retained Curzon's confidence whilst temporarily seizing the

[62] Gladys Pott to Curzon, 11 Apr. 1913. Curzon papers, MSS Eur F112/36.
[63] Gladys Pott to Curzon, 1 May 1913. Curzon papers, MSS Eur F112/36.
[64] Gladys Pott to Curzon, 2 May 1913. Curzon papers, MSS Eur F112/36.

initiative in anti-suffrage parliamentary organization. Personal qualities apart, her deeply held belief in the complementary strengths of men and women provided the basis for these bold female efforts in a common cause.

PUBLIC SUPPORT

The NLOWS aimed to bring the influence of public opinion to bear upon parliamentary decision-makers. Its achievements within Parliament were unimpressive, but its efforts to make public opposition to suffragism more visible achieved measurable results in terms of the growth of membership and branch activities. The purpose of local activity was to foster active male and female support, and also to demonstrate the existence of latent anti-suffragism at every level of society and in every part of Britain. From the viewpoint of Cromer and Curzon, the male electorate was the principal target of anti-suffrage propaganda. Women leaders, on the other hand, continued their earlier efforts to stir unenfranchised female public opinion. Was the amalgamated NLOWS more successful than the female-led WNASL in rousing public support? There is certainly some evidence to suggest that this was the case. The Annual Council of 1911 received welcome news of 72 new branches in the first year of amalgamation; in April 1912 the total had risen to over 230; by February 1913 there were some 270 League branches, and more than 33,000 members.[65] When Lady Tullibardine reported on NLOWS membership at the Annual Council Meeting in June 1914, she was able to announce a total of '42,000 subscribing members and 15,000 adherents at the end of six years work . . . a very good record which compares very favourably with the records of the associations organised by our opponents'.[66] Anti-suffrage speakers were often keen to drive home the links between militancy and the wider suffrage movement: as Lord Curzon put it in his address to the same meeting, 'These wild women are in a sense the most capable recruiting sergeants that we could have, and every one of them is an unconscious agent for our cause'.

However the League's strength could not be measured by membership numbers alone. Levels of commitment mattered too, and anti-suffragism's financial weakness stood in stark contrast to the financial successes of both moderate and militant suffragism. Despite suffragist accusations that the antis were bankrolled by plutocrats, the NLOWS faced periodic financial crisis as its activities expanded during 1912–14. Something of an internal stand-off developed among League organizers, as subscription income failed to meet rising costs yet Lord Curzon steadily refused to make up the shortfall by releasing more of his 1910 launch fund. Meanwhile Lady Tullibardine admitted to being impressed by the militant suffragists' large numbers of small-scale subscriptions, and by the high circulation

---

[65] *Anti-Suffrage Review*, 33 (Aug. 1911), 165; 41 (Apr. 1912), 82–6; 52 (Feb. 1913), 45.
[66] *Anti-Suffrage Review*, 69 (July 1914), 110. These figures included the Scottish membership.

of their newspapers. Speeches by Lord Curzon and Lord Weardale at the 1914 Annual Council frankly acknowledged that it was often an uphill struggle to convert anti-suffrage support into action, and action into income for the cause.

Alongside general evidence of membership and income, monthly branch reports in the *Anti-Suffrage Review* provide an informative, detailed picture of NLOWS efforts to build public support in the pre-war years. As Cromer had predicted to Mary Ward in 1910, there was widespread continuity in branch activity. Most WNASL branches remained in existence after the amalgamation, and retained their predominantly female leadership and membership. New branches were often simply offshoots of the existing ones, and usually followed the established pattern of upper-class or upper-middle-class female leadership and ladylike meetings in private drawing rooms. Though somewhat larger numbers of male speakers and office-holders were listed for the new NLOWS branches, the *Review* continued to record branch work as being predominantly organized by and for anti-suffrage women. In July 1911 the published list of Branch Presidents included 54 titled ladies and only 8 men (3 titled), out of a total of 119 names.[67] Some were mere figureheads, but most Presidents spoke at local meetings and sometimes hosted them at their own homes. Advice on starting new branches was occasionally offered through the *Review*, for example by Emily Simon in March 1911 and Ethel Harrison in May 1913. In both cases their emphasis was upon female activism within a conventional social context. Though Ethel Harrison remained confident of working-class support for anti-suffragism, her guidance to organizers made it clear that any mass meetings would be separate and subsequent to the main middle-and upper-class business of local committee-building. Lady Simon recommended well-structured meetings and the distribution of anti-suffrage literature, rather than the perils of public debate: 'we are, of course, deterred in this and in much of our work by difficulties which do not exist for our opponents, who will let their women and girls stand about in public places and at street corners, and who have undergone many hardening processes which we do not desire to emulate'.[68]

The NLOWS was aware of the potentially contradictory messages conveyed by women's public propaganda in support of their own abstention from parliamentary elections, but also reluctant to allow the more adventurous suffragists to monopolize effective publicity channels. An analysis of branch activities reported by the *Anti-Suffrage Review* in January 1913 and January 1914 shows that old and new methods were in practice side by side.[69] Alongside private drawing room meetings were listed larger 'At Home' gatherings in public venues, and a range of other public events including plays and concerts. Classes in public speaking for women were on offer from Ethel Colquhoun and Gladys Pott, in an attempt

[67] *Anti-Suffrage Review*, 32 (July 1911), 150–2.
[68] *Anti-Suffrage Review*, 28 (Mar. 1911), 47.
[69] *Anti-Suffrage Review*, 51 (Jan. 1913), 325–30; 63 (Jan. 1914), 275–8.

to resolve the long-standing problems of female reticence and male reluctance to supplement anti-suffrage platforms at local meetings. A small number of national speakers remained in heavy demand at local level, but there is also evidence in the 'Branch News' columns of dozens of local anti-suffrage speakers, the majority of whom were women. In January 1914 League branches reported a total of 40 women speakers, alongside only 20 men; 66 other women and 41 other men were named participants in meetings large and small. Larger meetings were, of course, more likely to receive a public report. Formal meetings addressed by a balanced combination of male and female speakers continued to attract audiences of several hundreds in many provincial towns, and were increasingly prone to end with a vote manifesting support for the anti-suffrage cause.

Despite their hazards, public suffrage debates were growing in popularity. A small number of branches took the still greater risk of organizing open-air meetings. These generally relied upon a male speaker—for example, Mr Samuels's successful series of meetings in Cheltenham, at which the local suffragist MP was taken to task for ignoring his constituents' views—but were sometimes led by a combination of a man and a woman, as in the case of nine open-air meetings in Bolton during a December 1912 by-election. More rarely, a woman anti-suffragist speaker was prepared to take on an open-air (usually mainly male, working-class) audience. In January 1913 an enthusiastic Miss Hughes wrote that she had 'addressed a meeting of about 40 men at Messrs. Jones and Leach's timber yard', and achieved a unanimous vote against women's suffrage. The undisputed heroine of such encounters was Mrs Gladstone Solomon, who was to be found in September 1912 addressing 'a very large and enthusiastic crowd' in Aberystwyth at a two-hour meeting, as well as a series of 'dinner hour meetings' for working women in Berkhamstead.[70] This energetic speaker conducted a tour of north and west Wales in November 1912, addressing a total of twenty meetings which included three in the open air and three for 'workmen only'.[71] In January 1914 she spoke at the Bradford Mechanics' Institute, and by July 1914 had graduated to a speaking tour in Scotland which included addresses to mass audiences on Clydeside.

In January 1911 the *Anti-Suffrage Review* published an impressive photograph of 'Mrs Stewart addressing a crowd of (about 5000) workmen at Messrs Singers' Works, Clydebank'; a graceful, well-dressed figure in white amid a sea of cloth caps, she had attracted the attention and curiosity of several young women onlookers as well as of the male workforce acknowledged by the caption.[72] Like Mrs Gladstone Solomon, Agnes Stewart appears to have been an enthusiast sponsored by NLOWS headquarters to conduct short, intensive campaigns which diverged from the quietly ladylike norm of female anti-suffragism. A member

[70] *Anti-Suffrage Review*, 51 (Jan. 1913), 329; 47 (Sept. 1912), 220.
[71] *Anti-Suffrage Review*, 50 (Dec. 1912), 286.
[72] *Anti-Suffrage Review*, 26 (Jan. 1911), 8.

of the Brixton branch, she worked in collaboration with Miss Gemmell of the Scottish Anti-Suffrage League, and by May 1911 the Glasgow branch boasted 20 honorary members, 102 members, 90 associates, and 1,825 socially mixed 'adherents'.[73] This success prompted further Scottish 'tours' by Agnes Stewart herself (November 1911), Ethel Colquhoun (December 1911), Helena Norris (January 1912), and Cordelia Moir (February 1912), sometimes with limited male assistance, sometimes timed to coincide with parliamentary by-elections, and in all cases including elements of populist propaganda. At the other end of the social spectrum, Miss Ermine Taylor and others were organizing the third annual ball of the Girls' Anti-Suffrage League. This attempt to appeal to the younger generation (believed particularly vulnerable to suffragette propaganda) had been launched in January 1911 'to bring together girls of the upper classes for the purpose of giving social entertainments to collect funds for the League and with leisure time to undertake work that may be helpful in forwarding the Anti-Suffrage cause'.[74]

Anti-suffrage branches were unlikely to match their suffragist equivalents in terms of continuous campaigning and lively sociability among like-minded women. However, many were reasonably active, and not entirely dependent upon the League's national organizers and speakers for their propaganda work. The NLOWS had a life of its own at local level, even if it was a relatively quiet and unadventurous one. Though the bias of anti-suffrage organization remained towards southern England, a fairly broad spread of modest activity was apparent between 1910 and 1914. Persistent, and largely unsuccessful, efforts were made to achieve an anti-suffrage breakthrough in the north-west, where more democratic methods were judged necessary in response to the established strength of suffragism. The local records of the Manchester branch survive, offering a discouraging picture of setbacks and membership apathy.[75] In Scotland, too, organizational progress seems to have been uncertain. Optimism in the aftermath of the great Glasgow meeting of November 1912 was tempered by a number of organizational setbacks during the previous two years (outlined in an anonymous organizer's memorandum to Lord Curzon),[76] and the *Anti-Suffrage Review* usually had limited Scottish or Irish branch news to report beyond Edinburgh and Dublin. The Scottish League's aristocratic patrons apparently had little interest in the humdrum work of branch organization, and failed to capitalize on sporadic campaigning by visiting speakers. Despite the continuous existence of a single Irish branch of the NLOWS, again under aristocratic female patronage, there was little evidence of anti-suffrage activism in Ireland

---

[73] *Anti-Suffrage Review*, 30 (May 1911), 102.   [74] Ibid. 17.

[75] See analysis by Pugh, *March of the Women*, 162. The records of the Manchester NLOWS are in Manchester Central Library.

[76] See an unsigned report on the outcome of the Nov. 1912 Glasgow meeting, addressed to 'Mr Chairman' of the NLOWS, which dwelt on the previous weaknesses. A relaunch was deemed necessary, with the help of a professional organizer. Curzon papers, MSS Eur F112/34.

and the 'Dublin Notes' section of the *Anti-Suffrage Review* was merely another political comment column by an individual, unnamed author. During 1913 a grandiosely titled 'All-India Federation of the NLOWS' surfaced briefly in Mussoorie, enlisting over two hundred members in three weeks but proving still more transitory than the northern outposts in British cities.[77]

However, it would be unfair to judge the success of NLOWS local organization entirely on the basis of its weaker links. Turning to the London branches, and to strongholds such as Kent, Berkshire, Sussex, Cheltenham, and Bristol, an altogether more positive picture emerges. League branches were at their most confident when they pursued their natural bent for social hierarchy, and social events or formal meetings which reflected this. Propaganda forays into working-class districts were rare, and still more rarely linked to effective branch-building. Mainly in the context of predictable and 'safe' propaganda work, the NLOWS was able to build upon the middle- and upper-class support gained by the WNASL during 1908–10. It expanded its network of branches in a steady if unspectacular manner, and was able to make use of these organized supporters to implement several major national propaganda initiatives.

Mass petitioning of Parliament was one long-established means by which organized anti-suffragism extended and manifested its public support. The WNASL petition of 1908–9 was supplemented by further male and female signatures during the first two years after amalgamation, and in February 1913 the *Anti-Suffrage Review* reported that Arnold Ward had presented a fourth instalment of signatures, bringing the total to 430,808 men and women.[78] However, by this date the NLOWS had begun to diversify, achieving some of its most effective propaganda through more striking methods. The WNASL had initiated a canvass of women municipal electors in several London boroughs during 1910. The results were startling: with remarkable (or, according to the suffragists, suspicious) consistency, two-thirds of women who already possessed the local government vote expressed their unwillingness to exercise the parliamentary franchise. Naturally, male anti-suffrage leaders were delighted, and keen to press ahead with more widespread use of the same strategy within the NLOWS. The impressive overall outcomes of the League's canvassing were published in the *Anti-Suffrage Handbook* of 1912: 'Out of an electorate of 135,481 canvassed, replies were received from 78,369. Of these *47,286 women were against the suffrage and only 21,725 for it. The number of neutral replies was 9,358.*'[79] A total of 103 districts had been canvassed, in rural and urban England, and it was noted that the higher the response rate, the bigger the anti-suffrage majority.

Of course the suffrage camp could not allow these results to go uncontested. Suffrage counter-propaganda soon emerged, and for many months arguments

---

[77] *Anti-Suffrage Review*, 60 (Sept. 1913), 194.
[78] *Anti-Suffrage Review*, 52 (Feb. 1913), 31.
[79] NLOWS, *The Anti-Suffrage Handbook* (London: National Press Agency, 1913), 70.

raged over methodologies of canvassing and the reliability of their outcomes. Suffragist householders in canvassed areas wrote to national and local newspapers claiming to have been deliberately missed out of the count,[80] while behind the scenes the London Society for Women's Suffrage received much anxious as well as indignant correspondence ('Have you enough data yet to write and refute this?').[81] Suffragists conducted their own canvasses, with very different outcomes. In Liverpool 1,611 of 3,185 women electors signed a suffrage petition carried round by 'educated, experienced and thoroughly trustworthy ladies', while a mere 471 refused.[82] It was claimed that 70 per cent of Cambridge women supported suffragism: a complete reversal of the anti-suffrage figures.[83] In an attempt to counter suffrage criticisms of paid canvassers on the one hand,[84] and of the 'well-dressed lady armed with the latest form of fountain pen and an ingratiating smile' on the other,[85] the National League began to canvass purely on the basis of reply-paid postcards bearing a neutral question. In January 1912 a triumphant Gladys Pott informed readers of *The Times* that four London boroughs tested by this means had produced anti-suffrage majorities comparable to those of earlier canvasses.[86] Such results provided endless fodder for speeches, leaflets, and the ongoing press debate, and eventually drove the suffragists into a preference for other methods of gauging their support.

Open debates were a popular form of propaganda among suffragists, and could be presented in the press as an instant test of public opinion. Anti-suffragists were forced to respond in kind, and achieved some successes which were proudly reported in the *Anti-Suffrage Review*. Many debates between NLOWS speakers and their opponents were mounted by other organizations as a form of public education (and entertainment), so the results were unpredictable. Naturally both sides preferred to rig the circumstances of the debate in their own favour wherever possible. Mary Ward's humiliating defeat by Millicent Fawcett at her own Passmore Edwards settlement in February 1909 was an example of misplaced faith in the power of argument over the power of efficient organization, and lessons were duly learned. The NLOWS did lose some major set-piece debates in later years, but it also won many others with the help of male as well as female speakers. The records of the London suffragists suggest that debating tactics were taken equally seriously by both sides. In November 1911 the NLOWS refused

---

[80] In *The Times*, 28 Nov. 1910, 6, a Hampstead lady complained indignantly that 'my servants, in my absence, were invited to sign the anti-suffrage petition, the nature of which was not disclosed to them'.

[81] E. Dimock to London Society for Women's Suffrage, 2 Aug. 1910 (annotated press cutting), Women's Library, 2/LSW 298/3.

[82] E. Rathbone in the *Manchester Guardian*, 13 Jan. 1911, Bodl., NLOWS, Newspaper Cuttings book, 2474c25.

[83] H. Dowson in the *Nottingham Daily Express*, 24 May 1911. NLOWS Cuttings book, 2474c25.

[84] E. Rathbone in *Manchester Guardian*, 13 Jan. 1911. NLOWS Cuttings book, 2474c25.

[85] J. Phillips in the *Liverpool Post*, 16 Dec. 1910. NLOWS Cuttings book, 2474c25.

[86] *The Times*, 19 Jan. 1912, 8.

to send a speaker, after detailed questioning from Lucy Terry Lewis about the terms of a proposed suffragist debate.[87] In April 1913 a suffragist speaker found herself out-argued and outvoted at a debate in Stepney which had included a speech by Captain Furber of the NLOWS (who favoured penal servitude for suffragettes). Suffrage headquarters penitently accepted its share of responsibility for this outcome.[88] Meanwhile the *Anti-Suffrage Review* 'Branch News' reported the mixed fortunes of local debaters, with a natural emphasis upon the positive. In January 1913 a total of 13 debates resulted in 7 anti-suffrage victories, 4 defeats, and 2 inconclusive results. In January 1914 there were 14 debates, with 6 victories, 3 defeats, and 5 indecisive encounters (a chivalrous decision not to take a vote was sometimes agreed before the debate began, where the speakers were women).

Evidently both suffragists and anti-suffragists were eager to prove their large-scale public backing on every possible occasion, and equally determined not to see this disproved by their opponents. In an era before public opinion polls, petitions, canvassing, and debates were all seen as valid methods of testing mass support. Still more effective, in the eyes of many anti-suffragists, would have been the weapon of a nationwide, single-issue referendum. Experienced parliamentarians doubted that the many practical obstacles to this stratagem could be overcome, preferring to emphasize the need for public pressure upon election candidates and sitting MPs. However, many of the leading women anti-suffragists were enthused by the outcomes of American state referenda, and keen to adopt a tactic which could give female opponents of the vote a more influential voice. This tactic remained under debate on the eve of the war, and became linked into progressive anti-suffrage women's wider discussion of constitutional alternatives to the parliamentary vote. The demand for a national referendum was to resurface as anti-suffrage policy during the final throes of the suffrage campaign in 1917–18.

OFFICE POLITICS, PROPAGANDA, AND THE ANTI-SUFFRAGE REVIEW

The NLOWS chalked up organizational successes as well as failures, only for these to be later eclipsed by the defeat of its general cause. Lord Curzon's anti-suffrage archive has also done the League's reputation few favours, for it tends to focus upon the areas in which its weaknesses were most prominent. The well-documented amalgamation process indicated that joint organizational and propaganda work by men and women would be an uphill task, and Lord

---

[87] Lucy Terry Lewis to Miss Deverall, 2 and 7 Nov. 1911. Women's Library, 2/LSW 298/3.

[88] Correspondence between Mary Fielden and Assistant Secretary, London Society for Women's Suffrage, 28 and 29 Apr. 1913. 2/LSW 298/3.

Curzon's correspondence between 1910 and 1914 apparently bears this out. The leadership of the NLOWS was severely impeded by recurrent gender conflicts between men and women on the paid staff and within the executive committee. Though such conflicts were often construed by contemporaries as the fault of the personalities involved, or due to straightforward disagreements over political tactics, retrospectively it seems evident that more fundamental issues were at stake. These issues were intimately bound up with the cause for which the League had been created, for they concerned the roles and relationships of men and women as well as the conduct of the League's day-to-day business. Arguments over policy and practice did not always produce a straightforward gender divide, as we have already seen in relation to the forward policy. However, those women who most strongly supported the forward policy, and who had offered the most effective leadership within the WNASL, found themselves embroiled in disagreements with the male leaders over other matters. The League's most important policy debates will be considered in the next chapter. Here, it is time to turn to the later stages of Lord Cromer's conflict with Lucy Terry Lewis, and to weigh up other women's dissatisfaction with the running of the NLOWS central office and with the direction of its anti-suffrage propaganda work. The manifest weaknesses of the *Anti-Suffrage Review* reflected unresolved problems in these two areas.

It is clear that Lord Cromer's earliest objections to the efficient and popular WNASL administrator related to her gender rather than to any other issue. As early as 4 August 1910 he was weighing up a possible male candidate to take over many of Lucy Terry Lewis's existing responsibilities within the future amalgamated League, and a week later spelling out to Curzon his view that 'some man should be put in a leading position at our office'.[89] Understandably annoyed at this demotion, and encouraged by the support of leading anti-suffrage women, Lucy Terry Lewis soon proved uncooperative as an office partner to a succession of inexperienced male organizers. By early November Cromer was forced to admit that 'there is not room for two important people, a man and a woman, at the head office . . . it is perfectly clear to me that with Miss Lewis, who I admit has done, and is doing admirable work, neither Mr Scott nor any other man appointed in his place will have the least chance'.[90] New arrangements were put in place, giving Mr Scott greater financial autonomy and a 'roving' brief as Organizing Agent for the League. However, office problems continued, as a male Assistant Secretary was brought in alongside Miss Lewis to deal with correspondence from the (mainly female) branches, and Mr Scott proved extravagant and a poor record-keeper. The following summer Cromer was looking for 'a really good man to be President of the Organisation Committee', rather than a mere administrator or secretary.[91] By November the office situation was once again

[89] Cromer to Curzon, 4 and 11 Aug. 1910. Curzon papers, MSS Eur F112/33B.
[90] Cromer to Curzon, 3 Nov. 1910. Curzon papers, MSS Eur F112/33B.
[91] Cromer to Curzon, 15 June 1911. Curzon papers, MSS Eur F112/34.

at crisis point, and he had reached the axiomatic conclusion that 'any attempt to put any man under any woman is quite sure to break down unless both the man and the woman possess such very exceptional qualities as to be practically undiscoverable'.[92]

Cromer's jaundiced views on gender collaboration were being simultaneously reinforced by his disagreements with women committee members over the forward policy. In December, a combination of poor health and recalcitrant female colleagues had forced him to the point of resignation. 'I really am in despair at the state of things at Caxton House,' he wrote to Curzon, 'all the more so because I feel that somebody with more youth, energy and vigour than myself ought to be at the head . . . I am physically incapable of doing eternal battle with all these rampaging women'.[93] Whilst it might seem improbable that office politics alone could reduce a man of Cromer's stature to such helpless fury, there is no doubt that the conflict with Miss Lewis had played a prominent part. In the same letter his gendered conclusions on that conflict were spelt out: 'With her ideas of the way to treat the male sex, Miss Lewis ought really to be a suffragist, it is a mere accident that she has drifted into our camp. If anybody wants to be convinced of the disastrous consequences which would ensue from allowing us to be governed by women, he need only go through the experience which I have had recently, not so much with our opponents as with our friends.'[94]

Cromer stayed in office for a few more weeks, while Lucy Terry Lewis was sacked, with the agreement of some (but not all) of the women on the executive. Meanwhile new men were brought in to shore up the League's organization, alongside the 'businesslike and conciliatory' Mrs Moberly Bell as temporary League Secretary.[95] Mr Howe was a reasonably successful branch organizer, but Captain Creed, the new face of male authority at head office, soon provoked a resumption of hostilities over NLOWS policy and administration. Mary Ward's correspondence with the Harrisons shows how she tried to enlist Ethel Harrison's help on the executive committee in January 1912, to support her insistence on 'a *lady* in the office, and in command of the women clerks—responsible also to the committee and dismissible only by them'. She added that Captain Creed's 'ideas about women—between ourselves—are rather of the three-tailed Bashaw order'.[96] This allegation was borne out by the turn of events over the next few months, for Creed backed Cromer against the leading women over the practical arrangements to facilitate Curzon's succession as President, as well as in relation to the forward policy. Colonel Lewis was appointed to chair the executive committee, and protect Curzon from the daily business which Cromer had found so trying. His gentlemanly manner temporarily appeased female critics,

---

[92] Cromer to Curzon, 23 Nov. 1911. Curzon papers, MSS Eur F112/34.
[93] Cromer to Curzon, 15 Dec. 1912. Curzon papers, MSS Eur F112/34.   [94] Ibid.
[95] Cromer to Curzon, 20 Feb. 1911. Curzon papers, MSS Eur F112/35.
[96] Mary Ward to Frederic and Ethel Harrison, 13 Jan. 1912. BLPES, LSE, F. Harrison papers, 1/113.

but he did nothing to restrain Captain Creed from endorsing and circulating Sir Almroth Wright's offensively misogynist propaganda letter on the League's behalf. In April 1912 Curzon was forced to mediate in yet another gendered office war.

A few months later Percy Creed was once again treading on dangerous gender territory as he became embroiled in the delicate question of how the League should best respond to suffragist attempts to link the franchise question with the cause of social purity. A private letter from him to Violet Markham in June 1912 provides interesting insights into his gender outlook, especially alongside her very different anti-suffrage correspondence with Mary and Dorothy Ward in the same period. As well as assuming her agreement with him on policy matters, Creed attempted to cheer her sickbed with a jolly, masculine account of recent League events: at the Annual Council, he had found that, in contrast to the suffragettes, 'our people all look normal human beings, a great relief'; Lady Tree had made a surprisingly good speech at a Mayfair branch reception—'I don't know whether the composition was her own, but the matter was for the most part admirable'.[97] Such underlying condescension towards the League's women supporters could not fail to provoke further conflicts in the future. Colonel Lewis left in July, after a conflict with Curzon over League finances; in November Creed followed him, no doubt to the immense relief of leading women. His boastful resignation letter was labelled 'insufferable' by Ethel Harrison. Her message to Curzon on this occasion included the sagacious comment that 'Our Society must in the main depend upon women. Women have to destroy a women's movement'.[98]

Gladys Pott's era of authority at central office opened in rather unpromising circumstances, but soon became living proof of Lady's Jersey's wisdom in recommending first-rate women above second-rate men. Not only did she display feminine tact in her relations with the leading men, whilst remaining close to the 'forward' women; in addition, she understood the importance of propaganda to the anti-suffrage cause, and had the talents needed to introduce constructive improvements. For a considerably lower salary than any man, she was prepared to take on many of the responsibilities of Mrs Moberly Bell and Captain Creed, delegating where necessary, and to combine her administrative work with some writing and much public speaking on the League's behalf. At last peace fell at Caxton House, but it was not the peace of conservative inaction. Curzon received a number of boldly innovatory proposals from the new secretary, at least some of which he agreed to convert into action. Though he rejected her suggestion of a Conservative Anti-Suffrage League (to counter the successful Conservative and Unionist Women's Franchise Association), he was more than happy to follow her lead on the Church Congress issue and on the improvement of communications with Members of Parliament, and to

---

97 Percy Creed to Violet Markham, 23 June 1912. Markham papers, 26/30.
98 Ethel Harrison to Curzon, 28 Nov. 1912. Curzon papers, MSS Eur F112/35.

allow her to take the initiative in combating suffrage allegations related to the League's finances and the League's policy on working women's wages. Closer to home, Miss Pott impressed him with closely argued memoranda on internal organization. In April 1913, when domestic commitments prompted her to cut her own office hours, she outlined a scheme to divide the work into three departments, each with a 'permanent official' in charge, with herself as 'a sort of figurehead and when necessary a "Referee" to whom the permanent officers can apply in a case of doubt'.[99] Six months later, as she announced her resignation due to 'private family duties', she had the satisfaction of reporting that the new, delegated arrangements were working extremely well.[100]

Despite this resourceful display of what has since been labelled typically feminine management technique, Gladys Pott had not been able to achieve all her objectives. A second organizational memorandum dwelt on points needing 'special consideration' in the months ahead. Her list of priorities was headed by the need for the League to raise its propaganda profile. After outlining the future role of an enhanced Press and Information Department, she wrote solemnly: 'I desire to place on record my own firm conviction that publicity in the Press is *our greatest need* and *our opponents' chief advantage over us.* Unless we improve in this respect, I do not believe that we shall make headway with the public.'[101] The media-savvy tactics of suffragism were undoubtedly worthy of imitation, to the extent that this could be achieved without resorting to illegality or unfeminine spectacle. Gladys recommended a systematic approach to securing news coverage for anti-suffragism, not only through its own journal but also (more importantly) through the mass-circulation local and national press. Well-informed counter-propaganda was essential. Among her many achievements during 1912, Gladys Pott had already supervised the compilation of *The Anti-Suffrage Handbook*, an invaluable compendium of anti-suffrage arguments, facts, and figures for use by the League's speakers and propagandists at every level of the organization.

The NLOWS Annual Report in 1914 suggests that at least some of her later proposals for improving propaganda work also came to fruition. Lady Tullibardine commented upon 'the growth of the journalistic work', including systematic 'watching' of the Press, and the opening of an anti-suffrage Information Bureau to support speakers and writers.[102] However, Lord Curzon was unsympathetic to Lily Frere's plea at the same meeting for greater expenditure on League publicity. On behalf of the Paddington branch, she proposed a special subcommittee to raise an advertising fund 'in view of the great increase of advertisement of Suffrage Societies'. Her appeal was directed particularly to the League's women. Curzon's response was to criticize both her mistaken sense of priorities and her lack of

[99] Gladys Pott to Curzon, 11 Apr. 1913. Curzon papers, MSS Eur F112/35.
[100] Gladys Pott to Curzon, 17 Oct. 1913. Curzon papers, MSS Eur F112/36.
[101] Ibid. (Memorandum).
[102] *Anti-Suffrage Review*, 69 (July 1914), 110. Members were also encouraged to subscribe to American anti-suffrage journals.

financial grasp: 'Money is best raised by one or two influential individuals . . . We would gladly undertake the work if we had not more important work to do, and I hope she will not think it necessary to move her resolution.' Suitably cowed, she 'agreed to withdraw her resolution'.[103] A public female challenge to the leadership's propaganda policy was much less acceptable than Gladys Pott's well-reasoned private proposals which made no troublesome links to extra expenditure or to the League's predominantly female membership.

Meanwhile, the *Anti-Suffrage Review* itself remained ripe for reform. A degree of caution was needed in contemporary female criticisms of the *Review*. As Gladys Pott would have been well aware, the League's journal had never endeared itself to the proconsuls, and was potentially under threat of closure during the 1913 search for financial savings and more effective ways of using existing resources. Her second memorandum took care to mention recent improvements and recent economies by the current editor, though she had earlier written that 'If there is a question between the relative values of the "Review" and other Press work my own opinion is that the latter is of greater service to the League'.[104] In December 1914 Curzon confided to Cromer his opinion that 'the Review has always been a flabby milk and water performance'.[105] During 1913 he lamented its expensiveness and the weaknesses of its (male) editor. Probably both Presidents disliked their journal's close association with Mary Ward, who continued to use the *Review* for discreet 'forward' propaganda even after it had been conceded during 1912 that anti-suffrage local government work must be organized independently. In addition, the *Review* had failed to achieve either popularity or journalistic distinction. A brief flurry of innovation at the time of amalgamation had not been maintained: coloured front pages, commercial advertisements, cartoons, detailed parliamentary reports, and weighty contributions from distinguished writers came and went, leaving unexciting continuity in dull editorials, informational announcements, and 'Branch News'. Early in 1914 a curious new attempt was made to boost circulation, through a would-be entertaining and 'non-political' women's page. Titled 'Controversy Apart', in April 1914 it contained snippets of Society news, notification of a 'shopping service' for busy ladies, and tips on Easter eggs, fashion, cookery, and church flower arrangements. In leaden prose, the male editor explained that the page was suitable for the 'many lady readers who are only rarely called upon to defend or explain their anti-suffrage position'.[106] The confused and uncertain purposes of the *Review* are manifest in this initiative. Effortful attempts to achieve the lighter touch conveyed male antis' derogatory views on lightweight femininity as well as their wish to obtain more readers. The non-campaigning women's page appeared oddly out of place

---

103 Ibid. 113.
104 Gladys Pott to Curzon, 11 Apr. 1913. Curzon papers, MSS Eur F112/36.
105 Curzon to Cromer, 2 Dec. 1914. Cromer papers, FO633/23.
106 *Anti-Suffrage Review*, 66 (Apr. 1914), 50.

alongside the energetic attempts of Mary Ward and others to promote the forward policy, and certainly did not reflect the continuing importance of female activism to NLOWS anti-suffrage work.

By 1914 it was clear that working with men had proved an uncomfortable experience for many leading anti-suffrage women. This feeling was more than reciprocated by their male counterparts. Despite consensus on the tactical advantages of collaboration, and theoretical agreement on the importance of demonstrating complementary and collaborative working practices, the men and women leaders found themselves jostling for position and influence within their amalgamated organization. They also had unexpected difficulties in communicating freely between the differently gendered social worlds of men and women, as many assumptions and conventions proved non-transferable into a mixed-sex organization. From the point of view of Lord Cromer, Lord Curzon, and their male supporters, the National League was a predominantly male body campaigning in defence of national and imperial interests, with a focus upon events in Parliament. From the point of view of many (but not all) anti-suffrage women, it was a strengthened version of the WNASL, a body launched to ensure the defeat of the women's suffrage movement by women themselves. There were many potential meeting points between these perspectives, evidenced by successful joint activities at local and national levels in the pre-war years. But there were also a number of intractable problem areas, concerning gender beliefs as well as organizational tactics. The development of gender ideology within the NLOWS, and through dialogue between suffragists and women anti-suffragists, requires closer investigation in the chapter which follows.

9

Suffrage, Sexuality, and Citizenship

ANTI-SUFFRAGISM AND THE CONFLICT OF IDEAS

Anti-suffrage women had few pretensions as theoreticians. Though a number of the women leaders wrote books and articles about their reasons for opposing the vote, they were far less prolix than their suffragist counterparts and their ideas received less attention from supporters and critics. As discussed in Chapter 4, the most widely read female advocacy of anti-suffragism came from novelists and journalists, few of whom played an active role in collective, organized opposition. In contrast, the prestigious male leaders of the NLOWS achieved prominence for their ideas upon public platforms as well as in print, and confidently imposed their views upon the League's organization and policies. Organized women antis were sometimes willing to defer to male ideologues because the success of the mixed-sex NLOWS depended upon a public display of unity. Within an organization which stood committed to gendered hierarchy in public affairs, there was also much genuine deference to male expertise in the formulation of anti-suffrage ideas. However, the internal debates of the NLOWS show that anti-suffrage women also persisted in the expression of their own divergent opinions. Conflicts with male colleagues could be interpreted purely as a matter of competing egos, laced by gender differences and jealousies. Yet this would be to underestimate conservative women's contributions to the ideological debates over gender, sexuality, and citizenship which characterized not merely organized suffragism and anti-suffragism, but also the broader public discussion of the Woman Question in Edwardian Britain.

This chapter will consider some of the more problematic issues facing women anti-suffragists, as they struggled to make a success of their collaborative campaign during the pre-war years. Disagreements over the potential for an alternative female citizenship, constructed around feminine duty towards families and local communities, had already begun to surface within the WNASL in 1908 and proved a growing source of conflict within its mixed-sex successor. Still more difficult for the NLOWS to accommodate were the debates over sexuality which underlay so many other aspects of the suffrage and anti-suffrage campaigns in this period. Victorian supporters of votes for women were initially wary of too close an association between their support for the vote and their deeply felt opposition to sexual double standards. The cause of social purity eventually helped to convince thousands of women of the need for direct female representation in Parliament, but its associations with generalized hostility towards men remained uncongenial to the more conservative suffragists into the twentieth century. Anti-suffragists were often eager to take advantage of their opponents' discomfiture, but faced their own problems in discussing the highly sensitive topic of sexuality and suffrage. Whilst novelists exercised their licence to delve into imaginary relationships and to explore undercurrents of sexuality in the ways sanctioned by literary convention, the adherence of most women antis to strict ideals of feminine modesty seriously impeded direct discussion of the sexual side of gender relations. The continuing existence of sexual double standards, the prospect of a 'sex war' stoked by suffragette militancy, and the incipient threat of 'feminist' sexual deviance all seemed to demand anti-suffrage denunciation, but how could these evils be denounced without transgression of conservative gender norms? As well as implementing a conventionally respectable taboo on discussions of sexuality, women antis more than shared the moderate suffragists' reluctance to antagonize their male supporters. Harmonious collaboration between men and women was a founding principle of the WNASL, and still more so of the NLOWS. Moreover anti-suffrage men proved particularly resentful of female criticism, which they associated with suffragism and especially with the man-hating and socially disruptive spectre of 'feminism'.

The task of addressing sexual matters was an unwelcome one for most anti-suffrage women, but became inescapable in the pre-war years. Inhibitions were gradually shed, as controversial issues related to both male and female sexual behaviour surfaced with increasing regularity. To the problems of feminine modesty and masculine aversion to criticism were added the problems of conflict among anti-suffrage women, as they found themselves at odds with each other and sometimes in closer agreement with moderate suffragists than with fellow-antis over such difficult issues as prostitution, social purity, and divorce reform. The anti-suffrage movement suffered from its inability to take a united, principled stand on these issues. On the other hand, male and female antis were united by their belief in the importance of women's combined biological and spiritual role as wives and mothers. The anti-suffrage movement drew strength from its women leaders' increasingly confident criticisms of suffragist departures from this bedrock of sexual orthodoxy. A minority of radical female thinkers had begun to move beyond suffragism and into the much more dangerous territory of reconfigured beliefs about the family and about sexual relationships. Anti-suffrage women were drawn after them in hot pursuit. The reciprocity of suffragist and anti-suffragist ideas is clearly illustrated by some of the more extreme critiques of 'feminism' in the pre-war years. Not all anti-suffrage women were prepared to follow their most outspoken leaders into such territory. Debates over sex and suffrage thus continued to divide as well as to unite anti-suffragism, setting women against each other as well as some anti-suffrage men against some anti-suffrage women.

The first half of the chapter will examine women's commentaries on aspects of sexuality from within the confines of organized anti-suffragism. The second half connects these sexuality debates to the anti-suffragists' extended discussion of a constructive forward policy. The more progressive women anti-suffragists were as determined as any suffragists to escape from the straitjacket of narrowly defined biological determinism. They tried to promote an alternative female citizenship which would release women from the restrictive confines of 'the Sex', both by enhancing respect for their sexual role and by fostering knowledge of its wider social value. The organized anti-suffragists' rejection of sexual radicalism, and their support for aspects of sexual reform, helped to draw them closer to conservative suffragism at the height of the militant campaign. To the dismay of male anti-suffrage leaders, some anti-suffrage women defied their prohibitions and insisted on moving beyond a negative campaign of opposition to the vote into an exploration of constructive alternatives. The polarities of suffragism and anti-suffragism were further diminished by tentative talk of a suffrage truce in 1913–14, as progressive anti-suffragists speculated upon a future of female collaboration in defence of womanly values and in support of feminized forms of government and citizenship.

MILITANCY AND SEXUALITY

The launch of the WNASL coincided with an escalation of suffragette militancy. Campaigners were not slow to take advantage of this fact, and early issues of the *Anti-Suffrage Review* rang with denunciations of the suffragettes' unfeminine and threatening behaviour. Far from being a divisive issue, condemnation of militant excesses provided a major plank of the anti-suffrage propaganda platform over the following years, uniting male and female leaders and winning thousands of supporters for the cause. Much of this condemnation related militancy directly or indirectly to women's innate sexual weaknesses, or alternatively to 'feminist' sexual deviance, rather than simply to a deplorable abandonment of female gentility. The January 1909 issue of the *Review* reported the 'ugly violence' of disruptive heckling at the Royal Albert Hall as 'an event . . . which has been of enormous advantage to the cause of those who are fighting the advance of Woman Suffrage', before going on to generalize about its lessons: 'What we are watching is, in truth, the letting loose, on the ground of politics, of certain illimitable capacities for excitement and hysteria . . . which are the permanent other side, the inevitable shadow, so to speak, of woman's special powers and functions in the State'.[1] This opaque comment would have conveyed clearly enough to most readers the connection between militancy and feminine frailty dictated by

---

[1] *Anti-Suffrage Review*, 2 (Jan. 1909), 1.

sexual function. Suffragettes were displaying the biologically determined flaws of their sex, thus proving their inability to participate usefully in Parliamentary politics. Moreover their challenging behaviour exposed all women to the dangers of a future breakdown in masculine chivalry towards the weaker sex: 'Alas! the scenes at the Albert Hall are only the climax in a long process which has been undermining that old chivalrous respect for woman as woman which used to be our national pride. Woman has gone down into an arena for which she is physically incapacitated, having deliberately divested herself of her natural armour'.[2]

As militancy continued to escalate, there were abundant opportunities for female anti-suffrage commentators to embellish these arguments both publicly and privately. Tactically it made good sense to tar all suffragists with the same brush, and Gladys Pott and others made sustained efforts to prove the connections between militant and moderate supporters of women's suffrage long after Mrs Fawcett and other moderate leaders had begun to distance themselves from extremism.[3] Anti-suffrage men and women continued to relate general conclusions based upon suffragette behaviour to all those women who defied nature by taking up the masculine trade of politics, whether or not they supported militancy. On the one hand, militancy provided evidence of female 'hysteria': a subject earnestly discussed in private correspondence between Violet Markham and John St Loe Strachey during 1909.[4] On the other hand, suffragettes provided the clearest possible warning of the denaturalizing impact of politics upon the female mind and body. From the late nineteenth century onwards, male commentators had argued that suffragists and other New Women risked becoming asexual beings, deprived of their feminine attributes whilst at the same time incapable of successfully emulating men.

These arguments were also powerfully expressed by a woman doctor, Arabella Kenealy, in the pages of the *Nineteenth Century* journal,[5] as well as by the novelists Eliza Lynn Linton and Marie Corelli. They were still more stridently asserted by Ethel Colquhoun in the context of Edwardian anti-suffragism. Between 1912 and 1914 she published a series of scathing attacks upon women who were in 'revolt against nature', as well as guilty of abandoning their 'racial duty'.[6] Like many other contemporary commentators, Ethel Colquhoun frequently elided the terms 'sex' and 'gender' and ostentatiously practised conventional sexual reticence, but her attacks on suffragism and the still greater dangers of 'feminism'

---

[2] *Anti-Suffrage Review*, 2.

[3] e.g. see Gladys Pott's letters to *The Times* on 8 Mar. 1912 and 8 June 1914. She tirelessly hunted down evidence of cross-membership and of financial links between 'moderate' and 'militant' organisations.

[4] See Strachey's letters to Violet Markham on 11 Oct. and 2 Dec. 1909. BLPES, LSE, Markham papers, 26/30.

[5] A. Kenealy, 'Woman as an Athlete', *Nineteenth Century*, 45 (1899), 633–45; 'Woman as an Athlete: A Rejoinder', *Nineteenth Century*, 45 (1899), 915–29.

[6] E. Colquhoun, *Vocation of Woman* (London: Macmillan, 1913), 40.

were sometimes made in unambiguously sexual terms. From the starting point that 'Woman was obviously intended by nature to become a mother',[7] she concluded that the differentiation between the sexes lay at the heart of social as well as biological evolution. Highly educated feminists posed a particular danger to society, as well as to their own happiness, as they rejected their feminine inheritance and their maternal duty.[8] The rush towards equality threatened not only to devalue motherhood, and to debase 'the standards of sex relations'; it also introduced the prospect of a descent into sexual hybridity, where 'manly' women and 'demasculinised' men would hold disastrous sway.[9] A dilution of gender difference could eventually undermine masculine strength and the powers of masculine imperial government, but male resistance to the advance of feminism would meanwhile endanger all women. With direct reference to sexualized male violence provoked by suffragette militancy, Ethel warned in 1914 that 'women must refrain from awakening the sleeping savage in man, individually or collectively'. Even an anti-suffrage woman speaker could no longer rely upon chivalrous treatment at public meetings, since she would be 'treated merely as a woman', and was therefore open to sexual insult and potential assault.[10] 'Sex war' had always been dreaded by female anti-suffragists: suffragette militancy and male responses to it seemed to be bringing that nightmare scenario into the realm of everyday politics.

Female denunciations of the sexual threat posed by militant suffragism aroused no public criticism from within the anti-suffrage ranks, and probably helped convince some readers to support the campaign against the vote. Far more controversial was the intervention into the same debate of a distinguished male doctor, Sir Almroth Wright. His notorious letter on 'Militant Hysteria', published in *The Times* on 27 March 1912, caused serious offence to many anti-suffrage women as well as to the suffragists whom he dismissed as embittered, sexless spinsters needing marriage more than votes.[11] Taking his stand upon professional rank, he claimed that 'no doctor can ever lose sight of the fact that the mind of woman is always threatened with danger from the reverberations of her physiological emergencies'. Suffragettes were accused of wanting to 'convert the whole world into an epicene institution', thus undermining the effective work (as well as the masculinity) of government.[12] Anti-suffrage reactions to this diatribe were varied and interesting. At the offices of the NLOWS, Captain Creed tried to capitalize on what he perceived as a valuable propaganda coup by circulating copies of the Wright letter to the members of both Houses of

---

[7] Ibid. 1.   [8] Ibid. 329.   [9] Ibid. 335, 285–6.

[10] E. Colquhoun, 'Woman and Morality', *Nineteenth Century and After*, 75 (1914), 132–3.

[11] This letter was republished, in an expanded form, as *The Unexpurgated Case Against Woman Suffrage* (London: Constable, 1913).

[12] Ibid. 77, 78. Wright accused the suffragists of pursuing a 'programme of feminism' which would result in their economic independence and an invasion of male institutions 'until we shall have everywhere one vast cock-and-hen show' (ibid. 61).

Parliament in the League's name.[13] Meanwhile the more 'forward' women antis began to voice private and public dismay over this crudely misogynist attack upon women's motives and abilities. Mary Ward corresponded anxiously with her son (who seemed inclined to minimize the importance of the controversy), before launching an indignant riposte in *The Times*, and successfully insisting that the NLOWS official endorsement of Wright's views should be retracted.[14] Violet Markham explained her reservations privately to St Loe Strachey, as well as writing her own public rebuttal.[15] The Curzon papers reveal that other anti-suffrage women joined in the criticism, helping to make Creed's position untenable. Ethel Colquhoun was not among them, lending support to the possibility that Wright's views helped to shape her own.

It is apparent that Almroth Wright had unintentionally succeeded in disrupting the anti-suffrage camp, whilst at the same time uniting militant and moderate suffragists in scornful denunciation of his views. His offence lay partly in his unvarnished presentation of a viewpoint within which sexual prejudice was disturbingly evident. Women anti-suffragists accused him of more than merely bad manners. Mary Ward suggested that 'a discussion so ruthless' would have been better suited to a medical journal than to *The Times*, before going on to accuse him of 'unjust and intolerable exaggeration' in his one-sided portrayal of women's unfitness for professional and public life. Rejecting aggressive anti-suffrage sloganizing which might foster antagonism between men and women as surely as suffragette militancy itself, she expressed her own faith in women's powers.[16] Her arguments moved the debate back from the dangerous territory of overtly sexual politics into the more comfortable and familiar context of maternal reformism.

Violet Markham's public response set out 'the anti-suffrage position as it appears to many women': 'His intervention will not help to further that ideal of womanhood, strong, sane, self-respecting, which surely sober-minded suffragists and anti-suffragists alike should cherish as a common end'.[17] Moderate suffragists duly welcomed this olive branch through *The Times* letter page, but not without also seeking to drive a deeper wedge between male and female anti-suffragists.[18] More acerbic versions of the anti-suffrage defence of womanhood were presented

[13] Percy Creed to Lord Curzon, 2 Apr. 1912. BL, Curzon papers, MSS Eur F112/35. Lady Robson voiced an immediate protest to Lord Curzon against this action, on her own and Lady Jersey's behalf.

[14] See Arnold Ward to Dorothy Ward, 8 Apr. 1912 and Arnold Ward to Mary Ward, 17 Apr. 1912, UCL Archives, D. Ward papers MS Add. 202.115; Mary Ward letter in *The Times*, 12 Apr. 1912, 15; M. Ward to Lord Curzon, 6 Apr. 1912, Curzon papers, MSS Eur F112/35.

[15] See St Loe Strachey to Violet Markham, 9 Apr. 1912, Markham papers, 26/30; Violet Markham's letter to *The Times*, 8 Apr. 1912, pointed out that 'Sir Almroth deprecates a sex war, but he himself throws fuel by handfuls on the flames'. Bodl., NLOWS Cuttings book, 2474c23.

[16] Mary Ward letter, *The Times*, 12 Apr. 1912, 15.

[17] Violet Markham letter, *The Times*, 8 Apr. 1912.

[18] See responses to Violet Markham's letter from Lady Chance and Lady Aberconway in *The Times*, 11 Apr. 1912. NLOWS Cuttings book, 2474c23.

in other contexts. Helena Norris told an Ipswich audience containing many suffragist hecklers that 'It mattered most to the nation not what women did but what women were . . . It was sex pride that was at the root of the anti-suffrage movement'.[19] Ethel Colquhoun dismissed claims that masculine and feminine virtues could be combined within the same person as 'one of those fallacies dear to the hearts of women who have no real confidence in their own sex'.[20] Although she was more willing than most other women writers to endorse physiological arguments about women's unsuitability for politics, she shared many female anti-suffragists' desire to defend gender differentiation on the basis of women's unique moral and physical strengths, rather than their psycho-sexual weaknesses.

THE FEMINIST THREAT

The term 'feminism' was only beginning to move into common currency during the Edwardian period and already signified different things to different people. It was being favourably used by a growing number of suffragists to convey general support for women's self-organization to promote their collective rights and opportunities. By the early twentieth century the label was also being self-applied by a minority of advanced and innovatory thinkers whose ideas intersected with the emergent discourses of individualism and modernism.[21] But amongst the women anti-suffragists of the NLOWS, its usage was almost invariably hostile. Feminism was perceived as the darker and more threatening side of suffragism: as a descriptor for the havoc which women's suffrage could wreak in gender relations, and the consequent damage likely to be inflicted upon society as a whole. Sexual deviance lay at the heart of the feminist threat. On the one hand, feminists (including militant suffragists) were accused of spurning their own femininity, rejecting female heterosexual roles, and undermining male protective instincts towards the weaker sex. Contrastingly, feminists were also sometimes portrayed as sexual predators, as promiscuous practitioners of 'free love', and generally as a danger to family life because of their defiance of gender norms through sexual excess.

The discussion of feminist promiscuity did not fit comfortably within anti-suffrage rhetoric. Women anti-suffragists hesitated to enter such delicate territory because of conventional prudery, but also because most were well aware of

---

[19] *East Anglian Daily Times*, 7 Oct. 1913. NLOWS Cuttings book, 2474c32.
[20] Colquhoun, *Vocation of Woman*, 285.
[21] See Lucy Delap's full discussion of contemporary usages of 'feminism', and her analysis of the avant-garde (and sometimes anti-suffrage) trends within this diverse movement, in Delap, *The Feminist Avant-Garde: Transatlantic Encounters, 1900s to the 1920s* (Cambridge: Cambridge University Press, 2007). She argues that feminism and anti-feminism, still more than suffragism and anti-suffragism, represented 'not polarised positions but different positions within a shared discourse about gender' (p. 85).

the unrepresentative nature of more radical versions of feminism. They were reluctant, even at the height of the suffrage debate, to launch unwarranted attacks upon suffragists who might include personal friends and close allies within other women's organizations. General accusations of suffragist sexual impropriety would have lacked credibility at any stage of the campaign. Yet the activities of a minority of feminists provided irresistibly emotive arguments for anti-suffrage women. From the 1890s onwards, anti-suffrage writers had linked the advent of the New Woman to sexual immorality. Among the younger generation of women antis, Violet Markham, Ethel Colquhoun, and Gladys Pott were particularly worried by the threat of sexual licence embedded within suffragism; their private as well as public pronouncements on this subject add an important extra dimension to our understanding of their anti-suffrage motives. All three women became involved in a pre-war controversy over the impact of feminist teachers upon the minds and morals of young girls which tapped into wider public anxieties over sexuality and suffrage.

Violet Markham's sensitivity on sexual matters was reflected in private correspondence relating to H. G. Wells's novel of feminist ideals, *Ann Veronica*, during 1909. St Loe Strachey accepted her view that the novel promoted immorality with the loaded comment that 'Under Socialism and free love women must and do sink to the level of the squaw or the kaffir's wife'.[22] He would have been familiar with her writings on South Africa, which dwelt at length upon race relations, and reflected her fears of physical as well as cultural contact between different races.[23] Later correspondence with Leo Maxse, editor of the *National Review*, on the evils of 'Girl Scouts', was equally revealing of her deep-seated fears of sexual transgression and (in this case) gender inversion.[24] During 1912 the appearance of the *Freewoman* magazine provided fresh impetus to anti-suffrage accusations of links between feminism, suffragism, and sexual deviance. Founded by WSPU dissidents, this journal has been analysed as a seminal contribution to the development of women's ideas around suffragism and feminism, marking a separation of these causes for women who were becoming conscious of the limitations of the vote as an instrument of wider female self-fulfilment.[25] The journal's male and female authors contributed articles which ranged across sexual controversies, many insisting that truly radical reforms needed first to address women's subjugation within marriage and heterosexual relations. The paper itself was short-lived, but its existence fuelled heated debate in both suffrage and

[22] St Loe Strachey to Violet Markham, 2 Dec. 1912. Markham papers, 26/30.

[23] See J. Bush, *Edwardian Ladies and Imperial Power* (London: Leicester University Press, 2000), ch. 7, for a discussion of Violet Markham's views on race relations.

[24] Violet Markham to Leo Maxse, 21 Feb. 1910. West Sussex Record Office, Maxse papers, 461/583.

[25] See L. Garner, *Stepping Stones to Women's Liberty* (London: Heinemann, 1984); L. Delap, ' "Philosophical vacuity and political ineptitude": The *Freewoman*'s Critique of the Suffrage Movement', *Women's History Review*, 11/4 (2002), 613–30; ead., *Feminist Avant-Garde*.

anti-suffrage circles. In a letter to *The Times*, Mary Ward linked 'the suffragist or feminist movement' to the *Freewoman* and its advocacy of unmarried motherhood: 'this dark and dangerous side of "the women's movement"' was no 'mere negligible quantity', though she accepted that many suffragists would wish to repudiate it.[26] Maude Royden and Frances Balfour were among those who rose indignantly to the bait, providing Mary Ward with a further opportunity to assert the *Freewoman*'s suffragist pedigree.[27] Two months later controversy was still raging, as the suffragist Julia Chance countered anti-suffrage discoveries of other 'unnatural and indecent' literature upon suffragist bookstalls.[28]

Perhaps partly in deference to such critics, Ethel Colquhoun tried to highlight the sexual dangers of feminism while avoiding accusations of doing so in indecently frank terms. Her references to the *Freewoman* were trenchant, but preserved the anonymity of the offending journal so as to avoid 'gratuitous advertisement'. Moderate suffragists' disclaimers were dismissed as cowardice and prevarication, in the face of evidence that 'a distinct and influential body of opinion is being formed among educated women which (to put it mildly) is hostile to marriage as a social institution and to the conception of the home as woman's particular care'.[29] Letters in the *Anti-Suffrage Review* provide further evidence of how powerfully criticism of feminism, and especially its sexual dimensions, resonated with female anti-suffragists. In August 1914 Mrs Kingsbury Waterman spoke for many conservative women when she described feminism as 'a direct attack on the home'; it was 'perfectly consistent that feminists should support any or all of the following ideas: easier divorce, free love, State nurseries, wages for wives, co-operative housekeeping, economic independence after marriage, trial marriages, equal pay, militancy and socialism'.[30] The connectedness of these diverse causes seemed evident enough to anti-suffrage women who believed socialism and conventional family life to be incompatible, and dreaded the advancing democratic labour movement almost as much as advancing feminism itself.

Leading anti-suffragists' views on feminism and sexual deviance can also be investigated through more private sources. Lord Cromer's correspondence during 1913 contains anxious letters from Violet Markham, Gladys Pott, and Ethel Colquhoun on this difficult subject. No doubt they anticipated a sympathetic response, for Cromer was among the many male writers who denounced feminism in this period, notably in a *National Review* article of 1913 which again linked together suffragism, feminism, socialism, and divorce reform.[31] Soon afterwards

---

[26] *The Times*, 19 June 1912, 14.

[27] *The Times*, 27 June 1912, 6. Mary Ward castigated the NUWSS newspaper, *Common Cause*, for the earlier welcome it had extended to the *Freewoman*: 'this carelessness in their chief organ in the Press illustrates the difficulty there is in drawing a sharp dividing line between the suffrage beliefs we all respect and a feminism which would uproot the moral landmarks of our race'.

[28] *The Times*, 13 Aug. 1912, 2.   [29] Colquhoun, *Vocation of Woman*, 209.

[30] *Anti-Suffrage Review*, 70 (Aug. 1914), 142.

[31] Lord Cromer, 'Feminism in France', *National Review*, 62 (1913–14), 403–8.

Gladys Pott sent Cromer a recent sample of suffrage literature on sexual subjects, adding comments which illustrate the antis' organizational dilemma and her own awareness of the overlap as well as divergence between organized anti-suffragism and broader anti-feminism: 'I have again to-day been approached by Anti-Suffrage ladies who are infuriated with the writings of the extreme Suffragists on sex questions; but it appears to me impossible for our League as a body to deal with the point. What we really need is an Anti-Feminist League of tactful ladies, and I have a faint hope that such a one may be started.'[32]

Violet Markham, meanwhile, was exulting in Cromer's favourable review of her own new book on South Africa. In a rather surprising burst of confidentiality, she wrote to him from the Far East about her fears for the future of womanhood:

I am growing increasingly concerned with the feminist movement—the suffrage seems to me only a by-product of a deeper and more prevailing spirit of anarchy in my sex. I am going to tell you something quite frankly though it's pleasant neither to write not to read . . . I was struck there [in South Africa]—struck and dismayed—by the sort of *loose spirit* which seemed to have come over the relations of men and women . . . And here again in Asia I have been up against exactly the same thing . . . last night I went to a dance here and looked on at Turkey Trots, Bunny Hugs, Tangoes and the like. The actual dances in themselves were harmless. Some women danced them and looked charming. But there were others who ought to have been turned out of the room. What sort of feeling of respect can men have for women apparently so devoid of every instinct of reticence and dignity? And what shall it profit a woman to gain the vote and lose all the dignity and sweetness of her womanhood? . . . The suffrage movement is one expression of it, but the evil is of deeper growth even than that, I fear, though of course it is the suffrage movement which has helped to fling open the floodgates. I don't wonder at your indignation. I am full of it myself.[33]

Violet's unresolved personal dilemmas over her own sexuality helped to frame this particular *cri de cœur*. However, her sense of a broader social and political context to sexual behaviour, and of a latent, sexualized, feminist threat looming behind even the more conservative forms of suffragism, was shared by many other anti-suffragists. Such mingled social and sexual fears provided a half-articulated subtext to more reasoned expressions of anti-suffrage faith by both men and women in this period.

Ethel Colquhoun made her own private approaches to the male anti-suffrage leaders on these difficult issues. In October 1912 she warned Curzon that 'The discussion, from a feminist point of view, of sex relations is certainly responsible for the wide spread of suffragism, especially among young girls and young women . . . suffragism is only the *effect*, the cause is psychological and also physiological'. She believed that young women were being 'corrupted

---

[32] Gladys Pott to Lord Cromer, 24 Sept. 1913. Cromer papers, National Archives, FO633/22.
[33] Violet Markham to Lord Cromer, 10 Dec. 1912. Cromer papers, FO633/22.

and spoilt', not merely by the open discussion of sexuality at public meetings, but more specifically by suffragist insistence upon male sexual depravity and 'an everlasting moan over the sufferings of women'. Gladys Pott had already provided a sympathetic audience for these ideas, but the two women were 'in agreement that to take it up in any public way, or as part of our anti-suffrage propaganda is simply to feed the evil'. Ethel was 'inclined to think we must do it as Anti-Feminists, not Anti-Suffragists. We shall then isolate the disease, which will cease to have the moral support of many suffragists who are not conscious of the feminist side of the propaganda.'[34] Though Curzon was apparently wary of giving Ethel Colquhoun the indirect support she sought for her anti-feminist crusade, Cromer delighted her by agreeing to review *The Vocation of Woman* for the *Spectator*. She introduced her work to him as 'the first Anti-Feminist book by a woman . . . a very serious and earnest attempt to get to the bottom of the extraordinary state of affairs prevailing in the ranks of my sex today'. Underlining her perception of the dangerous connections between suffragism, feminism, and sexuality, she claimed that 'The discussion, from a feminist point of view, of sex relations is certainly responsible for the wide spread of suffragism, especially among young girls and young women'. [35]

A week later, a second letter helpfully spelt out Ethel Colquhoun's authorial intentions, making it clear that she viewed the general relationship between anti-suffragism and anti-feminism in much the same light as Gladys Pott:

I am very anxious that it should not be thought to be merely an Anti-Suffrage publication, for important as the actual question of the suffrage is, it is, to my mind, secondary to the conditions of education and training which are turning out every year vast numbers of 'educated' (so-called) women for whom there is no proper niche in the world. I am convinced that this army of spoilt and damaged females are contributing, first of all, to the degeneracy of men, because they strive to be manly, and manly women beget feminine men, and second, to the spread of all sorts of morbid diseases among women, of which 'suffragitis' in its most extreme form is one.[36]

Cromer's review, published in December 1913, did not disappoint her. After noting that the franchise issue occupied 'a very secondary place in Mrs Archibald Colquhoun's thoughtful and acutely analytical work', he went on to outline her condemnation of 'the flimsy arguments of the feminists'. Their belief that 'Nature has erred' led them to conclude that women should aim to eliminate gender differences, including those related to the all-important sexual and moral functions of motherhood. Of suffragism's malign consequences, 'none

---

[34] Ethel Colquhoun to Lord Curzon, 24 Oct. 1912. Curzon papers, MSS Eur F112/35. She opened the subject by claiming that 'The discussion, from a feminist point of view, of sex relations is certainly responsible for the wide spread of suffragism, especially among young girls and young women'.

[35] Ethel Colquhoun to Lord Cromer, 30 Oct. 1913. Cromer papers, FO633/22.

[36] Ethel Colquhoun to Lord Cromer, 5 Nov. 1913. Cromer papers, FO630/22.

has been more deplorable than this—that it has brought into prominence a number of fundamental sex-issues which lie at the root of the social system, and which cannot form the subject of general discussion without doing much harm'.[37]

Despite their reluctance to 'feed the evil', many anti-suffrage women felt obliged to publicize their strong views on the sexual threat which feminist teachers posed to young women. Ethel Colquhoun was once again to the fore in condemning these teachers' evil impact through their fostering of general discontent and a pathological view of heterosexual relations. Though some anti-suffrage women had played a part in launching women's higher education, there was a widespread acceptance by 1912 that the universities were being captured by suffragism, and a fear that the contagion of feminism (in both its asexual and promiscuous forms) was seeping through into girls' secondary schools. In a *National Review* article titled 'Suffragette Factories', Helen Hamilton wrote that 'a system of education which tends to rob the woman of her sex-attributes must be radically wrong . . . educate her like a boy, and she is almost bound to develop into a bad imitation of a man; in other words, into the Suffragette type of woman'. Worse still, this experienced high school teacher observed that 'The man *versus* the woman spirit permeates the atmosphere of secondary schools and colleges', threatening to produce girls who would choose 'a mutual admiration society of spinsters' above the rewards of marriage and motherhood.[38] The theme of feminist infiltration into education was taken up by many anti-feminist commentators over the next two years. Letters to *The Times* condemned the suffragists' 'nauseous publications' and their links to feminist sex education in schools.[39] Ethel Harrison wrote in the *Nineteenth Century* that girls' schools were fostering 'the fierce sex antagonism displayed everywhere', whilst feminism was undermining the family as 'a sacred possession'.[40]

The *Anti-Suffrage Review* helped to fuel these protests. In January 1914 a group of five women published a direct attack on 'Woman Suffrage Propaganda in Girls' Schools'. Suffragism flourished among those who 'for one reason or another, have given up the normal family life of women and specialised in the professions'; it was 'more than a political question; it connotes a radical divergence of view of the function of women in the world'.[41] The following month a letter linked the schools issue to the 'tide of dirty literature' corrupting young girls who were being encouraged by suffragists to take up the cause of sexual reform.[42] In August 1914 another letter attacked suffragist recruitment of impressionable young women beneath the title 'The Poisoning of Young

[37] Lord Cromer, *Spectator*, 13 Dec. 1913. Cromer papers, FO633/30.

[38] H. Hamilton, 'Suffragette Factories', *National Review*, 60 (1913), 591–2, 595, 598.

[39] See *The Times*, 12 and 18 Apr. 1912. The term 'nauseous publications' was coined by the suffragist Maud Royden, and taken up with enthusiasm by the women antis.

[40] E. Harrison, 'Abdication', *Nineteenth Century*, 74 (1913), 1331, 1332.

[41] *Anti-Suffrage Review*, 63 (Jan. 1914), 274.　　　　　[42] Ibid., 64 (Feb. 1914), 10.

Minds'.[43] Meanwhile the anti-suffrage cause was being doughtily defended from within the teaching profession by Elizabeth Burgwin and other male and female antis.[44] The *Anti-Suffrage Review* gave gleeful coverage to majority votes against suffrage resolutions at successive conferences of the National Union of Teachers. A special male-authored NLOWS leaflet targeted teachers at their 1912 conference, stoking up the equal pay debate and informing them that the women's suffrage movement was 'a dangerous and insidious one, for, although the rank and file of Suffragists do not know it, the movement is being engineered by "feminists", who wish for more fundamental things than the vote, only they dare not say in public what they wish for'.[45] Whether as promoters of 'sex war' and spinsterism, or as purveyors of dangerous sexual knowledge, feminist teachers were an easy target for organized anti-suffragism, as well as among the stock villains of anti-suffrage fiction.

REFORMING SEX AND MARRIAGE

The climax of the suffrage and anti-suffrage campaigns coincided with an important stage in women's long-standing campaign for sexual and marital reform. Despite some initial hesitation, close alliances had been forged between Victorian suffragism, the repeal of the Contagious Diseases Acts, ongoing promotion of sexual purity, and an end to the male double standards which provided prostitutes with their clients and threatened innocent wives with venereal disease. Millicent Fawcett was at the forefront of the campaign for the Criminal Law Amendment Act of 1885 which raised the age of consent, restricted brothels, and outlawed homosexual practices.[46] Meanwhile suffragists were also among the most enthusiastic supporters of legislation to improve women's legal status within marriage through the Married Women's Property Act of 1882 and laws to restrain domestic violence and improve women's rights of access to children after marital breakdown. During the Edwardian period pressure grew for stronger legislation to control male sexual behaviour and for further reforms of existing marriage law, including more equal and accessible divorce. Undoubtedly both these causes benefited from the expansion of a suffrage campaign which was slowly becoming more willing to identify itself publicly with feminist demands

[43] *Anti-Suffrage Review*, 70 (Aug. 1914), 143. A suffragette and feminist teacher was the villain of Mary Ward's *Delia Blanchflower* (London: Ward, Lock and Co., 1915).

[44] See H. Kean, *Deeds Not Words* (London: Pluto Press, 1990), 40–3.

[45] *Anti-Suffrage Review*, 30 (May 1911), 90; 42 (Apr. 1912), 89; 67 (May 1914), 68. The leaflet, by Arthur Gronno, was titled 'The Attempt to Capture the NUT by Women-Suffragists. Important to Members of the NUT' (London: NLOWS, 1912).

[46] See L. Bland, *Banishing the Beast: English Feminism and Sexual Morality 1885–1914* (London: Penguin, 1995); B. Caine, *Victorian Feminists* (Oxford: Oxford University Press, 1992); S. Kingsley Kent, *Sex and Suffrage in Britain 1860–1914* (London: Routledge, 1990).

for fundamental changes in the relations between men and women. However, suffragists were far from unanimous in their views on these broader issues. Anti-suffrage women shared the more conservative suffragists' doubts over how far sexual and marital reforms should proceed, and over whether such reforms might either antagonize men or undermine the sanctity of marriage. Their position was a particularly difficult one, for they faced the tactical resistance of male leaders to any involvement with such matters, alongside distrust by male (and some female) antis of what was widely seen as a dubiously feminist cause.

At the same time, female public opinion had been stirred. In 1912 the issue of 'white slavery' provoked a second moral panic, on a similar scale to that which had preceded the 1885 Criminal Law Amendment Act. The government agreed to support further legislation to control prostitution, after severe pressure from an extra-parliamentary 'Pass the Bill' committee sponsored by the National Vigilance Association and many suffragists. A neutral stance on this question seemed to many anti-suffrage women to be both impossible and indefensible: for some, official neutrality by the NLOWS would have amounted to a betrayal of their own moral principles. Consequently, the League's office found itself besieged in the summer of 1912 by female members demanding a statement of anti-suffrage support for the new Criminal Law Amendment Bill.[47] Behind the scenes the leading men and women corresponded anxiously with each other, and not for the first time a split threatened to open up on gendered lines. Mary Ward and Dorothy Ward both assumed Violet Markham's support in pressing Lord Curzon and Captain Creed to adopt a more conciliatory tone towards NLOWS branches caught up in the general sexual reform fervour.[48] Meanwhile, in an unusual display of uncertainty, Gertrude Bell sought Violet's views on the 'Pass the Bill' committee, whose (mainly suffragist) names 'fill me with distrust'.[49]

In June 1912 the NLOWS executive committee issued a diplomatic policy statement aimed at appeasing the female membership. Based upon a memoran-dum from Lord Charnwood, it simultaneously defended the male sex from some of the grosser allegations of moral reform campaigners; reiterated the dangers of 'sex war' between men and their feminist critics; and expressed qualified anti-suffrage approval of further social purity legislation. The League's anti-suffrage work 'would suffer if it were diverted into other channels'; nevertheless, organized anti-suffragism must counter 'the fallacious arguments which not infrequently emanate from suffrage sources on these subjects'.[50] The Wards decided to tolerate this official statement, but the strong feelings aroused by the whole episode were reflected in Mary Ward's insistence upon amending an accompanying letter from Curzon to the League's (mainly female) branches. Dorothy reported to Violet

---

[47] See Colonel Lewis to Lord Curzon, 14 and 18 May 1912. Curzon papers, MSS Eur F112/35.
[48] Dorothy Ward to Violet Markham, 15 June 1912. Markham papers, 26/30.
[49] Gertrude Bell to Violet Markham, 27 July 1912. Markham papers, 26/30.
[50] Proof copy of Lord Charnwood's memorandum. Markham papers, 26/30.

Markham that, following 'a long consultation with Lady Jersey', her mother had drawn up 'two long paragraphs to be worked in, the gist of which was *sympathy* with all wise efforts to improve legislation for women and children'. She added that '*Personally* I would rather the Executive had gone a step further and *had* passed a Resolution definitely in favour of this Bill. Mother also would have been really glad if they had felt that way.'[51] Percy Creed, on the other hand, wrongly assumed a sympathetic hearing from Violet Markham when he wrote to her a week later condemning all suffragist campaigning on the 'White Slave Traffic' as 'absurd and calculated to stir up sex antagonism or arouse dangerous curiosity in innocent minds'.[52]

The issue of divorce reform aroused less public controversy in the same period, but in some ways was a still more problematic one for women anti-suffragists. There was no easy bandwagon to join, as a Royal Commission received conflicting evidence between 1909 and 1912 on the desirability or otherwise of equal, cheaper, and easier access to divorce for men and women of all social classes.[53] The Royal Commission heard a number of women witnesses, including Millicent Fawcett and Helena Swanwick, and its members included the distinguished suffragists Lady Frances Balfour and May Tennant (a close personal friend of Violet Markham). The NLOWS was evidently conscious of an indirect link between the Commission's deliberations and the protracted debate over gender roles which provided its own ideological context, for extensive reports on divorce reform were carefully preserved in its press cuttings archive. The combined rewards and stern social necessities of marriage had always been central to the anti-suffrage cause. Ethel Harrison repeatedly linked her defence of marriage with public opposition to easier divorce, which she and many others saw as a manifestation of the general feminist slide towards immorality and social anarchy. In an article titled 'A Woman's View of Divorce', published in the *Nineteenth Century* in 1911, she argued that women should have played a far larger part on a Commission whose outcomes would affect them profoundly. Raising and protecting the position of women in marriage was 'of supreme importance . . . it is a national question, second to none, to secure for the children of our country a worthy upbringing by worthy parents'. A recent suffragist 'Woman's Charter' had urged reforms in the marriage service, but Ethel rejected adaptations to suit modern couples' prejudices, at the expense of an emphasis on love, duty, and 'social obligation'. Using anecdotes to illustrate her points, she claimed that few working-class women wanted easier divorce. Though some minor improvements might be possible, 'We are persuaded that

---

[51] Dorothy Ward to Violet Markham, 15 June 1912. Markham papers, 26/30.
[52] Percy Creed to Violet Markham, 23 June 1912. Markham papers, 26/30.
[53] See R. Phillips, *Untying the Knot: A Short History of Divorce* (Cambridge: Cambridge University Press, 1991), ch. 7, for an interesting analysis of the ambivalences of Victorian and Edwardian divorce law reform.

in any loosening of the marriage tie women must lose infinitely more than they can gain, and immeasurably more than men'.[54]

Mary Ward's views on divorce were equally apocalyptic, and expressed at length in her melodramatic novel *Daphne, or Marriage a la Mode*, written in the year when she decided to rededicate herself to active anti-suffragism.[55] Though the novel dwelt upon the suffering of a wronged man, it concluded with the sorrows of a woman who has lost both husband and child, and found feminist politics of little consolation. Mary seems to have contemplated an importation of the divorce debate into organized anti-suffragism in Britain, but apparently recoiled from the issue as its difficulties became apparent. In August 1908 she wrote to Louise Creighton about her American experiences: 'a part of the strong opposition to the suffrage comes there from the feeling that it is the suffragists who are helping in the disintegration of the family'.[56] *Daphne* caused predictable offence to many Americans, and even Mary Ward must have hesitated to press British parallels which would have been still more offensive to the highly respectable leaders of British suffragism. She quietly dropped the subject in her later propaganda.

Though some anti-suffrage attacks on feminism included hostile references to suffragist links to divorce, there were few determined attempts to demonstrate a strong connection. This may have been simply because many anti-suffragists supported a limited measure of divorce reform as strongly as many suffragists: even Ethel Harrison granted the possibility of introducing greater fairness and stronger safeguards for women's custody of their children. As in the case of the Criminal Law Amendment Bill, the women antis were reluctant to concede promising ground to the suffrage cause, and anxious to demonstrate that they too were devoted to the welfare of women and children. At the same time most male leaders of the NLOWS were deeply reluctant to enter the divorce debate, which they saw as inherently divisive between men and women as well as a distraction from the anti-suffrage campaign. In May 1912 Cromer wrote to Curzon explaining his views on both the Criminal Law Amendment Bill and divorce reform. After expressing personal sympathy with League members who felt 'a special moral obligation' to support the proposed reforms from an anti-suffragist perspective, he set forth his 'equally strong opinion that the work of our League should be wholly confined to resisting the grant of the Parliamentary

[54] E. Harrison, 'A Woman's View of Divorce', *Nineteenth Century and After*, 69 (1911), 329, 330, 332, 333. In the *Anti-Suffrage Review* she noted that women's enfranchisement would lead to immediate divorce law reform, commenting that 'Divorce, so far as the writer knows, has not greatly occupied the attention of anti-suffrage women. They have been more intent upon the constructive side of marriage and family life.' *Anti-Suffrage Review*, 30 (May 1911), 94.

[55] M. Ward, *Daphne or Marriage à la Mode* (London: Cassel, 1909). After her own marital breakdown the anti-heroine becomes 'a "Feminist"—and particularly associated with those persons in the suffrage camp who stood for broad views on marriage and divorce' (p. 253).

[56] Mary Ward to Louise Creighton, 23 Aug. 1908. Pusey House Library, Oxford, M. Ward papers, 3/3/1.

vote'. Disagreements over the details of the Criminal Law Amendment Bill were rife among suffragists and anti-suffragists alike, whilst as for divorce reform: 'I can conceive no more difficult question, or one where there is more likely to be a difference of opinion'. It was inconceivable that the League should be allowed to develop 'a general roving commission to deal with all the real or supposed grievances of women'.[57] Perhaps fortunately for the anti-suffrage campaign, the Royal Commission's recommendations for divorce law reform did not reach the statute book until after the First World War. Another divisive internal debate with uncomfortable gender dimensions had been successfully avoided.

AN ALTERNATIVE FEMALE CITIZENSHIP?

The emergence of an anti-suffrage forward policy has been described in relation to the WNASL and its difficult amalgamation into the mixed-sex NLOWS. As we have seen, a majority of the most active women anti-suffragists were determined to explore constructive alternatives to suffragism. Convinced of women's unique capabilities and social importance, they sought answers to the question of how (rather than whether) women could play an influential role in public life without jeopardizing male imperial government and their own femininity. The answer seemed to lie in an expansion of specialized women's work related to the family and to the welfare of local communities. These anti-suffragists' predilection for a stronger feminine role in local government is not surprising, in an era which saw both the establishment of democratized local authorities and the launch of various welfare policies which relied upon a combination of local government initiative and voluntary collective effort for successful delivery. Feminine local government was not a universal panacea, but it did seem to offer prospects of improving the lives of British women and children, and thus strengthening the imperial nation, without the risks inherent to female involvement in parliamentary politics. Anti-suffrage women needed an inspiring vision of combined social reform and social consolidation to set against the utopian promises of suffragism. Though local government all too often failed to inspire the wider anti-suffrage constituency of conservative women, the forward policy maintained its hold over the leading anti-suffrage women until 1914. It represented a distinctive enclave of anti-suffrage ideas and activities, both within the NLOWS and (after successful distancing tactics by the male leadership) outside it. It also helped to sustain anti-suffrage women's contact with the many suffragists committed to the wider women's movement of organized social action and good works. Ultimately the forward

---

[57] Lord Cromer to Lord Curzon, 20 May 1912. Cromer papers, FO633/21. In his review article 'Feminism in France', published the following year, Cromer expressed his own condemnation of large-scale divorce reform, and his belief in its links to both suffragism and feminism. *National Review*, 62 (1913–14), 405.

policy brought progressive antis and conservative suffragists closer together, or at the very least helped to prevent them from drifting further apart at the height of the suffrage debate.

Violet Markham provided the 'forward' women with probably the most eloquent and successful exposition of their ideas ever made, when she spoke at the National League's great Albert Hall gathering on 28 February 1912. Rising to the challenges of a particularly fraught period in the League's history, as well as of a dauntingly large audience, she inspired both men and women with her account of women's citizenship in a modernizing society and an imperial nation. Her opening sentences condemned suffragism as 'disastrous to the Empire, disastrous to the nation—last, but not least, disastrous to the cause of that womanhood, which it professes to serve'. Gracefully conceding the discussion of 'directly political issues' to the male statesmen present, she took her stand as a woman addressing 'the woman's side of the question' from an affirmative, rather than a negative, point of view. The passage which followed summarized the essence of the forward policy:

In the first place, we are here to affirm that a woman's citizenship is as great and as real as that of any man, that her service is as vitally necessary to the State. But unlike our Suffragist friends, we do not fly in the face of hard facts and natural law. We believe that men and women are different—not similar—beings, with talents that are complementary, not identical, and that, therefore, they ought to have different shares in the management of the State that they severally compose.

Violet Markham went on to demolish suffragist arguments by portraying them as a pursuit of sectional interests, rather than of 'the highest interest of the nation as a whole'. National efficiency would not be served by a female franchise which, logically, must extend to include universal suffrage for both men and women regardless of fitness to vote. The second half of her speech dwelt at some length upon the 'special aptitudes' of women for certain forms of public service:

If the work of Imperial Parliament belongs more naturally to men, the work of Local Government, with its splendid opportunities for civic betterment and the uplifting of the race belongs more naturally to women. Here her powers of citizenship and service can find the fullest and noblest expression.

A swingeing attack upon suffragist neglect of municipal reform followed next, before a peroration which portrayed local government work as feminine in its methods as well as its social welfare content. Anti-suffragism was 'the symbol of disinterested service', in contrast to suffragist ambition for a place in the limelight. To 'loud and prolonged cheers', Violet told her audience of thousands: 'we hold that it is through the faithful fulfilment of duty, through service, not self-assertion, that woman will arrive at a true conception of her place in the body politic'.[58]

---

[58] V. Markham, *Miss Violet Markham's Great Speech at the Albert Hall, February 28th*, 1912 (London: NLOWS, 1912).

The success of this speech owed much to its faithful reflection of current male and female anti-suffragist views on women's innate qualities, skilfully combined with a positive depiction of female powers and opportunities which could be exercised without the parliamentary vote. Inevitably some members of the audience focused on the former, whilst others (including the forward women) rejoiced in the latter.[59] An emphasis on innate difference and on the duties of social and familial service was entirely compatible with faith in a female gender role determined first and foremost by biological attributes, and linked in turn to women's combined sexual and moral qualities as prospective (or actual) wives and mothers. However, the biological imperative took on a more original aspect when elevated into a demand for distinctive female citizenship. Violet Markham's speech triumphantly squared the circle linking sexuality to citizenship by claiming an important public role for women whilst conceding both their innate and their socially determined unsuitability for parliamentary politics. Male anti-suffrage prejudices were appeased, while women antis could choose to read the speech as an affirmation of their responsibilities as feminine citizens and maternal reformers, rather than merely womanly carers within individual families. Supporters of the forward policy believed that this perspective combined a willing acceptance of natural function, and a rejection of disruptive feminism, with necessary progress towards greater responsibilities for women in public life.

Though Violet Markham's speech was essentially a statement of anti-suffrage ideals, it also contained practical policy proposals and reflected a particular stage in the development of the NLOWS as a campaigning organization. Progressive anti-suffrage ideas emerged from a context of political debate which included the internal gender conflicts of organized anti-suffragism as well as the evolving tactics and alliances of the suffrage campaign itself. During 1910–14 the forward women leaders tried simultaneously to make a success of the amalgamated League and to implement their own views on female citizenship. The Albert Hall meeting coincided with the crisis within the NLOWS which led to the resignation of Lord Cromer as President soon afterwards. The meeting was immediately preceded by the controversial sacking of Lucy Terry Lewis, the League's leading female administrator. Both these departures were tied to the underlying problems of a forward policy which had never been fully accepted by Cromer and Curzon, despite their grudging assent to a League constitution which committed them to promoting women's role in local government. When Cromer complained to Curzon of 'these infernal women' within the League, three weeks before the

---

[59] Congratulatory letters included one from Marion Mortley: 'With your great intellectual powers and ability, you were able to give voice to what I believe to be still the convictions and the spirit of the great majority of women of all classes.' Edna Dalton wrote to express the enthusiasm of 'three of my working class friends . . . they cannot find words to express their admiration and also their hearty agreement with all you said'. Markham papers, 26/30.

Albert Hall meeting, he was referring to a controversy still more bitter than that over Miss Lewis's impending dismissal.[60] Violet Markham, together with Mary Ward, Gertrude Bell, and other leading women, had become embroiled in a severely embarrassing dispute which related directly to women's role in local government. The unusually plentiful surviving correspondence around this episode presents a vivid picture of the clash of ideas, as well as of personalities, within the League. The leading women corresponded with each other as well as with Lord Cromer, in the process exploring their own views on issues well beyond the immediate question of whether or not to support female candidates in local elections primarily on the grounds of their gender.[61]

After a slow start, Mary Ward had gradually succeeded during 1911 in extending the League's paper commitment to 'clause b' into the establishment of a functioning local government subcommittee.[62] The *Anti-Suffrage Review* began to carry an increasing number of instructive and exhortatory articles on local government matters, and at the Annual Council in July a resolution reaffirmed the League's commitment to 'a sympathetic and generous attitude towards the cause of women in local government'.[63] Mary Ward's speech on this occasion pointed to the tactical advantages of seizing the initiative from suffragists in local government, as well as providing a ringing endorsement of 'forward' ideals. Seconding the resolution, Miss Trapnell described the successes of female anti-suffragists within Bristol local government, sometimes achieved in collaboration with suffragists.[64] Neither of these speeches can have given Lord Cromer much pleasure. Never more than an unwelcome distraction from his perspective, the local government committee became a severe embarrassment as it began to implement its policy of supporting promising female election candidates. In November 1911 Mary Ward announced that her committee had assumed the more independent status of an affiliate to the League, in deference to those who felt its work lay beyond 'the original purpose of the association'.[65] The corollary of this semi-detachment was greater independence of action, and within weeks the Local Government Advancement Committee (as it was now called) had taken the bold step of announcing its support for Dr Sophia Jevons as a candidate in the forthcoming West Marylebone county council by-election. Unfortunately,

[60] Lord Cromer to Lord Curzon, 8 Feb. 1912. Curzon papers, MSS Eur F112/35.

[61] See also J. Bush, 'British Women's Anti-Suffragism and the Forward Policy, 1908–1914', *Women's History Review*, 11/3 (2002), 431–54.

[62] See Mary Ward's letter to Lord Cromer, 11 Jan. 1911, requesting a private meeting to enable her to explain her views and assuage his concerns over the League's local government policy. Curzon papers, MSS Eur F112/34.

[63] *Anti-Suffrage Review*, 33 (Aug. 1911), 166.   [64] Ibid. 167.

[65] Ibid., 36 (Nov. 1911), 236. Dorothy Ward recorded gleefully in her diary on 26 July 1911 that her mother had persuaded the NLOWS executive to agree to a local government committee 'on new and better footing as LG Advancement Committee *affiliated* to the League, *not* a sub-committee, and with its own Secretary and £300 a year subsidy!' But the first meeting of the LGAC did not take place until 5 Dec. 1911. Diary 1911, D. Ward papers, 202.47.

her male opponent turned out to be an anti-suffragist Conservative crony of Lord Cromer: his annoyance at this turn of events ensured that the private correspondence about the situation would be both plain-spoken and politically revealing.

A sympathetic Lord Curzon was the first to receive news of Cromer's fury over this new example of female insubordination, in a letter proclaiming 'I really have not the health, strength, youth or, I may add, the temper to go on dealing with these infernal women'.[66] Violet Markham, who had tried on the same day to defend Dr Jevons and Mary Ward, received an equally angry but more politely phrased response. Explaining her support for the committee's forward policy and for the candidate personally, she outlined Dr Jevons's unusually good qualifications for local government work, adding reassuringly that she was 'not a member of a suffrage society, or in any case is not prominently identified with that cause'.[67] In reply, Cromer accused Miss Markham of looking at only 'one side of a very complicated and difficult question'; both she and Mary Ward were 'extremists . . . who invite the ratepayers to vote for a woman merely on account of her sex, quite irrespective of her opinions on other questions'.[68] The following day Violet Markham stood her ground, claiming to be 'chastened, but I fear at heart impenitent'. Rejecting the accusation of prioritizing gender alone, she explained her dislike of party politics imported into local government. Setting forth the fundamental premises of the forward policy, she claimed that 'women who serve in Local Government deal with social facts'; for this very reason, and because many women had 'special knowledge of social work', their influence in local government needed to increase:

I cannot but feel that it would be a real disaster for our cause if we give even the least impression, however unjustified, of being anti-women. There is a large body of centre opinion which I feel it should be our object to conciliate and detach from the Suffragist side. But to do this we must show that we take positive views of women's work and do not meet the whole feminist movement with a blunt *non possumus*.[69]

Even Cromer's resignation, which had occurred two days before this letter was sent, could not shake such convictions. Mary Ward and her supporters were reluctantly prepared to accept the need for a complete organizational separation of their local government committee from the National League, but they were not willing to jettison their faith in woman-centred social action as a vital component of female citizenship. The intersection with suffragist views on women's place in local government was plain enough, and another reason for Lord Cromer's dismay. However the anti-suffrage 'forward' women believed

---

[66] Lord Cromer to Lord Curzon, 8 Feb. 1912. Curzon papers, MSS Eur F112/35.
[67] Violet Markham to Lord Cromer, 8 Feb. 1912. Cromer papers, FO633/21.
[68] Lord Cromer to Violet Markham, 9 Feb. 1912. Markham papers, 26/30.
[69] Violet Markham to Lord Cromer, 10 Feb. 1912. Cromer papers, FO633/21. Later the same day she wrote regretting his resignation as President of the NLOWS.

that their local government work was a strongly preferable alternative, rather than merely a supplement, to participation in parliamentary politics. During 1912 the anti-suffrage women maintained uneasy communications on areas of joint interest with the suffrage-leaning (but officially suffrage-neutral) Women's Local Government Society. Mary Ward, despite earlier friendly relations, had fallen out with the leaders of this organization.[70] Violet Markham, on the other hand, was genuinely concerned to refute the Local Government Society's hostile attack on her Albert Hall speech.[71] Correspondence between these two women shows that, despite their shared support for the forward policy, their views were far from identical.[72] Mary Ward wished her reconstituted Local Government Advancement Committee to become an overtly anti-suffragist alternative to the long-established Women's Local Government Society, while Violet Markham had by this stage decided that a true separation of activities was necessary. Her preference for a suffrage truce in local government was clearly reflected in her increasingly critical relationship to Mary Ward's committee, ended abruptly by her mother's death in April 1912 and her own temporary withdrawal from political work of all kinds.

Meanwhile Mary Ward was trying to shore up her support among other anti-suffrage women. By August 1912 her Local Government Advancement Committee included such NLOWS stalwarts as Gertrude Bell, Gladys Pott, Emily Simon, Katharine Tullibardine, and Edith Long Fox (all listed as executive committee members), as well as 'General Committee' members including Elizabeth Burgwin, Ethel Harrison, Margaret Jersey, Violet Montrose, Harriet Wantage, Lucy Soulsby, Maud Hamilton, and Lucy Terry Lewis. Distinguished male antis were also nominally included on the committee list, published in *The Times* below a letter claiming that the work of women in local government was 'the true alternative to the suffrage agitation'.[73] However, Dorothy Ward's private diary suggests that the reality of committee meetings during 1912 fell a long way short of expectations.[74] Though Gertrude Bell was noted by Cromer as a strong supporter of Mary Ward,[75] and Gladys Pott continued to be a regular

[70] Mary Ward's critical comments were reported in the *Standard*, 12 Nov. 1912. NLOWS Cuttings book, 2474c25. Dorothy Ward echoed these criticisms in the *Hampstead and Highgate Express*, 5 July 1913. NLOWS Cuttings book, 2474c27.

[71] See *Anti-Suffrage Review*, 43 (May 1912), 107.

[72] Mary Ward to Violet Markham, 10, 11, and 14 Feb. and 24 Mar. 1912; Violet Markham to Mary Ward, ? March 1912. Violet's lengthy letter expressed her reservations about Mary Ward's anti-suffragist plans for the newly independent LGAC. Her own draft Memorandum on local government work insisted upon the right of individuals to support any candidate, suffragist or non-suffragist. Markham papers, 26/30.

[73] *The Times*, 6 Aug. 1912, 7.

[74] See entries in Dorothy Ward's diary for 21 May, 25 June, 9 July, 17 July, 9 Oct. 1912. D. Ward papers, MS Add. 202.48.

[75] Lord Cromer to Lord Curzon, 23 Feb. 1912, Curzon papers, MSS Eur F112/35. See also Gertrude Bell to Violet Markham, 13 Feb. 1912, Markham papers, 26/30. Cromer had forwarded Violet Markham's letters on the West Marylebone affair to Gertrude, no doubt hoping for her help

visitor to her home, the reconstituted and independent committee was soon faltering. In January 1913 Mary Ward tried to take its work in a new direction by linking support for an extended municipal franchise to the possibility of a future referendum on parliamentary votes for women.[76] Gladys Pott, soon after, publicly re-emphasized the committee's lack of formal connections to organized anti-suffragism, though her personal commitment to local government work remained strong.[77] Dorothy Ward's slightly incongruous excursion into local government in March 1913, as the leading supporter of Miss Willoughby's hopeless candidature in a Hoxton municipal by-election, was a brave experiment which led nowhere.[78] By the end of the year Mary Ward was casting around for more effective and inspiring ways of embodying the forward policy vision of an alternative female citizenship. Prominent women antis continued to advocate greater female involvement in local government during 1914, but it was clear that the committee had failed to galvanize strong support either for local government work or for anti-suffragism itself. The ideal of local government by women was often more attractive to anti-suffragists than the humdrum, strenuous reality.

FEMINIZING THE CONSTITUTION

Some of the anti-suffragists who promoted women's work in local government were also eager to explore the possibility of new constitutional channels for female influence upon national policy. How might the machinery of government be modified to give women a voice without immersing them in the masculine world of parliamentary politics? This interesting question was repeatedly addressed by women during the era of organized anti-suffragism.[79] Progressive antis were anxious to protect the integrity of imperial government. At the same time they wished to extend their forward policy, based upon women's strengths, into the realms of policy-making as well as policy implementation.

The idea of a separate 'women's chamber', dealing exclusively with policy areas where women were believed to have special expertise, was popular with some anti-suffrage women from 1907 onwards. Ethel Harrison put this suggestion forward in her book *The Freedom of Women*. Without developing the idea in any detail,

in resolving the conflict. She assured Violet that 'I am all on your side in principle', whilst at the same time urging her to accept the complete separation of the LGAC from the NLOWS as 'the least evil' choice available.

[76] Mary Ward letter, *The Times*, 31 Jan. 1913, 8.

[77] Gladys Pott letter, *The Times*, 6 Feb. 1913, 8.

[78] See Dorothy Ward's diary entries for the period 18 Feb.–6 Mar. 1913. D. Ward papers, MS Add. 202.49.

[79] There was also more limited masculine interest in this question. See e.g. S. Mitra, 'Voice for Women—Without Votes', *Nineteenth Century and After*, 74 (1913), 998–1007. He described himself as 'an Indian fellow-subject' with friendly intentions. Leo Maxse, editor of the *National Review*, was also supportive.

and with the proviso that most women currently had no wish for extra powers, she observed, 'when, if ever, the ten millions of Englishwomen of whom we have spoken demand and get the vote, with parliamentary representation and the rest, let us trust that it will be in a Diet of Women outside Imperial Parliament'.[80] The same idea was taken up and developed in more detail by Caroline Stephen and Violet Markham. Caroline was the sister of two distinguished Victorian scholars and aunt to two leading Edwardian women intellectuals, as well as a religious writer and active philanthropist in her own right. As a Quaker, she had experienced the Society of Friends' debates over the admission of women to their governing body in the 1890s, and probably regretted the subsequent decision to abolish a separate Women's Yearly Meeting.[81] Her *Nineteenth Century* article on 'Women and Politics', published in 1907, presented a maternal reformist defence of women's 'own special work', and of their moral influence over men. It also expressed the view that 'In a certain sense, no doubt, public affairs are the province of us all. There are many questions coming before Parliament on which it would be most desirable that the opinion of wise and experienced women should be heard'. Perhaps a 'third House' might be developed, 'with or without legislative power', giving a voice to women and leavening parliamentary debate?[82] A letter in the *Anti-Suffrage Review* in January 1909 made it clear that Caroline preferred an advisory to a legislative role for women. She now proposed 'a Consultative Chamber for Women, elected by women only, and meeting during the session of Parliament to consider and offer suggestions on such Bills as either House might at its own discretion think fit to lay before it . . . for the first time we should hear a really feminine voice in national affairs—a voice which we must remember that the Suffrage can never give'.[83] Her fear that enfranchised women would find their views swamped by those of men within a male-dominated Parliament proved eventually to be well founded.

Meanwhile Violet Markham and Mary Ward had also begun to consider the possibility of separate representation for women at Westminster. Mary daringly hinted at the possibility of constitutional reform in her launch speech for the Women's League in July 1908, adding that 'we have no hard and fast plan'.[84] Not only were such proposals likely to be divisive within the new League; she was herself genuinely uncertain of the best way forward. The practicalities of building

---

[80] E. Harrison, *Freedom of Women*, 29.

[81] For details of Quakers' internal reforms, see T. Kennedy, *British Quakerism 1860–1920* (Oxford: Oxford University Press, 2001), ch. 6. For the Quakers' engagement with suffragism see S. Holton, 'Kinship and Friendship: Quaker Women's Networks and the Women's Movement', *Women's History Review*, 14/3–4 (2005), 365–84; also L. Lauer, 'Women in British Non-Conformity 1880–1920, with Special Reference to the Society of Friends, Baptist Union and Salvation Army', D.Phil. thesis (Oxford, 1994).

[82] C. Stephen, 'Women and Politics', *Nineteenth Century and After*, 61 (1907), 230–1.

[83] *Anti-Suffrage Review*, 2 (Jan. 1909), 7.

[84] *Women's National Anti-Suffrage League: Speech by Mrs Humphry Ward*, WNASL pamphlet no. 3 (London: WNASL, 1908), 10.

the anti-suffrage organization soon supervened, leaving Violet Markham to take up the baton. During 1909 she corresponded over the desirability of a Women's Chamber with St Loe Strachey as well as Mary Ward, preparing the way for a major article in the *National Review*. Her article set forth what she described as a 'scheme of conciliation', designed to convert the constructive spirit behind women's anti-suffragism into 'an active force'. Taking her stand upon grounds of principle, rather than mere anti-suffrage tactical advantage, she outlined her social evolutionary belief in 'the scientific fact of specialisation'. Female sexual difference meant that 'Nature herself has marked out one great primary set of duties for woman', comprising responsibility for home-making and 'the bearing and rearing of healthy citizens'. Women were incapable of exercising the 'physical sanction' of imperial government. Their 'perfectly reasonable' desire for 'a definite share in the management of the State' would therefore need to be met through different means: a combination of local government work with 'the creation of a Women's Council, elected by women'. Violet sketched out a two-way process through which women's resolutions would be sent to the House of Commons, while 'on the other hand, the Commons would seek the opinion of the Council'. The goal would thus be achieved of 'giving women some body of their own, which can voice their opinions without detriment to the sovereign power as a whole'. More positively, 'their own special gifts would be turned to the greatest national advantage'.[85] A mixed reaction greeted this bold proposal, even from the anti-suffrage friends whom she consulted in advance of publication. Mary Ward explained to Violet her own preference for a different form of Women's Council, based upon a national gathering of female local government representatives, and the *Anti-Suffrage Review* soon after reflected this position in a critical editorial.[86] Sir Alfred Lyall was privately sympathetic, but both St Loe Strachey and Lord Cromer wrote dismissive letters, the former commenting on 'the extreme danger of women acting together' while the latter objected both on grounds of principle and practicality.[87]

The idea of a Women's Council went temporarily into abeyance as anti-suffrage women concentrated upon the difficult task of holding together conservatives and progressives within the WNASL, then upon making a success of the amalgamated NLOWS. During 1912 it re-emerged in a different context. The setbacks to gender collaboration caused by the sacking of Miss Lewis, the resignation of Lord Cromer, and the breach between the League and the Local Government

---

[85] V. Markham, 'A Proposed Woman's Council', *National Review*, 55 (1910), 1029–38.

[86] Mary Ward to Violet Markham, 29 Sept. 1909. Markham papers, 26/30. Inviting Violet for 'a good talk' and an overnight stay, she wrote suggesting triennial meetings of women councillors connected in the future to a permanent women's local government committee with links to government departments. See also *Anti-Suffrage Review*, 22 (Sept. 1910).

[87] Alfred Lyall to Violet Markham, 10 Sept. 1910, Markham papers, 26/30; St Loe Strachey to Violet Markham, 11 Oct. 1909, Markham papers, 26/30; Lord Cromer to Violet Markham, 11 Aug. 1910, Cromer papers, FO633/19.

Advancement Committee made the idea of separate male and female organizations once more attractive. In the heat of the moment, Lord Cromer confided to Lord Curzon his belief that 'it would, as events have turned out, have been better not to amalgamate. But that cannot be helped now.'[88] As the dust settled on these events, Gertrude Bell wrote to Violet Markham in July 1912 describing a new initiative to establish some form of representative organization for women, with a role in national government which would be both helpfully separate from and usefully integrated with the male machinery of parliamentary rule. Making a direct connection with Violet's earlier ideas, she explained that 'The question of a Women's Council has come up again in a rather different form'. A series of meetings had taken place, beginning with a luncheon party at her own house where four women (including Gladys Pott) 'sketched out' two parallel committees, one of male legislators specially interested in women's issues and the other of 'women . . . to whom they could go for advice and help, and who would also be ready to suggest matters that the MP committee ought to take up'. An 'unofficial origin' could actually help this plan along, postponing any demand for 'official sanction and enlarged powers' until it had 'proved its value'. Gertrude went on to list women who might play a leading role, including Violet herself, Miss Pott ('subject to Lady Wantage's approval which I have no doubt we would get'), Lady Evelyn Grey, and possibly sympathetic suffragists such as May Tennant and Una Pope-Hennesy: 'I would like to see a good proportion of pronounced antis, such as Miss Pott, who would see that the violent suffragists would not collar the whole organisation'. Her letter opened with the information that she had spent the previous Sunday with Mary and Dorothy Ward, and there can be little doubt that they too were regarded as potential recruits.[89]

Both Gertrude Bell and Violet Markham moved off into other activities during the second half of 1912, but discussion of similar ideas continued among leading anti-suffrage women during the following year. The internal conflicts of the National Union of Women Workers provided additional impetus, as Mary Ward gradually decided to launch a new organization titled the Joint Parliamentary Advisory Committee. In October 1913, as her final defeat and departure from the NUWW loomed, press reports appeared of her determination to 'enlarge and strengthen the protest movement, and to provide it, if possible, with a new centre and rallying point for social work, involving, probably, active co-operation with a certain number of Members of Parliament who, on wholly neutral grounds from which the question of the Suffrage, for and against, has been altogether excluded, desire the help and advice of women in social legislation'.[90] Louise Creighton, as President of the NUWW, had been reluctantly forced into

    [88] Lord Cromer to Lord Curzon, 5 Jan. 1912. Curzon papers, MSS Eur F112/34.
    [89] Gertrude Bell to Violet Markham, 27 July 1912. Markham papers, 26/30.
    [90] Mary Ward statement, reported in *Eastern Morning News*, 10 Oct. 1913. NLOWS Cuttings book, 2474c.28.

the eye of the storm over its formal commitment to suffragism. She received a series of letters from her old friend which prove that the Joint Advisory Committee was formed on the rebound from Mary's defeat within the NUWW, but at the same time show the ambitious scope of this new scheme.

In December 1913 Mary Ward was already optimistically describing the JAC as 'a kind of Standing Committee composed equally of members from all parts of the House of Commons, and both sides of the Suffrage question—and women of experience in social work . . . it *ought* to be very useful, and to develop into a permanent adjunct of the House of Commons'. A plea for 'friendly relations with the Union' followed next, and was to be frequently (and fruitlessly) repeated during the months ahead. The JAC was 'no Anti conspiracy!—but a bona-fide attempt to get Antis and Pros to work together on really equal terms'.[91] By early April the Conservative suffragists had 'come in splendidly'. The lack of Liberal and Labour women seemed likely to be alleviated by the adherence of two Labour Members of Parliament and the 'really hopeful' presence of Violet Markham at the opening meeting.[92] Later the same month Mary Ward predicted a future body of '70 women with 30 or 40 Members of Parliament'. Future feminine influence upon parliamentary business seemed guaranteed, and 'looking round the Westminster Hall Committee room, one felt it *might* be the germ of great things—who knows?'[93] Dorothy Ward's diary recorded both the JAC's modest success and her mother's understandable delight at having demonstrated in practice, rather than merely in theory, that women could make their presence felt in national government on non-suffrage terms.[94]

Mary Ward was also centrally involved in another constitutional discussion during the spring of 1914. The potential of federal forms of government was of great contemporary interest in relation to imperialist hopes for closer cohesion between Britain and her 'white settler' dominions. The same concept filtered through into the suffrage debate, as some anti-suffrage women began considering the possibility of expanding the powers of British local government in order to provide an acceptable alternative to parliamentary votes for women. Could the appropriately feminine character of local government be carried forward into regional assemblies, holding devolved powers from national government in relation to the social issues which most concerned women as local voters and representatives? Would this leave Parliament with a clearer remit to focus upon its imperial duties, including military and foreign affairs and the fostering of a stronger, more united empire? Might moderate suffragists—by this date

---

[91] Mary Ward to Louise Creighton, 18 Dec. 1913. M. Ward papers, 3/3/1.
[92] Ibid., 6 Apr. 1914. M. Ward papers, 3/3/1.
[93] Ibid., 24 Apr. 1914. M. Ward papers, 3/3/1.
[94] See Dorothy Ward's diary entries on 20 Mar. and 3, 6, 7, 15, 21, and 22 Apr. 1914, when 'Mummy came home really happy' from the first full meeting of the JAC at the House of Commons. D. Ward papers, MS Add. 202.50.

often appalled at militant outrages and their consequences—be won over to support such a scheme? Such ideas lay on the more imaginative outer fringes of anti-suffrage constitutional theory, but their connectedness to the dual causes of empire and of social reform gave them a certain currency.

This was especially the case among anti-suffrage women who had conservative suffragist friends and shared their wish to reunite the British women's movement in support of long-term social improvement. Violet Markham, as an executive member of the imperialist Victoria League as well as a committed social reformer, corresponded with her male imperialist friends about federalism from 1910 onwards.[95] In one of his earliest letters to her, Lord Cromer expressed his own uncertainties over federalism, with the affable rider: 'Possibly the solution lies in the direction which you suggest, and which has also occurred to me, namely that of extending the powers of County Councils'.[96] Her *National Review* article in 1910 drew parallels between the legislative duties of Australasian states and 'those of Local Government in this country . . . They can call women to their councils without running the risks which must attend that experiment in Great Britain.'[97] Anti-suffragists were fond of minimizing both the remit and the impact of women's enfranchisement in Australia and New Zealand, even at the risk of offending national pride in those parts of the Empire.[98] Similar arguments were deployed to turn aside suffragist boasts about the success of female enfranchisement in several American states.[99] Violet Markham was again to the fore during 1913 when a combined effort was made by suffragists and a minority of anti-suffrage women to investigate the realities of the female vote within the federal constitution of the United States.[100]

Mary Ward's interest in federalism was related to her enthusiasm for the Empire as well as to her faith in women's public service through local government. In November 1913 she publicly refuted suffragist accusations that her Local Government Advancement Committee aimed primarily to undermine

---

[95] Violet Markham's friendships with Lord Milner and members of his South African 'Kindergarten' of imperialist supporters, as well as with Earl Grey and Mackenzie King in Canada, placed her close to the heart of contemporary debates over imperial federation.

[96] Lord Cromer to Violet Markham, 11 Aug. 1910. Cromer papers, FO633/19.

[97] Markham, 'A Proposed Woman's Council', 1036.

[98] See *Anti-Suffrage Review*, 58 (Aug. 1913), on 'The Vote in Australia' and 'Woman Suffrage in New Zealand', 173 and 178.

[99] See e.g. Mary Ward's comments on the limitations of American enfranchisement in the *Anti-Suffrage Review*, 16 (Mar. 1910), 4, and 18 (May 1910), 8. After the success of the suffragists in the Californian referendum of 1911, she countered Millicent Fawcett's triumphalism by claiming that 'the general result . . . in the suffrage States . . . is certainly nearer to English local government than to our Parliamentary system'. *The Times*, 19 Oct. 1911, 7.

[100] See Maud Selborne's letter to Violet Markham, 11 July 1913, relating to their exchanges over the joint American enquiry, but also commenting at length upon the common ground between some suffragists and some anti-suffragists. Markham papers, 26/30. The outcomes of this enquiry were published in 'Woman Suffrage at Work in America', *Nineteenth Century and After*, 75 (1914), 415–33.

the long-standing Women's Local Government Society, claiming the political high ground through her assertion of faith in federalism. The imperial Parliament was 'destined to become the Parliament not of the United Kingdom only, but the Empire'; in consequence, 'a great mass of social and domestic legislation' would need to be referred to 'the provincial councils of the future'. Anti-suffragists regarded it as vital 'on the one hand, to protect the Imperial Parliament of the near future' from women voters, and 'on the other, to secure that women should have their full ultimate share in the domestic and social powers of an organised nation'.[101] In May 1914 the same ideas resurfaced in a different context. Mary Ward was anxious to turn aside suffragist criticism of her Joint Advisory Committee, and believed there was a real possibility of wooing large numbers of conservative suffragists into willing collaboration with this step towards greater female influence upon national government. With or without the vote, closer cooperation between women social workers and the Parliament remained desirable and achievable. An interesting press debate developed, as Mary tried to convince the suffragists of her honourable intentions, as well as of the virtues of 'local Parliaments'. As usual *The Times* provided a willing platform for her opening salvo, under the title 'Minor Parliaments and Woman Suffrage'. After outlining a future division of imperial and local powers 'which corresponds broadly to the natural differences between the sexes', she boldly predicted 'the rise of a middle suffrage party—in which many who have hitherto been opponents might find themselves working side by side in the promotion of a settlement by consent'. This settlement would, of course, be dependent upon a suffragist pledge to accept a clear demarcation between local assemblies and 'the Central Imperial Parliament'.[102]

Suffragist responses to this seemingly placatory offer were polite but cautious. It was never likely that leading suffragists would renounce their campaign for the parliamentary vote in favour of a federalist compromise, and Mary Ward can scarcely have expected their eager assent. However, she did have some basis for believing that much common ground existed between moderate suffragists and progressive anti-suffragists. Women on both sides of the suffrage divide were showing interest in the possibility of building upon what united them, rather than concentrating purely upon short-term hostilities over the franchise issue. Suffragette militancy had polarized debate and provided the antis with new evidence to support their cause. But it had also driven some women towards more thoughtful acknowledgement of the middle ground shared by a majority of female reformers.

[101] Mary Ward letter in the *Standard*, 12 Nov. 1913. NLOWS Cuttings book, 2474c25.
[102] *The Times*, 15 May 1914, 9. Mrs Fawcett and others responded, providing Mary Ward with further opportunities to demonstrate her own constructive and conciliatory attitude, which she contrasted with the suffragists' reluctance to compromise, in *The Times*, 20 May 1914, 13; and 26 May 1914, 11.

WAS A SUFFRAGE TRUCE POSSIBLE?

The press debate over federalism illustrated both the possibilities and the limitations of conciliatory behaviour among suffrage and anti-suffrage women in 1914. Mary Ward was not a natural conciliator, for all her awareness of the tactical advantages of a suffrage truce, and for all her genuine faith in the female solidarity underpinning much philanthropic social reform. Her responses to suffragist criticism of her 'Minor Parliaments' proposals soon threatened to revert to habitual anti-suffrage point-scoring. It is necessary to look elsewhere for more convincing evidence of the potential for an eventual suffrage truce.

In the first place, leading suffragists and anti-suffragists were to be found collaborating in support of non-political causes throughout the suffrage campaign. Many women's associations, including the very large Anglican organizations as well as smaller female imperialist societies and a multitude of social reform groups, made a deliberate effort to avoid divisive suffrage debates which would impede their work.[103] Some women's societies, such as the Personal Service Association established in 1909, made a founding principle out of their desire to bridge the suffrage divide in pursuit of more fundamental purposes. There were thus plenty of precedents for Mary Ward's appeal for combined suffrage and anti-suffrage support for her JAC scheme. Even the NUWW, which became acrimoniously divided over its formal commitment to suffragism in 1912–13, produced evidence of suffrage supporters' strong desire to conciliate anti-suffragist colleagues. Behind the scenes, and amongst the majority of women who were not deeply committed to collective public action, there were still more plentiful examples of friendships and joint activities among suffrage and anti-suffrage women. Many women were uncertain of their own position, or held fluctuating views on the female franchise influenced by personal and family prejudices as much as by rational political argument. Even among the leading activists in the suffrage and anti-suffrage campaigns, there are numerous examples of friendships and family ties quite unaffected by differing views on the female vote. Mary Ward's friendship with Louise Creighton was tried and tested more than most by the suffrage conflict, but survived into old age. Violet Markham enjoyed her closest friendships with suffragist fellow Liberals; more strikingly, she also befriended Maud Selborne and Edith Lyttelton across both party political and suffrage barriers. The suffrage question was often frankly discussed within such friendships, which helped to consolidate shared ideas as well as providing opportunities for private debate.

There were, of course, parallel examples of single-minded conviction and of genuine hostility between suffrage and anti-suffrage women. The escalation of

---

[103] See Ch. 3, above, also Bush, *Edwardian Ladies*, ch. 10.

militancy, and of official and unofficial reactions to militancy, drove women apart as well as threatening a 'sex war' between men and women. On the other hand, as has been noted earlier in this chapter, dislike of militancy and of the 'ultra-feminism' with which it was sometimes associated could also bring women together in support of conservative gender ideals. A telling example of both unity and division occurred within the NLOWS during the summer of 1913. Gertrude Elliott, a member of the League's Berkshire branch, took the initiative in drafting a collective letter addressed from anti-suffrage women to Millicent Fawcett and Maud Selborne, appealing for a united front against militancy and 'extremism'. The fourteen signatories included Beatrice Chamberlain, Violet Markham, Lucy Soulsby, Charlotte Toynbee, Katharine Tullibardine, Lady Weardale, Mary Ward, and Harriet Wantage. Its text provided the clearest possible statement of shared purpose: 'We maintain that Constitutional Suffragists have more in common with us than they have with the extremists of their own party, for we seek the same ultimate end, namely the improvement of the position of women and through it the purifying and raising of the whole human race; and we both profess to seek it through legal and peaceful means.'[104] However, the letter never reached its intended recipients. Lady Haversham objected strongly to its contents and forwarded it to Lord Curzon with the scathing comment: 'There is a section of our Party, which is always trying to show how much they have in common with our opponents, and try and combine with them on some common platform. I thought you, as our Head, had better read the enclosed proposal which I cannot think will meet with your approval.'[105]

A veto was duly imposed, but not before Curzon had been made aware of the extent of female support for Miss Elliott's stance. Gertrude Elliott herself wrote to defend her letter, explaining its tactical value in separating militants from moderates and emphasizing that Lady Jersey was 'cognizant of our purpose'.[106] Margaret Jersey followed up with a letter informing Curzon that Miss Elliott had acted 'in consultation with Lady Wantage who is a near neighbour of hers and I understand anxious to have it sent'. She restated the tactical purpose of the letter, making it clear that she had indeed approved it, apart from having no desire to offend one of the League's 'most consistent and generous' supporters.[107] Gertrude Elliott's eventual climbdown provides further evidence of Curzon's personal stature and of masculine control over League policy.[108] This incident also illustrates once again the divisions among the anti-suffrage women themselves, as well as among the suffragists whose disunity Gertrude Elliott's letter had attempted to highlight.

---

[104] 'Miss Elliott's proposed letter, August 1913'. Curzon papers, MSS Eur F112/36.
[105] Lady Haversham to Lord Curzon, 12 Aug. 1913. Curzon papers, MSS Eur F112/36.
[106] G. Elliott to Lord Curzon, 22 Aug. 1913. Curzon papers, MSS Eur F112/36.
[107] Margaret Jersey to Lord Curzon, 27 Aug. 1913. Curzon papers, MSS Eur F112/36.
[108] In her letter on 1 Sept. 1913, confirming that she had agreed to withdraw her letter, Miss Elliot wrote, 'May I add that it is solely out of respect to *your* opinion that I consent to take this course'. Curzon papers, MSS Eur F112/36.

Despite so many overlapping ideas and so much joint female work in other causes, there was little realistic prospect of a formal suffrage truce before the First World War. The constraints of organized campaigning were too great. Though there is considerable evidence of fluidity and diversity of opinion on both sides of the suffrage divide, public confrontation between rival organizations inevitably tended to polarize public discussion. The male leaders of the NLOWS and their more diehard female followers believed that public exploration of shared ideals would fatally weaken their cause. Yet exploration of the ideological middle ground persisted in the teeth of such disapproval, both among forward women anti-suffragists and between these women and the more conservative suffragists. Innovative thinking, as well as social conservatism, characterized the public and private views of some leading anti-suffrage women on the eve of the First World War. It remained to be seen how far the upheaval of war would draw women together through common work undertaken in unprecedented circumstances. The context of the debate over suffrage, sexuality, and citizenship was about to be transformed, with unpredictable results.

10

Anti-Suffragists at War

THE IMPACT OF WAR

The outbreak of the First World War surprised anti-suffrage campaigners as much as nearly everybody else. At the height of summer holidays, and in the midst of preoccupying domestic conflicts over Ireland, suffrage, and labour unrest, Britain's future as a world power was suddenly at stake. Worse still, the precious lives of friends and relatives were under threat, though nobody yet foresaw the full extent of the devastation which lay ahead. Like their suffrage counterparts, many anti-suffrage women hesitated as they contemplated both public and private dangers. However, the leading anti-suffragists' dilemma over war support was short-lived. Without exception, they proved loyal to their established faith in male imperial government and the values it sought to defend. As suffragists agonized over their duty as internationalists, and (in some cases) their allegiance to peace-loving socialism, anti-suffrage women stood ready to support masculine 'physical force' through to its logical conclusion. Never had the manliness of men and the womanliness of women been put to a sterner test. The war promised to purge the nation of its weaknesses and to reinforce the gender differences which characterized an advanced civilization. Anti-suffragists had long viewed the suffrage campaign as a damaging distraction from women's vital purpose as the linchpins of family life, inspirers of men, social carers, and guardians of morality. Their particular virtues and capacities would be needed more than ever in wartime, to provide the bedrock of national and imperial strength.

Gendered patriotism took many different forms over the following four years. In August 1914 there was little or no expectation of prolonged conflict and unprecedented loss, ending in a victory which would coincide with women's enfranchisement. Yet both suffragists and anti-suffragists were soon declaring the relevance of their gender beliefs to Britain's eventual military success, as they simultaneously suspended their political campaigning. 'Today we are at grips with realities', announced the first wartime issue of the *Anti-Suffrage Review*. A stern editorial commented on 'the fact' of physical force as 'the ultimate basis of all existence', before proceeding to a condemnation of the final pre-war suffragist peace rally: an object lesson in the threat posed by 'theorists who would render the counsels of the nation effeminate'. Victory depended ultimately upon 'the virility of the nation's counsels', as much as upon military might. Meanwhile the wartime division of gender responsibilities seemed clear enough: 'When face to face with realities men and women take up instinctively the posts which Nature allots them. While men mount guard or give battle to the foe, women tend the home and make provision for the sick and the wounded . . . Both roles are essential to the welfare of the nation, and no-one would dream of saying that women are despised by men because they are not taken with them into the firing line'.[1] As well as echoing the (male) editor's call for 'Patriotism before Politics', and a clear separation of wartime gender roles, Gladys Pott provided a supplementary female viewpoint in her own first public commentary upon 'Anti-Suffragists in the Time of War'. The auxiliary duties of patriotic women must be shared by suffragists and anti-suffragists, but her own local branch of the NLOWS was already showing the best way forward by practical collaboration between male and female members to instil patriotism and organize war work. As anti-suffrage gentlemen took to local recruiting platforms and donated their money for patriotic purposes, women performed a multitude of quietly useful roles, with 'no advertisement, no showy report, no brag, no public emotionalism'. Anti-suffrage women were needed to provide a style of wartime leadership which contrasted with the 'undisciplined zeal' of selfishly ambitious women who neglected 'the daily routine of life' in order to indulge in showy displays of patriotic commitment.[2]

Within the first weeks of the war it was clear that the suffrage conflict would be only semi-submerged by the flood of women's war work, despite the general sense of altered priorities during a national emergency. The Pankhursts' campaign for military recruitment, alongside the suffragist drive to organize voluntary war work and later to mobilize a wartime female labour force, are much better known than their anti-suffrage equivalents.[3] Suffrage leaders spared no effort to ensure that this was the case. Despite the obvious handicap of pacifist dissent within their own ranks, the main suffrage organizations were extremely successful in reinventing themselves in the eyes of the government, the national press, and the wider public. Suffragist volunteer bureaux and hospital units made no secret of their political inspiration, and by the summer of 1915 Mrs Pankhurst and Lloyd George, the Minister for Munitions, were standing side by side to review a WSPU-led procession of women demanding the 'right to serve'. Meanwhile women anti-suffragists were by no means politically idle. For all their protestations of patriotic impartiality, many of the leading women were deeply

---

[1] *Anti-Suffrage Review*, 71 (Sept. 1914), 154.   [2] *Anti-Suffrage Review*, 71 (Sept. 1914), 157
[3] For accounts of suffragists at war, see J. Alberti, *Beyond Suffrage: Feminists in War and Peace, 1914–1928* (Basingstoke: Macmillan, 1989); L. Garner, *Stepping Stones to Women's Liberty 1900–1918* (London: Heinemann,1984); S. Holton, *Feminism and Democracy* (Cambridge: Cambridge University Press, 1986); ead., *Suffrage Days* (London: Routledge, 1996); M. Pugh, *Women and the Women's Movement in Britain 1914–1959* (Basingstoke: Macmillan, 1992); A. Smith, *Suffrage Discourse in Britain during the First World War* (Aldershot: Ashgate, 2005).

resentful of suffragist wartime opportunism. Some continued to work through the auspices of the NLOWS, its journal, and its local branches throughout the war in order to prove that anti-suffrage patriotism was an equally active and effective practical force. Many directed their efforts into alternative channels, but without altering their views on the undesirability of female suffrage. Others, including ultimately Violet Markham, made a gradual and pragmatic shift away from anti-suffragism. When women's suffrage resurfaced as a parliamentary issue in the final years of the war, its active opponents were a somewhat attenuated force. However, they still included prominent women and were still highly confident of the support of a silent female majority. War had transformed many lives and some women's political outlook, but this experience was by no means universal. Gender conservatism was a powerful force in 1918, and in some respects had been reinforced by the war. Those men and women who fought suffragism to the last ditch framed their final arguments around a plea for a referendum which would 'Let Women Say!'[4]

Over recent years there has been much debate among historians over the significance of the war for the achievement of women's suffrage in Britain. Did the war delay the inevitable, or did it unwittingly create the political context which transformed the female franchise into an acceptable policy, or at least a safe risk? Did a wartime shift in parliamentary opinion, and the well-publicized 'conversion' of several leading politicians, reflect a wider sea change in public attitudes towards women's capabilities and their role as citizens? Or was the eventual enfranchisement of women a conservative measure designed to shore up the pre-war gender order? It has become increasingly clear that a longer-term perspective, and a skilful integration of many different historical approaches, is required in order to tackle these complex questions at all adequately. The final chapter of this book will attempt to set the consequences of the war for suffragism and anti-suffragism in the context of inter-war developments in British government and the British women's movement. The present chapter considers the impact of war upon organized anti-suffragism, and upon the activities and outlook of its leading women, during the period 1914–18. This selective focus tends to reinforce scepticism over interpretations of the 1918 suffrage success as primarily a reward for women's selfless patriotism. Though it suited politicians to collude with such an explanation,[5] there is abundant evidence that suffragists and anti-suffragists alike were the pawns of political circumstance so far as the detailed, short-term conclusion of the matter was concerned. For all their efforts to claim credit for women's war work, suffragists were no more successful

---

[4] See M. Ward, 'Let Women Say! An Appeal to the House of Lords', *Nineteenth Century and After*, 58 (1918), 47–59.

[5] This type of explanation was also endorsed by many suffragists: e.g. M. Fawcett, *What I Remember* (London: Fisher Unwin, 1924), records 'the great change in public opinion' (p. 240) as well as the changed views of politicians and of Lord Northcliffe. Like other suffrage leaders, Mrs Fawcett naturally also credited the efforts of her own movement.

than their defeated opponents in proving their case through deeds rather than words (to borrow the WSPU's pre-war slogan). Brian Harrison has provided a convincing history of the parliamentary decision-making process during the war.[6] This now needs to be supplemented by a fuller account of the extra-parliamentary role of the opponents as well as the supporters of the eventual outcome.

The war years provided the most committed anti-suffrage women with fresh opportunities to demonstrate their opposition to the vote. Though the outcome of the suffrage campaign was not, and could not have been, significantly altered by their efforts, these merit some belated historical recognition. Wartime challenges and controversies served to highlight and even strengthen some of the pre-war characteristics of the female anti-suffrage cause. Women's faith in their indispensability as mothers and home-makers, and in their centrality to civic virtue and national greatness, found plenty of new outlets through voluntary war work bolstered by growing government support. The more contentious issues of women's wartime employment, and their expanding opportunities for economic and social independence, also helped to promote frank expression of conservative gender views. Though the suffrage cause was lost in 1918, the cause of female social conservatism still had many years to run. The debacle of January 1918, when the NLOWS President conspicuously failed to lead the anti-suffrage cause in Parliament and was publicly censured by women leaders for his actions, provided a fitting climax to a long-running history of gender tensions within organized anti-suffragism. The well-recorded final rounds between Lord Curzon and Mary Ward make stirring reading, but this drama should not be allowed to eclipse the equally interesting record of the final League Council meeting a few weeks later. On this valedictory occasion, male leaders left it almost entirely to the women diehards to defend anti-suffragism's achievements and to make a plausible case for its post-war legacy.[7]

ANTI-SUFFRAGE WOMEN'S PATRIOTISM

The anti-suffragists' wholehearted support for the war effort was predictable, given their predilection for the gendered cause of the British Empire. As anti-suffragists took patriotically to the press and the recruiting platforms, and Lord Curzon, Lord Milner, and Neville Chamberlain moved eventually to the forefront of a coalition government, the leading women found their own pathways into patriotic service. Individual experience was coloured by private circumstances, as well as by the women's varied talents and somewhat varying outlook on gender politics and on the war itself. For four of the National League's most outstanding women, the war offered an unexpected route into responsible

---

[6] B. Harrison, *Separate Spheres*, ch. 10.
[7] See *Anti-Suffrage Review*, 113 (Apr. 1918), 19–22.

government work which lasted in different forms for the rest of their lives. Violet Markham graduated from service on the National Relief Fund Committee in 1914 to a place on the Central Committee on Women's Employment in 1915, and eventually a leading role as deputy director of the women's section of the National Service Department. She also took a trusted role in several government inquiries, including an investigation into the alleged immorality of members of the Women's Army Auxiliary Corps stationed in France in 1917.[8] Gladys Pott, whose pre-war reluctance to set public work before family duty has been noted, gradually moved beyond voluntary work in Berkshire to join the Board of Agriculture as a travelling inspector and official propagandist for female agricultural labour in wartime.[9] Gertrude Bell, after an initial flurry of voluntary work for the Red Cross in France, devoted her many skills to government service in the Middle East.[10] Most unexpectedly of all, Mary Ward found herself working as an official propagandist on behalf of the British government and at the request of Theodore Roosevelt from late 1915 onwards. Meanwhile her London play-schemes achieved national fame and major government funding, as war casualties underlined the importance of childcare to future military strength.[11]

The connections between dedicated war service and enthusiastic patriotism were clear enough, in the lives of each of these women. The relevance of anti-suffragism to their war work can also be surmised, though it was usually indirect. Possibly these women's reputation as conservative anti-suffragists helped to make their appointments more congenial in like-minded government circles; certainly their pre-war anti-suffragism had helped provide them with useful training in the skills and stratagems of public life. Their prominent war work focused substantially upon women's lives in every case except that of Gertrude Bell, and provided them with new opportunities to make influential pronouncements on the gender issues which continued to preoccupy organized anti-suffragism in wartime. Conservative gender beliefs apparently posed no obstacle to their assumption of heavy public responsibilities in wartime, and proved compatible with their post-war government service too.

---

[8] Violet Markham's war work is described in her autobiography, *Return Passage* (London: Oxford University Press, 1953), ch. 16, as well as extensively evidenced in her archive, BLPES, LSE, Markham papers.

[9] Gladys Pott's war work was reported in the *Anti-Suffrage Review* throughout the war, by herself and others.

[10] Gertrude Bell's war work was recorded to some extent in her correspondence, but the secret nature of her intelligence work in the Middle East has obscured its true nature until quite recently. See an interesting analysis in S. Goodman, *Gertrude Bell* (Leamington Spa: Berg, 1985), ch. 8. The same author concludes that her anti-suffrage views persisted throughout the war. She remained nominally an executive member of the NLOWS until 1918, and the *Anti-Suffrage Review* occasionally noted her war service with proprietorial pride.

[11] Mary Ward's war work is reported in her correspondence with Louise Creighton and her Parisian friends M. and Mme Chevrillon. Pusey House, Library, Oxford, M. Ward papers, 3/3 and 3/2. It is also represented in her letters to *The Times* and her wartime propaganda tracts, *England's Effort* (London: Smith, Elder, 1916) and *Towards the Goal* (London: Murray, 1917).

It was as patriots, rather than primarily as anti-suffragists, that Violet Markham, Gladys Pott, and Mary Ward gave vociferous public support to the war effort. Their unconditional support for the war perhaps owed a certain amount to their own good fortune in suffering fewer bereavements than many others, though both men and women discovered that private grief could also fuel a grim determination to vindicate the deaths of loved ones.[12] Violet Markham surprised most of her acquaintance by marrying a professional army officer in February 1915. Her heartfelt patriotism is nowhere more vividly illustrated than in her intimate letters to her friend Hilda Cashmore during 1914–15. As she celebrated the joys of a late romance in the early days of the war, she also contemplated the possibility of bereavement, weighing it in the balance alongside the justice of the national cause: 'the thought of the loss and suffering would be absolutely unbearable if one wasn't sustained by the most deep belief that we are standing in this appalling catastrophe for the right principles . . . I feel it is a great privilege to be able to give one's dearest to England in her need. And if I never see his face again I shall feel that all is very well for both of us.'[13] Later in the war, having herself avoided the ultimate test of such sentiments, Violet worried privately over the wilting patriotism of others, asserting the general responsibility of the educated classes for sustaining morale and pitting her own formidable administrative powers against the unthinkable possibility of British defeat.[14] In the letters column of *The Times* she wrote of the importance of war production and the contributions of women workers, and responded to German air attacks in October 1917 with an uncompromising demand for 'a steady air offensive over German towns'.[15]

Gladys Pott's patriotism was also expressed through the national press and the *Anti-Suffrage Review*, as well as through her own practical war work. Suffragist pacifism provided her with a double target which she assaulted with her usual relentless vigour, the more so since one of its leading proponents was her pre-war adversary Maud Royden. Her tireless behind-the-scenes efforts to keep the cause of organized anti-suffragism afloat were equally intended to contribute towards safeguarding imperial strength. Patriotic rhetoric was the wartime stronghold of Mary Ward. As the undisputed literary queen of anti-suffragism by this date, she played a uniquely important propaganda role before taking up the reins of anti-suffrage leadership for one final time in the last year of the war. Like Violet Markham and Gladys Pott, she had always seen anti-suffragism as a patriotic

---

[12] Less fortunate anti-suffragists included Gertrude Bell, whose married lover died at Gallipoli, and Ethel Harrison and Louise Creighton, who each lost a son. Edward Mitchell Innes and Rudyard Kipling also lost sons. Mary Ward lost three nephews. She wrote tenderly to Louise to comfort her in her bereavement, recalling beliefs of T. H. Green encountered during their shared Oxford youth (5 May 1918). M. Ward papers, 3/3.

[13] Violet Markham to Hilda Cashmore, 6 Aug. 1914. Markham papers, 25/12.

[14] Correspondence between Violet Markham and John St Loe Strachey, Jan. 1918. Markham papers, 25/78.

[15] *The Times*, 5 Oct. 1917, 10.

cause, as well as the cause of true womanhood and of maternal social reform. Her wartime tracts were a fervent defence of British values and of a British way of life characterized by the selflessness of brave men and devoted women, rather than by aggressive militarism.

Despite the universal patriotism of its leaders, the NLOWS faced a difficult task as it attempted to keep the anti-suffrage cause alive during the war without courting accusations of divisiveness or irrelevance. In the autumn of 1914 the League's executive followed the example of the major suffrage organizations by declaring their own political truce in support of a swift and single-minded British victory. Office staff were despatched to distribute relief to soldiers' families, whilst the Oxford Street anti-suffrage information centre was soon converted into a Patriotic Bureau, accepting and commissioning war work from middle-class volunteers.[16] However, a gradual departure from this high-minded pose of suffrage neutrality became necessary during the months which followed. By December Gladys Pott was urging Alfred Howe, the League's remaining paid organizer, to counter suffragist propaganda over women's war work by proving to the British public that anti-suffragists were no less active and no less patriotic.[17] In March 1915 he presented the NLOWS executive with an impressive list of war work undertaken by its local branches, as well as by individuals.[18] Exemplars of collective anti-suffrage war work were doubly useful, since they showed the suffragists that their opponents were still active and that anti-suffragism was directly relevant to the war effort. Considerable efforts were made to collect and publicize the necessary local evidence, but with mixed results. The League's own collection of press cuttings demonstrates the much greater success of the suffragists in linking their cause to the national relief effort in the autumn of 1914. Surviving correspondence from anti-suffrage branches during the same period includes members' patriotic protests against the NLOWS's attempted propaganda push, alongside reports of crumbling organization and diverted energies.[19] Anti-suffrage women all over Britain were willing enough to undertake voluntary war work, but only the most determined opponents of the female franchise accepted the need to link their patriotic service overtly to the organized anti-suffrage cause.

Despite these problems, the NLOWS held some patriotic advantages over its suffragist rivals during the early years of the war. Above all the League was never threatened, as the suffragists were, by damaging internal divisions linked

[16] *Anti-Suffrage Review*, 72 (Oct. 1914), 161; and 75 (Jan. 1915), 1.
[17] Gladys Pott to Alfred Howe, 5 Dec. 1914. Bodl., NLOWS Scrapbooks 19A, 2474d.68.
[18] Alfred Howe's Report to NLOWS on Anti-Suffrage War Relief Work, Mar. 1915, NLOWS Scrapbooks 19A Two, 2474d.68.
[19] e.g. a note to Gladys Pott from the Ipswich NLOWS branch (n.d.) rejecting the idea of anti-suffrage press publicity for war work, since the author's time was entirely taken up by work for the Soldiers and Sailors Families Association; Gladys Medwin to Gladys Pott from the Bournemouth branch, 7 Jan. 1915, commenting on lack of activities 'bar holding the meeting in November to collect funds for the Belgian refugees'. NLOWS Scrapbooks 19A, 2474d.68.

to pacifism. From the earliest days of the war, the antis found it hard to resist the temptation to score points off many suffragists' commitment to international peace. Even Emmeline and Christabel Pankhurst failed to carry all their supporters with them as they campaigned along feminist lines for unconditional support for the war. Meanwhile Millicent Fawcett, for so long the undisputed leader of the largest suffrage organization, initially found herself in a minority upon her own national executive as she rejected all talk of peaceful compromise in the autumn of 1914. During 1915 she stood firm against participation in the suffragist Hague Peace Conference and gradually won over many British women to her own patriotic stance. But it was impossible to avoid the negative publicity attached to pacifist resignations from the main suffrage organizations, as well as to the anti-war and anti-conscription campaigning of suffragist minorities. The leading anti-suffrage women rapidly joined their male colleagues in self-righteous condemnation of those seeking to undermine the war effort. 'Suffragists have closely identified themselves in connection with this war with every variety of peace movement', declared the *Anti-Suffrage Review* in April 1915.[20] In the same issue Gladys Pott commented acidly: 'One may be devoutly thankful that at the critical period when British honour was hanging in the balance Miss Royden had not the power of the vote, and one may hope that she may never have the opportunity of putting into practice her overwhelming desire to destroy our every means of defence both of Empire and honour'.[21] By June the *Anti-Suffrage Review* was gloating over suffragist disarray around the international women's peace conference, and jesting at the inconsistencies of 'Mrs Physical Fawcett' and other suffrage patriots.[22] 'While women talk, men die', warned Violet Markham sternly.[23] A few months later Mary Ward weighed in with a heavy-handed press correspondence which highlighted the contrasting patriotic legacy of the executed heroine Edith Cavell.[24] The revival of the suffrage issue in Parliament during the final years of the war gave the antis further incentive to drive home 'the intimate association between Suffragism and Pacifism'.[25] But by this stage the patriotic suffragists had largely succeeded in moving the main gender role debate onto more favourable territory.

ANTI-SUFFRAGE SOCIAL ACTION

Support for the war was seldom debated between women activists in terms of politics and diplomacy, and only occasionally weighed up as an issue of morality.

---

[20] *Anti-Suffrage Review*, 78 (Apr. 1915), 29.   [21] Ibid.

[22] *Anti-Suffrage Review*, 80 (June 1915), 45 and 48.

[23] *Daily Chronicle*, 3 May 1915. NLOWS Scrapbooks 26, 2474d.72.

[24] *The Times*, 23 Oct. 1915, 8; 27 Oct. 1915, 9.

[25] *Anti-Suffrage Review*, 107 (September 1917), 67.

Instead, most suffragists and anti-suffragists sought to prove their patriotism through the less controversial channels of wartime social action. Though somewhat damaged by pacifist associations, the leading suffrage organizations more than made up lost ground through the success of their voluntary war work campaign. Suffragist war work, it was claimed, demonstrated the highest form of womanly patriotism. Moreover it usefully enhanced the philanthropic social service which had so powerfully characterized the pre-war middle-class women's movement. Women anti-suffragists had vainly tried to prevent the National Union of Women Workers from falling into the hands of a suffragist leadership before the war. They now found themselves fighting an uphill battle to remind the government and the country that wartime commitment to social service was by no means solely the province of those who supported votes for women.

In the first weeks of the war the philanthropic efforts of female patriots centred upon relief work with the families of serving soldiers, unemployed women, and Belgian refugees. Millicent Fawcett recognized the healing value for her own divided suffrage organization of a collective focus upon humanitarian endeavour, and the considerable resources and organizing power of the NUWSS quickly swung into action. The suffragist publicity machine was equally quick off the mark. Though the national press carried encouraging reports of collaboration between former suffrage opponents, there was also wide coverage of exclusively suffragist ventures into war relief. In November 1914 the *Ladies' Field Supplement* published an elaborately illustrated account of 'The Woman Suffrage Movement and the War', linking admiring accounts of war work to commentaries by suffrage leaders which spelt out perceived links between the war effort and the political aims of their various organizations.[26]

It is not surprising that Gladys Pott was anxious for the NLOWS to make up lost ground. The League's catalogue of anti-suffrage war work soon made impressive reading. By the end of 1914 Lady Jersey was presiding over the Soldiers and Sailors' Families Association in Oxfordshire, Mrs Benyon was doing the same in Berkshire, Lady Wantage was a member of the Central Relief Committee, Mrs Lewis Harcourt was heading up the American Women's War Hospital, Miss Bell was reported to be 'at the Boulogne office for tracing the missing', Beatrice Chamberlain was amongst a red-pencilled list of anti-suffrage donors to the French Wounded Emergency Fund, while the Havershams and Lady Dimsdale had donated motor cars and hospital beds.[27] By the time Mr Howe presented his summary to the NLOWS executive, a satisfying amount of female social action could also be linked to specific League branches. An announcement of the League's patriotic war work policy had earlier been circulated to over

---

[26] *Ladies Field Supplement*, 21 Nov. 1914. NLOWS Scrapbooks 19B, 2474d.69.

[27] Gladys Pott to Alfred Howe, 5 Dec. 1914. Direct news from Gertrude Bell had reached Gladys Pott on a postcard posted from France on 2 Dec. Other news was gleaned from press cuttings assembled into a scrapbook titled 'The War. Anti-Suffrage Work Only'. NLOWS Scrapbooks 19A, 2474d.68.

two hundred local newspapers, with gratifying results. Anti-suffrage war workers were encouraged to make their own contribution towards the publicity drive by contacting their local press individually, Gertrude Bell's letter to the *Yorkshire Post* offering a model of how this should be done. A warning notice to League branches, marked 'confidential and important', observed: 'Evidence is accumulating that many Suffragists—though not *all* Suffrage societies—are exploiting the terrible European War to their own aggrandisement, by sending communications to the Press advertising their doings in the relief societies'.[28] Some rank-and-file members certainly shared the leadership's growing concern over suffrage opportunism. As one lady wrote indignantly in the *Church Family Newspaper*, 'there is a danger lest we shall find when the war is over that every sock we have knitted and every help we have given to our country, has gone to swell public opinion in favour of votes for women'.[29]

Promising anti-suffrage war work initiatives in the spring of 1915 included Ethel Colquhoun's free 24-hour buffet for travelling servicemen at Paddington station. With due regard for the League's patriotic reputation, and the need to bolster this at branch level, she appealed directly to its members: 'We want workers and money . . . 1) Will you, on behalf of your Branch, guarantee 5/- or 10/- per week? 2) Will you be responsible for a day once a fortnight?'[30] Presumably the response was positive, for over the following months the *Anti-Suffrage Review* gave extensive publicity to the success of this venture. Members of the Kensington branch alone gave 'nearly £100 in a few days', and by August 1915 between 800 and 1400 men each day were benefiting from anti-suffrage hospitality. The War Office warned Ethel Colquhoun against using the NLOWS name in the buffet's title, but the *Review* reported proudly that 'The Committee is confined to members of the League, and the days are apportioned to honorary secretaries of the London Branches, so that the credit of the work will eventually belong to the Anti-Suffragists'.[31]

The latent tension between upholding a wartime truce and sustaining the NLOWS as an active and purposeful organization was reflected in these reports, and was still more clearly spelt out at the meeting of London branches which substituted for the usual Annual Council in July 1915. The League's Chairman, Edward Mitchell-Innes, acknowledged that continuing suffrage activism made suspension of the Annual Council a controversial decision, before voicing his pride in anti-suffragists' 'loyal observance' of their own political truce. He went on to claim that the war had undermined the political basis of suffragism by

    [28] This undated notice enclosed Gertrude Bell's letter dated 15 Aug. 1914, publicizing the NLOWS executive's decision to drop propaganda work and urging members to undertake war work through 'societies which are already in existence rather than in an attempt to start fresh organisations' (an implied criticism of the London suffragists' Women's Service Bureau and similar organizations elsewhere). NLOWS Scrapbook 19A, 2474d.68.
    [29] *Church Family Newspaper* (n.d. [1914/15]). NLOWS Scrapbook 19A, 2474d.68.
    [30] *Anti-Suffrage Review*, 79 (May 1915), 33.   [31] *Anti-Suffrage Review*, 85 (Nov. 1915), 84.

demonstrating 'with new and terrible force . . . the existence of a natural and insuperable demarcation between the functions of men and women'. Gladys Pott used her speech to emphasize the central role of women within the League's patriotic social service. She admitted that 'One of the hardest things Anti-Suffragists had to face was the accusation that while Suffragists were making so much clamour, Anti-Suffragists were doing nothing. However much we might know this accusation to be false, it was very trying . . . Patriotism did not consist in carrying out war service with the ulterior motive of exploiting the nation's need for the benefit of one's particular political or personal interests'.[32]

Deliberate abstention from political activity threatened to leave the NLOWS in a defensive and ultimately unsustainable position. Anti-suffragists who adhered loyally to the wartime political truce feared they were missing opportunities to proselytize for their own cause, as well as allowing the suffragists to steal an unfair advantage. The temptation to promote wartime social action as a beneficial extension of women's natural gender role was a hard one for anti-suffragists to resist, whether or not this assertion was accompanied by a sideswipe at the self-promoting 'patriotic' suffragists. Maternal reformism, as well as female patriotism, seemed to be coming into its own as the British government gradually realized that the long haul of a world war required more from women than mere short-term relief work. Both suffragists and anti-suffragists were eager to prove their capability as contributors towards long-term social improvement, rather than merely in response to wartime needs. Incentives both to collaboration and to competition between suffragist and anti-suffragist maternal reformers therefore became stronger as the war progressed. The result was an uneasy combination of joint effort and rivalry, especially in relation to those aspects of social policy which most closely defined female gender roles. While Ethel Colquhoun 'mothered' tired and hungry soldiers at Paddington station, other anti-suffrage women came forward to offer many other kinds of practical help for women and children. Such work rested upon pre-war voluntarist foundations, yet was cumulatively moving social action towards greater reliance upon government intervention. An undercurrent of gender debate accompanied many wartime innovations in social policy, both at government level and within the organizations which supported or opposed votes for women. The ambivalent relationship between anti-suffragists, suffragists, and government policy-makers can best be illustrated through more detailed studies of anti-suffrage women's response to several specific wartime issues.

One of the earliest gendered social policy initiatives of the war years was the formation of voluntary women's patrols in the autumn of 1914, followed eventually by the launch of a government-backed female police force. The scheme for women's patrols was closely associated with the NUWW, being coordinated by a group of women under Louise Creighton's leadership. The object of these middle-class volunteers was initially to patrol the sexual behaviour

---

[32] *Anti-Suffrage Review*, 82 (Aug. 1915), 60–1.

of young people in the neighbourhood of military camps: a cause close to the hearts of the many women who had campaigned for moral reform before the war. Wholehearted anti-suffrage support for such a scheme might have been predicted. But the source of this innovation aroused initial suspicion and jealousy, due both to the recent suffragist coup within the NUWW and to the parallel development of a second female policing scheme linked more directly to suffragism.[33] Rather than extending maternal moral influence, it was feared both schemes might result in women challenging gender boundaries and usurping the authority of uniformed male police. This fear was reinforced by the inclusion of the women patrols in the *Ladies Field Supplement*'s account of suffragist war work.[34]

In December 1914 the *Anti-Suffrage Review* openly voiced its criticism of the patrols, making unfavourable comparisons with the conventionally patriotic and feminine Legion of Honour which was 'more closely in touch with the spirit of the times than any organisation over which the demon of notoriety broods and blights the worthiest intentions with the canker of political controversy'.[35] The presence of several highly conservative women on the NUWW organizing committee should have offered some reassurance, but Ethel Harrison claimed that female patrols in pursuit of sexual deviance 'would inevitably provoke unseemly scenes in the streets'. She felt that there had already been 'altogether too much scolding and hectoring on the part of women'.[36] Edith Milner echoed this criticism in the same issue of the *Review*, with her comment that 'Though the majority of women are content to do what their hand finds to do quietly, the aggressive ego has gained too much prominence'.[37] Women patrols did indeed help to open up opportunities for women to join the police force in the long run, but the *Anti-Suffrage Review* gradually overcame its scruples in the light of experience and in response to growing Home Office support for wartime policewomen. A sympathetic account by an insider was published in December 1915, and by 1917 the *Review* was even willing to commend the social value of women police.[38] Violet Markham had repeatedly expressed her strong dislike of women in uniform in the early years of the war, yet also came to agree that women police played a useful role in wartime as her own responsibilities expanded. Her official report on industrial welfare in Coventry, published in November 1916, included a significant final section on 'moral questions' which praised policewomen's 'preventive' work in terms familiar to all maternal reformers.[39]

---

[33] See records of the NUWW, LMA ACC3613, for information on the NUWW's pre-war commitment to 'Police Matrons', and on its 1914 campaign for women patrols. On women police more generally, see A. Woodeson, 'The First Women Police: A Force for Equality or Infringement?', *Women's History Review*, 2/2 (1993), 217–32.

[34] *Ladies Field Supplement*, 21 Nov. 1914. NLOWS Scrapbook 19B, 2474d.69.

[35] *Anti-Suffrage Review*, 74 (Dec. 1914), 178.   [36] *Anti-Suffrage Review*, 76 (Feb. 1915), 12.

[37] Ibid. 13.   [38] *Anti-Suffrage Review*, 86 (Dec. 1915), 93; 102 (Apr. 1917), 32.

[39] V. Markham, 'Report on Industrial Welfare Conditions in Coventry', Nov. 1916. Markham papers, 3/33.

The War Babies controversy of 1915 provoked further expressions of anti-suffrage gender anxiety, reinforcing dual fears of suffrage opportunism and of a lurking feminist agenda. Whilst women patrols had raised spectres of gender subversion in an arena of masculine authority, suffragist proposals to succour the illegitimate children of serving soldiers threatened to undermine respect for marriage. In the spring of 1915 a full-scale moral panic developed from ill-founded press reports of huge numbers of abandoned expectant mothers. Departing soldiers were believed to be responsible, so that some women (including several leading suffragists) promised support for their babies as an act of patriotism as well as of social duty. Emmeline Pankhurst further politicized the situation by her personal decision to adopt four baby girls. Her subsequent appeals for financial support invoked the feminist principle of shared parental responsibility, as well as the more straightforward issue of patriotic maternal care.[40] But enthusiasm for this particular wartime social cause proved limited, after the first excitement had died down. The WSPU failed to provide the hoped-for levels of financial support for the Pankhurst babies, and closer investigation by various women's organizations soon revealed the exaggerated scale of the original scare.

Whilst interest in the issue lasted, it was intense. Ethel Colquhoun and Gladys Pott attended women's conferences on War Babies in April and May 1915, as representatives of the NLOWS, and in June the *Anti-Suffrage Review* warned that 'It is desirable that Anti-Suffragists should interest themselves keenly and actively in the subject, because the whole question of marriage is closely bound up with the treatment of the unmarried mother'. The issue 'bristled with difficulties', since most anti-suffragists stood equally committed to the defence of marriage and to the welfare of infants.[41] Complexity was still further increased as prominent suffragists publicly disagreed with each other and related the unfortunate War Babies to wider debates over nation and motherhood. Anti-suffragists no doubt enjoyed the spectacle of these suffrage divisions, but must also have shared in widespread relief when an inquiry chaired (again) by Louise Creighton discovered the lack of statistical basis for current rumours. It is interesting to note that Violet Markham, in the midst of her many other patriotic concerns, found time to make her own enquiries about War Babies among her friends and relatives in different parts of the country, with equally reassuring results.[42]

The War Babies scare was relatively short-lived, but the general subject of maternal and child welfare continued to provide both suffragist and anti-suffragist women with their most important social cause for the remainder of the war. Children were acknowledged to be a national asset, as casualties mounted and a determined government began to intervene more strongly in their defence than

---

[40] See Emmeline Pankhurst's circular letter appealing for support, 20 May 1915. Markham papers, 25/62.

[41] *Anti-Suffrage Review*, 80 (June 1915), 43.

[42] See correspondence on War Babies during Apr. 1915. Markham papers, 2/1.

during the pre-war years of cautious social reform. Mary Ward was among many women reformers who found themselves pushing at an open door when they requested additional government support for their work. Like those who founded maternity clinics and schools for mothers, Mary was building upon a pre-war foundation of voluntary work and benefiting indirectly from reformist currents within the Liberal party and the labour movement, as she extended her London play-schemes to meet wartime needs. This did not lessen her personal pride in her achievements; nor did it deter the anti-suffrage movement from trying to share the mantle of her success.

Mary Ward's annual play-centres appeal in *The Times* was already an established institution by 1914. Over the following years she developed the theme of play centres as 'a war claim', offering shelter from darkened streets for the children who were 'the nation's hope for the future'.[43] In 1915 she could claim the 'express sanction and approval of the heads of the police'. A year later she was rejoicing in Board of Education grants which would cover half her costs, and offering to promote a national expansion of her scheme.[44] By January 1918 the Board itself was 'pressing for a wide extension of the play centre movement'.[45] At the end of the war more than 60,000 London children were crowding to her doors, and Mary Ward was privately reflective on the relationship between gender, voluntarism, and social policy. Her long-standing belief in the special ability of philanthropic women to resolve social issues related to their maternal role had survived intact, as she rejected the idea of state-run play-schemes. In a letter to Louise Creighton in January 1917, Mary Ward boasted that she herself had 'written a great deal of the Board Circular—this is of course only for your private ear!—and been consulted on all the regulations'.[46] The responsibilities of fund-raising and administration were a heavy burden, but she never ceased to believe that the centres would 'mortally degenerate' if handed over to the London County Council.[47]

Suffragist and anti-suffragist reformers had plenty of pre-war collaborative experience to draw upon in their attempts to improve the conditions of motherhood. The pressures and opportunities of wartime made such work more urgent than ever before. The issue of the franchise sank into the background as successful maternity schemes around the country reflected a fruitful combination of private philanthropy and state-funded local government initiative. But political tensions were never entirely absent, even in this field of shared womanly endeavour. Gladys Pott became a somewhat unlikely proponent of 'schools for mothers' and baby clinics during the war, and her writings on these subjects in the *Anti-Suffrage Review* linked practical reform proposals indirectly

---

[43] *The Times*, 21 Dec. 1914, 10.   [44] *The Times,* 6 Dec. 1915, 10.
[45] *The Times*, 10 Jan. 1918, 10.
[46] Mary Ward to Louise Creighton, 28 Jan. 1917. M. Ward papers, 3/3.
[47] Mary Ward to Louise Creighton, 22 Sept. 1918 and 26 Oct. 1919. M. Ward papers, 3/3.

to anti-suffrage propaganda. In November 1915 she claimed that 'the special needs of the mothers of Great Britain during the war' deserved 'more assistance from patriotic women than they usually receive'. Whilst the number of maternity centres and the sum of government funding were both increasing, 'instances of the desertion of normal voluntary workers from maternity centres have been brought to my notice, such deserters having offered themselves as unskilled munition workers . . . necessitating the curtailment of the assistance given to the sickly babies, who, we hope and trust, will take the places of our fallen and falling heroes'. Recalling pre-war debates over infant mortality, Gladys reiterated her conviction that 'careful, voluntary effort is . . . the clue to success; personal, not official, labour'.[48] Two months later she returned to this theme in an article on 'Mother and Wage Earner'. Women reformers, she believed, should devote themselves to removing mothers from the labour market in the future, rather than to the provision of workplace crèches. Not even the welcome presence of women upon town councils could guarantee an improvement in standards of childcare, which rested ultimately upon the shoulders of individual mothers and the volunteers who advised them in their own homes.[49]

The logic of Gladys Pott's arguments against working mothers was to be severely tested by her own official involvement in the recruitment of female agricultural workers in the latter stages of the war. However, there can be little doubt that her scepticism over maternal employment and state-provided childcare found a responsive echo among many anti-suffrage women. Social action was seen by socially conservative middle-class women as an extension of their own family responsibilities into less fortunate homes, not as a substitute for individual maternal responsibility at any level of the social scale. Some of the most highly conservative anti-suffrage women responded to the social upheavals of wartime by placing an even stronger emphasis upon each woman's primary responsibility to her own family. Alongside records of widespread social action, and admiring reports on anti-suffrage leaders whose war service had helped thousands of fellow women, the *Anti-Suffrage Review* carried articles which reflected this outlook. In April 1915 Norah Sedgwick condemned the overindulgent childcare of a suffragist friend. 'The home training of our boys and girls' was at the heart of national progress: 'If she can so little grasp the duties, responsibilities and opportunities of "home service", how is she fit for a wider scope with a vote, and possibly later on a seat in Parliament?'[50] Edith Clifford continued to contribute articles on anti-suffrage needlework, dedicated to the needs of the wartime home as well as to serving soldiers who were portrayed as family members rather than anonymous national heroes; the industrial-scale needlework organized by the Patriotic Bureau was similarly reported in comfortably domestic terms. Wartime cookery found its place in the *Review*, as a family as well as a patriotic duty.

[48] *Anti-Suffrage Review*, 85 (Nov. 1915), 85.   [49] *Anti-Suffrage Review*, 87 (Jan. 1916), 4.
[50] *Anti-Suffrage Review*, 78 (Apr. 1915), 28.

The epitome of small-scale, domesticated wartime social action was represented by the regular reports of the Scottish anti-suffragist Griselda Cheape, whose 'Beehive' organization resisted any departure from pre-war standards of prayerful, small-scale philanthropy dispensed by individuals to deserving individuals ('the Beehive . . . like the violet, grows in the shade').[51]

Meanwhile suffrage links with the dangerous sexual politics of feminism came under more severe criticism than ever before, as both men and women worried lest the disruption of family life imposed by the war would be deliberately prolonged into peacetime. The women patrols and the War Babies debates were both symptomatic of conservative women's anxiety over lax sexual behaviour encouraged by the war. Disagreements among suffragists over such issues under-lined once again the enduring common ground between conservatives like Louise Creighton and many anti-suffrage women. A more general anxiety over sexual licence was reflected in the appointment of a government committee of inquiry in 1917 to investigate allegations of immoral behaviour by members of the Women's Army Auxiliary Corps serving in France. Violet Markham's leading role as secretary to this committee was linked to her personal concerns over feminism and sexuality in the pre-war period, as well as marking official recognition of her skills in social research. She could be relied upon to cast a stern eye over the situation, though (perhaps due partly to the evolution of her own private life) she eventually penned a tolerant report. Earlier in the war she had also courted controversy by supporting unmarried 'wives' in their claims for official war relief.[52]

The *Anti-Suffrage Review* remained vigilant, meanwhile, against the combined threats of suffragism, feminism, and the subversion of family values. An alarmist report in October 1916 claimed that 'Miss Clementina Black and *The Common Cause* have decided that an Englishman's home must no longer be his castle. Houses in future should be built on the kraal or native compound system, with a central cookhouse and eating system.' Commenting on the absence of childcare provision from such socialistic plans, the anonymous article concluded that 'Miss Black's scheme is essentially a Feminist suggestion. As it enjoys the warm support of the official organ of the National Union of Women's Suffrage Societies, the nation can learn betimes the trend of Suffragism'.[53] The suffrage question had never been far below the surface of women's social action during the war, as suffrage and anti-suffrage war workers jostled for public recognition and the government's wartime needs opened up new channels for feminine intervention. By the end of 1916 this question was moving once more to the forefront of

---

[51] *Anti-Suffrage Review*, 96 (Oct. 1916), 79.
[52] Markham, *Return Passage*, 148. In contrast, Barbara Ord's indignant protest against government support for 'unmarried wives' was published in the *Anti-Suffrage Review*, 73 (Nov. 1914), 174.
[53] *Anti-Suffrage Review*, 96 (Oct. 1916), 76.

national affairs, and the political truce over votes for women was virtually at an end.

THE QUESTION OF WOMEN'S EMPLOYMENT

Unemployment among working-class women attracted the benevolent attention of middle-class volunteers during the early months of the war. The mass mobilization of Britain's armed forces severely damaged female employment opportunities until munitions production began to gather speed in the late autumn of 1914. Thousands of women were then sucked into the war economy, filling the places of departed men as they supplied military and civilian needs.[54] A major expansion in female employment, and especially the prospect of huge numbers of married women workers, was far from welcome to those who believed in women's primary responsibility for their homes and families. Anti-suffrage women's pre-war anxieties over married women's work were sharply resurrected from 1915 onwards, in the difficult context of patriotic demands for extra labour to win the war, reinforced by press adulation for women workers and by suffragist-led demands for 'the right to serve'. Despite some differences of emphasis over the direction of wartime social policy, and a good deal of covert rivalry over its delivery, there was substantial agreement among suffrage and anti-suffrage women over such priorities as relief for the poor, support for soldiers' families, the defence of moral standards, and the improvement of maternity and child welfare. This was much less the case in relation to the problematic subject of paid employment. Wartime debates over women's work threatened to deepen the already well-established divide between suffragists promoting women's employment opportunities, and anti-suffragists who identified married women's employment with neglect of wifely and maternal duty. Nor were the anti-suffragists themselves entirely united over workplace reforms which threatened permanently to reduce the differentiation between male and female roles in employment and family life.

Gladys Pott's fears over the seductive effect of well-paid munitions work have already been quoted. Working-class mothers as well as maternity clinic volunteers threatened 'desertions' which would jeopardize efforts to improve infant welfare. However, the question of female employment could not be judged solely in relation to maternity reform. When the shells shortage worsened during 1915, Violet Markham showed her willingness to set aside some of her earlier views on women's labour in order to press for a mass mobilization of women workers. As

---

[54] For analysis of women's war work and its impact upon gender debates in Britain, see G. Braybon, *Women Workers in the First World War* (London: Croom Helm, 1981); C. Culleton, *Working-Class Culture: Women and Britain, 1914–1921* (Basingstoke: Macmillan, 2000); D. Thom, *Nice Girls and Rude Girls: Women Workers in World War I* (London: I. B. Tauris, 1998); A. Woolacott, *On Her Their Lives Depend: Munitions Workers in the Great War* (Berkeley and Los Angeles: University of California Press, 1994).

a member of the government's Central Committee on Women's Employment, then later Deputy Director of the Women's Section of the National Service Department, she was fully implicated in the expansion of the female workforce. A letter to *The Times* in March 1915 spelt out both her confidence in 'the power of women to assist the industrial needs of the nation', and her conviction that this could be achieved 'without prejudice to those permanent industrial interests which sooner or later will have to resume their normal place'.[55] The problem was one of organization, as well as of principles. Many patriotic anti-suffrage women were prepared to follow Violet's lead in promoting female employment whilst also demanding safeguards for a returning male workforce after the war. However, her insistence upon the temporary nature of female employment was more popular among the antis than her defence of higher female wages and her demand for the full representation of women workers on negotiating bodies, which was misinterpreted as a surrender to suffragist labour policies. Mary Ward backed up Violet Markham's support for a large and adequately paid female workforce, from the sentimental perspective of her own propaganda writings on munitions production. Rejecting female trade unionists' further efforts to improve wages and working conditions as 'mischievous and unpatriotic', she claimed never to have seen 'a healthier, brighter set than the women in the munitions works' after her tour of northern cities during 1916: 'For the woman worker in the flesh I have simply nothing but the *warmest* admiration and sympathy. She is really saving the country at the present moment. What an honour for women!—and they know it.'[56]

From a different perspective, well-paid women workers were regarded by some anti-suffragists as a serious threat to the established gender order. In June 1915 Ethel Colquhoun wrote to the *Evening Standard* condemning equal pay for women as 'fundamentally unsound' and linking the employment of married women once again to high infant mortality.[57] The following month Frances Low set out her view that expanded women's employment was inevitable both in agriculture and in munitions production, but not at the expense of equal pay, and not as a substitute for greater efficiency in the home.[58] The *Anti-Suffrage Review* also praised 'The Woman who Stayed at Home': her domestic devotion was more important to victory than the spectacular achievements of female munitions workers.[59] Gladys Pott, meanwhile, reported evidence contradicting the growing belief that women were capable of direct substitution for men in industrial

---

[55] *The Times*, 26 Mar. 1915, 11. Violet Markham had little patience with trade union resistance to female 'dilution' of the workforce, writing to Hilda Cashmore on 1 Feb. 1916: 'I cannot conceive how men can argue about the details of dilution when the delay is being expressed daily in terms of other men's lives . . . For me only one thing exists today—England and her need'. Markham papers, 25/12.

[56] Mary Ward to Louise Creighton, 23 June 1916. M. Ward papers, 3/3.

[57] *Evening Standard*, 4 June 1916. NLOWS Scrapbook, 2474d.70.

[58] *Standard*, 23 July 1915. NLOWS Scrapbook, 2474d.70.

[59] *Anti-Suffrage Review*, 84 (Oct. 1915), 75.

employment. Employers remained aware of 'the eternal difference between the economic value of the two sexes', and were therefore as justified in refusing equal wages as they were in refusing to accept 'the permanent displacement of men by women'. The family wage, earned by men who preferred to keep their wives at home, was justified on strictly economic grounds as well as being essential to the long-term defence of distinctive gender roles.[60] Anti-suffrage opposition to equal pay related mainly to the position of married women, but was sometimes extended to encompass general distrust of female economic independence and of the attitudes which went with it.

The suffragists were also far from unanimous in their views on women's war work, but it suited the *Anti-Suffrage Review* to emphasize their widespread enthusiasm for substitute female labour and for equal wages, in contrast to anti-suffragist insistence upon the importance of male jobs and of women's familial responsibilities outside the workplace. The Pankhursts' coup in obtaining government backing for their war work pageant in July 1915 fuelled jealous accusations that the suffragists were taking advantage of the crisis to advance their own political cause. This belief was further reinforced by suffragist commentaries upon the lasting social and economic transformations produced by the war. 'In one year many prejudices which interfered with the employment of women have been swept away by the force of this hurricane', observed Maud Selborne approvingly, before expressing her support for equal pay and for more equal opportunities for women in the professions.[61] Millicent Fawcett was convinced from an early stage that there could be no return to working women's pre-war status, and did not hesitate to yoke this view to the question of female suffrage even at the height of the political truce.[62]

Violet Markham privately endorsed such opinions when she referred to women's war work in a letter which explained to Lord Cromer her own changed views on the suffrage question. In the same letter she wrote revealingly: 'The man as worker, the woman as home maker remains my ideal of society. But in this difficult world one has to take facts as they are . . . Little though I like it women are going to play an ever larger part in industry and public life.'[63] It is impossible to gauge how many other anti-suffrage women shared this reluctant, pragmatic adjustment of political outlook. But it seems clear that the employment of women was central to a general wartime reconsideration of gender roles, as well as to the narrower suffrage debate. The high-profile involvement of suffrage leaders in promoting women's war work helped to ensure that some anti-suffragists would continue to resist the whole concept of expanding opportunities for women in the workplace, tolerating it only as a patriotic necessity to be swiftly reversed after victory had been achieved.

---

[60] Ibid., 76–7.   [61] *Daily Graphic*, 6 Oct. 1915. NLOWS Scrapbook, 2474d.71.
[62] e.g. in *The Times*, 24 May 1916, 9.
[63] Violet Markham to Lord Cromer, 2 Nov. 1916. Markham papers, 26/30.

Interestingly, there seems to have been a hierarchy of anti-suffrage distaste for female employment. For reasons which were never fully explained, many women found the idea of rural, agricultural war work much more acceptable than its urban, industrial equivalent. Gladys Pott led the way in presenting this less threatening face of war work to anti-suffrage audiences long before she herself took on official responsibilities at the Board of Agriculture. In the spring of 1915 she began to publicize the initiative taken by 'a few Berkshire ladies' to train dairymaids and thus protect the national milk supply, as well as providing suitable employment for local working-class women.[64] It is easy to see why this scheme appealed to conservative women as a contribution to the war effort. Philanthropic in origin, and linked into the work of one of the largest local anti-suffrage branches, it was small-scale and 'eminently practical', with reassuring connections both to a traditionally female branch of farm work and to the nutritional needs of small children. Soon Gladys was propagating her scheme at national level, whilst at the same time deprecating many aspects of female munitions work. By the following year she had obtained the expert support of University College, Reading and also attracted the interest of the government, which helped her to organize an expedition to France for 'a small party of selected women workers . . . in order to give them an opportunity of seeing how French women are carrying on the agricultural industries of the country, while men are serving with the colours'.[65] The *Anti-Suffrage Review* published a detailed account of this somewhat surreal visit. Though hampered by 'extremely bad weather, and the fact that the great battle of Verdun began just at the moment the mission entered the army zone affected', the British women saw enough to encourage their confidence in female farm workers as well as to fire their enthusiasm for the war effort: 'the sight of village women carrying on the necessary agricultural work undeterred by the terrible struggle which was raging within earshot, and in which their own relations were concerned, afforded an object lesson of the deepest value'.[66] Gladys Pott returned to share this lesson with audiences around the country, and to develop her government contacts into the foundations of a later public service career.

ANTI-SUFFRAGE WOMEN IN GOVERNMENT SERVICE

The employment of women in wartime included government service which, in the case of anti-suffrage women, almost invariably arose from evidence of

---

[64] *Anti-Suffrage Review*, 79 (May 1915), 36 and 37. Gladys Pott's publicity for her scheme included a visit to Dorothy Ward's 'little Conference on "War Service for Women on the Land" ' in Watford on 7 May 1915: 'really interesting, though just as small as I feared—about 16 people'. Dorothy Ward's diary, in UCL Archives, D. Ward papers, MS add. 202.51.

[65] *Anti-Suffrage Review*, 89 (Mar. 1916), 20.   [66] *Anti-Suffrage Review*, 90 (Apr. 1916), 29.

their previously successful voluntary work. As individuals, were they conscious of contradictions between their cautious attitude to the expanding female workforce and their own promotion into positions of official authority and (in some cases) financial reward? There seems to be no evidence that this was the case. On the contrary, as the possibility of military defeat loomed, these patriotic women revelled in their own achievement of influential positions, and enjoyed their opportunity to prevent the suffragists from monopolizing female influence over policies concerning women. Both Violet Markham and Mary Ward expressed some frustration at the exclusion of women from the counsels of wartime government in the early stages of the war. Violet's letters to *The Times* in the first two years of the war were a very public attempt to influence policy, and included (in March 1915) the direct suggestion that women representatives should have been invited to the Treasury Conference on munitions production.[67] Mary Ward, on the other hand, made common cause with Louise Creighton when she wrote privately in July 1915: 'I suppose all women's societies are equally furious at the scant attention that has been paid them by Hayes Fisher and the Government . . . I suppose the united voice of women of all sorts may succeed in putting more women on the committees.'[68] Expanding government recognition of women's voluntary war work, as well as their rapidly growing consultative and administrative involvement in many aspects of home front policy, helped assuage such criticisms without necessarily undermining anti-suffrage faith in unofficial and indirect womanly influence. It seems likely that wartime government service was often valued by the government itself in terms of womanly influence, rather than as a step towards political equality or a permanent concession to women's growing role in the workplace and the professions. Certainly the *Anti-Suffrage Review* had no hesitation in celebrating anti-suffrage women's appointments to official committees and even to paid government service. Such appointments became all the more welcome as the suffragists flaunted their success in government circles, particularly in relation to women's employment and various aspects of social service.

Though Violet Markham's experience of government work led indirectly to her conversion to suffragism, she was at pains to explain both to Lord Cromer and to posterity (through her autobiography) that her change of view on the vote was not accompanied by a recantation of all her earlier views on gender difference and on women's citizenship. Throughout the war she retained a strong respect for middle-class women's voluntary effort and opposed government control of the details of social policy. The war emergency had revealed the inadequacy of 'amateurism' in the management of labour force supply. As Violet contemplated the prospects for post-war social work, she developed proposals for a reformed voluntarism, linking women's social action with government

[67] *The Times*, 26 Mar. 1915, 11.
[68] Mary Ward to Louise Creighton, 19 July 1915. M. Ward papers, 3/3.

policies to the benefit of both.[69] Local government remained her own preferred arena of womanly political intervention into the inter-war era.[70] Gladys Pott's work for the Board of Agriculture also led her eventually into a post-war role in female emigration which drew strongly upon established traditions of women's voluntary social service.[71] Mary Ward's careful balancing act between welcoming government support for her play-schemes, and maintaining elements of voluntary female control, has already been described. The survival of her pre-war Joint Advisory Committee into the war years, and through to the reconstruction era, is evidence of her ongoing search for innovative, feminine ways of influencing government policy which might provide an alternative to the female suffrage. There were some tangible JAC successes in modifying aspects of legislation which particularly concerned her. For example, she collaborated with Violet Markham in 1916 to secure improvements to women's war pensions through the mechanism of this committee. Violet paid special tribute to the JAC's effectiveness in her autobiography, commenting that it 'did very good work in examining Bills affecting women and children' and 'might with advantage have been revived after the war'.[72] The inclusion of compulsory provision for disabled children's education in the 1918 Education Act was another JAC success.[73] But by this date the Representation of the People Act had brought organized anti-suffragism to its final defeat.

THE DEFEAT OF ORGANIZED ANTI-SUFFRAGISM

Historians continue to debate the significance of the pre-war suffrage movement and have reached varying conclusions about the suffrage leaders' role in the final stages of the campaign. There is now general consensus around the view that the changed political circumstances of the war determined the eventual timing of women's franchise legislation. Wartime evolution of public attitudes towards women, and women's own shifts of gender outlook and political consciousness, have also been much analysed and debated.[74] However, proof of a sea change in

[69] e.g. Violet Markham to Elizabeth Macadam, 13 Feb. 1918. Markham papers, 2/3.
[70] Markham, *Return Passage*, 172.
[71] See U. Monk, *New Horizons: A Hundred Years of Women's Migration* (London: HMSO, 1963).
[72] Markham, *Return Passage*, 99.
[73] See Mary Ward to Louise Creighton, 23 June 1918. M. Ward papers, 3/3.
[74] See, e.g. work on suffragism and the war, cited above, by Alberti, Garner, Harrison, Holton, and Pugh; work on women's employment and the war, cited above, by Braybon, Culleton, Thom, and Woollacott; work on women, literature, and the war, including J. Potter, *Boys in Khaki, Girls in Print: Women's Literary Responses to the Great War 1914–1918* (Oxford: Oxford University Press, 2005); A. Smith, *The Second Battlefield: Women, Modernism and the First World War* (Manchester: Manchester University Press, 2000); C. Tylee, *The Great War and Women's Consciousness: Images of Militarism and Womanhood in Women's Writings, 1914–1918* (Iowa City: University of Iowa

public opinion was clearly not an essential precondition for the parliamentary enfranchisement of women in 1918. Rejecting calls for a referendum on the subject, male politicians went ahead and decided the matter for themselves in a series of debates which are fully summarized in Brian Harrison's account of the defeat of anti-suffragism.[75] Martin Pugh has expanded upon the view that neither the pressure of wartime suffrage campaigners, nor a change in public attitudes due to women's war work, played a major part in an essentially political decision.[76] Historians who attribute greater influence to suffrage activism both before and during the war have broadened the explanation of suffrage victory,[77] but so far without expanding upon Harrison's brief summary of the decline of anti-suffrage organization, and without challenging his claim that the NLOWS suffered heavily from male military service because it was 'a predominantly male organisation'[78] by this stage of its existence. A fresh perspective is provided in the analysis which follows. Though the NLOWS was defeated in 1918, and impotent in the face of political events, it maintained some continuity of organization and argument throughout the war. Its modest achievements in wartime, still more than in peacetime, rested substantially upon women leaders and women supporters. The League's final stand in Parliament was planned and actively supported not only by anti-suffrage peers but also by anti-suffrage women who remained outspoken in defence of their cause even as most male leaders surrendered to short-term political expediency and the longer-term advance of democratic gender equality.

The suffrage debate was never completely extinguished by the war, as this chapter has already demonstrated. The revival of active campaigning during 1916 was directly linked to government recognition that franchise reform was required in order to secure adequate political representation of British servicemen. An all-party Speaker's Conference was set up in October 1916 to devise a compromise parliamentary solution which always seemed likely to include a measure of female enfranchisement, given the cessation of militancy, the extent of support for suffragism, and women's well-publicized contributions to the war effort, alongside the predicted political advantages of a female electorate.

Press, 1990); also, more generally, L. Abrams, *The Making of Modern Woman* (London: Longman, 2002), G. Braybon and S. Summerfield, *Out of the Cage: Women's Experiences in Two World* Wars (London: Pandora, 1987), M. R. Higonnet and J. Jenson (eds.), *Behind the Lines: Gender and the Two World Wars* (New Haven: Yale University Press, 1987), S. Kingsley Kent, *Making Peace: The Reconstruction of Gender in Inter-War Britain* (Princeton: Princeton University Press, 1993) and *Gender and Power in Britain, 1640–1990* (London: Routledge, 1999).

[75] B. Harrison, *Separate Spheres*, ch. 10, and 'Women's Suffrage at Westminster, 1866–1928', in M. Bentley and J. Stevenson (eds.), *High and Low Politics in Modern Britain* (Oxford: Clarendon Press, 1983).

[76] Pugh, *Women and the Women's Movement*; *The March of the Women* (Oxford: Oxford University Press, 2000).

[77] See e.g. Holton, *Suffrage Days*, ch. 10, and J. Purvis, *Emmeline Pankhurst: A Biography* (London: Routledge, 2002), ch. 11.

[78] B. Harrison, *Separate Spheres*, 203.

Suffrage organizations were undoubtedly in a stronger position to respond to this opportunity than their anti-suffrage opponents. Despite leadership divisions over the war question, and some loss of membership as war work consumed women's energies, the suffragists were quick to mobilize a franchise campaign in the press and in Parliament. Anti-suffrage leaders, on the other hand, remained handicapped by their wish to prioritize the war effort and hesitant in the face of their own organizational weakness. As we have seen, the NLOWS had honoured its self-imposed political truce during 1915 by postponing its usual Annual Council meeting. This decision was criticized by the women members of several London branches, and in consequence an informal general meeting was organized in London instead.

As early as March 1915 Helena Norris had warned of the importance of continuing to counter suffragist propaganda.[79] She was not alone in holding such views and branch secretaries' meetings seem to have continued throughout the war, mainly under Gladys Pott's aegis.[80] Some branches undertook their own successful war work, as we have seen in the cases of the Paddington station buffet and the Berkshire dairymaids scheme. The Woking branch, and possibly others too, suspended directly political work but continued to collect subscriptions which were donated to the Soldiers and Sailors Families' Association.[81] The Annual Council of the League eventually reconvened in July 1916, by which date the *Anti-Suffrage Review* reflected widespread alarm at the extent of renewed suffrage agitation. The June edition carried an attack on Mrs Fawcett's suffrage 'blackmail', headed 'Patriotism—at a Price'. An article on 'The Broken Truce' posed (but did not answer) the question: 'What is to be the attitude of Anti-suffragists in the face of this recrudescence of the Suffrage campaign?'[82] The 1916 Council meeting suggested one line of response, by passing resolutions from the Paddington and Kensington branches of the League which demanded 'immediate action' from their executive committee. Anti-suffrage Members of Parliament were also criticized at the Council for not having 'taken the Government more strongly to task' over its support for the Pankhursts' war work campaign. Encouraging messages from Cromer and Curzon and the Chairman's rather defensive speech were fully reported by the *Review*, but the published attendance list and the critical branch resolutions suggest that the main impetus towards stronger tactics was already coming from women members.[83]

---

[79] *Anti-Suffrage Review*, 77 (Mar. 1915), 23.

[80] *Anti-Suffrage Review*, 100 (Feb. 1917), 14. The *Review* reported continuous monthly meetings of London and south-eastern branch secretaries and workers over the past 'six or seven years', chaired by Miss Pott and with secretarial support from Miss Manisty. Both ladies were now required elsewhere for war work, but Mrs Macmillan and Mrs Willmot were appointed to take up their organizing roles.

[81] *Anti-Suffrage Review*, 105 (July 1917), 53.

[82] *Anti-Suffrage Review*, 92 (June 1916), 41–2.

[83] *AntiSuffrage Review*, 94 (Aug. 1916), 61.

Over the following months the NLOWS stirred slowly back to life as an organized opposition, though it continued to operate mainly in reactive mode. An executive resolution after the 1916 Council reiterated that anti-suffrage public meetings were 'undesirable' in wartime, but also encouraged members to counter suffragist propaganda: 'private meetings of sympathisers' should be held, both to promote war work and to strengthen local organization ready for a post-war resumption of campaigning.[84] A formal letter of protest against suffrage opportunism was also sent by the NLOWS to Members of Parliament and to the press. In November 1916 this was reinforced by a letter in *The Times* from twenty male and fifteen female anti-suffragists, warning that women's suffrage would be accompanied by universal adult suffrage and claiming that 'the present Parliament has no moral right to deal with the matter'.[85] Though Violet Markham had reached the point of defection by this stage, the signatories included many of the women who had taken a leading role in pre-war anti-suffragism, among them Margaret Jersey, Beatrice Chamberlain, Elizabeth Burgwin, Violet Montrose, Catherine Robson, Harriet Wantage, Gladys Pott, and Mary Ward.

The NLOWS publicly traded conflicting claims over the extent of suffrage support with Millicent Fawcett during January 1917, and Oxford and Cambridge pro-suffrage memorials provoked strong anti-suffrage responses soon after.[86] But it was left to Mary Ward to make one of the most powerful press interventions. Her letter to *The Times* on 23 May 1917 reiterated old arguments about the weak parliamentary mandate and the dangers of adult suffrage before proposing an alternative measure of sweeping local government reform which would supply 'a large body of women electors from whom a referendum on the subject of the Parliamentary suffrage could be taken', as well as giving women the benefits of 'that share in the local administration of matters concerning their daily life which has been too long their due'. The Empire was invoked, both as the object of patriotic government and as a future context for creative constitutional reform. Finally, Mary Ward turned her experiences as an official wartime propagandist to eloquent effect. Whilst sharing national pride in the achievements of women munitions workers, she drew an emotional contrast between their relatively good working conditions in 'large and cheerful factories, well warmed and ventilated' and the desolate battlefields which she herself had briefly witnessed.[87]

During the remainder of the year the League's protests against advancing suffragism became steadily stronger. There was no Annual Council, but a Special Meeting on 18 April 1917 discussed organization and tactics, drawing members from fifty-nine English and Scottish branches to London. Branch delegates heard a detailed report on protest activities organized from the NLOWS headquarters,

---

[84] *Anti-Suffrage Review*, 95 (Sept. 1916), 69.

[85] *The Times*, 17 Nov. 1916, 3. Missing signatories included Ethel Harrison, who had died in July, and Ethel Colquhoun, who had remarried and emigrated to Rhodesia (from whence she continued to send supportive messages through the *Review*).

[86] *The Times*, 20 Jan. 1917, 9; 28 Feb. 1917, 3.   [87] *The Times*, 23 May 1917, 9.

including parliamentary meetings and vain attempts to persuade the Prime Minister to receive an anti-suffrage deputation, before pledging themselves to exert local anti-suffrage pressure and formally recording 'an emphatic protest against the question of Woman Suffrage being dealt with by the present Parliament'.[88] A statement titled 'The Political Truce Violated' was widely circulated through the national and provincial press, where it created 'a very large response from new sympathizers'. Meanwhile Arnold Ward had returned from an inglorious stint in the army to lead the parliamentary opposition. Defeats for anti-suffragism in the House of Commons in May 1917 were followed by further small-scale branch protests, including a 'lightning canvass' of public opinion in St Andrews.[89]

Funds were necessary to make protest effective, and during the spring the League's executive unanimously asked Lord Curzon to release the remainder of the anti-suffrage fund he had raised in 1910. In this connection, Edward Mitchell-Innes privately told Curzon that the provincial branches of the League were 'practically non-existent'[90]—an assertion which is cast into doubt by the number of branches represented at the Special Meeting.[91] Like Curzon himself, and probably Arnold Ward too, Mitchell-Innes evidently had limited confidence in the potential value of (mainly female) extra-parliamentary pressure. A tactical meeting of anti-suffrage leaders in June 1917 resulted in a firm decision to continue the fight into the House of Lords. An anti-suffrage parliamentary conference in the same month heard speeches from male and female antis and passed a resolution which was circulated to all members of both Houses and published in *The Times*.[92] During the autumn of 1917 Mitchell-Innes wrote on the executive's behalf to local branches, urging them to take action. But it was not until Mary Ward resumed the helm of the NLOWS in November that a truly determined effort was made to return the League to its roots, as an organization which had always encouraged women to take the rejection of the female franchise into their own hands.

Mary Ward's private confession to Lord Cromer that the war had strengthened suffragism has been quoted to suggest that she knew the cause was lost well before the end of 1917.[93] However, it is difficult to understand why she would have subjected herself to the trials and tribulations of the final weeks of the campaign if she had been without any hope of a successful outcome, or at least

---

[88] *Anti-Suffrage Review*, 103 (May 1917), 38.

[89] *Anti-Suffrage Review*, 104 (June 1917), 43.

[90] Edward Mitchell-Innes to Lord Curzon, 6 Apr. 1917, Curzon papers, MSS Eur F112/37.

[91] Branches represented at the Special Meeting included 17 from London and 43 other English and Scottish branches.

[92] *Anti-Suffrage Review*, 105 (July 1917), 52–53.

[93] Mary Ward to Lord Cromer, 9 July 1915, National Archives, Cromer papers, FO633/24, quoted by Purvis, *Emmeline Pankhurst*, 276. Violet Markham claimed in her autobiography that 'most of the "anti" protagonists realised by 1918 that the game was lost, whether or not their own views had changed', *Return Passage*, 100.

a delayed decision. Her public statements on anti-suffragism continued to ring with conviction, if not with confidence. On 5 November she wrote to Lord Curzon requesting a '20 minute talk' on the prospects for the House of Lords campaign and advancing her own agenda for linking suffrage reform to a future scheme of imperial federation.[94] The following day she urged the centrality of the referendum as a delaying tactic. A few days later she was still hoping for a meeting with Curzon to discuss drafting a Referendum Bill to be introduced alongside suffrage legislation.[95] In the same week John Massie, the League's faithful and efficient Treasurer, was already addressing Curzon on the subject of winding up NLOWS finances after defeat.[96] But Mary Ward was by now on fire with new ideas for proving that women did not want to vote, and still convinced that this could be made into the central plank of a House of Lords strategy for defeating women's suffrage. On 7 December she took up the chairmanship of the League, while Mitchell-Innes departed to America on war duties. With a fine disregard for the crushing burdens upon Curzon as a member of the War Cabinet at a critical stage of the war, she continued to press for his active support.[97]

At the same time, Dorothy Ward's diary entries provide vivid evidence of the energy her mother put into campaigning initiatives directed mainly towards female anti-suffragists. A Women's Memorial was launched, to counter one sent by suffragists to the House of Lords, and a blizzard of individual letters was required to produce signatures as quickly as possible. While Lady Ilchester, Lady Bathhurst, and the Duchess of Montrose approached their fellow peeresses, Mary Ward concentrated upon obtaining support from women war workers.[98] On 30 December her daughter had no time to go to church or to enjoy her brother-in-law's military leave, due to anti-suffrage work: '*Oh* dear! Mother worked at letters on the subject like a nigger—personal letters—but I worked at the main "hack" letters, most of which Gladys nobly typed!'[99] On New Year's Day 115 postcards were despatched to anti-suffrage branches. Results soon flowed from these efforts. Mary reported to Curzon on 7 January that she had despatched her Memorial to the Lords, and that signatures were 'still coming in by every post'. In an echo of the 1889 campaign, she told him that there were 'a great many distinguished names, but it is not of course so "intellectual" as the suffrage list—not so many women doctors, or MA's, or members of R[oyal] C[ommission]s! It is perhaps for that very reason it seems to me the more broadly representative of the mass of Englishwomen—hard-working, patriotic and intelligent'.[100]

---

[94] Mary Ward to Lord Curzon, 5 Nov. 1917. BL, Curzon papers, MSS Eur F112/37.
[95] Mary Ward to Lord Curzon, 9 Nov. 1917. Curzon papers, MSS Eur F112/37.
[96] John Massie to Lord Curzon, 13 Nov. 1917. Curzon papers, MSS Eur F112/37.
[97] Mary Ward to Lord Curzon, 23 Dec. 1917. Curzon papers, MSS Eur F112/37.
[98] Mary Ward to Lord Curzon, 27 Dec. 1917. Curzon papers, MSS Eur F112/37.
[99] Dorothy Ward's diary, 30 Dec. 1917 and 1 Jan. 1918. D. Ward papers, MSS Add. 202.53, 55.
[100] Mary Ward to Lord Curzon, 7 Jan. 1918. Curzon papers, MSS Eur F112/37.

Mary Ward also mobilized contributors to a special edition of the *Anti-Suffrage Review*, designed to influence the parliamentary outcome through further evidence of 'distinguished' support. In December 1917 ten women set out their case against women's suffrage in the *Review*, alongside ten well-known male antis.[101] Together these female contributors summarized most of the familiar women's arguments against the vote, including the view that women's special work would suffer from parliamentary involvement, and that their interests could be better represented through participation in local government. They condemned the timing and manner of enfranchisement as strongly as the measure itself—some stating they were ready to accept the franchise if it proved to be the will of the country. Mrs Robinson of the Women's Anti-Suffrage Association of Massachusetts backed up calls for a more democratic decision, asserting that 'England is doing what the Suffragists in America have tried in vain to persuade this country to do—force Woman Suffrage upon the country without giving the people a voice in the matter'. Mary Ilchester believed that public opinion had changed far less than the politically motivated opinions of Members of Parliament. At the same time the political fears of Conservative ladies were evident enough in condemnations of 'a rising tide of State socialism'. War work was invoked as evidence that 'women's real power lies in higher regions than the dust and strife of the political arena'; though Ellen Desart claimed that 'the war work argument fairly makes my blood boil . . . Had they *really* considered us inferior beings, incapable of devotion, of self-sacrifice, of patriotism?' As in earlier years, the arguments of anti-suffrage men and women were differently inflected. Women's confident assertions of their gendered capability and sense of civic responsibility contrasted with masculine warnings that female weaknesses were 'a danger to the State'.

Mary Ward's own final public statement of her anti-suffrage beliefs took the form of a full-length article in the *Nineteenth Century and After*, published in January 1918.[102] Under the title 'Let Women Say!' she appealed both to the House of Lords and to 'Conservative men and women of all classes, and, if one may put it so, of all parties', whose duty it was to halt the threat of a 'revolutionary' change in the British constitution. With recent events in Russia hovering not too far in the background, she developed an argument which rested upon both negative and positive claims. Political calculation was driving forward changes which would soon benefit the Labour party above all others. Suffragism represented 'sham equality with men' and 'rivalry with men, tending in the case of many women to a position of sex hostility'. Women's interests would be far better defended by 'the complementary action, through different institutions, of men and women', allied to women's participation in local government. Above

    101 *Anti-Suffrage Review*, 110 (Dec. 1917), 89–100.
    102 M. Ward, 'Let Women Say! An Appeal to the House of Lords', *Nineteenth Century and After*, 58 (1918), 47–59.

all, 'the women of this country have indeed every right to be consulted before this thing is done'. Outlining possible scenarios for a national referendum, she emphasized that 'the Women's Referendum is in fact all that matters. If they really wish for the vote, no subsequent Referendum of men will deny it to them. Nor would any of us who, in the interests of our sex, have opposed Women's Suffrage, continue to fight any further.' On a more personal note, Mary Ward concluded by reflecting back on a thirty-year debate. She believed more strongly than ever that 'nothing could be achieved by Women's Suffrage that could not be attained in other ways'; and that 'Women's Suffrage would tend to make women the mere political tools of men, and thereby to endanger the stability and safety of the British State'. The arguments of 'the Manifesto of 1889' had stood the test of time.

The success of the Women's Memorial encouraged Mary Ward to organize a deputation of signatories to the House of Lords. More than two thousand women had by now signed the Memorial, including representatives of all the main branches of women's war work. But before the anti-suffrage women could deliver their message in person, their cause had gone down to defeat. On 10 January the House of Lords voted through the women's suffrage clause, following a startling speech from Lord Curzon. Though still President of the NLOWS, he capped his summary of anti-suffrage arguments with a warning to fellow peers to avoid a clash with the Commons on the suffrage issue, and himself abstained from voting on the grounds of his membership of the War Cabinet. Five days later referendum proposals were also voted down. Dorothy Ward recorded her mother's exhaustion 'after all the strain and tension'. She was 'full of fight, bless her, to the last', but also full of fury against Curzon's apparent betrayal.[103] An unwise accusatory correspondence followed, both in public and in private.[104] Determined to defend himself, and never a great admirer of Mary Ward, Curzon preserved most of the letters he received, including some from male leaders of the League who accepted his exculpatory version of events.[105] On 5 February he attended the League's executive in person to defend himself against a censure motion on his behaviour. The motion was somewhat toned down, but eventually passed in a form which provoked his angry resignation.[106]

[103] Dorothy Ward's diary, 12 Jan. 1918. D. Ward papers, MS Add. 202.55.

[104] Mary Ward published criticisms of Lord Curzon in the *Morning Post*, as well as addressing angry letters to him directly on 14 and 16 Jan. 1918. Curzon papers, MSS Eur F112/37.

[105] e.g. letters from Lord Charnwood on 25 Jan. 1918 and from Alfred Maconachie on 30 Jan. 1918. Curzon papers, MSS Eur F112/37. The former was privately abusive towards Mary Ward—'that holy woman'—whom he implausibly accused of lying 'in the hope of getting personal advertisement out of the defeat of our common cause'. The latter had reached the sycophantic conclusion that Curzon's parliamentary action was 'not only constitutionally correct but of lofty patriotism . . . your judgement on such a matter is infinitely sounder than mine'.

[106] The final resolution was forwarded to Lord Curzon by Viva Jeyes on 7 Feb. 1918. Curzon papers, MSS Eur F112/37. It had been somewhat moderated, in response to Curzon's vigorous

For most of the male leaders of the NLOWS, as well as for Lord Curzon himself, the history of organized anti-suffragism ended on this negative note. However, there were formalities to complete. The organization wound up its business, closed down its journal, and on 12 April 1918 held a Special Council Meeting to approve its own demise. By this date a calmer and more cheerful mood had set in. Lord Weardale presided over the final meeting, but the attendance was more than ever predominantly female. Unusually, women speakers also dominated the platform and made most of the speeches. Lord Weardale summarized recent history, thanked Mary Ward for her efforts, paid tribute to Lord Cromer, and declared his own and the League's determination to 'go down with our flag flying'. Then a succession of leading anti-suffrage women rose to deliver their valedictions. Margaret Jersey declared her wish 'to put what seems to me the woman's point of view of the present position'. She reminded women members of the League that 'They did not come into existence merely because they wanted to be "anti" . . . They banded themselves together against it because they felt that woman had a large and definite share of the world's work committed to her . . . Let us still continue in the future, as we have done in the past, to try to do the work which is lawfully ours to the very best of our ability.' Mary Ward spoke next, recalling nostalgically that 'when the question first came to be debated I was at Oxford and taking a rather active part in the organisation of women's education at Oxford'. Over the past ten years the League had 'kept up the fight', achieving 'great success' in its pre-war appeals to the country. The outcome might have been different had not the war intervened, and the female support received in the final weeks proved that 'we were perfectly right to fight the great fight on behalf of those hundreds and thousands of women throughout the country who would have preferred not to take upon themselves the great responsibility of the vote'. It was now necessary to 'go forward in a different scene and under a different sky . . . above all, we have got to hold over us a flag of womanly steadfastness, womanly help, womanly service to our country'.

After a brief financial report from John Massie, Gladys Pott proposed a vote of thanks to honorary officers, singling out six leading women. It was left to Beatrice Chamberlain to complete the speeches with a vote of thanks to the chairman. Departing from conventional practice, she used this opportunity to deliver a final message of heartfelt female patriotism to her audience of women anti-suffragists. Thus far only the opponents of the vote were fully conscious of the extent of their new responsibilities, but 'we see what we have to do next . . . we do perceive the importance of what is now expected from women, there is therefore a great work for us to do, to try to bring it home to our country'. Anti-suffragists had succeeded in postponing women's enfranchisement for long enough to enable

---

self-defence, but remained a motion of censure, passed by a majority of 9 to 5 committee members. Curzon was sufficiently angry to begin scribbling notes for a reply—which he apparently did not send.

Britain to organize for victory. The war itself was now helping to prepare women for their newly enfranchised citizenship, but 'More remains for us to do'. In the post-war future, female anti-suffragists must undertake the vital task of teaching other women to use their votes well: 'We have done a great work. We are doing a great work. Our work is not ended, it is beginning.'[107]

[107] *Anti-Suffrage Review*, 113 (Apr. 1918), 19–22.

11

A Retrospective View of Failure

LOOKING FORWARD, LOOKING BACK

During 1918 the leading anti-suffrage women faced up to the defeat of their cause with remarkable equanimity, given their own past predictions of the catastrophic consequences of votes for women. In the short term the war and its aftermath overshadowed all other issues. In the longer term, it seemed probable that post-war reconstruction would present opportunities to press ahead with important social reforms advocated by suffragists and anti-suffragists alike. Though the parliamentary vote offered no guarantee of a better future for women, and indeed threatened an unwelcome diversion of their energies, it could perhaps be tamed through appropriate political education. The primary tasks of improving women's lives and rebuilding national strength might then move steadily forward, rather than being undermined by a revolution in established gender roles. Certainly there had never before been such a widespread acknowledgement of the value of women's contributions both to family life and to Britain's future. Women's role as citizens must now be reshaped to accommodate their new political role alongside a reassertion of their essential gifts and responsibilities as social carers and custodians of moral and patriotic values. As the male leaders of the NLOWS turned away to other matters, many anti-suffrage women looked forward to immersing themselves in citizenship education and the congenial work of the women's movement alongside their former suffrage adversaries. There was also palpable relief among both men and women anti-suffragists at the ending of an uncomfortable NLOWS gender alliance which had always promised more advantages in theory than it had been able to deliver in organizational practice.

The final chapter of this book will weigh up the extent to which anti-suffrage hopes of protecting and reinforcing distinctive gender roles were matched by developments in public life during the inter-war years. Would gender conservatism successfully curb the dangers of feminist subversion in the home, the wider community, and the imperial Parliament itself? Would formerly anti-suffrage women succeed in finding new avenues for their gendered public service, linked to a continuation of pre-war social action and its most promising wartime offshoots? Would women's enfranchisement fulfil the more hopeful predictions of anti-suffragists by failing to deliver a new world, and also failing to disrupt the old one? These questions will first be considered in relation to the post-war careers of the leading anti-suffrage campaigners whose ideas and activism have provided much of the substance of previous chapters. Continuity and change will then be discussed in the context of parliamentary politics and government, before turning to the evolution of the non-political women's movement during the first two decades of female enfranchisement. Some further comment is also required on the evolving gender views of the 'ordinary woman', that unorganized and under-recorded construct whose (usually silent) beliefs had been so frequently invoked by both camps during the suffrage campaign. This retrospective survey of post-war expectations and outcomes prepares the way for some summative conclusions on the women anti-suffragists' achievements and long-term historical importance.

WOMEN LEADERS AFTER THE SUFFRAGE DEFEAT

Mary Ward had more reason than most to sigh with relief as the NLOWS dissolved itself and its male and female leaders went their separate ways. 'Well now, thank goodness it is over...', she wrote to Louise Creighton in March 1918; 'Now the question is what the women will do with their vote. I can only hope that you and Mrs Fawcett are right and I am wrong.' Her first concern was to ensure that gullible women were not misled into supporting 'a merely shameful and temporary peace'. With typical confidence in her own ability to channel the tide of public opinion, she proposed a patriotic summer tour in the socialistic north of England to educate 'those at home who don't or can't read'.[1] The steady advance of government-approved children's play-schemes across Britain was a source of consolation and an assurance of her continued public influence. So, too, was her success in using the still-extant Joint Parliamentary Advisory Committee to insert a clause into the 1918 Education Act making schools for the physically disabled part of compulsory education provision. By June, Mary Ward was informing Louise of her first ideas for a remapping of the landscape of women's politics which would combine the old with the new.[2] But ill health intervened to prevent her following through any fresh initiatives to strengthen women's influence upon social legislation through means other than parliamentary politics. Like many other anti-suffrage leaders, she was becoming old and weary. Grappling with financial problems, her son's loss of his parliamentary seat in the 1918 election, and her husband's illness as well as her own, she produced a third patriotic tract and two final novels in the last year of her life. Her memoirs also appeared at the end of the war,

---

[1] Mary Ward to Louise Creighton, 14 Mar. 1918. Pusey House Library, Oxford, M. Ward papers, 3/3.

[2] Mary Ward to Louise Creighton, 23 June 1918. M. Ward papers, 3/3.

with anti-suffragism and most of her other non-literary achievements discreetly expunged from the record. An honorary doctorate from Edinburgh University brought welcome recognition of her contributions to literature, philanthropy, and education, while her nomination during 1919 as one of the first female magistrates was another source of pleasure to a dedicated social activist who had always supported women's entry into those arenas of public life where they could most appropriately offer their gendered service to the nation.

Mary Ward died of heart failure on 24 March 1920. Her departure added another name to the roll-call of senior anti-suffragists whose lives and work ended while the consequences of votes for women still remained largely unknown. The demographic of the female anti-suffrage movement tended to bear out suffragist jeers against their innate Victorianism. Amongst her fellow women writers, Eliza Lynn Linton had died in 1898, Mary Kingsley in 1900, Charlotte Yonge in 1901, and Ouida in 1908. The religious writer Caroline Stephen died in 1909, and the social reformer Octavia Hill in 1912. Marie Corelli lived on till 1924, but her public reputation never recovered from a (contested) prosecution for food hoarding in 1917. The war took its toll on other women too, leaving a trail of deaths, bereavements, and retirements among former anti-suffrage campaigners. Ethel Harrison lost a son in military action, and herself succumbed to grief and illness the following year. Harriet Wantage retired from public life after the death of her husband during the war. Margaret Jersey was also widowed and lost her son-in-law during the war. Though she continued as president of the Victoria League until 1926 and lived on till the age of 95, her public work became more muted and she too turned to the task of suffrage-free autobiography. Honourable wartime retirements included the anti-suffragist educators Lucy Soulsby and Elizabeth Burgwin. Elizabeth Wordsworth had retired from Lady Margaret Hall in 1909, after apparently accepting the inevitability of votes for women, and continued to distance herself from political controversy till her death in 1932. Louise Creighton, another pre-war suffrage convert, remained active in public life into the 1920s, but was equally reluctant to take up political duties. Her preference remained the womanly work of Anglican Church reform and voluntary social service. She memorialized her son's death as an army chaplain in April 1918, before completing her own memoir with its cryptic references to anti-suffragism and to the evils of party politics ('I have always hated everything that was concerned with parties').[3]

Beatrice Chamberlain's unexpected death in November 1918 added to the thinning of anti-suffragist ranks at the end of the war. Aged only 56, she fell victim to influenza after a busy wartime career of patriotic public service. Her father's death in 1914 had released her from family ties, and her combative speech at the final meeting of the NLOWS suggested that she was more than

---

[3] L. Creighton, *Memoir of a Victorian Woman*, ed. J. Covert (Bloomington: Indiana University Press, 1994), 145.

ready to take up the challenge of defending traditional gender ideals within the new context of female enfranchisement. Tributes poured in after her death, including an obituary in *The Times* which recorded her work for government committees and her enthusiasm for the Empire which her father had helped to create and to idealize.[4] At a more humble level, Dorothy Ward commemorated her work for the Children's Country Holidays Fund and the South Fulham Group of Special Schools passed a resolution acknowledging that she had 'for twenty-eight years unsparingly devoted her time and thought to the Elementary and Special Schools in the Borough'.[5] Beatrice Chamberlain was a stalwart of Mary Ward's Joint Advisory Committee, and its secretary recorded that she had 'worked resolutely and untiringly, not only in the service of the great political party to which she belonged, but also in the interests of education and the poor, without any thought of party'.[6] Unlike most other women antis, Beatrice had a long record of engagement with Unionist party politics. In 1920 her party paid her a posthumous tribute by republishing a speech she had made on the eve of enfranchisement: 'Women must not advance selfish and exclusive claims against the interests of the nation as a whole, but we may and should especially urge reforms in regard to health, housing and child welfare, wherein women are naturally experts'.[7] Here was a prototype for the emergence of gendered parliamentary politics from the ruins of anti-suffragism. As suffragists debated the merits of a Women's Party, anti-suffragists hoped to combine voluntary social action and innovatory JAC lobbying with judicious work for an auxiliary Women's Unionist Association working 'hand in hand with the men's association of the same party'.[8]

Beatrice Chamberlain did not live to carry her post-war plans into action. But she was not alone in foreseeing positive ways of combining old and new beliefs about women's role in politics. Several younger leaders of the NLOWS provided outstanding public and political service during the following two decades, whilst at the same time remaining loyal to the conservative gender ideals which had underpinned their former anti-suffragism. Gladys Pott, who before the war had struggled to fit the demands of her NLOWS job alongside the claims of family duty, had discovered new talents and priorities during her work for the Board of Agriculture and emerged from the war as the chairman of the Society for Oversea Settlement of British Women from 1920 to 1937. This semi-official organization built directly upon the labours of voluntary female imperialist associations devoted to assisted emigration. As an arm of the Dominions Office,

[4] *The Times*, 22 Nov. 1918, 11.

[5] Tribute sent by A. Crossley, London County Council, 21 Nov. 1918. University of Birmingham Library, Chamberlain papers, BC5/8/20.

[6] Margaret Turvey on behalf of JAC, 22 Nov. 1918. Chamberlain papers, BC5/8/22. Beatrice Chamberlain had acted as Treasurer and as Chairman of the JAC.

[7] B. Chamberlain, 'A Call for Recruits', *Home and Politics*, 3 (repr. Nov. 1920).

[8] Ibid.

the Society received government funding in return for a measure of government direction, and was only too happy to expand its protective and educational work to include the settlement of ex-servicewomen alongside thousands of other women seeking work and matrimony in 'Greater Britain'. The Victoria League's (suffragist) secretary was appointed as Gladys Pott's deputy, enabling her to travel the world as an unelected government representative and even to act as an adviser on women's issues at the International Labour Conference in Geneva in 1926.[9]

Violet Markham's post-war career trajectory was still more remarkable, for another anti-suffragist woman who had rejected previous opportunities to extend her formal education and establish the career path which her abilities merited. Again purely on the basis of official nominations, and as a reward for her successes in philanthropy and social research, she advanced rapidly in both local and national government. Her wartime experience of government had led her to conclude that the female franchise was necessary, though it brought with it the dangers of mass female ignorance. Voluntary and professional social work, and political education for women, would be vital adjuncts of the reforming legislation promised in the reconstruction era. Violet Markham allowed herself to be flattered into the bold step of standing for Parliament in 1918, as an un-couponed Liberal candidate in her late brother's Mansfield constituency. Her surprise and pleasure at the suffragist Eleanor Rathbone's offer of active support reveals both her consciousness of her anti-suffrage past and her acceptance of the need for future bridge-building.[10] The immediate outcome was a heavy election defeat. Violet's correspondence shows that this was not entirely unwelcome, for her dislike of direct campaigning had never been overcome and she would probably have found considerable difficulty in adjusting herself to the masculine demands of Parliament. Instead she followed her husband abroad for an interlude of domesticity, before resuming a public service career which accorded better with her faith in feminine skills and influence. Like Mary Ward and Margaret Jersey she was nominated for the magistracy, as well as continuing her philanthropic and local government work in her native Chesterfield. At a national level she joined various government committees on social issues, before becoming the statutory woman member of the Unemployment Assistance Board in 1934.[11] As an intimate friend of leading imperialists, she also persisted in her behind-the-scenes interventions in imperial affairs, taking particular pride in her influential friendship with the Canadian Prime Minister, Mackenzie King. John Buchan,

[9] See U. Monk, *New Horizons: A Hundred Years of Women's Migration* (London: HMSO, 1963).

[10] V. Markham, *Return Passage* (London: Oxford University Press, 1953), 156–7; S. Pederson, *Eleanor Rathbone and the Politics of Conscience* (Yale: Yale University Press, 2004), 176–7.

[11] See H. Jones, (ed.), *Duty and Citizenship: The Correspondence and Papers of Violet Markham, 1896–1953* (London: The Historians' Press, 1994), ch. 3. Helen Jones comments that 'Violet Markham gained a permanent foothold in Whitehall . . . with more power than many women on more orthodox career paths'. H. Jones, *Women in British Public Life 1914–1950: Gender, Power and Social Policy* (London: Pearson Education, 2000), 18.

who became Governor General of Canada in 1935, had been Violet Markham's friend since his days as a fellow acolyte of Lord Milner in South Africa; his wife was a fellow organizer within the Edwardian circles of female social imperialism.

Two more of the leading anti-suffrage imperialist ladies created post-war careers for themselves which owed nothing to female enfranchisement. Gertrude Bell crowned her wartime career as an oriental specialist and British agent in the Middle East with an important intervention in the affairs of post-war Iraq. As an advocate of British influence exerted through friendly Arab rulers, she helped King Feisal to assume the throne in 1921, and became involved both officially and unofficially in many aspects of nation-building. As a linguist and archaeologist, she played a leading role in the creation of the Iraqi National Museum in Baghdad before her premature death in 1926.[12] More than most other anti-suffrage leaders, Gertrude had always devoted only a limited amount of her public work to the particular needs of women. However, her preferred methods of private influence were entirely consonant with an anti-suffragist distrust of democracy and dislike of party politics. Her old Oxford friend Janet Courtney recalled that when a parliamentary career was suggested to her in the 1920s, her reaction was instantly dismissive: 'she hated politics in the narrower sense; what she cared for was the good government of an Eastern people'.[13]

Ethel Colquhoun seemed an equally unlikely candidate for elected office, despite her pre-war links with the Women's Unionist Association. After her husband's sudden death in December 1914 she found consolation in taking up his editorial duties at the Royal Colonial Institute alongside her work for the anti-suffragist station buffet. Soon another continuity was established when she made a second imperialist marriage to John Tawse Jollie, a Rhodesian farmer settled on the lands which Archibald Coloquhoun had helped Cecil Rhodes to annex to British interests twenty years earlier. Ethel departed to a new life in the sun, though not without some journalistic contributions to the latter stages of the anti-suffrage campaign. By 1917 she was working for a different political cause, as a founder member of the Responsible Government Campaign which resisted Rhodesia's incorporation into the new Union of South Africa. Ironically, this campaign led eventually to her own election in 1923 as the first woman member of any colonial legislature. Ethel's anti-suffragism had always been closely linked to her hostility to the social consequences of 'feminism', and as a Rhodesian parliamentarian she continued to associate herself with conservative gender views as well as with a racially defined vision of British imperialism.

---

[12] See S. Goodman, *Gertrude Bell* (London: Berg, 1985). Goodman speculates that Gertrude Bell's death was probably a case of suicide, linked to her exhaustion and ill health and to the death of her lover during the war.

[13] J. Courtney, *An Oxford Portrait Gallery* (London: Chapman and Hall, 1931), 87.

Her extra-parliamentary activities included support for female immigration and for Rhodesian women's voluntary organizations which promoted patriotic maternalism.[14]

Clearly there were many ways in which a former anti-suffragist could develop her public work without departing altogether from her earlier principles. Indeed anti-suffrage maternal reformism, imperialism, and anti-feminism often merged seamlessly with their suffragist equivalents during the inter-war years, once again illustrating the existence of a complex web of views within the British women's movement rather than a straightforward opposition between pro-suffrage and anti-suffrage standpoints. Aspects of anti-suffrage thinking continued to be reflected in post-war lives and careers as pragmatic adjustments were made by the younger women leaders to the accomplished fact of female enfranchisement. Anti-suffragism did not prove a career impediment, though womanhood itself sometimes did. In fact the reverse may even have been true, as male-led governments sought cooperative (as well as competent) women to take on a limited range of public roles and help meet the anticipated needs and expectations of female voters.

The later career of the Marchioness of Tullibardine, better known as the Duchess of Atholl from 1917 onwards, provides a particularly striking example of successful adjustment to changed circumstances.[15] Her prominence within the anti-suffrage movement was relatively short-lived, dating from her appearance alongside Lord Curzon at the great Glasgow meeting of the Scottish National Anti-Suffrage League in 1912. On this occasion and others, she made clear her adherence to the anti-suffrage forward policy, with its insistence upon women's public as well as private social duties. Her anti-suffragism was linked to her high social status and her devotion to her husband's career of military imperialism, as well as to her established work in female philanthropy. During the war this work expanded through government committees, as well as including support for the Red Cross and the organization of entertainments and welfare programmes for thousands of troops. In 1919 she took up service on her local education authority, then as a member of the Scottish Board of Health's consultative council for the Highlands and Islands. But still greater responsibilities beckoned, as Lloyd George suggested she would make an excellent MP and her husband duly gave her permission to stand for election. In 1923 Katharine Atholl became the first Scottish woman Member of Parliament and by 1929 she was the first woman member of a Conservative government, serving as Parliamentary Secretary to

[14] See D. Lowry, in I. Fletcher, L. Nym Mayhall, and P. Levine (eds.), *Women's Suffrage in the British Empire* (London: Routledge, 2000), ch. 11. Also Ethel Colquhoun's Rhodesian publications, e.g. *The Future of Rhodesia* (Bulawayo, 1917), *The Rhodes Idea: Portrait of a Great Imperialist* (n.d. ?1930); and her articles in British periodicals, e.g. 'Britain's Youngest Colony', *National Review* (Nov. 1923), 447–57.

[15] See K. Atholl, *Working Partnership* (London: Arthur Baker, 1958) and S. Hetherington, *Katharine Atholl 1874–1960: Against the Tide* (Aberdeen: Aberdeen University Press, 1989).

the Board of Education. During the 1930s her relative independence of party politics was demonstrated by her strong stand on a number of foreign policy issues, including opposition to greater Indian self-rule, support for women's health interests in Africa, and criticism of British appeasement of Franco and of Hitler. Her departure from the front benches gave her time to devote to a didactic book on *Women and Politics*, published in 1931.[16] Three years earlier she had opposed further extension of the female franchise, on the well-worn grounds of women's ignorance and their numerical majority among voters. Her book rehearsed arguments familiar to an earlier generation of anti-suffragists, with its emphasis upon women's special gifts and responsibilities as potential mothers themselves and as part of a Mother Country watching over 'women of the backward races of the Empire'. She believed that British women were already making their distinctive influence felt as they voted in relation to questions of family life, housing, health, employment, and international peace. In her conclusion, she invoked women's ability 'to promote greater and much-needed unity in our national life' by helping to heal 'unnecessarily wide and needlessly embittered' divisions between the political parties.[17]

It would be an exaggeration to claim huge influence for Katharine Atholl's views on women and politics. But she helped to define and represent, as well as attempting to swell, a current of conservative female opinion which was already flowing strongly and included many women less powerful than herself. This will be illustrated by a consideration of women's participation in parliamentary politics between the wars, before we turn to the more indirect evidence of the non-political women's movement and to the still more elusive political outlook of unorganized women.

GENDER CONSERVATISM AND POST-WAR POLITICS

While some anti-suffrage women leaders faded away after the suffrage defeat, others tried to fulfil the brave promises of the NLOWS at its moment of dissolution. They could soon draw fresh hope from the growing evidence that millions of women were adapting to changing times whilst holding fast to long-established, fundamentally conservative beliefs about their gendered participation in public life. How far did newly enfranchised women meet the varied expectations of suffragist and anti-suffragist activists during the interwar period? The nature of these expectations, and particularly the outcomes in terms of female voting and legislation related to 'women's subjects', have

---

[16] K. Atholl, *Women and Politics* (London: Philip Allan, 1931).

[17] Ibid. 172–6. In the same passage she reflected upon the potentially valuable links between maternity and a more womanly style of politics, and warned against the dangers of excessive female separatism.

provided material for much historical debate. Brian Harrison's study of the willing conservatism of female voters, of the limited achievements of women in Parliament, and of the 'prudence' of inter-war feminists has been supplemented by Martin Pugh's analysis of female participation and self-organization in both parliamentary and extra-parliamentary arenas.[18] From different perspectives, Barbara Caine, Harold Smith, Susan Kingsley Kent, and Helen Jones have all tended to confirm the general scenario of disappointing political outcomes for former suffragist campaigners, reflecting post-war hostility to feminism as well as the resilience of the male establishment.[19] On the other hand more positive assessments, related to the diversity of suffragist political ambitions, have been presented by Johanna Alberti, Cheryl Law, Amanda Vickery, and Pat Thane.[20] It is nowadays generally accepted that women's political contribution cannot be measured solely in terms of their direct impact upon elections, political parties, legislation, and the composition of Parliament and governments. However, these traditional routes to political power were assumed to be crucial during the suffrage campaign, so for present purposes it seems sensible to begin from Parliament, and the electoral route to Westminster.

How much did women actually achieve from the Representation of the People Act, 1918? Clearly, not everything which the more radical suffragists had hoped for, and not as much as their anti-democratic opponents had feared. The limitations of the 1918 franchise were necessary to ensure its acceptance by Parliament. The new female electorate represented less than 40 per cent of the total vote, rather than the much-dreaded 'petticoat rule' by an ignorant, gullible majority. By 1928, when women were enfranchised for the first time on the same terms as men and the new female electorate reached over 52 per cent of the total, Parliament had been reassured that women voters were relatively harmless. In fact, all the main parties had some hopes of rendering them positively useful. In the first place women must be persuaded to use their votes, and to use them wisely. There was much ill-informed speculation about

[18] See B. Harrison, *Separate Spheres*, ch. 11; *Prudent Revolutionaries: Portraits of British Feminists between the Wars* (Oxford: Clarendon Press, 1987); 'Women's Suffrage at Westminster 1866–1928', in M. Bentley and J. Stevenson (eds.), *High and Low Politics in Modern Britain* (Oxford: Clarendon Press, 1983); 'Women in a Men's House: The Women MPs 1919–1945', *Historical Journal*, 29/3 (1986), 623–54. See M. Pugh, 'Domesticity and the Decline of Feminism', in H. Smith (ed.), *British Feminism in the Twentieth Century* (Aldershot: Edward Elgar, 1990); *Women and the Women's Movement in Britain, 1914–1959* (London: Macmillan, 1992).

[19] See B. Caine, *English Feminism 1780–1980* (Oxford: Oxford University Press, 1997); Smith (ed.), *British Feminism in the Twentieth Century*; S. Kingsley Kent, *Making Peace: The Reconstruction of Gender in Interwar Britain* (Princeton: Princeton University Press, 1993) and *Gender and Power in Britain 1640–1990* (London: Routledge, 1999); Jones, *Women in British Public Life*.

[20] See J. Alberti, *Beyond Suffrage: Feminists in War and Peace 1914–1928* (London: Macmillan, 1989) and 'A Symbol and a Key: The Suffrage Movement in Britain, 1918–1928', in J. Purvis and S. Holton (eds.), *Votes for Women* (London: Routledge, 2000); C. Law, *Suffrage and Power: The Women's Movement 1918–1928* (London: I. B. Tauris, 2000); A. Vickery, *Women, Privilege and Power: British Politics, 1750 to the Present* (Stanford: Stanford University Press, 2001); P. Thane, 'What Difference Did the Vote Make?', in Vickery (ed.), *Women, Privilege and Power* (2001).

women's participation rates in the elections of the 1920s, but little or no firm evidence exists to show that women were more reluctant to go to the polls than men. Did they vote differently when they got there? Martin Pugh quotes research which supports the view that the Labour party was disadvantaged by the female electorate, especially after it expanded in 1928.[21] Obviously multiple variables determine election results, and more recently Pat Thane has argued strongly against received wisdom on women's lower participation rates, tendency to vote under male influence, and assumed Conservative tendencies.[22] Insecure statistical evidence has often been used to support a general picture of the disappointments of female enfranchisement in its early decades. However, it does seem certain that women failed to vote as a gendered bloc in the 1920s and 1930s, thus allaying anti-suffragist fears and confounding some suffragists' hopes for the establishment of a separate Women's Party.

Christabel and Emmeline Pankhurst made an abrupt decision to launch such a party in November 1917, as the enfranchisement of women became inevitable. Their initiative drew credibility from their suffragist past and from dislike of masculine party politics among women on both sides of the suffrage divide, but the circumstances of the launch linked the new party irrevocably to anti-Bolshevism and hostility to the organized labour movement, as well as to militant patriotism and the Pankhurst style of personal leadership.[23] Despite government support in the 1918 election, Christabel was narrowly defeated in a mainly working-class constituency and soon after withdrew from the political scene. There seems to have been insufficient agreement among other women leaders and women's organizations to press forward with any alternative version of gendered electoral organization. Meanwhile the counter-organization of the established parties was moving into gear, reminding women voters of the full range of political issues at stake in the era of post-war reconstruction and reassuring them that their particular concerns would receive due attention. Anti-suffragists like Beatrice Chamberlain, as well as many suffragists, were eager to use the party propaganda machinery as well as the organizations of the women's movement to educate the new female electorate as rapidly as possible. However, there is evidence of some continuing support for the concept of women's politics organized by independent women. Moderate suffragists challenged the eligibility of Mrs Ogilvie Gordon to preside over the National Council of Women in 1918–19, because of her close association with the Coalition government and the Conservative party; the defeat of this challenge was followed by much discussion of party-neutral political education.[24] In the field of local government, where women's special interests had long been advocated by both suffragists and

---

[21] Pugh, *Women and the Women's Movement*, 152.   [22] Thane, 'What Difference'.
[23] See Pugh, *Women and the Women's Movement*, 66–71; J. Purvis, *Emmeline Pankhurst: A Biography* (London: Routledge, 2002), ch. 21.
[24] See National Council of Women, *Handbook and Report 1918–1919* (London: NCW, 1919).

anti-suffragists, there was even some short-term success in organizing electoral support for independent women candidates.[25] But reluctance among more conservative women to mount an apparently feminist challenge to mixed-sex politics soon curbed such experiments at local as well as national level.

Women's incorporation into the main political parties provided an object lesson in the difficulty of obtaining a distinctive voice for women within the bounds of conventional British politics. The anti-suffragists had consistently argued the need to advance women's interests by indirect means. In effect, a somewhat enhanced indirect hearing was what resulted from women's admission to parliamentary politics organized by men and upon men's terms. Female enfranchisement went hand in hand with much rewriting of party constitutions. Women were invited to collaborate, but this led to a complementary and subordinate role in determining party policies and organizing elections, rather than to equal opportunities of standing for Parliament and entering government. In 1918 the Conservative party committed itself to a low membership fee and to one-third representation of women on its committees. This was sufficient to draw in a mass female membership of over a million by 1928. David Jarvis has investigated the inner workings of what he describes as 'a primarily exploitative relationship' between men and women in the party.[26] An unequal division of responsibilities reflected current gender beliefs as well as the practical circumstances of most Conservative women activists' lives; continuities with the semi-political female propaganda work of the Primrose League were also clearly apparent. Liberal party women had an equally long history of voluntarily servicing male politics, despite the links between the Women's Liberal Federation and the suffrage campaign from the 1880s onwards. However, the party was in decline during the inter-war years and failed to build upon its potential attractions for women voters, despite the Liberal politics of the leaders of many extra-parliamentary women's organizations.[27]

The Labour party apparently held better prospects for women, as it regrouped around its new constitution in 1918 and began to recruit a mass membership in the constituencies alongside its traditional trade union support.[28] Women had a guaranteed minority of seats on the national executive, and the party was supportive towards the social reform policies being advocated by the non-political women's movement. However, a class-based party dominated by the interests of organized labour was never likely to surrender its resistance to more

[25] See P. Hollis, *Ladies Elect: Women in English Local Government 1865–1914* (Oxford: Clarendon Press, 1987), ch. 10; Pugh, *Women and the Women's Movement*, 56–61.

[26] D. Jarvis, in A. Vickery (ed.), *Women, Privilege and Power*, ch. 9, p. 303.

[27] Pugh, *Women and the Women's Movement*, 141.

[28] See P. Graves, *Labour Women: Women in British Working-Class Politics, 1918–1939* (Cambridge: Cambridge University Press, 1994); C. Collette, 'Questions of Gender: Labour and Women', in B. Brivati and R. Heffernan, (eds.), *The Labour Party: A Centenary History* (Basingstoke: Macmillan, 2000); G. Scott, *Feminism and the Politics of Working Women* (London: UCL Press, 1998).

challenging women's demands. Though many constituencies developed a large and committed female membership, national policy debates around employment issues remained dominated by trade union interests, while at local level there was little sympathy for placing gender equality before class solidarity and the defence of male breadwinners. Labour often claimed to be the natural party of women between the wars, but its organization and policies demonstrated a lack of warmth towards egalitarian ambitions. The women anti-suffragists' dread of a future slide towards socialism and allied forms of immoral feminism proved wide of the mark, as millions of working-class women voters confirmed their electoral support for a Labour party which stood committed to masculine leadership and support for most aspects of the existing gender order.

Turning to legislative outcomes for evidence of the impact of female enfranchisement, we enter upon contested territory. By the late 1920s many suffragists took immense comfort from the unprecedented volume of social legislation which had been passed during the first post-war decade. The social welfare agenda of the organized women's movement was finally being addressed and laws improving women's legal status were also reaching the statute book.[29] But women's widespread support for these reforms does not prove that they were primarily a result of female enfranchisement, rather than a logical extension of pre-war reform programmes. Anti-suffrage women had always argued that social reform did not require the female vote, since many powerful men shared their desire to improve the lives of women and children and understood this to be in the national interest. Though social reforms were prominent in election propaganda aimed at women voters, none of the political parties proved willing to legislate at the former suffragists' command. Major disappointments for many former suffragists included the refusal of equal pay for women teachers and civil servants, the prolongation of the marriage bar, the continuation of protective legislation restricting women's employment opportunities, and the deliberate loopholes within some of the new equalities legislation. Much of the successful legislation seemed designed to consolidate women's role as wives and mothers, rather than to open up new opportunities. Whilst this may well have been what most 'ordinary women' would have chosen for themselves, it represented only a limited success for the more radical reformers. On the basis of her study of women's inter-war influence in Whitehall and Westminster, Helen Jones has concluded that 'women's role in policy-making did not really move beyond that of pressure groups'.[30] Even Pat Thane's more upbeat account of women's

---

[29] e.g. by the Maternity and Child Wefare Act (1918), the Criminal Law Amendment Act (1922), the Infanticide Act (1922), the Matrimonial Causes Act (1923), the Widows, Orphans and Old Age Contributory Pensions Act (1925); and, in relation to legal status, the Sex Disqualification Removal Act (1919), the Married Women's Property (Scotland) Act (1920), the Guardianship of Infants Act (1925), and the Acts which gave women the right to stand for Parliament and to vote on an equal basis to men.

[30] Jones, *Women in British Public Life*, 134.

achievements emphasizes the continuing need for traditional extra-parliamentary lobbying in order to achieve reform legislation.[31]

Historians remain divided on the subject of connections between female voting and reforms benefiting women. The complexity of the debate is increased by contemporary disagreements among women, sometimes within the same women's organizations, over the desirability of reforms which might disturb established patterns of gender authority at home or in the workplace. This subject will be further considered in the next section, for much of the evidence belongs in the extra-parliamentary arena. At the level of national politics and government, it remains to examine briefly the entry of enfranchised women to the British Parliament. How far did women achieve a direct voice in the counsels of the nation during the 1920s and 1930s? Legal barriers to equality had been removed in 1918, but did the results meet suffragist expectations? The answer from many contemporaries, and especially from most modern historians, seems to be an emphatic negative.[32] The House of Commons remained overwhelmingly a 'Men's House', while the House of Lords continued to exclude women altogether until the 1950s. As is well known, the number of women MPs remained consistently low until almost the end of the twentieth century, never exceeding 15 out of a total of 615 Members in the decades before the Second World War. Other measures of achievement include women's promotion or non-promotion into government; the number, quality, range, and impact of their contributions to debates and other parliamentary work; and their ability to make a collective impact upon the masculine way in which Parliament conducted its business. In all these areas progress was extremely slow. The women who did achieve selection against the odds, then election on a party platform, chose their own varied survival strategies, but were usually eager to demonstrate their ability to do a man's job in a feminine manner. Transforming that job, or departing from party loyalty in other ways, was scarcely an option. The parliamentary record, as well as the more subjective evidence of autobiographies and other memoirs, confirms that the pioneer women MPs faced huge obstacles to the achievement of fundamental changes within Parliament, even supposing that they harboured such transformational intentions.

Anti-suffrage women had often warned that parliamentary politics meant politics on men's terms, and this very largely proved to be the case. Pat Thane has suggested that unrealistic expectations of what might be achieved by a first generation of enfranchised women should not be allowed to overshadow the significance of female political activity which 'made some indentations in the political order'.[33] But it was evident during the inter-war years to former

---

[31] Thane, in Vickery (ed.), *Women, Privilege and Power*, 280.

[32] See B. Harrison, 'Women in a Men's House'; Pugh, *Women and the Women's Movement*, ch. 6.

[33] Thane, in Vickery (ed.), *Women, Privilege and Power*, 288.

suffragists and anti-suffragists alike that the polling booth, the political parties, and the actions of Parliament represented no substitute for the ongoing work of a long-established and largely non-political women's movement.

CONSERVATIVE IDEALS AND THE INTER-WAR WOMEN'S MOVEMENT

In many respects the successes of the extra-parliamentary women's movement stand in stark contrast to the small-scale advances of women within the formal political system. By the 1930s there were thousands more organized women than ever before, mostly within single-sex organizations which were committed to some degree of social improvement as well as to providing congenial company, education, and entertainments. There was a considerable overlap between the more political and less political women's organizations, in terms of membership and policy, but for purposes of analysis it is helpful to separate out those organizations which were direct descendants of the women's suffrage societies from those which have been described as 'mainstream'.[34] This distinction is in itself suggestive, and became increasingly significant to contemporaries. It was certainly not anticipated by the victorious suffragists in 1918, as they planned to harness even such a large-scale 'umbrella' organization as the National Council of Women to a non-party legislative programme benefiting all women, and agreed to support Women's Citizens' Associations, if not a separate Women's Party.[35] The commitment to educating women towards active, responsible citizenship was of course shared by leading anti-suffragists, who hoped to capitalize upon the assumed conservatism of the majority of 'ordinary women'. In the early 1920s prospects seemed good for collaboration between the more conservative suffragists and the more progressive former antis, both at local level and within many national women's organizations. Yet as the most active suffragists rallied around the National Union of Societies for Equal Citizenship, successor to the National Union of Women's Suffrage Societies, many anti-suffrage women were already turning quietly back to their established activities within less politicized voluntary organizations such as the National Council of Women, the imperialist Victoria League, the Anglican women's societies, or the newly founded Women's Institutes and Townswomen's Guilds which were expanding steadily across Britain.

The history of NUSEC is largely beyond the scope of this study, but its problems from the mid-1920s onwards help to demonstrate the continuing

[34] See C. Beaumont, 'Citizens not Feminists: The Boundary Negotiated between Citizenship and Feminism by Mainstream Women's Organisations in England, 1928–1939', *Women's History Review*, 9/2 (2000), 411–29.

[35] See S. Innes, 'Constructing Women's History in the Interwar Period: The Edinburgh Women's Citizens' Associations', *Women's History Review*, 13/4 (2004), 621–47.

relevance of conservative gender ideals linked to anti-suffragism, long after that cause had been defeated. There is now a considerable historical literature on the successes and failures of 'new' and 'old' feminism between the wars, and on the relationship between the two.[36] In 1918 Eleanor Rathbone inherited Millicent Fawcett's leadership role, and over the next few years led her organization towards formulation of a programme of welfare reforms aimed primarily at improving the lives of working-class wives and mothers. Family allowances (the endowment of motherhood) and support for birth control occupied a central place in this programme of 'new feminism', despite their unpopularity with many male trade unionists, and in contrast to the 'old feminist' emphasis upon full legal equality and greater economic equality for women in the workplace. In retrospect it was always likely to be impossible to hold together the varied coalition of women who had supported the pre-war campaign for votes for women. Welfarism and egalitarianism intersected at many points, but the difference of emphasis was sufficient to divide suffragists against each other, and also to alienate many working-class women from middle-class-led, gender-based politics. After the achievement of a first raft of social legislation for women in the 1920s, NUSEC lost impetus and fragmented into a number of separate organizations with differing agendas: some committed to egalitarian feminism, others resting upon a social reform programme which was criticized by the more radical women as non-feminist and designed to reinforce conservative ideals of gender difference and domesticity. Former suffrage activists seemed increasingly out of tune with female public opinion, even on the more conservative wing of political 'feminism'. During the 1930s NUSEC and the smaller organizations formed from it went into steep decline, under the combined influences of mass unemployment; the growth of alternative, non-feminist organizations for women both inside and outside the main political parties; and other conservative social and cultural trends since characterized as an 'anti-feminist backlash'.[37] These trends included a reconfiguration of idealized domestic life, centred on the well-equipped private home and the expert housewife and mother.

Historians continue to debate whether or not the women's movement was in full-scale retreat by the 1930s. Developments within NUSEC and related suffragist organizations are open to more positive interpretation, taking fuller account of the obstacles created by unfavourable social, political, and economic circumstances as well as by a divided leadership. An inevitable, and often friendly, diversity of policies and tactics among women leaders could be a source of future strength as well as weakness. From the perspective of anti-suffrage women, the divisions among former adversaries created welcome new possibilities of

---

[36] See works cited above by Alberti, Caine, Harrison, Jones, Kingsley Kent, Law, Pederson, Pugh, Thane.
[37] The 'backlash' argument receives strong support from Kingsley Kent, *Gender and Power*, ch. 12, as well as from Pugh, *Women and the Women's Movement*, ch. 4.

constructive partnership by removing any threat of a feminist takeover of the
wider women's movement. The term feminism was in much more general use by
the post-war decades. It was often employed as a general descriptor of collective
attempts by women to improve their own lives, but had not lost its negative
connotations for many socially conservative women, including most former
antis. These women continued to believe that feminism represented aspirations
towards new, less-differentiated gender identities and changed patterns of family
life, rather than merely towards improved opportunities and living conditions
for women. Feminism was also understood to be critical of male oppression,
and therefore linked to sex antagonism. The overextended and somewhat
anachronistic use of this term by some modern historians has since become a
complicating factor in discussion of developments within the women's movement
in this period.[38] However, it is clear enough that during the inter-war period
a large number of women's organizations existed, and indeed flourished, whilst
deliberately distancing themselves from the feminist label. Before the war anti-
suffrage women had fiercely resisted the claims of suffragists, and still more
of feminists, to speak for British womanhood. An 'anti-feminist backlash' may
indeed have helped to weaken NUSEC, as the direct descendant of suffragism,
but the same social trend also helped to strengthen the relatively conservative,
mainstream organizations which had always been more attractive to anti-suffrage
and non-suffrage women.

The early chapters of this book explored some of the interconnections between
conservative gender ideals and the organized women's movement in the pre-war
decades. Many of the same women's organizations were still in existence between
the wars, holding fast to their core gender beliefs whilst successfully adapting
their activities to changed times. The National Council of Women (formerly the
NUWW) provides an interesting case study of adaptation and change, especially
given the pre-war strife over its formal commitment to suffragism.[39] The conflict
and eventual schism over the suffrage issue had been immensely distressing to
its supporters, including many suffragists as well as the defeated minority of
antis. For these women the issue at stake had been the future solidarity of
a tolerant, non-political women's movement, rather than merely the franchise
question. As the war ended, the NCW debated its prospects of influencing future
governments in women's interests, both through its own lobbying and through
the mass of female voters who were being shepherded into affiliated Women
Citizens' Associations. A careful path had to be steered between the NCW's
commitment to developing informed political participation by women citizens,
and its commitment to an inclusive, non-party-political stance. In 1918 Mrs

---

[38] For a discriminating analysis of the history of early 20th-cent. feminism, see L. Delap, *The
Feminist Avant-Garde* (Cambridge: Cambridge University Press, 2007).
[39] See Beaumont, 'Citizens not Feminists'; D. Glick, *The National Council of Women of Great
Britain: The First One Hundred Years* (London: NCW, 1995) and Ch. 3, above.

Ogilvie Gordon successfully defended her own non-political credentials as NCW President, whilst freely admitting her Conservative party links outside the NCW and devoting much of her conference address to the impact of enfranchisement upon women. In 1920 the NCW formed a joint committee with NUSEC aimed at promoting the election of more women to Parliament. At the same time the NCW was equally active in developing its support for women candidates in local government elections, and successfully perpetuated its traditional role as a hub for middle-class women's voluntary work.

There was no question of a takeover by parliamentary or party political concerns, especially as the prospects for a distinctively female impact upon Westminster quickly faded. In 1926 the NCW participated in a Hyde Park demonstration in favour of an equal parliamentary suffrage for women, but in the same year the Six Point Group (an egalitarian, 'old feminist' offshoot of NUSEC) was refused affiliation on the grounds that it was too political. The NCW was sometimes accused of political bias by its members, following its critical responses to proposed social legislation. In 1925 the government itself refused to allow women civil servants to affiliate, lest their political neutrality should be compromised. Yet the non-political basis of the NCW was by and large successfully maintained, and its inclusiveness reinforced by rule changes which marked a retreat from the strong line taken to enforce the suffragist victories in 1912 and 1913. Belatedly, and in the spirit of Louise Creighton's earlier conciliatory suggestions, an opt-out (or 'stand-aside') clause was adopted by the Council, enabling dissenting organizations to make a formal record of their viewpoint without being driven to withdraw their affiliation. This procedure proved useful when divisive issues such as divorce law reform and birth control came before the Council during the 1920s and 1930s. By 1938 the NCW had reached a total of 15,488 members, 86 branches, and 1,219 locally affiliated organizations.[40]

The largest and most long-standing affiliates of the NCW included religious women's societies such as the Mothers' Union, the Girls' Friendly Society, the Young Women's Christian Association, and the Catholic Women's League. As we saw in Chapter 3, such organizations attracted much anti-suffrage support and gave important religious sanction to gender conservatism, whilst distancing themselves from any direct participation in the suffrage fray. During the inter-war years church attendance declined and organized religion seemed often to be on the back foot, but many religious women's societies continued to expand. The Girls' Friendly Society suffered setbacks due to its inherent dependence upon outmoded social hierarchy, but the Mothers' Union carried all before

---

[40] *NCW Handbook 1937–1938* (London: NCW, 1938), 59. In 1938 the NCW had 131 nationally affiliated societies. The totals of affiliates and branches had fallen from its post-war peak, but the NCW individual membership and the membership of its largest affiliates had substantially increased.

it as it consolidated its maternal reformism and extended its imperial reach, as well as satisfying members' social and religious needs.[41] By 1939 it had 538,000 members, spread across all regions of Britain. The sanctity of marriage, responsible motherhood, and the importance of prayer remained at the heart of the Union, as it grappled with the moral implications of twentieth-century reforms related to women. Divorce, and still more abortion, were definitely taboo subjects, though birth control received some muted support from the Union. Lobbying for and against government legislation took a far larger share of the Union's attention after enfranchisement, especially at leadership level. Members could also participate as elected members of the Anglican Church's lay bodies on equal terms with men from 1919 onwards.[42] This cause had been strongly supported by Louise Creighton, who served as one of the first female representatives on the Church National Assembly, and was also backed by anti-suffragists seeking an appropriate female role in public affairs. The success of the Mothers' Union owed little or nothing to suffragism or feminism. Equally conservative, and also very successful in this period, were the YWCA, with 42,000 mainly young, working-class members by 1938; and the Catholic Women's League, with 22,000 mainly middle-class members deeply committed to opposing 'immoral' legislation such as divorce reform.[43]

The only women's organization which could rival the growth of the Mothers' Union between the wars was the Federation of Women's Institutes. Founded in 1915 by a Canadian lady who received support from the Board of Agriculture to improve British villages, the Women's Institutes soon became an indispensable adjunct to rural life.[44] Maggie Andrews has made the case for adding the WI to the firmament of feminist organizations, but not without spelling out her intention of transplanting her modern understanding of this term into an earlier era. In fact, the WI succeeded because of its inclusiveness and its avoidance of controversy, especially at local level. Anti-suffrage and non-suffrage women found a comfortable berth alongside suffragists (and some feminists) within a society which prioritized pleasant socializing alongside a mild degree of education in home-making and related matters. Like the NCW, the WI was sometimes unfairly accused of political bias at national leadership level, and incurred jealous male criticism of its single-sex status, but its national support for important legislation benefiting women did not alter its fundamentally conservative gender outlook. The WI helped to improve the morale and self-confidence of women

---

[41] See C. Moyse, 'The History of the Mothers' Union 1876–2001', unpublished manuscript, 2002.

[42] See B. Heeney, *The Women's Movement in the Church of England 1850–1930* (Oxford: Clarendon Press, 1988).

[43] Statistics are from Beaumont, 'Citizens not Feminists'.

[44] See M. Andrews, *The Acceptable Face of Feminism: The Women's Institute as a Social Movement* (London: Lawrence and Wishart, 1997); S. Goodenough, *Jam and Jerusalem* (Glasgow: Collins, 1977).

living in sometimes isolated communities, without threatening to subvert the domestic order. It is interesting to find the *Anti-Suffrage Review* reporting approvingly on the organization from its earliest days, and slightly poignant to note that Dorothy Ward sought consolation at an introductory meeting on the WI movement in the same week that the anti-suffrage cause suffered its final parliamentary defeat.[45] One of the WI's first historians was to be none other than Janet Courtney, Gertrude Bell's friend and former colleague on the executive committee of the NLOWS. Her history, published in 1933, made much of rural women's importance to the nation and their need for a voice within the organized British women's movement. Her own anti-suffrage past was clearly reflected in her jaundiced comments upon the female vote as 'a double-edged weapon of limited usefulness', involving women in 'the strife of parties' whilst denying them adequate parliamentary representation. In contrast, the WI offered 'a non-party all-embracing organisation in which the slow-speaking countrywoman, as much as her readier sisters, could make her voice heard'.[46] By 1937 the WI had 318,000 members, most of whom conformed to the not-unfriendly 'jam and Jerusalem' stereotype of local female activism dominated by regular celebrations of domesticity.[47]

A parallel organization of Townswomens' Guilds, founded in 1928, achieved a more middle-class membership of 54,000 on the eve of the Second World War. Its launch was closely linked to NUSEC and to the extension of the female franchise, but the Guild separated off from NUSEC after four years and became steadily less 'feminist' during the 1930s.[48] According to the Guild's historian, Margery Corbett Ashby decided to sideline her own political enthusiasms on becoming Guild president. She was 'very close to "ordinary" life, to the experience and feelings of women whose life-work was raising a family and caring for husband and home . . . what the majority of women were likely to want, first and foremost, was to share the interests they had in common, not battle across party or sectarian lines'. As the Guild's secretary retrospectively put it, 'We didn't want the Townswomens' Guilds to be available to people with an axe to grind. We were trying to recruit people who had not got around to serious thinking'.[49] This pragmatic approach relates closely to Janet Courtney's view of the WI, and to earlier anti-suffragist commentaries upon the apolitical (or even anti-political) outlook of the 'ordinary woman'. The aims of the non-political women's

[45] See report in the *Anti-Suffrage Review*, 91 (May 1916), 39; D. Ward diary, 17 Jan. 1918, in UCL Archives, D. Ward papers, MS Add. 202. 55.

[46] J. Courtney, *Countrywomen in Council* (Oxford: Oxford University Press, 1933), 144. She noted approvingly that the Women's Institutes 'take no narrow feminist view' (ibid. 149).

[47] It is interesting to find Pat Jacob, the National Chairman of the WI, proudly claiming 'Of course, we are still ordinary' in her introduction to Simon Goodenough's 'pictorial history of Britain's greatest women's movement', *Jam and Jerusalem* (London: Collins, 1977), 5.

[48] See M. Stott, *Organisation Woman: The Story of the National Union of Townswomen's Guilds* (London: Heinemann, 1978).

[49] Ibid. 18–19, 20–1.

organizations between the wars certainly included citizenship education and the general advancement of women's interests. However, this did not commit them to any form of feminism, as it was understood by more conservative women at the time; nor did it usually extend their political engagement beyond the minimal level of responsible voting and, at leadership level, selective lobbying of those in power. Mass support for the mainstream women's organizations apparently owed more to gender views previously advocated by the anti-suffrage movement than it did to the political leadership of former suffragists and suffragettes.

GENDER CONSERVATISM AND THE 'ORDINARY WOMAN'

The 'ordinary woman' was invoked by both sides in the suffrage campaign, first as a symbol of the advantages (or disadvantages) of votes for women and secondly as a representative of female public opinion. A conveniently malleable and overgeneralized construct, she encompassed the silent majority of women, including the poorer women who made up the bulk of the female population. Her support was therefore well worth claiming, though difficult to prove. Many suffragists made a sustained attempt to rouse working-class women's support for their cause, but the anti-suffragists were more ambivalent in their approach. Organized anti-suffragism was an overwhelmingly middle- and upper-class movement, and judged working-class women to be deeply unsuitable voters as well as indifferent or opposed to the prospect of the franchise. Class prejudice inhibited anti-suffrage efforts to muster working-class support, though such attempts were sporadically made by the women leaders. In the virtual absence of poorer women's involvement in the movement, anti-suffrage assertions that the vote would damage their lives were often made with general reference to the maternal imperative and the nation's need, rather than to more concrete details of daily experience. The views of the 'ordinary woman' remained an abstraction, and were treated by most male leaders as largely an irrelevance. On the other hand women leaders hoped to prove the reality of mass female support (or at least absence of mass female support for their opponents). Many were also determined to counter suffragist welfare campaigns with their own maternal reform programme, which required some understanding of women's attitudes as well as of their needs. For these reasons the records of organized anti-suffragism do include a small amount of evidence on the gender outlook of working-class women, as it related to the suffrage issue. This rather sparse evidence can be supplemented from the impressive research into working-class women's lives undertaken by various modern historians.[50] Most 'ordinary women' were

---

[50] e.g. J. Bourke, *Working Class Cultures in Britain 1890–1960* (London: Routledge, 1994); C. Chinn, *They Worked All Their Lives: Women of the Urban Poor in England 1880–1939* (Manchester:

working class, but the concept was often extended to include lower-middle-class women; sometimes its compass included all those women who chose to stand aside from public debate. The gender views of these largely unorganized women remain elusive, but social and cultural historians have again been at work, piecing together varied evidence which supports the general conclusion that most 'ordinary women' from all social classes were eager to prioritize the claims of domesticity and family life above those of paid employment and political activism. What is more, this was probably becoming more, rather than less, true during the first twenty years of parliamentary votes for women.

Turning first to direct evidence from anti-suffrage sources, we find the women antis testing out pre-war female opinion in a number of different contexts. In the first issue of the *Anti-Suffrage Review* Ethel Harrison claimed to have found 'all the working women on our side' whilst canvassing for petition signatures in her Kent village.[51] Later reports on the petition sometimes emphasized the presence of working-class women's support: for example, John Massie boasted to the House of Commons that its signatories included 'authors, journalists, secretaries, school-mistresses, from the Universities to elementary schools, farmers, shopkeepers, typists, clerks, domestic servants, mill hands, shop assistants, fishwives, coastguards' wives, soldiers' and sailors' wives, charwomen, caretakers, and many others'.[52] The April 1909 edition of the *Review* gleefully reported the same information, in response to a suffragist attack on the upper-class composition of the WNASL, claiming proof that 'The last thing which the women workers desired was to see the Government of the country entrusted to themselves and their sisters'.[53] Another pleasing propaganda coup was achieved when suffragist claims of support from 'all the wardresses in Holloway' were tested out by a League member, and 68 out of 72 wardresses agreed to sign the anti-suffrage petition.[54] The first Annual Council Meeting of the WNASL received a resolution from the Chelsea branch asking for suggestions 'as to the means of getting really into touch with working people, to educate them'.[55]

Manchester University Press, 1985); A. Davin, *Growing Up Poor: Home, School and Street in London 1870–1914* (London: Rivers Oram Press, 1996); J. Giles, *Women. Identity and Private Life in Britain 1900–1950* (Basingstoke: Macmillan, 1995); J. Lewis (ed.), *Labour and Love: Women's Experience of Home and Family 1850–1940* (Oxford: Basil Blackwell, 1986); J. Liddington, and J. Norris, *One Hand Tied Behind Us* (London: Virago, 1978); E. Roberts, *A Woman's Place: An Oral History of Working Class Women 1890–1940* (Oxford: Basil Blackwell, 1984).

[51] *Anti-Suffrage Review*, 1 (Dec. 1908), 7. Ethel Harrison contrasted working-class women's strong support for anti-suffragism with false suffragist claims; suffragism was not a working class movement: 'if it *were*, our task would be infinitely harder'.

[52] *Anti-Suffrage Review*, 8 (July 1909), 3. Working-class women's support was also emphasized by several speakers when a formal anti-suffrage deputation visited the Prime Minister in June 1910. *Anti-Suffrage Review*, 20 (July 1910), 4.

[53] *Anti-Suffrage Review*, 5 (Apr. 1909), 3.   [54] Ibid.

[55] *Anti-Suffrage Review*, 8 (July 1909), 5. Miss Mary Backhouse commented that 'in her opinion cottagers were practically all for Anti-Suffrage'; Lady Jersey invited other ladies to share their relevant experience through the League office.

At least two of the early leaflets from the Women's League were subsequently aimed at working-class women.[56] These provide some hint of the anti-suffrage arguments which were expected to appeal to such women: centred, of course, on the primacy of home duties and on a woman's pride in devoting herself to these without the distractions of male politics. A vivid sketch of working-class attitudes appeared on the front page of the *Review* in January 1909. 'House to house canvassing among the poor' included a doorstep exchange in which the canvasser was wrongly identified as a suffragist: 'a darkly suspicious look comes over the face, and the door begins to close'. However, a short, clear explanation soon set matters right: ' "It is for women—who *don't*—want votes. Do you want a vote?" "Not me!" . . . then I am invited in, and asked to sit down while the opinion of another woman worker starts on its journey to the Government'.[57]

Some working-class women, it appears, expressed active hostility to suffragism as soon as they were given a chance. However, many more were simply indifferent to the issue. This was a less satisfying, but still reasonably satisfactory, outcome for anti-suffrage canvassers anxious to counter suffragist claims of support. The fullest descriptions of anti-suffrage canvassing in a working-class district were produced by Dorothy Ward during Miss Willoughby's hopeless campaign in the Hoxton LCC election of March 1913. Spurred on by her mother's Local Government Advancement Committee, Dorothy spent several uncomfortable weeks tramping much less inviting territory than Ethel Harrison's Kent village. Her report for the *Review* was determinedly upbeat, again emphasizing the unpopularity of suffragism among women on the doorstep. However, her overwhelming impression was of 'the degraded and degrading poverty of some of those streets, those little courts and alleys in which Hoxton abounds! The dirt, the miserable condition of some even of the big blocks of dwellings; the swarming masses of children'.[58] Some of the canvassing, she confessed privately, had produced 'rather extra poor results',[59] and the experiment was not repeated. Dorothy found a kinder reception at meetings of 'ordinary' women in her Hertfordshire home constituency,[60] but prospects were never good for enlisting working-class women as active League members. The League struggled in its northern recruitment campaigns, and even the largest branches in Kensington, Berkshire and Bristol seem to have been almost entirely middle class. Anti-suffrage outdoor campaigns in Scotland and Wales reached large, friendly working-class audiences, both male and female, but with very limited branch-building results.[61] Only in Oxford

[56] *Votes and Wages*, WNASL leaflet No. 3, Women's Library anti-suffrage leaflets; *A Word to Working Women*, advertised at 2s. 6d. per 1,000 in *Anti-Suffrage Review*, 13 (Dec. 1909), 8.

[57] *Anti-Suffrage Review*, 2 (Jan. 1909), 1.   [58] *Anti-Suffrage Review*, 54 (Apr. 1913), 79.

[59] Dorothy Ward diary, 28 Feb. 1913. D. Ward papers, MS Add. 202.49.

[60] e.g. an afternoon meeting in Berkhamsted on 26 Feb. was 'very much "worthwhile"—quite 70 working women, of Miss Hyrom's Anti-Suffrage branch . . . they *were* so candid and interested'. D. Ward diary, 26 Feb. 1913. D. Ward papers, MS Add. 202.49.

[61] See Chs. 7 and 8, above, on branch-building by the WNASL and the NLOWS.

does house-to-house canvassing seem to have resulted in some measurable success in poorer areas; 147 associate members were signed up at a reduced fee in 1909, though it seems doubtful that they joined meetings held at the heart of the university.[62]

In July 1910 Gladys Pott was reported as having given 'a series of lectures to working women to discuss various controversial points'.[63] During 1912 the indefatigable Mrs Gladstone Solomon addressed 'a large and interested audience of working women' in Berkhamsted: 'the resolution against Woman Suffrage was passed unanimously, and all those who did not already belong to the League (eleven in number) joined'.[64] Despite the fact that the project of recruiting a socially mixed membership soon faded as an ambition for the Women's League, its leaders remained deeply convinced of their passive support among 'ordinary women'. Mrs Greatbatch explained this viewpoint at the second Annual Council Meeting: 'They stoutly maintained that the bulk of women throughout the country did not want the vote. Nine-tenths of the women of the country were utterly indifferent to the whole franchise question, and would be thankful to be allowed to remain indifferent. To many of them the idea of the vote was repugnant. It was as unwise as it was unnecessary.'[65] Her elision of passive and active supporters represented an important plank of the anti-suffrage platform, and was probably the best case that could be made for mass female anti-suffragism.

The range of evidence gathered by modern historians seems to confirm the view that the 'ordinary woman' had little interest in the vote before the war, and only limited interest once it had been finally placed in her hand.[66] Organized anti-suffragism made only a minimal contribution towards this state of affairs, but could plausibly claim that lack of female support for the vote strengthened the pre-war case against enfranchisement. The widespread persistence of entrenched gender differences after the First World War was a welcome relief to many former anti-suffragists. It confirmed their faith in the 'natural' distinction between male and female citizenship, whilst at the same time disproving earlier alarmism over the disruptive threat of votes for women. The historical evidence shows that poorer working-class women lived lives severely constricted by lack of money,

---

[62] Annual Report of WNASL Oxford Branch 1909–10, Bodl.: 'After the Long Vacation, a series of small Cottage Meetings were held in various districts of Oxford, at which members of the committee gave informal addresses to the wives of working men . . . Many associates have been enrolled at these meetings, which it is hoped will be continued as opportunity offers'. The associates contributed 10s. 6d. in subscriptions, compared to £16. 0s. 4d. from an almost equal number of full members in the same year.

[63] *Anti-Suffrage Review*, 20 (July 1910), 8.   [64] *Anti-Suffrage Review*, 47 (Sept. 1912), 220.

[65] *Anti-Suffrage Review*, 20 (July 1910), 9.

[66] See Roberts, *A Woman's Place*, 2, and conclusion. Out of 160 elderly people interviewed in Barrow, Lancaster and Preston, only two expressed support for suffragism. Most women expressed 'indifference, with a feeling that this particular movement was not theirs and did not represent their particular needs or interests'. Moreover, such political indifference persisted among family-centred working-class women until the Second World War.

time, and space as well as by lack of education and a narrow gender outlook.[67] Employment opportunities remained limited for married women burdened by the heavy demands of caring for inconvenient homes and over-large families. In these circumstances, the male breadwinner model of family life seemed inevitable, and even desirable. Its widespread acceptability among women as well as men was inextricably tied into gendered notions of social respectability and working-class conformity. The evidence of contemporary social investigators, of working-class autobiographers and of oral history underlines the centrality of mothers to poor families' very existence, as well as to their social status and emotional well-being.[68] Working-class women's power in their own homes should not be underestimated, however limited their political ambitions. Though valid generalization is difficult, several historians have built up an impressive picture of working-class matriarchy at work in urban communities, controlling family expenditure and social norms in equal measure. What is more, important continuities in working-class lifestyles and attitudes extended across the First World War, undisturbed by the advent of female democracy and by a slow rise in living standards.[69] During the inter-war years politicians from all parties were to be found adapting their rhetoric to the home-and-hearth values of their constituents, as huge numbers of middle-class as well as working-class women chose to link their aspirations to evolving domesticity and associated gender conservatism.

The 'ordinary woman' was a political and media invention, but she deserves to be taken as seriously by historians as she was by contemporaries. Anti-suffrage women were guilty of wishful thinking when they asked working-class housewives to provide active support for organized opposition to the vote. However, they were not unrealistic in assuming that unambitious women preoccupied with raising their own families may often have shared some version of the anti-suffragists' high regard for women's distinctive social role, and have valued this above any direct participation in the masculine game of parliamentary politics. Resistance or indifference to voting could represent pride in feminine priorities, as well as reflecting the demands of poorer women's overburdened lifestyles.

---

[67] See esp. the evidence provided by female social investigators: F. Bell, *At the Works* (1907; London: Virago, 1985); M. Llewellyn Davies (ed.), *Maternity: Letters from Working Women* (1915; London: Virago, 1978); M. Pember Reeves, *Round About A Pound A Week* (1913; London: Virago, 1979); M. Spring Rice, *Working Class Wives: Their Health and Conditions* (London: Penguin, 1939).

[68] See esp. the evidence of autobiographers: G. Foakes, *Between High Walls: A London Childhood* (London: Shepheard-Walwyn Ltd., 1972); A. Jasper, *A Hoxton Childhood* (London: Cresset Press, 1969); R. Roberts, *The Classic Slum: Salford Life in the First Quarter of the Century* (Manchester: Manchester University Press, 1971); D. Scannell, *Mother Knew Best: An East End Childhood* (London: Macmillan, 1974). See also the wider evidence provided by Chinn, *They Worked All Their Lives*; Ross, *Love and Toil*; Davin, *Growing Up Poor*; and by all the social investigators, above.

[69] It is notable that social and cultural historians, in contrast to many political counterparts, have frequently chosen to periodize across the First World War and up to the Second: e.g. Chinn, *They Worked All Their Lives*; Giles, *Women, Identity and Private Life*; Lewis, *Labour and Love*; S. Oldfield, *This Working Day World: Women's Lives and Culture(s) in Britain 1914–1945* (London: Taylor and Francis, 1994); Roberts, *A Woman's Place*.

Large numbers of women in inter-war Britain did eventually make the leap of political faith required to link female suffrage, political party membership, and even entry into Parliament into their personal dreams of a better life; yet millions did not. Anti-suffragism was at its most convincing as a reflection of this fundamental lack of political conviction. The female anti-suffrage leaders did not represent (or influence) the 'ordinary woman' in any true sense. But their views, for all their anti-democratic elitism and maternal condescension, did resonate with some of her most basic gender prejudices.

WOMEN AGAINST THE VOTE: SOME CONCLUSIONS

Women's organized opposition to the parliamentary vote ended in 1918, yet it is clear that many of the beliefs and attitudes which had motivated this opposition survived into the inter-war years and beyond. From this longer-term perspective, it is now necessary to re-evaluate women's contribution to the anti-suffrage campaign and to reposition it in relation to the suffrage movement and the organized women's movement in Britain. The female antis deserve greater prominence within the history of women's political activism. As self-appointed spokeswomen for gender conservatism, they also merit recognition within wider British social and cultural history.

The anti-suffrage campaign has previously been analysed mainly from the perspective of its male leaders, and in the context of parliamentary debates. Analysis from the perspective of women leaders and supporters is still in its early stages, but already offers fresh insights into the nature of the campaign as a whole. A close study of the leading women helps us to understand their distinctive view of the suffrage issue in conjunction with other aspects of their lives. The narrow question of the vote was rarely the main driving force behind these women's often reluctant engagement with national politics. As the early chapters of this book demonstrated, the women who converged in their opposition to the vote were already connected to each other, and sometimes also to the leading men, through ideas and social networks arising from other causes. In this sense anti-suffragism was always a social as well as a political movement, and it was always a movement of women as well as of men. The most active and influential female leaders were deeply committed to ideals of maternal social reform. They engaged in a wide variety of philanthropic work which had usually originated in an (often religious) commitment to individual charity, but grew to encompass the collective, gendered voluntarism of middle-class women's social action, and eventually edged closer to national and local government too. Suffrage and anti-suffrage women combined to help open up new opportunities in relation to the improvement of women's education. They then pressed forward together in pursuit of other social reforms aimed at improving the lives of women and children from all social classes. Civic maternalism, which enhanced responsibilities for women as citizens as well as social carers, was widely embraced by women on both sides of the suffrage divide. Female alliances established through joint social action expanded rapidly in the late Victorian period, and proved strong enough to survive the strains imposed by the final decade of the suffrage campaign.

Another significant source of female influence within the anti-suffrage campaign was the work of women writers, some of whom were also social reformers. Though most of these writers resisted direct involvement in collective political action, they offered continuous support to the movement through their published journalism and fiction. For each anti-suffrage woman novelist there were many thousands of anti-suffrage women readers, using books and magazines to explore and express their views on gender relations, family life, and female morality. Female anti-suffragism could scarcely have found a more effective means of publicly developing its sexual politics. Women antis who turned to the weighty periodical press to denounce the perils of suffragism found a receptive audience whose reasoned views on the Woman Question had been reinforced by popular literature fostering the popular prejudices of both sexes in favour of manly men and womanly women.

Ideas linked to social evolutionism found indirect expression in fiction, as well as in the work of both male and female social commentators. At the beginning of the twentieth century anti-suffragism was ploughing fertile territory when it dwelt upon the threat of mutating gender roles to the future of the family, the nation, and the empire. The relationship between private sexual anxiety, public gender debate, and uncertainty over Britain's future world status has received much historical attention in recent years. Anti-suffragism positioned itself at the heart of these linked concerns. Despite the inhibitions imposed by social convention, women antis felt it their particular responsibility to bring home to their fellow women the true perils of feminism. This perjorative label was used to condemn the more radical end of the spectrum of suffragist opinions, and was linked to the sexual dangers of promiscuity, sexual inversion, and 'sex war'. The most outspoken opponents of feminism within the anti-suffrage movement were also leading imperialists. The role of male imperialists within the movement is well documented, and can now be supplemented by a fuller understanding of the ideas and actions of a range of anti-feminist female imperialists, many of whom were also active as writers and maternal reformers. The Edwardian female imperialist associations provided another site for suffragist and anti-suffragist collaboration in a common cause; but the commitment of some leading anti-suffrage women to these associations was as strongly linked to their anti-feminism as to their benign imperialist vision of maternal reform.

The women leaders' contribution to the anti-suffrage movement was a diverse one. Overlapping networks of maternal reformers, women writers, and female imperialists have been identified for purposes of analysis, but this configuration hardly does justice to the diversity of ideas and motivation which becomes apparent from a closer study of individuals. Recent revisionist work on the suffrage movement has highlighted the role of varied personal and political experience in shaping individual participation; the importance of local and regional variation; and the complexity and shifting nature of a suffragist coalition which collaborated and feuded over the years. Anti-suffrage women merit the same detailed analysis, drawing upon their life histories and exploring their ideas as well as identifying their organizational contributions to the movement. This is more easily achieved for well-known, outspoken women than for those conservative and conventional anti-suffragists who prided themselves upon their lack of political self-assertion, even in the cause of opposing votes for women. The leaders of organized anti-suffragism included a number of highly conservative women, some of whom were forceful individuals. The divergence between the 'negatives' (as Lady Jersey called them) and the more progressive women anti-suffragists has received some attention in this book. The greater eloquence of the latter is reflected in the balance of coverage. An imbalance in favour of the more progressive women is justified by the importance of their organizational role in the anti-suffrage movement, as well as by the distinctive and interesting nature of their political ideas. The presence of ultra-conservative women in the anti-suffrage Leagues was a source of satisfaction to male leaders uncertain of their authority in the face of stubborn female criticism. It illustrated the important fact that many anti-suffrage women were only too happy to defer to male authority, both in private and in public life. For this reason, as well as many others, women's opposition to female suffrage cannot be studied in isolation from the men's movement. The present book consciously set out to redress the gender balance. It should now be read alongside the older histories focused upon male campaigners, and eventually integrated within a more comprehensive revision of anti-suffrage and wider anti-feminist history.

Mary Ward took the lead in advocating a more positive stance for female anti-suffragism, but she did not act alone. Her vision of an alternative female citizenship, based upon differentiated political structures at national level as well as upon an expansion of women's role in local government, was shared with an important group of colleagues within the Edwardian anti-suffrage Leagues. Progressive anti-suffragists made various practical suggestions to support their theoretical viewpoint. These included proposals for a separate Women's Chamber, a Ministry for Women, or a standing Joint Advisory Committee bringing together women's representatives and Members of Parliament on a non-political basis. Other suggestions sought to enlarge the sphere of local government as well as to increase female participation, possibly by linking regional self-government in Britain to the development of federal government across a more united empire. All these proposals aimed to provide an appropriately gendered setting for women's influential participation in public life.

Far from desiring a total separation of public and private spheres, the 'forward' anti-suffragists hoped to see a more productive integration between women's specialized work, centred upon their families and local communities, and the functions of national government. This aspiration was of little or no interest to the male leaders of the NLOWS, and has subsequently received scant attention from historians. Yet modern political theorists have demonstrated the continuing need for research into the inadequacies of 'gender-blind' democracy as a route to women's full participation in public affairs. Carole Pateman, Ruth Lister, and Joni Lovenduski have recently analysed the reasons why, many decades later, female enfranchisement has still failed to deliver genuine political equality for women, concluding that women continue to be disadvantaged both by social obstacles and by institutional barriers.[70] The setbacks experienced by early women MPs were the inevitable result of a 'deeply embedded culture of masculinity' within the British Parliament, and have been perpetuated to some extent into the twenty-first century.[71] The latest major survey of women's overall participation in British politics found that in 2004 women remained 'less active in formal politics than men as well as being less interested in national politics';[72] on the other hand this 'activism gap' disappeared in relation to informal, 'cause-oriented' politics and voting in local elections.[73] Perhaps the time has come to revisit the female anti-suffragists' prediction that egalitarian democracy would prove a disappointment to women who valued their own distinctive contribution to national life. Their search for alternatives was purely speculative, but far from irrelevant to political realities.

The women leaders' contributions towards organized opposition to the vote have been examined in some detail in this book. No attempt has been made to replicate the detailed research into the world of (male) parliamentary anti-suffragism undertaken by earlier historians, but a fuller account of the extra-parliamentary dimensions of the movement, with a focus upon women's role, must inevitably somewhat alter our view of the anti-suffrage movement as a whole. The famous 1889 Appeal Against Women's Suffrage was no mere put-up job, undertaken by women at the behest of men. Neither did female anti-suffragism grind to a halt in the following two decades, though it found mainly indirect public expression. There is no longer any justification for eliding the histories of the WNASL and the NLOWS, in the process diminishing the role of women as leaders, administrators, and members of both organizations. Without

---

[70] See C. Pateman, *The Disorder of Women* (Cambridge: Polity Press, 1989); R. Lister, *Citizenship: Feminist Perspectives* (Basingstoke: Macmillan, 1997); J. Lovenduski, *Feminizing Politics* (Cambridge: Polity Press, 2005).

[71] Lovenduski, *Feminizing Politics*, 48.

[72] The Electoral Commission, *Gender and Political Participation* (London: The Electoral Commission, 2004), 53.

[73] Ibid. The Electoral Commission concluded that 'using local campaigns may motivate women to become more involved generally' (ibid. 65). Patricia Hollis had already concluded in 1987 that 'the most effective way of strengthening women's participation in politics may be to devolve power to where women are, that is to local government, rather than to seek to bring women to where power currently resides, at Westminster'; she also conjured with the view that 'Local government could do far more and central government far less if we so chose'. Hollis, *Ladies Elect*, 484.

contesting that Parliament held the ultimate power of decision over the female franchise, it can be concluded that women were always at the heart of organized anti-suffragism.

The WNASL was an almost entirely female organization, at every level. Though it suffers by comparison with the growth rates and dedicated commitment of the suffrage movement in the same period, its achievements in launching a network of national branches, as well as an ongoing propaganda campaign, were far from negligible. The NLOWS was dominated by its distinguished male leaders, especially the imperial proconsuls Cromer and Curzon, but behind the scenes the former leaders of the WNASL put up a spirited defence of their position and also made a sustained attempt to incorporate their 'forward' ideas into the new organization. Records of the difficult relationship between male and female leaders provide a ringside view of unexpected conflict among gender conservatives who had everything to gain from public displays of harmonious unity. Clearly, disagreements were rooted in differing views of the optimum roles for men and women in public life. Though personality clashes did occur, they were insufficient to explain the depth of frustration experienced by men and women ostensibly committed to a shared cause. By 1914 women leaders were on the retreat within the NLOWS, and the organization was suffering a loss of dynamism related to this factor as well as to its parliamentary setbacks. However, the League's membership remained overwhelmingly female. During the war anti-suffrage women turned their energies to other, more immediate causes. But organized support for anti-suffragism in the country did not entirely disappear and last-ditch efforts by the women leaders to resist enfranchisement in 1917–18 centred upon one final attempt to demonstrate, through a petition and proposed referendum, that the female majority still rejected votes for women.

The women's anti-suffrage movement was ultimately inseparable from male support and from the parliamentary cause. This was accepted by all the female leaders, and indeed welcomed as a manifestation of their wider faith in the complementary gender roles of men and women. However, acceptance of female dependency upon men in some political contexts did not translate into a rejection of single-sex organization for more exclusively feminine purposes. As we have seen, women's social action was often distinctively gendered in practice as well as in motivation. This reflected the current realities of conventional middle- and upper-class female lifestyles, as well as embodying aspirations towards feminine ideals and 'womanly' work. Female anti-suffragism was a women's social cause, as well as an important adjunct of a male political campaign. In this guise, it is not surprising to find that it sought, and usually found, acceptance within the gender-conscious network of female organizations which together constituted the British women's movement.

The National Union of Women Workers (National Council of Women) represented most fully the breadth and diversity of late nineteenth- and early twentieth-century women's voluntarism. For this reason suffragists were keen to enlist its formal support. Their eventual success in doing so was a severe blow for female anti-suffragism, but did not prevent the antis from continuing to play a major part within many affiliated organizations and some NUWW branches. After the war the National Council of Women made a conscious effort to restore its commitment towards inclusive, non-political representation of the full range of women's voluntary organizations. As we have seen, the inter-war growth of these organizations owed more to a widespread acceptance of conservative views on women's role in the family and the home than it did to any collective desire for radical reform. Further research is still needed into the largest and least politicized twentieth-century women's associations, from the perspectives of contemporary social conservatism rather than those of modern feminism. Organized female anti-suffragism was no longer a factor in the inter-war years; but the non-political women's organizations drew upon its former supporters as well as inheriting aspects of anti-suffrage gender ideology. The undemanding conservatism of the inter-war women's organizations helped to realign the boundaries between organized and unorganized womanhood. More women than ever before became involved in associational activity. Their chosen forms of organization went some way towards substantiating long-standing anti-suffrage claims about what women really wanted and needed from their lives. At the same time, the carefully targeted political lobbying of these organizations perpetuated older traditions of feminine political influence which did not depend upon the still largely masculine game of party politics, nor upon women's presence in Parliament. Despite underlying changes in the demographic and economic basis of female gender roles, and the cultural challenges posed by a new generation of modernist women writers and other social thinkers, former anti-suffragists were reassured by the continuities in gender attitudes apparent within the mainstream women's organizations between the wars.

The history of the British women's movement is gradually becoming more securely grounded in its wider social and political context, as historians move beyond celebratory accounts of female achievement and discussion of its significance for modern feminism. The suffrage movement is likely to retain its historical status as one of the defining features of the nineteenth- and twentieth-century historical landscape, yet suffragism no longer stands in lonely eminence and looks less and less monolithic. A detailed study of women's role as opponents as well as supporters of the female franchise confirms the integration of suffragism and anti-suffragism within a wider British women's movement, whilst also illustrating the interdependence of men and women within the anti-suffrage movement itself. Women opposed the vote for many of the same reasons as men, and often turned to men for an authoritative exposition of their cause. At the same time many anti-suffrage women remained deeply immersed in womanly work which continuously reinforced their links to their suffrage opponents. This did not make them into feminists, in any sense which they themselves would have been prepared to accept. On the contrary, feminism remained the most dangerous enemy of the female conservatism which the anti-suffrage movement embodied. Women antis sometimes joined with the more conservative suffragists in deploring the divisive impact of the suffrage campaign. A full resumption of collaborative work to advance the interests of women was eagerly anticipated as the campaign drew to a close, and was in fact swiftly achieved. This shows that the histories of suffragism and of female anti-suffragism were very much closer to each other than has often been assumed. Conservative suffragists and progressive anti-suffragists met on the common ground of a maternalist, patriotic, and mainly middle-class women's movement. Rather than being opposites, they should be reconceptualized as connecting facets of a many-sided debate over ideal gender roles, current social changes, and related forms of women's citizenship.

The contribution of male thinkers and a minority of male supporters to the suffrage movement has recently received due acknowledgement. It is now time to restore the anti-suffrage women to their due place in history, as thinkers and activists as well as passive supporters of the masculine campaign against the vote. Theirs was a majority role within the organized anti-suffrage movement, and their fundamental gender outlook was widely supported by women at every social level. From a longer-term perspective, it is apparent that these women's sturdy defence of gender difference was also far from irrelevant to later generations. Organized anti-suffragism plainly failed to hold back the advance of democracy, but it did succeed in giving voice to important currents of conservative opinion in the late nineteenth and early twentieth centuries. The rediscovery of women against the vote forms part of a broader project to restore neglected conservative dimensions to British women's history.

Bibliography

INDIVIDUALS' PAPERS

Gertrude Bell (University of Newcastle Library)
James Bryce (Bodleian Library, Oxford)
Beatrice Chamberlain (University of Birmingham Library)
Louise Creighton (Lambeth Palace Library, London)
Evelyn Baring/Lord Cromer (National Archives, London)
George Curzon (British Library, London)
Ethel Harrison (British Library of Political and Economic Sciences (BLPES), London School of Economics (LSE))
Frederic Harrison (BLPES, LSE)
Margaret Jersey (London Metropolitan Archives)
Violet Markham (BLPES, LSE)
Dorothy Ward (University College London Archives)
Mary Ward (Pusey House Library, Oxford)
Elizabeth Wordsworth (Lady Margaret Hall, Oxford)

ORGANISATIONAL RECORDS

Church Congress (Lambeth Palace)
Church League for Women's Suffrage (Women's Library, London)
Female Emigration Societies (Women's Library)
Gerritsen Collection—American suffrage and anti-suffrage on-line archive (British Library)
Girls' Friendly Society (GFS, London)
London Society for Women's Suffrage (Women's Library, London)
Men's League for Opposing Woman's Suffrage (Women's Library)
Mothers' Union (Mothers' Union and British Library, London)
National League for Opposing Woman's Suffrage (Bodleian Library)
National Union of Women Workers/National Council of Women (London Metropolitan Archive, BLPES)
Victoria League (Victoria League, London)
Women's National Anti-Suffrage League (Women's Library)

NEWSPAPERS AND JOURNALS

Anti-Suffrage Review
Contemporary Review
Fortnightly Review
Friendly Words
Friendly Leaves
Mothers in Council

National Review
Nineteenth Century
Occasional Paper (NUWW)
Positivist Review
Quarterly Review
The Times
United Empire
Victoria League Notes

Newspaper cuttings collection in NLOWS scrapbooks, Bodleian Library, Oxford (includes extensive range of national and provincial press, 1909–15)

BOOKS AND ARTICLES

Abrams, L., *The Making of Modern Woman* (London: Longman, 2002).

Adams, P., *Somerville for Women: An Oxford Women's College 1879–1973* (Oxford: Oxford University Press, 1996).

Alberti, J., *Beyond Suffrage: Feminists in War and Peace, 1914–1928* (Basingstoke: Macmillan, 1989).

Anderson, O., 'The Feminism of T. H. Green: A Late-Victorian Success Story?', *History of Political Thought*, 12/4 (1991), 671–93.

Andrew, A., 'The Great Ornamentals: New Viceregal Women and their Imperial Work 1884–1914', D.Phil. thesis (University of Western Sydney, 2004).

Andrews, M., *The Acceptable Face of Feminism: The Women's Institute as a Social Movement* (London: Lawrence and Wishart, 1997).

Ardis, A., *New Women, New Novels: Feminism and Early Modernism* (New Brunswick: Rutgers University Press, 1990).

Atholl, K., *Women and Politics* (London: Philip Allan, 1931).

——— *Working Partnership* (London: Arthur Baker, 1958).

Bailey, G. (ed.), *Lady Margaret Hall: A Short History* (London: Oxford University Press, 1923).

Bartley, P., *Prostitution: Prevention and Reform in England, 1860–1914* (London: Routledge, 2000).

Battiscombe, G., *Reluctant Pioneer: A Life of Elizabeth Wordsworth* (London: Constable, 1978).

Beaumont, C., 'Citizens not Feminists: The Boundary Negotiated between Citizenship and Feminism by Mainstream Women's Organisations in England, 1928–1939', *Women's History Review*, 9/2 (2000), 411–29.

Beetham, M., *A Magazine of Her Own? Domesticity and Desire in the Woman's Magazine 1800–1914* (London: Routledge, 1996).

——— and Boardman, K. (eds.), *Victorian Women's Magazines* (Manchester: Manchester University Press, 2001).

Bell, F., *At the Works* (1907; London: Virago Press, 1985).

Bell, G., *Syria: The Desert and the Sown* (London: Heinemann, 1908).

——— *Amurath to Amurath* (London: Heinemann, 1911).

——— *The Letters of Gertrude Bell*, ed. Lady F. Bell (London: Ernest Benn Ltd., 1927).

——— *The Earlier Letters of Gertrude Bell*, ed. E. Richmond, (London: Ernest Benn Ltd., 1937).

Bentley, M., and Stevenson, J. (eds.), *High and Low Politics in Modern Britain* (Oxford: Clarendon Press, 1983).

Betts, R., 'Included or Excluded? Elizabeth Burgwin on the NUET/NUT Executive 1885–96', *Journal of Educational Administration and History*, 34/2 (2002), 106–14.

Bernard, H. and M., *Woman and Evolution* (London: Frank Palmer, 1909).

Birch, D. (ed.), *Ruskin and Gender* (Basingstoke: Palgrave, 2002).

Birkett, D., *Mary Kingsley, Imperial Adventuress* (London: Macmillan, 1992).

——— *Spinsters Abroad: Victorian Lady Explorers* (Stroud: Sutton Publishing, 2004 edn.).

Bland, L., *Banishing the Beast: English Feminism and Sexual Morality 1885–1914* (London: Penguin Books, 1995).

Bock, G., and Thane, P., *Maternity and Gender Policies: Women and the Rise of the European Welfare States 1880s–1950s* (London: Routledge, 1991).

Bolt, C., *The Women's Movements in the United States and Britain from the 1790s to the 1920s* (Hemel Hempstead: Harvester Wheatsheaf, 1993).

Bourke, J., *Working Class Cultures in Britain 1890–1960* (London: Routledge, 1994).

Boyd, C. (ed.), *Mr Chamberlain's Speeches* (London: Constable, 1914).

Brandon, R., *The New Women and the Old Men: Love, Sex and the Woman Question* (London: Flamingo, 1991).

Braybon, G., *Women Workers in the First World War* (London: Croom Helm, 1981).

——— and Summerfield, P., *Out of the Cage: Women's Experiences in Two World Wars* (London: Pandora, 1987).

Brittain, V., *The Women at Oxford: A Fragment of History* (London: George Harrap and Co., 1960).

Brivati, B., and Heffernan, R. (eds.), *The Labour Party: A Centenary History* (Basingstoke: Macmillan, 2000).

Brock, M., and Curthoys, M. (eds.), *The History of the University of Oxford, vii. Nineteenth-Century Oxford* (Oxford: Clarendon Press, 2000).

Burdett-Coutts, A. (ed.), *Woman's Mission* (London: Samson, Low, Marston and Co., 1893).

Burgoyne, E., *Gertrude Bell from Her Personal Papers 1889–1914* (London: Ernest Benn Ltd., 1958).

Burton, A., *Burdens of History: British Feminists, Indian Women, and Imperial Culture, 1865–1915* (Chapel Hill: University of North Carolina Press, 1994).

Bush, J., *Edwardian Ladies and Imperial Power* (London: Leicester University Press, 2000).

——— 'British Women's Anti-Suffragism and the Forward Policy, 1908–1914', *Women's History Review*, 11/3 (2002), 431–54.

——— ' "Special strengths for their own special duties": Women, Higher Education and Gender Conservatism in Late Victorian Britain', *History of Education*, 34/4 (July 2005), 387–405.

——— 'The National Union of Women Workers and Women's Suffrage', in M. Boussahba-Bravard (ed.), *Suffrage Outside Suffragism* (London: Palgrave, 2007).

Caine, B., 'Beatrice Webb and the "Woman Question" ', *History Workshop*, 14 (1982), 23–43.

——— *Destined to be Wives: The Sisters of Beatrice Webb* (Oxford: Clarendon Press, 1986).

——— *Victorian Feminists* (Oxford: Oxford University Press, 1992).

——— *English Feminism 1780–1980* (Oxford: Oxford University Press, 1997).

——— *Bombay to Bloomsbury: A Biography of the Strachey Family* (Oxford: Oxford University Press, 2005).

Caird, M., *The Daughters of Danaus* (1894; New York: Feminist Press, 1989).

Callan, H., and Ardener, S. (eds.), *The Incorporated Wife* (London: Croom Helm, 1984).

Camhi, J., *Women Against Women: American Anti-Suffragism 1880–1920* (New York: Carlson, 1994).

Cannadine, D., *Aspects of Aristocracy* (London: Penguin, 1995).

—— *The Decline and Fall of the British Aristocracy* (London: Macmillan, 1996 edn.).

Chase, Beatrice, 'Woman's "Emancipation" (By one who does not want it)' (*c.*1912).

Chaudhuri, N., and Strobel, M. (eds.), *Western Women and Imperialism: Complicity and Resistance* (Bloomington: Indiana University Press, 1992).

Chinn, C., *They Worked All Their Lives: Women of the Urban poor in England 1880–1939* (Manchester: Manchester University Press, 1985).

Coleridge, C., *The Daughters Who Have Not Revolted* (London: Wells Gardner and Co., 1894).

Colley, L., *Britons: Forging the Nation 1717–1837* (New Haven: Yale University Press, 1992).

Colquhoun, E., *Two on Their Travels* (London: William Heinemann, 1902).

—— *The Vocation of Woman* (London: Macmillan, 1913).

Corelli, M., *The Sorrows of Satan* (1895; Oxford: Oxford University Press, 1998).

—— *Free Opinions Freely Expressed on Certain Phases of Modern Social Life and Conduct* (London: Archibald Constable and Co., 1905).

—— *Woman, or Suffragette? A Question of National Choice* (London: C. Arthur Pearson Ltd., 1907).

—— *Innocent—Her Fancy and His Fact* (London: Hodder and Stoughton, 1914).

Coleridge, C., *Charlotte Mary Yonge: Her Life and Letters* (London: Macmillan, 1903).

Courtney, J., *An Oxford Portrait Gallery* (London: Chapman and Hall, 1931).

—— *Countrywomen in Council* (Oxford: Oxford University Press, 1933).

Covert, J., *A Victorian Marriage: Mandell and Louise Creighton* (London: Hambledon and London, 2000).

Creighton, L., *A Purpose in Life* (London: Wells Gardner, Darton and Co., 1901).

—— *The Art of Living* (London: Longmans, Green and Co., 1909).

—— *Memoir of a Victorian Woman*, ed. J. T. Covert (Bloomington: Indiana University Press, 1994).

Earl of Cromer, *Modern Egypt* (London: Macmillan, 1908).

Culleton, C., *Working-Class Culture, Women and Britain, 1914–1921* (Basingstoke: Macmillan, 2000).

Curzon, G., *Subjects of the Day: Being a Selection of Speeches and Writings of Earl Curzon of Kedleston*, ed. D. M. Chapman-Huston (London: George Allen and Unwin Ltd., 1915).

—— in *Memorial to the late Earl of Cromer* (London: H. R. Stokes, 1920).

Daly, C., and Nolan, M. (eds.), *Suffrage and Beyond: International Feminist Perspectives* (Auckland: Auckland University Press, 1994).

Darley, G., *Octavia Hill: A Life* (London: Constable, 1990).

Davenport Adams, W., *Stories of the Lives of Noble Women* (London: Thomas Nelson and Sons, n.d.).

Davidoff, L., and Hall, C., *Family Fortunes: Men and Women of the English Middle Class 1780–1850* (London: Hutchinson, 1987).

Davin, A., 'Imperialism and Motherhood', *History Workshop Journal*, 5 (1978), 9–65.

—— *Growing Up Poor: Home, School and Street in London 1870–1914* (London: Rivers Oram Press, 1996).

Delap, L., '"Philosophical vacuity and political ineptitude": *The Freewoman's* Critique of the Suffrage Movement', *Women's History Review*, 11/4 (2002), 613–30.

____ 'Feminist and Anti-Feminist Encounters in Edwardian Britain', *Historical Research*, 78/201 (2005), 377–99.

____ and Heilmann, A. (eds.), *Anti-Feminism in Edwardian Literature* (London: Thoemmes Continuum, 2006).

____ DiCenzo, M., and Ryan, L. (eds.), *Feminism and the Periodical Press* (London: Routledge, 2006).

Dicey, A. V., *Letters to a Friend on Votes for Women* (London: John Murray, 1909).

Dundas, L., *Lord Cromer* (London: Hodder and Stoughton, 1932).

Dyhouse, C., *Girls Growing Up in Late Victorian and Edwardian England* (London: Routledge and Kegan Paul, 1981).

____ *Feminism and the Family in England 1880–1939* (Oxford: Basil Blackwell, 1989).

____ *No Distinction of Sex? Women in British Universities 1870–1939* (London: UCL Press, 1995).

E.A. and B.H.S. (eds.), *Impressions of L.H.M.S.* (Brondesbury: Manor House School, 1927).

____ ____ and P.H. (eds.), *The Letters of S.S.S. and L.H.M.S. (Mrs and Miss Soulsby)* (Brondesbury: Manor House School, 1929).

Eldridge Miller, J., *Rebel Women: Feminism, Modernism and the Edwardian Novel* (London: Virago, 1994).

Electoral Commission, *Gender and Political Participation* (London: The Electoral Commission, 2004).

Faraut, M., 'Women Resisting the Vote: A Case of Anti-Feminism?', *Women's History Review*, 12/4 (2003), 605–21.

Fawcett, M., *Home and Politics* (London: Women's Printing Society, 1894).

____ *Women's Suffrage: A Short History of a Great Movement* (London: T. C. and E. C. Jack, 1912).

____ *What I Remember* (London: T. Fisher Unwin, 1925).

Federico, A., *Idol of Suburbia: Marie Corelli and Late Victorian Literary Culture* (Charlottesville: University Press of Virginia, 2000).

Finlayson, G., *Citizen, State and Social Welfare in Britain 1830–1990* (Oxford: Oxford University Press, 1994).

Fix Anderson, N., *Woman against Women in Victorian England: A Life of Eliza Lynn Linton* (Bloomington: Indiana University Press, 1987).

Fletcher, I., Nym Mayhall, L., and Levine, P. (eds.), *Women's Suffragism in the British Empire* (London: Routledge, 2000).

Flint, K., *The Woman Reader 1837–1914* (Oxford: Clarendon Press, 1993).

Foakes, G., *Between High Walls: A London Childhood* (London: Shepheard-Walwyn Ltd., 1972).

Garner, L., *Stepping Stones to Women's Liberty 1900–1918* (London: Heinemann, 1984).

Giles, J., *Women. Identity and Private Life in Britain 1900–1950* (Basingstoke: Macmillan, 1995).

Gill, S., *Women and the Church of England from the Eighteenth Century to the Present* (London: SPCK, 1994).

Gilmour, D., *Curzon* (London: John Murray, 1994).

Gleadle, K., *British Women in the Nineteenth Century* (Basingstoke: Palgrave, 2001).

Gleadle, K. and Richardson, S. (eds.), *Women in British Politics, 1760–1869: The Power of the Petticoat* (Basingstoke: Macmillan, 2000).

Glick, D., *The National Council of Women of Great Britain: The First One Hundred Years* (London: NCW, 1995).

Gollin, A., *Proconsul in Politics* (London: Anthony Blond, 1964).

Goodenough, S., *Jam and Jerusalem* (Glasgow: Collins, 1977).

Goodman, S., *Gertrude Bell* (Leamington Spa: Berg, 1985).

Graves, P., *Labour Women: Women in British Working-Class Politics, 1918–1939* (Cambridge: Cambridge University Press, 1994).

Grewal, I., *Home and Harem: Nation, Gender, Empire, and the Cultures of Travel* (London: Leicester University Press, 1996).

Hall, C., McClelland, K., and Rendall, J., *Defining the Victorian Nation: Class, Race, Gender and the Reform Act of 1867* (Cambridge: Cambridge University Press, 2000).

Halperin, F., *Lord Milner and the Empire: The Evolution of British Imperialism* (London: Odhams Press, 1952).

Hammerton, J. A., '"The Perils of Mrs Pooter": Satire, Modernity and Motherhood in the Lower Middle Classes in England, 1870–1920', *Women's History Review*, 8/2 (1999), 261–76.

Hannam, J., Auchterlonie, M., and Holden, K., *International Encyclopedia of Women's Suffrage* (Santa Barbara: ABC-CLIO, 2000).

Harris, J., *Private Lives, Public Spirit: Britain 1870–1914* (London: Penguin Books, 1994).

Harrison, A., *Frederic Harrison: Thoughts and Memories* (London: William Heinemann, 1926).

Harrison, B., 'For Church, Queen and Family: The Girls Friendly Society 1874–1920', *Past and Present*, 61 (1973), 107–38.

_____*Separate Spheres: The Opposition to Women's Suffrage in Britain* (London: Croom Helm, 1978).

_____'Women's Suffrage at Westminster 1866–1928', in M. Bentley and J. Stevenson (eds.), *High and Low Politics in Modern Britain* (Oxford: Clarendon Press, 1983).

_____'Women in a Men's House: the Women MPs 1919–45', *Historical Journal*, 29/3 (1986), 623–54.

_____*Prudent Revolutionaries: Portraits of British Feminists between the Wars* (Oxford: Clarendon Press, 1987).

_____(ed.), *The History of the University of Oxford*, viii. *Twentieth-Century Oxford* (Oxford: Clarendon Press, 1994).

Harrison, E., *The Freedom of Women* (London: Watts and Co., 1908).

Harrison, F., *Memoir and Essays of Ethelbertha Harrison* (Bath: Sir Isaac Pitman and Sons, 1917).

Harrison, J., *'Homo Sum': Being a letter to an anti-suffragist from an anthropologist* (London: NUWSS, n.d. [*c*.1910]).

Harrison, P., *Connecting Links: The British and American Women's Suffrage Movements 1900–1914* (Westport: Greenwood Press, 2000).

Hart, H., *Woman Suffrage: A National Danger* (London: P. S. King and Son, 1912).

Heeney, B., *The Women's Movement in the Church of England 1850–1930* (Oxford: Clarendon Press, 1988).

Heilmann, A., *New Woman Fiction: Women Writing First Wave Feminism* (Basingstoke: Macmillan, 2000).

_____ *Feminist Forerunners: Womanism and Feminism in the Early Twentieth Century* (London: Rivers Oram, 2001).

_____ *New Woman Strategies: Sarah Grand, Olive Schreiner, Mona Caird* (Manchester: Manchester University Press, 2004).

_____ and Beetham, M. (eds.), *New Woman Hybridities: Femininity, Feminism and International Consumer Culture, 1880–1930* (London: Routledge, 2004).

Hetherington, S., *Katharine Atholl 1874–1960: Against the Tide* (Aberdeen: Aberdeen University Press, 1989).

Higonnet, M. R., and Jenson, J. (eds.), *Behind the Lines: Gender and the Two World Wars* (New Haven: Yale University Press, 1987).

Hollis, P., *Ladies Elect: Women in English Local Government 1865–1914* (Oxford: Clarendon Press, 1987).

Holton, S., *Feminism and Democracy* (Cambridge: Cambridge University Press, 1986).

_____ *Suffrage Days: Stories from the Women's Suffrage Movement* (London: Routledge, 1996).

_____ 'Kinship and Friendship: Quaker Women's Networks and the Women's Movement', *Women's History Review*, 14/3&4 (2005), 365–84.

Hunt, F. (ed.), *Lessons for Life: The Schooling of Girls and Women 1850–1950* (Oxford: Basil Blackwell, 1987).

Huws Jones, E., *Mrs Humphry Ward* (London: Heinemann, 1973).

Innes, S., 'Constructing Women's History in the Interwar Period: The Edinburgh Women's Citizens' Associations', *Women's History Review*, 13/4 (2004), 621–47.

Jablonsky, T., *The Home, Heaven and Mother Party: Female Anti-Suffragism in the United States, 1868–1920* (New York: Carlson, 1994).

Jasper, A., *A Hoxton Childhood* (London: Cresset Press, 1969).

Joannou, M., 'Mary Augusta Ward (Mrs Humphry) and the Opposition to Women's Suffrage', *Women's History Review* 14/3&4 (2005), 561–80.

_____ and Purvis, J. (eds.), *The Women's Suffrage Movement: New Feminist Perspectives* (Manchester: Manchester University Press, 1998).

John, A. (ed.), *Our Mothers' Land: Chapters in Welsh Women's History 1830–1939* (Cardiff: University of Wales Press, 1991).

_____ and Eustance, C. (eds.), *The Men's Share? Masculinities, Male Support and Women's Suffrage in Britain, 1890–1920* (London: Routledge, 1997).

Jones, H. (ed.), *Duty and Citizenship: The Correspondence and Papers of Violet Markham, 1896–1953* (London: The Historians' Press, 1994).

_____ *Women in British Public Life 1914–1950: Gender, Power and Social Policy* (London: Pearson Education, 2000).

Kean, H., *Deeds Not Words* (London: Pluto Press, 1990).

Kennedy, T., *British Quakerism 1860–1920* (Oxford: Oxford University Press, 2001).

Kenney, A., *Memories of a Militant* (London: Edward Arnold, 1924).

Kingsley Kent, S., *Sex and Suffrage in Britain 1860–1914* (Princeton: Princeton University Press, 1987).

_____ *Making Peace: The Reconstruction of Gender in Inter-War Britain* (Princeton: Princeton University Press, 1993).

_____ *Gender and Power in Britain, 1640–1990* (London: Routledge, 1999).

Koven, S., and Michel, S., *Mothers of a New World: Maternalism, Politics and the Origins of Welfare States* (London: Routledge, 1993).

Lauer, L., 'Women in British Non-Conformity 1880–1920, with special reference to the Society of Friends, the Baptist Union and the Salvation Army' (Oxford D.Phil. thesis, 1994).

Law, C., *Suffrage and Power: The Women's Movement 1918–1928* (London: I. B. Tauris, 2000).

Layard, G., *Mrs Lynn Linton: Her Life, Letters and Opinions* (London: Methuen, 1901).

Ledger, S., *The New Woman: Fiction and Feminism at the Fin de Siecle* (Manchester: Manchester University Press, 1997).

Leneman, L., *A Guid Cause: The Women's Suffrage Movement in Scotland* (Aberdeen: Aberdeen University Press, 1991).

Leonardi, S., *Dangerous by Degrees: Women at Oxford and the Somerville College Novelists* (New Brunswick: Rutgers University Press, 1989).

Levine, P., *Feminist Lives in Victorian England: Private Roles and Public Commitment* (Oxford: Basil Blackwell, 1990).

Lewis, J. (ed.), *Labour and Love: Women's Experience of Home and Family 1850–1940* (Oxford: Basil Blackwell, 1986).

_____ *Before the Vote Was Won: Arguments For and Against Women's Suffrage 1864–1896* (London: Routledge and Kegan Paul, 1987).

_____ *Women and Social Action in Victorian and Edwardian England* (Stanford: Stanford University Press, 1991).

Liddington, J., and Norris, J., *One Hand Tied Behind Us: The Rise of the Women's Suffrage Movement* (London: Virago, 1978).

Lister, R., *Citizenship. Feminist Perspectives* (Basingstoke: Macmillan, 1997).

Llewellyn Davies, M. (ed.), *Maternity: Letters from Working Women* (1915; London: Virago, 1978).

Lonsdale, S., *The English Poor Laws: Their History, Principles and Administration* (London: P. S. King and Son, 1897).

Lovenduski, J., *Feminizing Politics* (Cambridge: Polity Press, 2005).

Low, F., *Press Work for Women: A Textbook for Young Women Journalists* (London: L. Upcott Gill, 1904).

_____ 'Principal Childs on Woman Suffrage: a Rejoinder', *The Hibbert Journal* (Oct. 1910), 163–8.

Lynn Linton, E., *The Rebel of the Family* (London: Chatto and Windus, 1888).

_____ *In Haste and at Leisure*, i. (London: William Heinemann, 1895).

Lytton, C., *Prisons and Prisoners* (London: William Heinemann, 1914).

Mackenzie, J., *Propaganda and Empire: The Manipulation of British Public Opinion, 1880–1960* (Manchester: Manchester University Press, 1986).

_____ (ed.), *Imperialism and Popular Culture* (Manchester: Manchester University Press, 1986).

Markham, V., *South Africa, Past and Present* (London: Smith, Elder and Co., 1900).

_____ *The New Era in South Africa* (London: Smith Elder and Co., 1904).

_____ *Return Passage* (London: Oxford University Press, 1953).

Marlowe, J., *Milner, Apostle of Empire* (London: Hamish Hamilton, 1976).

Marsh, P., *Joseph Chamberlain, Entrepreneur in Politics* (New Haven: Yale University Press, 1994).

Marshall, S., *Splintered Sisterhood: Gender and Class in the Campaign Against Woman Suffrage* (Wisconsin: University of Wisconsin Press, 1997).

Martineau, V., *Recollections of Sophia Lonsdale* (London: John Murray, 1936).

Midgley, C., *Women Against Slavery: The British Campaigns 1780–1870* (London: Routledge, 1992).

_____ (ed.), *Gender and Imperialism* (Manchester: Manchester University Press, 1998).

Milner, A., *The Nation and the Empire* (London: Constable, 1913).

Moberly Bell, E., *Octavia Hill* (London: Constable, 1942).

_____ *Flora Shaw* (London: Constable, 1947).

Monk, U., *New Horizons: A Hundred Years of Women's Migration* (London: HMSO, 1963).

Murphy, C., *The Women's Suffrage Movement and Irish Society* (Hemel Hempstead: Harvester Wheatsheaf, 1989).

Oldfield, S., *This Working Day World: Women's Lives and Culture(s) in Britain 1914–1945* (London: Taylor and Francis, 1994).

Owen, H., *Woman Adrift: The Menace of Suffragism* (London: Stanley Paul and Co., 1912).

Owen, R., *Lord Cromer: Victorian Imperialist, Edwardian Proconsul* (Oxford: Oxford University Press, 2004).

Oxford Dictionary of National Biography (Oxford: Oxford University Press, 2004).

Pankhurst, C., *Unshackled: The Story of How We Won the Vote* (London: Hutchinson, 1959).

Pankhurst, E., *My Own Story* (London: Eveleigh Nash, 1914).

Pankhurst, E. S., *The Suffragette Movement* (London: Longman, 1931).

Pateman, C., *The Disorder of Women* (Cambridge: Polity Press, 1989).

Pederson, J. S., *The Reform of Girls' Secondary and Higher Education in Victorian England* (New York: Garland Publishing, 1987).

Pederson, S., *Eleanor Rathbone and the Politics of Conscience* (New Haven: Yale University Press, 2004).

Pember Reeves, M., *Round About A Pound A Week* (1913; London: Virago, 1979).

Peterson, M. J., *Family, Love and Work in the Lives of Victorian Gentlewomen* (Bloomington: Indiana University Press, 1989).

Phillips, R., *Untying the Knot: A Short History of Divorce* (Cambridge: Cambridge University Press, 1991).

Pickles, K., *Female Imperialism and National Identity: Imperial Order Daughters of the Empire* (Manchester: Manchester University Press, 2002).

Potter, J., *Boys in Khaki, Girls in Print: Women's Literary Responses to the Great War 1914–1918* (Oxford: Oxford University Press, 2005).

Powell, V., *Margaret, Countess of Jersey* (London: Heinemann, 1978).

Prochaska, F., *Women and Philanthropy in Nineteenth Century England* (Oxford: Clarendon Press, 1980).

_____ *The Voluntary Impulse and Philanthropy in Modern Britain* (London: Faber and Faber, 1988).

Pugh, M., *Women and the Women's Movement in Britain 1914–1959* (Basingstoke: Macmillan, 1992).

_____ *The March of the Women* (Oxford: Oxford University Press, 2000).

Purvis, J., *Emmeline Pankhurst: A Biography* (London: Routledge, 2002).

Purvis, and Holton, S. (eds.), *Votes for Women* (London: Routledge, 2000).

Raby, A., *Virginia Woolf's Wise and Witty Quaker Aunt: A Biographical Sketch of Caroline Emilia Stephen* (London: Cecil Woolf, 2002).

Ransom, T., *The Mysterious Miss Marie Corelli* (Stroud: Sutton Publishing, 1999).

Richardson, A., and Willis, C. (eds.), *The New Woman in Fiction and in Fact: Fin-de-Siecle Feminisms* (Houndmills: Palgrave, 2001).

Richter, M., *The Politics of Conscience: T. H. Green and his Age* (Lanham: University Press of America, 1983).

Roach, J., 'Victorian Universities and the National Intelligentsia', *Victorian Studies*, 3/2 (1959), 131–50.

Roberts, E., *A Woman's Place: An Oral History of Working Class Women 1890–1940* (Oxford: Basil Blackwell, 1984).

Roberts, R., *The Classic Slum: Salford Life in the First Quarter of the Century* (Manchester: Manchester University Press, 1971).

Rogers, A., *Degrees by Degrees* (Oxford: Oxford University Press, 1938).

Rose, K., *Curzon: A Most Superior Person* (London: Macmillan, 1985 edn.).

Rosen, A., *Rise Up Women! The Militant Campaign of the Women's Social and Political Union 1903–1914* (London: Routledge, 1978).

Ross, E., *Love and Toil: Motherhood in Outcast London 1870–1918* (Oxford: Oxford University Press, 1993).

Rover, C., *Women's Suffrage and Party Politics in Britain* (London: Routledge and Kegan Paul, 1967).

Rowbotham, J., *Good Girls make Good Wives: Guidance for Girls in Victorian Fiction* (Oxford: Basil Blackwell, 1989).

Rubinstein, D., *Before the Suffragettes: Women's Emancipation in the 1890s* (Brighton: Harvester Press, 1986).

Ruskin, J., *Sesame and Lilies*, ed. J. Bryson (London: J. M. Dent and Sons, 1970).

Sanders, V., *Eve's Renegade: Victorian Anti-feminist Women Novelists* (Basingstoke: Macmillan, 1996).

Scannell, D., *Mother Knew Best: An East End Childhood* (London: Macmillan, 1974).

Schneer, J., *London 1900: The Imperial Metropolis* (New Haven: Yale University Press, 1999).

Scott, G., *Feminism and the Politics of Working Women* (London: UCL Press, 1998).

Shaw, F., *Letters from South Africa* (London: *The Times*, 1893).

Smith, A., *Suffrage Discourse in Britain during the First World War* (Aldershot: Ashgate, 2005).

Smith, H. (ed.), *British Feminism in the Twentieth Century* (Aldershot: Edward Elgar, 1990).

Soulsby, L., *Brondesbury Ways, or Toys Old and New* (privately printed, 1916).

——— *Stray Thoughts on Reading* (London: Longman, 1897).

——— *A Woman's Movement* (London: Longmans, Green and Co., 1913).

——— *The Woman's Kingdom* (London: Longmans, Green and Co., 1910).

——— *Home Rule or Daughters of Today* (Oxford: James Palmer and Co., 1894).

Spring Rice, M., *Working Class Wives: Their Health and Conditions* (London: Penguin, 1939).

Stephen, C., *The Vision of Faith and Other Essays* (Cambridge: W. Heffer & Sons Ltd., 1911).

Stott, M., *Organisation Woman: The Story of the National Union of Townswomen's Guilds* (London: Heinemann, 1978).

Strachey, R., *The Cause: A Short History of the Women's Movement in Great Britain* (1928; London: Virago Press, 1978 edn.).

Sutherland, J., *Mrs Humphry Ward: Eminent Victorian, Pre-Eminent Edwardian* (Oxford: Oxford University Press, 1991).

Swanwick, H., *I Have been Young* (London: Victor Gollancz, 1935).

Thom, D., *Nice Girls and Rude Girls: Women Workers in World War I* (London: I. B. Tauris, 1998).

Thompson, A., *Imperial Britain: The Empire in British Politics c.1880–1932* (Harlow: Pearson Education Limited, 2000).

Thompson, N. (ed.), *Victorian Women Writers and the Woman Question* (Cambridge: Cambridge University Press, 1999).

Trevelyan, J., *The Life of Mrs Humphry Ward* (London: Constable, 1923).

Trodd, A., *Women's Writing in English* (Harlow: Addison Wesley Longman, 1998).

Tylee, C., *The Great War and Women's Consciousness: Images of Militarism and Womanhood in Women's Writings, 1914–1918* (Iowa City: University of Iowa Press, 1990).

Van Thal, H., *Eliza Lynn Linton: The Girl of the Period* (London: George Allen and Unwin, 1979).

Vickery, A. (ed.), *Women, Privilege and Power: British Politics, 1750 to the Present* (Stanford: Stanford University Press, 2001).

Villiers, M., Countess of Jersey, *Fifty-One Years of Victorian Life* (London: John Murray, 1922).

Vogeler, M., *Frederic Harrison: The Vocations of a Positivist* (Oxford: Clarendon Press, 1984).

Wallach, J., *Desert Queen* (London: Weidenfeld and Nicholson, 1996).

Ward, M., *Marcella* (1894; London: Virago Press, 1984 edn.).

———*Daphne or Marriage à la Mode* (London: Cassel, 1909).

———*Diana Mallory* (London: Smith, Elder and Co., 1908).

———*Delia Blanchflower* (1915; London: Ward Lock and Co., 1917 edn.).

———*England's Effort* (London: Smith, Elder, 1916).

———*Towards the Goal* (London: Murray, 1917).

———*A Writer's Recollections* (London: W. Collins and Sons, 1918).

Webb, B., *The Diary of Beatrice Webb*, ed. N. and J. MacKenzie, vol. i (London: Virago, 1982).

———*The Diary of Beatrice Webb*, ed. J. MacKenzie, 1-vol. edn. (London: Virago, 1986).

———*My Apprenticeship* (London: Pelican Books, 1938).

———*Our Partnership* (1948), ed. B. Drake and M. Cole (Cambridge: Cambridge University Press, 1975).

Woolacott, A., *On Her Their Lives Depend: Munitions Workers in the Great War* (Berkeley and Los Angeles: University of California Press, 1994).

Wordsworth, C., *Christian Womanhood and Christian Sovereignity* (London: Rivingtons, 1884).

Wordsworth, E., *First Principles in Women's Education* (Oxford: James Parker and Co., 1894).

_____ *Essays Old and New* (Oxford: Oxford University Press, 1919).

Wright, A., *The Unexpurgated Case Against Woman Suffrage* (London: Constable, 1913).

Yonge, C., *The Daisy Chain* (1856; London: Macmillan, 1888).

_____ *Womankind* (London: Mozley and Smith, 1876).

_____ *The Clever Woman of the Family* (1865; London: Virago, 1985).

Index